THE
ART
OF
COOKERY,

Made PLAIN and EASY;

Which far exceeds any THING of the Kind ever yet Published.

CONTAINING,

I. Of Roasting, Boiling, &c.
II. Of Made-Dishes.
III. Read this Chapter, and you will find how Expensive a *French* Cook's Sauce is.
IV. To make a Number of pretty little Dishes fit for a Supper, or Side-Dish, and little Corner-Dishes for a great Table; and the rest you have in the Chapter for *Lent*.
V. To dress Fish.
VI. Of Soops and Broths.
VII. Of Puddings.
VIII. Of Pies.
IX. For a Fast-Dinner, a Number of good Dishes, which you may make use for a Table at any other Time.
X. Directions for the Sick.
XI. For Captains of Ships.
XII. Of Hog's Puddings, Sausages, &c.
XIII. To Pot and Make Hams, &c.
XIV. Of Pickling.
XV. Of Making Cakes, &c.
XVI. Of Cheesecakes, Creams, Jellies, Whip Syllabubs, &c.
XVII. Of Made Wines, Brewing, *French* Bread, Muffins, &c.
XVIII. Jarring Cherries, and Preserves, &c.
XIX. To Make Anchovies, Vermicella, Ketchup, Vinegar, and to keep Artichokes, French-Beans, &c.
XX. Of Distilling.
XXI. How to Market, and the Seasons of the Year for Butcher's Meat, Poultry, Fish, Herbs, Roots, &c. and Fruit.
XXII. A certain Cure for the Bite of a Mad Dog. By Dr. *Mead*.

BY A LADY.

LONDON:

Printed for the AUTHOR; and sold at Mrs. *Ashburn*'s, a China-Shop, the Corner of *Fleet-Ditch*. MDCCXLVII.

[Price 3 s. stitch'd, and 5 s. bound]

SUBSCRIBERS TO THIS BOOK.

A
Mrs. ALLGOOD
Mrs. Adams
Mrs. Atwood
Mrs. Armorer
Mrs. Ayliffe
Miss Ayliffe
Dr. Anderson
Mr. Anderson
Capt. Ash.

B
Mrs. Butler
Mrs. Bedford, *Bread-street Hill*
Mrs. Bedford, *Chancery-lane*
Mrs. Bury, *Norfolk-street*
Mrs. Bury, *Peckham*
Miss Amy Bury
Miss Bedford
Mrs. Berrysford
Mrs. Bertie
Mrs. Barker
Mrs. Bugby
Mrs. Bathus
Mrs. Beckly
Mrs. Bromfield
Mrs. Brown
Mrs. Bird
Mrs. Bowman
Mrs. Brown, *Chancery-lane*
Mrs. Blunckley
Mrs. Bowdler
Mrs. Barrit
Mrs. Barlet
Mrs. Baker
Mrs. Boys
—— Barnet, Esq;
Dr. John Bedford
Mr. Back
Mr. Blanco
Mr. Bluck
Mr. Brickhill.

C
Hon. Mrs. Carmecheal
Mrs. Claxton, sen.
Mrs. Claxton, jun.
Mrs. Crofts
Mrs. Carter, *Hay-Market*
Mrs. Carter, *Bishopsgate-street*

Mrs. Churchill
Mrs. Cooke
Mrs. Cotesworth
Miss Coumbs
Miss Clokenhints
Miss Carlton
Mrs. Cheyney
Mrs. Cuttlar
Mr. Collice
Mr. Cove.

D
Lady Dudly
Mrs. Duan
Mrs. Driddon
Mrs. Deucon
Mrs. Dawson
Mrs. Denton
Mrs. Dent
Mrs. Dalows
Mr. Daverel.

E
Mrs. Edgerton
Mrs. Ebleso.

F
Mrs. Farmer
Mrs. Fitzwater
Mrs. Finch
Rev. Mr. Finch.

G
Lady Gunston
Mrs. Griffith
Mrs. Gandy
Mrs. Glasse, *Cary-street*
Mrs. Gordon
Mrs. Gritton
Mr. Glasse, Attorney at Law
Mr. Grear.

H
Mr. Hoar, *St. Martin's-lane*
Miss E. Hoar
Miss M. Hoar
Mrs. Hill
Miss Haftens
Mrs. Herriss
Mrs. Hatten
Mrs. Hendrick
Mrs. Harrison
Mr. Hanysut
Mrs. Ann Hooper.

SUBSCRIBERS to this BOOK.

I
Mrs. Joderell
Mrs. Jenkes
Dr. James
Mr. Jelf.

K
Mrs. Kegwig
Mr. Kirk
Mr. Keeble.

L
Lady Lee
Mrs. Lathbury
Mrs. Lembrey
Miss Lembrey
Mrs. Lilly
Mrs. Loyon
Mrs. Lee
Miss Lance
Miss Legrand
Mr. Lee
Mr. Licet
Mr. Lloyd
Mr. Lack, jun.

M
Mrs. Morant
Mrs. Medly-Coat
Mrs. Manering
Miss Manering
Mrs. Marshel
Mrs. Mombray
Mrs. Merrit
Mrs. Middleton
Mrs. Mathews
Mrs. Morell
Mrs. Mackcollo
Mrs. Mash
Mrs. Masterman
Hum. Morice, Esq;
Nic. Morice, Esq;
Mr. Morice, *Holborn*
Mr. Mathews
Mr. Macnamar
Mr. Masterman.

N
Mrs. Nicholas
Miss Nash
Mr. Norris.

P
Mrs. Pocock
Mrs. Proutford
Mrs. Phips, *Cheapside*
Mrs. Phips, *Bartholomew-Close*
Mrs. Pardo
Mrs. Pack
Mrs. Pettree
Mrs. Porter
Mrs. Pinson
Mrs. Pye
Mr. Perry
Mr. Powel.

Q
Mr. Quin
Mr. Quay.

R
Mrs. Ryder

Mrs. Roger
Mrs. Ranner
Mrs. Rily
Mrs. Roycroft, sen.
Mrs. Roycroft, jun.
Mrs. Rainby
Mrs. Ragshaw
Mrs. Richards, *St. Martin's-lane*
Mrs. Richards, *Holborn-hill*
Mrs. Raper
Mrs. Reed
Mrs. Roper.

S
Lady Smith
Mrs. Stone
Mrs. Stephenson
Mrs. Shardin
Mrs. Sheed
Mrs. Southern
Mrs. Sclater
Mrs. Swoen
Mrs. Shipton
Mrs. Slomaker
Mrs. Spence
Mrs. Shuttleworth
Mrs. Sharp
Mrs. Smith
Mrs. Soulby
Mrs. Stuart
Col. Stephenson
Mr. Jos. Sclater.

T
Mrs. Talar
Mrs. Tucker
Mrs. Tuder
Mrs. Thornhill
Mr. Thead, *Holborn*
Mr. Treadwell

V
Mrs. Veal.

W
Mrs. West
Mr. Warton
Mrs. Widdrington
Mrs. Ward
Mrs. Webb
Mrs. Whiten
Mrs. Watkins
Mrs. Wroughton
Miss Sophia Wroughton
Mrs. Williams
Mrs. Wollenston
Mrs. Wadmane
Mrs. Walker
Mrs. Woickester
Mr. Waits
Mr. Whitehead
Mr. Winsmore.

Y
Mrs. Yeldham.

Z
Mr. Zeman.

THE CONTENTS.

CHAP. I.
Of Roasting, Boiling, &c.

	Page
BEEF	3
Mutton and Lamb	4
Veal	ib.
Pork	ib.
To roast a Pig	ib.
Different Sorts of Sauce for a Pig	ib.
To roast the hind Quarter of a Pig, Lamb Fashion	ib.
To bake a Pig	5
To melt Butter	ib.
To roast Geese, Turkies, &c.	ib.
Sauce for a Goose	ib.
Sauce for a Turkey	ib.
Sauce for Fowls	ib.
Sauce for Ducks	ib.
Sauce for Pheasants and Partridges	ib.
Sauce for Larks	ib.
To roast Woodcocks and Snipes	ib.
To roast a Pigeon	6
To broil a Pigeon	ib.
Directions for Geese and Ducks	ib.
To roast a Hare	ib.
Different Sorts of Sauce for a Hare	ib.
To broil Steaks	ib.
Directions concerning the Sauce for Steaks	ib.
General Directions concerning Broiling	ib.
General Directions concerning Boiling	7
To boil a Ham	ib.
To boil a Tongue	ib.
To boil Fowls and House-Lamb	ib.
Sauce for a boiled Turkey	ib.
Sauce for a boiled Goose	ib.
Sauce for boiled Ducks or Rabbits	ib.
To roast Venison	ib.
Different Sorts of Sauce for Venison	8
To roast Mutton, Venison Fashion	ib.
To keep Venison or Hares sweet, or to make them fresh when they stink	ib.
To roast a Tongue or Udder	ib.
To roast Rabbits	ib.
To roast a Rabbit, Hare Fashion	ib.
Turkies, Pheasants, &c. may be larded	ib.
To roast a Fowl, Pheasant Fashion	ib.

	Page
Rules to be observed in Roasting	8
Beef	ib.
Mutton	9
Pork	ib.
Directions concerning Beef, Mutton, and Pork	ib.
Veal	ib.
House-Lamb	ib.
A Pig	ib.
A Hare	ib.
A Turkey	ib.
A Goose	ib.
Fowls	ib.
Tame Ducks	ib.
Wild Ducks	10
Teal, Wigeon, &c.	ib.
Woodcocks, Snipes and Partridges	ib.
Pigeons and Larks	ib.
Directions concerning Poultry	ib.
To keep Meat hot	ib.
To dress Greens, Roots, &c.	ib.
To dress Spinage	ib.
To dress Cabbages, &c.	ib.
To dress Carrots	ib.
To dress Turnips	11
To dress Parsnips	ib.
To dress Brockaley	ib.
To dress Potatoes	ib.
To dress Colliflowers	ib.
To dress French Beans	ib.
To dress Artichokes	ib.
To dress Asparagus	ib.
Directions concerning Garden Things	12
To dress Beans and Bacon	ib.
To make Gravy for a Turkey, or any Sort of Fowl	ib.
To draw Mutton, Beef, or Veal Gravy	ib.
To burn Butter for thickening of Sauce	ib.
To make Gravy	ib.
To make Gravy for Soops, &c.	ib.
To bake a Leg of Beef	13
To bake an Ox's Head	ib.
To boil Pickled Pork	ib.

CHAP.

CONTENTS.

CHAP. II.
Made-Dishes.

	Page
TO dress Scotch Collops	13
To dress White Scotch Collops	ib.
To dress a Fillet of Veal with Collops, &c.	ib.
To make Force-meat Balls	ib.
Truffles and Morells, good in Sauces and Soops	ib.
To stew Ox-Palates	14
To ragoo a Leg of Mutton	ib.
To make a Brown Fricasey	ib.
To make a White Fricasey	ib.
To fricasey Chickens, Rabbits, Lamb, Veal, &c.	ib.
A second Way to make a White Fricasey	ib.
A third of making a white Fricasey	ib.
To fricasey Rabbits, Lamb, Sweet-breads, or Tripe	ib.
Another Way to fricasey Tripe	15
To ragoo Hog's Feet and Ears	ib.
To fry Tripe	ib.
To stew Tripe	ib.
A Fricasey of Pigeons	ib.
A Fricasey of Lamb-stones and Sweat-breads	ib.
To hash a Calf's Head	ib.
To hash a Calf's Head White	16
To bake a Calf's Head	ib.
To bake a Sheep's Head	ib.
To dress a Lamb's Head	ib.
To ragoo a Neck of Veal	ib.
To ragoo a Breast of Veal	17
Another Way to ragoo a Breast of Veal	ib.
A Breast of Veal in Hodge-podge	ib.
To collar a Breast of Veal	ib.
To collar a Breast of Mutton	ib.
Another good Way to dress a Breast of Mutton	18
To force a Leg of Lamb	ib.
To boil a Leg of Lamb	ib.
To force a large Fowl	ib.
To roast a Turkey the genteel Way	ib.
To stew a Turkey or Fowl	ib.
To stew a Knuckle of Veal	19
Another Way to stew a Knuckle of Veal	ib.
To ragoo a Piece of Beef	ib.
To force the Inside of a Surloin of Beef	ib.
To force the Inside of a Rump of Beef	ib.
A rolled Rump of Beef	ib.
To boil a Rump of Beef the French Fashion	20
Beef Escarlot	ib.
Beef à la Daub	ib.
Beef à la Mode in Pieces	ib.
Beef Olives	ib.
Veal Olives	ib.
Beef Collops	ib.
To stew Beef Steaks	21
To fry Beef Steaks	ib.
A second Way to fry Beef Steaks	ib.
Another Way to do Beef Steaks	ib.
A pretty Side-Dish of Beef	ib.
To dress a Fillet of Beef	ib.
Beef Steaks rolled	ib.
To stew a Rump of Beef	22
Another Way to stew a Rump of Beef	ib.
Portugal Beef	ib.
To stew a Rump of Beef, or the Brisquit, the French Way	ib.

	Page
To stew Beef Gobbets	22
Beef Royal	ib.
A Tongue and Udder forced	23
To fricasey Neat's Tongue	ib.
To force a Tongue	ib.
To stew Neats Tongues Whole	ib.
To fricasey Ox Palates	ib.
To roast Ox Palates	ib.
To dress a Leg of Mutton à la Royale	24
A Leg of Mutton à la Hautgoût	ib.
To roast a Leg of Mutton with Oysters	ib.
To roast a Leg of Mutton with Cockles	ib.
A Shoulder of Mutton in Epigram	ib.
A Harrico of Mutton	ib.
To french a Hind Saddle of Mutton	ib.
Another French Way, called St. Menehout	25
Cutlets à la Maintenon, a very good Dish	ib.
To make a Mutton Hash	ib.
To dress Pigs Petty-toes	ib.
A second Way to roast a Leg of Mutton with Oysters	ib.
To dress a Leg of Mutton to eat like Venison	ib.
To dress Mutton the Turkish Way	26
A Shoulder of Mutton, with a Ragoo of Turnips	ib.
To stuff a Leg or Shoulder of Mutton	ib.
Sheeps Rumps with Rice	ib.
To bake Lamb and Rice	ib.
Baked Mutton Chops	27
A forced Leg of Lamb	ib.
To fry a Loin of Lamb	ib.
Another Way of frying a Neck or Loin of Lamb	ib.
To make a Ragoo of Lamb	ib.
To stew a Lamb's or Calf's Head	ib.
To dress Veal à la Bourgoise	28
A disguised Leg of Veal and Bacon	ib.
A Pillaw of Veal	ib.
Bombarded Veal	ib.
Veal Rolls	ib.
Olives of Veal, the French Way	29
Scotch Collops à la Francois	ib.
To make a savoury Dish of Veal	ib.
Scotch Collops Larded	ib.
To do them White	ib.
Veal Blanquets	ib.
A Shoulder of Veal à la Piemontoise	ib.
A Calf's Head Surprise	30
Sweet-breads of Veal à la Dauphine	ib.
Another Way to dress Sweet-breads	ib.
Calf's Chitterlings or Andouilles	ib.
To dress Calf's Chitterlings curiously	31
To dress a Ham à la Braise	ib.
To roast a Ham or Gammon	ib.
To stuff a Chine of Pork	ib.
Various Ways of dressing a Pig	ib.
A Pig in Jelly	32
To dress a Pig the French Way	ib.
To dress a Pig au Pere-douillet	ib.
A Pig Matelote	ib.
To dress a Pig like a Fat Lamb	33

To

CONTENTS.

	Page		Page
To roaft a Pig with the Hair on	33	A green Goofe	ib.
To Roaft a Pig with the Skin on	ib.	To dry a Goofe	ib.
To make a pretty Difh of a Breaft of Venifon	ib.	To drefs a Goofe in Ragoo	ib.
To boil a Haunch or Neck of Venifon	ib.	A Goofe à la Mode	43
To boil a Leg of Mutton like Venifon	34	To ftew Giblets	ib.
To roaft Tripe	ib.	Another Way	ib.
To drefs Poultry	ib.	To roaft Pigeons	ib.
To roaft a Turkey	ib.	To boil Pigeons	44
To make Oyfter-Sauce, either for Turkies or Fowls boiled	ib.	To à la Daube Pigeons	ib.
		Pigeons au Poir	ib.
To make Mufhroom-Sauce for White Fowls of all Sorts	ib.	Pigeons ftoved	ib.
		Pigeons furtout	ib.
Mufhroom-Sauce for White Fowls boiled	35	Pigeons in Compôte, with white Sauce	45
To make Sellery-Sauce either for roafted or boiled Fowls, Turkies, Partridges, or any other Game	ib.	A French Pupton of Pigeons	ib.
		Pigeons boiled with Rice	ib.
		Pigeons tranfmogrified	ib.
To make Brown Sellery-Sauce	ib.	Pigeons in Fricandos	ib.
To ftew a Turkey, or Fowl in Sellery Sauce	ib.	To roaft Pigeons with a Farce	ib.
To make Egg-Sauce, proper for roafted Chickens	ib.	To drefs Pigeons à Soliel	46
		Pigeons in a Hole	ib.
Shalot-Sauce for roafted Fowls	ib.	Pigeons in Pimlico	ib.
Shalot-Sauce for a Scraig of Mutton boiled	ib.	To jugg Pigeons	ib.
To drefs Livers with Mufhroom-Sauce	ib.	To ftew Pigeons	ib.
A pretty little Sauce	36	To drefs a Calf's Liver in a Caul	ib.
To make Lemon-Sauce for boiled Fowls	ib.	To roaft a Calf's Liver	47
A German Way of dreffing Fowls	ib.	To roaft Partridges	ib.
To drefs a Turkey or Fowl to perfection	ib.	To boil Partridges	ib.
To ftew a Turkey brown	ib.	To drefs Partridges à la Braife	ib.
To ftew a Turkey brown the nice Way	ib.	To make Partridges Pains	48
A Fowl à la Braife	37	To roaft Pheafants	ib.
To force a Fowl	ib.	A ftewed Pheafant	ib.
To roaft a Fowl with Chefnuts	ib.	To drefs a Pheafant a la Braife	ib.
Pullets à la Sainte Menehout	ib.	To boil a Pheafant	ib.
Chicken Surprize	ib.	To roaft Snipes or Woodcocks	49
Mutton Chops in Difguife	38	Snipes in a Surtout, or Woodcocks	ib.
Chickens roafted with Forced-Meat and Cucumbers	ib.	To boil Snipes or Woodcocks	ib.
		To drefs Ortolans	ib.
Chickens a la Braife	ib.	To drefs Ruffs and Reifs	ib.
To marinate Fowls	ib.	To drefs Larks	ib.
To broil Chickens	39	To drefs Plovers	50
Pulled Chickens	ib.	To drefs Larks Pear Fafhion	ib.
A pretty Way of ftewing Chickens	ib.	To drefs a Hare	ib.
Chickens Chiringrate	ib.	A jugged Hare	ib.
Chickens boiled with Bacon and Sellery	ib.	To ftew a Hare	ib.
Chickens with Tongues, a good Difh for a good deal of Company	40	A Hare Civet	ib.
		Portuguefe Rabbits	51
Scotch Chickens	ib.	Rabbits Surprife	ib.
To marinate Chickens	ib.	To boil Rabbits	ib.
To ftew Chickens	ib.	To drefs Rabbits in Cafferole	ib.
Ducks a la Mode	ib.	Mutton Kebob'd	ib.
To drefs a Wild Duck the beft Way	ib.	A Neck of Mutton, call'd the Hafty Difh	ib.
To boil a Duck or Rabbit with Onions	41	To drefs a Loin of Pork with Onions	52
To drefs a Duck with Green Peas	ib.	To make a Currey the Indian Way	ib.
To drefs a Duck with Cucumbers	ib.	To make a Pellow the Indian Way	ib.
To drefs a Duck à la Braife	ib.	Another Way to make a Pellow	ib.
To boil Ducks the French Way	42	To make Effence of Ham	ib.
To drefs a Goofe with Onions or Cabbage	ib.	Rules to be obferved in all Made-Difhes	ib.
Directions for roafting a Goofe	ib.		

CHAP.

CONTENTS.

CHAP. III.

Read this CHAPTER, *and you will find how expensive a French Cook's Sauce is.*

	Page		Page
THE French Way of Dressing Partridges	53	Cullis of Crawfish	54
To make Essence of Ham	ib.	A White Cullis	ib.
A Cullis for all Sorts of Ragoo	ib.	Sauce for a Brace of Partridges, Pheasants, or any thing you please.	ib.
A Cullis for all Sorts of Butcher's Meat.	ib.		
Cullis the Italian Way	54		

CHAP. IV.

To make a Number of little Dishes fit for a Supper, or Side-Dish, and little Corner-Dishes for a great Table; and the rest you have in the Chapter *for* Lent.

	Page		Page
HOG's Ears forced.	55	To force Cucumbers	58
To force Cocks Combs	ib.	Fry'd Sausages	ib.
To preserve Cocks Combs	ib.	Collup and Eggs	ib.
To preserve or pickle Pig's Feet and Ears	ib.	To dress cold Fowl or Pigeon	ib.
To pickle Ox Palates	ib.	To mince Veal	ib.
To stew Cucumbers	56	To fry cold Veal	ib.
To ragoo Cucumbers	ib.	To toss up cold Veal White	59
To make Jumballs	ib.	To hash cold Mutton	ib.
To make a Ragoo of Onions	ib.	To hash Mutton like Venison	ib.
A Ragoo of Oysters	ib.	To make Collops of Cold Beef	ib.
A Ragoo of Asparagus	ib.	To make a Florendine of Veal	ib.
A Ragoo of Livers	57	To make Salamongundy	ib.
To ragoo Colliflowers	ib.	Another Way	60
Stewed Peas and Lettice	ib.	A third Salamongundy	ib.
Cod-Sounds broiled with Gravy	ib.	To make little Pasties	ib.
A Forced Cabbage	ib.	Petit Patties for Garnishing of Dishes	ib.
Stewed red Cabbage	ib.	Ox Pallat baked	ib.
Savoys forced and stewed	58		

CHAP. V.

Of Dressing Fish.

	Page		Page
FISH Sauce with Lobster	61	To make Anchovy Sauce	61
To make Shrimp-Sauce	ib.	To dress a Brace of Carp with Gravy	ib.
To make Oyster Sauce	ib.		

CHAP. VI.

Of Soops and Broths.

	Page		Page
TO make Strong Broth for Soops or Gravy	62	A Crawfish Soop	ib.
Gravy for White Sauce	ib.	A good Gravy Soop	ib.
Gravy for Turkey, Fowl, or Ragoo	ib.	A Green Peas Soop	ib.
Gravy for a Fowl, when you have no Meat nor Gravy ready	ib.	A White Peas Soop	64
To make Mutton or Veal-Gravy	ib.	Another Way to make it	ib.
To make Strong Fish-Gravy	ib.	A Chesnut Soop	ib.
Plum-Porridge for Christmas	ib.	To make Mutton Broth	ib.
To make strong Broth to keep for Use	63	Beef Broth	ib.
		To make Scotch Barley Broth	65

To

CONTENTS.

	Page		Page
To make Hodge-Podge	65	To make Portable Soop	65
To make Pocket Soop	ib.	Rules to be observed in Soops or Broths	68

CHAP. VII.
Of Puddings.

	Page		Page
AN Oat Pudding to bake	68	A Yorkshire-Pudding	69
To make Calf's Foot Pudding	ib.	A Steak Pudding	ib.
To make a Pith Pudding	ib.	A Vermicella Pudding, with Marrow	ib.
To make a Marrow Pudding	69	Suet-Dumplings	70
A boiled Suet-Pudding	ib.	An Oxford Pudding	ib.
A boiled Plumb-Pudding	ib.	Rules to be observed in making Puddings, &c.	ib.

CHAP. VIII.
Of Pies.

	Page		Page
TO make a very fine Sweet Lamb or Veal Pye	70	A Goose-Pye	73
To make pretty Sweet Lamb or Veal Pye	ib.	To make a Venison-Pasty	ib.
A Savoury Veal Pye	71	A Calf's-Head Pye	74
To make a Savoury Lamb or Veal Pye	ib.	To make a Tart	ib.
A Calf's-Foot Pye	ib.	To make Mince-Pies the best Way	ib.
To make an Olive Pye	ib.	Tart de Moy	ib.
To season an Egg-Pye	ib.	To make Orange or Lemon Tarts	ib.
To make a Mutton-Pye	ib.	To make different Sorts of Tarts	75
A Beef-Steak Pye	ib.	Paste for Tarts	ib.
A Ham-Pye	ib.	Another Paste for Tarts	ib.
A Pigeon-Pye	72	Puff-Paste	ib.
To make a Gibblet-Pye	ib.	A good Crust for Great Pies	ib.
A Duck-Pye	ib.	A Standing Crust for Great Pies	ib.
A Chicken-Pye	ib.	A Cold Crust	ib.
A Cheshire Pork-Pye	ib.	A Dripping Crust	ib.
A Devonshire Squab-Pye	ib.	A Crust for Custards	76
A Shropshire Pye	73	Paste for Crackling Crust	ib.
A Yorkshire Christmas-Pye	ib.		

CHAP. IX.
For a Fast-Dinner, a Number of good Dishes, which you may make use of for a Table at any other Time.

	Page		Page
A Peas-Soop	76	A White-Pot	79
A Green Peas Soop	ib.	A Rice White-Pot	ib.
Another Green Peas Soop	ib.	Rice Milk	ib.
Soop Meager	ib.	An Orange Fool	ib.
An Onion Soop	77	A Westminster-Fool	ib.
An Eel Soop	ib.	A Gooseberry-Fool	ib.
A Crawfish Soop	ib.	Furmity	ib.
A Muscle Soop	ib.	Plumb-Porridge, or Barley-Gruel	ib.
A Scate or Thornback Soop	78	Buttered Wheat	80
An Oyster Soop	ib.	Plumb-Gruel	ib.
An Almond Soop	ib.	To make a Flour Hasty-Pudding	ib.
A Rice Soop	ib.	To make an Oatmeal Hasty-Pudding	ib.
A Barley Soop	ib.	To make another Sack-posset	ib.
A Turnip Soop	ib.	Or make it thus	ib.
An Egg Soop	ib.	To make a fine Hasty-Pudding	ib.
Peas-Porridge	79	To make Hasty-Fritters	ib.

b   To

CONTENTS

	Page
To make fine Fritters	81
Another Way	ib.
Apple Fritters	ib.
Curd Fritters	ib.
Fritters Royal	ib.
Skirret Fritters	ib.
White Fritters	ib.
Water Fritters	ib.
Syringed Fritters	82
Vine-Leaves Fritters	ib.
To make Clarye Fritters	ib.
Apple Frazes	ib.
An Almond Fraze	ib.
Pancakes	ib.
To make Fine Pancakes	ib.
A second Sort of Fine Pancakes	83
A third Sort	ib.
A fourth Sort call'd, A Quire of Paper	ib.
Rice Pancakes	ib.
To make a Pupton of Apples	ib.
To make Black Caps	ib.
To bake Apple Whole	ib.
To stew Pears	ib.
To stew Pears in a Sauce-pan	ib.
To stew Pears Purple	84
To stew Pippins Whole	ib.
A pretty Made-Dish	ib.
To make Kickshaws	ib.
Pain Perdu, or Cream Toasts	ib.
Salamangundy for a Middle Dish at Supper	ib.
To make a Tansey	ib.
Another Way	85
To make a Hedge-Hog	ib.
Or make it thus for Change	ib.
To make pretty Almond Puddings	ib.
To make Fry'd Toasts	ib.
To dress a Brace of Carp	86
To fry Carp	ib.
To bake a Carp	ib.
To fry Tench	ib.
To roast a Cod's Head	87
To boil a Cod's Head	ib.
To stew Cod	ib.
To fricasee Cod	ib.
To bake a Cod's Head	ib.
To broil Shrimp, Cod, Salmon, Whiting, or Haddocks	88
Or Oyster-Sauce made thus	ib.
To dress little Fish	ib.
To broil Mackerel	ib.
To broil Weavers	ib.
To boil a Turbut	ib.
To bake a Turbut	ib.
To dress a Jole of Pickled Salmon	89
To broil Salmon	ib.
Baked Salmon	ib.
To broil Mackerel Whole	ib.
To broil Herrings	ib.
To fry Herrings	ib.
To dress Herring and Cabbage	ib.
Water-Sokey	90
To stew Eels	ib.
To stew Eels with Broth	ib.
To dress a Pike	ib.
To broil Haddocks, when they are in High Season	ib.

	Page
To broil Cod-Sounds	90
To fricasee Cod-Sounds	ib.
To dress Salmon au Court-Bouillon	91
To dress Salmon a la Braise	ib.
Salmon in Cases	ib.
To dress Flat-Fish	ib.
To dress Salt Fish	ib.
To dress Lampreys	ib.
To fry Lampreys	92
To pitchcock Eels	ib.
To fry Eels	ib.
To broil Eels	ib.
To farce Eels with White Sauce	ib.
To dress Eels with Brown Sauce	ib.
To roast a Piece of Sturgeon	ib.
To roast a Fillet or Collar of Sturgeon	93
To boil Sturgeon	ib.
To crimp Cod the Dutch Way	ib.
To crimp Scate	ib.
To fricasee Scate or Thornback White	ib.
To fricasee it Brown	ib.
To fricasee Soals White	ib.
To fricasee Soals Brown	94
To boil Soals	ib.
To make a Collar of Fish in Ragoo, to look like a Breast of Veal collared	ib.
To butter Crabs, or Lobsters	ib.
To butter Lobsters another Way	95
To roast Lobsters	ib.
To make a fine Dish of Lobsters	ib.
To dress a Crab	ib.
To stew Prawns, Shrimps, or Crawfish	ib.
To make Collops of Oysters	ib.
To stew Muscles	ib.
Another Way to stew Muscles	96
A third Way to dress Muscles	ib.
To stew Scollops	ib.
To ragoo Oysters	ib.
To ragoo Endive	ib.
To ragoo French Beans	ib.
A Good Brown Gravy	ib.
To fricasee Skirrets	97
Chardoons fry'd and buttered	ib.
Chardoons a la Framage	ib.
To make a Scotch-Rabbit	ib.
To make a Welch-Rabbit	ib.
To make an English-Rabbit	ib.
Or do it thus	ib.
Sorrel with Eggs	ib.
A Fricasee of Artichoke-Bottoms	ib.
To fry Artichokes	ib.
A White Fricasee of Mushrooms	98
To make Buttered Loaves	ib.
Brockerly and Eggs	ib.
Asparagus and Eggs	ib.
Brockerly in Sallad	ib.
Potatoe-Cakes	ib.
A Pudding made thus	ib.
To make Potatoes like a Collar of Veal or Mutton	ib.
To broil Potatoes	ib.
To fry Potatoes	99
Mashed Potatoes	ib.
To grill Shrimps	ib.
Buttered Shrimps	ib.
To dress Spinage	ib.

CONTENTS.

	Page		Page
Stewed Spinage and Eggs	99	A Batter Pudding without Eggs	108
To boil Spinage when you have not Room on the Fire, to do by itself	ib.	A Grateful Pudding	ib.
		A Bread Pudding	109
Asparagus forced in French Role	ib.	A fine Bread Pudding	ib.
To make Oyster-Loaves	ib.	An Ordinary Bread Pudding	ib.
To stew Parsnips	100	A Baked Bread Pudding	ib.
To mash Parsnips	ib.	A Boiled Loaf	ib.
To stew Cucumbers	ib.	To make a Chesnut Pudding	ib.
To ragoo French Beans	ib.	A fine Plain Baked Pudding	ib.
A Ragoo of Beans with a French Force	ib.	To make pretty little Cheesecurd Pudding	110
Or this Way Beans ragoo'd with a Cabbage	ib.	An Apricot Pudding	ib.
Beans ragoo'd with Parsnips	101	The Ipswich Almond Pudding	ib.
Beans ragoo'd with Potatoes	ib.	A Vermicella Pudding	ib.
To ragoo Salary	ib.	Puddings for little Dishes	ib.
To ragoo Mushrooms	ib.	To make a Sweet-meat Pudding	ib.
A pretty Dish of Eggs	ib.	To make a fine Plain Pudding	111
Eggs a la Tripe	ib.	To make a Ratafia Pudding	ib.
A Fricasee of Eggs	ib.	A Bread and Butter Pudding	ib.
A Ragoo of Eggs	102	A Boiled Rice Pudding	ib.
To broil Eggs	ib.	A Cheap Rice Pudding	ib.
To dress Eggs with Bread	ib.	A Cheap Plain Rice Pudding	ib.
To farce Eggs	ib.	A Cheap Rice Pudding baked	ib.
Eggs with Lettice	ib.	A Spinage Pudding	ib.
To fry Eggs as round as Balls	ib.	A Quaking Pudding	ib.
To make an Egg as big as twenty	ib.	A Cream Pudding	112
A Grand Dish of Eggs	103	A Prune Pudding	ib.
A pretty Dish of Whites of Eggs	ib.	A Spoonful Pudding	ib.
To dress Beans in Ragoo	ib.	An Apple Pudding	ib.
An Amlet of Beans	ib.	Yeast Dumplings	ib.
A Bean Tansey	ib.	Norfolk Dumplings	ib.
A Water Tansey	104	Hard Dumplings	ib.
Peas Francoise	ib.	Another Way to make Hard Dumplings	113
Green Peas with Cream	ib.	Apple Dumplings	ib.
A Farce Meagre Cabbage	ib.	Another Way to make Apple Dumplings	ib.
To farce Cucumbers	ib.	To make a Cheesecurd Florendine	ib.
To stew Cucumbers	105	A Florendine of Oranges or Apples	ib.
Fry'd Salary	ib.	An Artichoke Pye	ib.
Salary with Cream	ib.	A Sweet Egg Pye	ib.
Colliflowers fry'd	ib.	A Potatoe Pye	ib.
An Oatmeal Pudding	ib.	An Onion Pye	114
A Potatoe Pudding	ib.	Orangeado Pye	ib.
A second Potatoe Pudding	ib.	A Skirret Pye	ib.
A third Sort of Potatoe Pudding	ib.	An Apple Pye	ib.
An Orange Pudding	ib.	To make a Cherry Pye	ib.
A second Sort of Orange Pudding	106	A Salt-Fish Pye	ib.
A third Orange Pudding	ib.	A Carp Pye	115
A fourth Orange Pudding	ib.	A Soal Pye	ib.
A Lemon Pudding	ib.	An Eel Pye	ib.
An Almond Pudding to bake	ib.	A Flounder Pye	ib.
An Almond Pudding to boil	ib.	A Herring Pye	ib.
A Sagoe Pudding	ib.	A Salmon Pye	ib.
A Millet Pudding	107	A Lobster Pye	ib.
A Carrot Pudding	ib.	A Muscle Pye	116
A Second Carrot Pudding	ib.	Lent Mince Pies	ib.
A Cowslip Pudding	ib.	To collar Salmon	ib.
To make a Quince, Apricot, or White Pear Plumb-Pudding	ib.	To collar Eels	ib.
		To pickle or bake Herrings	ib.
A Pearl Barley Pudding	ib.	To pickle or bake Mackerel, to keep all the Year.	
A French Barley Budding	ib.		
To make an Apple Pudding	ib.	To souse Mackerel	117
An Italian Pudding	ib.	To pot a Lobster	ib.
A Rice Pudding	108	To pot Eels	ib.
A second Rice Pudding	ib.	To pot Lampreys	ib.
A third Rice Pudding	ib.	To pot Charrs	ib.
A Custard Pudding to boil	ib.	To pot a Pike	ib.
A Flour Pudding	ib.	To pot Salmon	ib.
A Batter Pudding	ib.	Another Way to pot a Salmon	ib.

CHAP.

CONTENTS

CHAP. X.
Directions for Sick.

	Page
To make Mutton Broth	118
To boil a Scragg of Veal	ib.
Beef or Mutton Broth for very weak People, who take but little Nourishment	ib.
To make Beef Drink, which is ordered for weak People	ib.
Pork Broth	ib.
To boil a Chicken	ib.
To boil Pigeons	119
To boil a Partridge, or any other Wild Fowl	ib.
To boil a Plaife or Flounder	ib.
To mince Veal or Chicken, for the Sick or weak People	ib.
To pull a Chicken for the Sick	ib.
Chicken Broth	ib.
Chicken Water	ib.
To make White Caudle	ib.
To make Brown Caudle	120
To make Water Gruel	ib.
To make Panado	120
To boil Sego	ib.
To boil Salup	ib.
To make Ifinglass Jelly	ib.
To make the Pectoral Drink	ib.
Buttered Water, or what the Germans call Egg Soop, and are very fond of it for Supper, you have it in the Chapter for Lent	ib.
Seed Water	ib.
Bread Soop for the Sick	ib.
Artificial Afses Milk	121
Cows Milk next to Afses Milk done thus	ib.
A Good Drink	ib.
Barley Water	ib.
Sage Drink	ib.
For a Child	ib.
Liquor for a Child that has the Thrush	ib.
To boil Camphire Roots	ib.

CHAP. XI.
For Captains of Ships.

	Page
To make Ketchup to keep twenty Years	121
Fish Sauce to keep the whole Year	122
To pot Dripping to fry Fish, Meat, or Fritters, &c.	ib.
To pickle Mushrooms for the Sea	ib.
To make Mushroom Powder	ib.
To keep Mushrooms without Pickle	ib.
To keep Artichoke Bottoms dry	ib.
To fry Artichoke Bottoms	123
To ragoo Artichoke Bottoms	ib.
To fricafee Artichoke Bottoms	ib.
To drefs Fish	ib.
To bake Fish	ib.
To make a Gravy Soop	ib.
To make Peas Soop	ib.
To make a Pelow	123
To make Pork Pudding, or Beef, &c.	ib.
To make a Rice Pudding	124
A Suet Pudding	ib.
A Liver Pudding boiled	ib.
An Oatmeal Pudding	ib.
An Oatmeal Pudding to bake	ib.
A Rice Pudding baked	ib.
A Peas Pudding	ib.
A Fowl Pye	ib.
A Cheshire Pork Pye for Sea	125
To make Sea Venifon	ib.
To make Dumplings, when you have White Bread	ib.

CHAP. XII.
Of Hog's Puddings, Saufages, &c.

	Page
To make Almond Hog's Puddings	125
Another Way	ib.
A third Way	126
To make Hog's Puddings with Currans	ib.
To make Black Puddings	126
To make Fine Saufages	ib.
To make Common Saufages	ib.
To make Belony Saufages	ib.

CHAP.

CONTENTS

CHAP. XIII.
To Pot and Make Hams, &c.

	Page		Page
TO pot Pigeons, or Fowls	127	To make Dutch Beef	129
To pot a Cold Tongue, Beef, or Venison	ib.	To make Sham Brawn	ib.
	ib.	To souse a Turkey, in Imitation of Sturgeon	ib.
To pot Venison	ib.	To pickle Pork	ib.
To pot Tongues	ib.	A Pickle for Pork, which is to be eat soon	ib.
A fine Way to pot a Tongue	ib.	To make Veal Hams	ib.
To pot Beef like Venison	128	To make Beef Hams	ib.
To pot Cheshire-Cheese	ib.	To make Mutton Hams	130
To collar a Breast of Veal, or a Pig	ib.	To make Pork Hams	ib.
To collar Beef	ib.	To make Bacon	ib.
Another Way to season a Collar of Beef	ib.	To save potted Birds, that begin to be bad	ib.
To collar Salmon	ib.	To pickle Mackerel, call'd Caveach	ib.

CHAP. XIV.
Of Pickling.

	Page		Page
TO pickle Wallnuts Green	131	To pickle Codlings	134
To pickle Wallnuts White	ib.	To pickle Red Currans	ib.
To pickle Wallnuts Black	ib.	To pickle Fennel	ib.
To pickle Gerkins	132	To pickle Grapes	ib.
To pickle large Cucumbers in Slices	ib.	To pickle Barberries	ib.
To pickle Asparagus	ib.	To pickle Red Cabbage	135
To pickle Peaches	ib.	To pickle Golden Pippins	ib.
To pickle Reddish Pods	ib.	To pickle Stertion Buds and Limes, you pick them off the Lime-trees in the Summer	ib.
To pickle French Beans	133		
To pickle Colliflowers	ib.	To pickle Oysters, Cockels and Muscles	ib.
To pickle Beat-Root	ib.	To pickle young Suckers, or young Artichokes before the Leaves are hard	ib.
To pickle White Plumbs	ib.		
To pickle Nectarines and Apricots	ib.	To pickle Artichoke-Bottoms	ib.
To pickle Onions	ib.	To pickle Samphire	ib.
To pickle Lemons	ib.	Elder-Shoots in Imitation of Bamboo	138
To pickle Mushrooms White	134	Rules to be observed in Pickling	ib.
Pickle for Mushrooms	ib.		

CHAP. XV.
Of Making Cakes, &c.

	Page		Page
TO make a rich Cake	138	To make little Fine Cakes	140
To ice a great Cake another Way	ib.	Another Sort of little Cakes	ib.
To make a Pound Cake	ib.	To make Drop Biskets	ib.
A cheap Seed Cake	139	To make Common Biskets	ib.
To make a Butter Cake	ib.	French Biskets	ib.
To make Ginger-Bread Cakes	ib.	To make Maccaroons	141
To make a fine Seed or Saffron Cake	ib.	To make Shrewsbury Cakes	ib.
A rich Seed Cake, called the Nun's Cake	ib.	Madling Cakes	ib.
To make Pepper Cakes	ib.	To make light Wigs	ib.
Portugal Cakes	ib.	To make very good Wigs	ib.
A pretty Cake	140	To make Buns	ib.
To make Ginger-Bread	ib.	To make little Plumb-Cakes	ib.

CHAP.

CONTENTS.

CHAP. XVI.
Of Cheesecakes, Creams, Jellies, Whip Syllabubs, &c.

	Page		Page
To make fine Cheesecakes	142	To make Ratafia Cream	144
To make Lemon Cheesecakes	ib.	To make Whipt Cream	ib.
A second Sort of Lemon Cheesecakes	ib.	To make Whipt Syllabubs	ib.
To make Almond Cheesecakes	ib.	To make Everlasting Syllabubs	ib.
To make Fairy Butter	ib.	To make Hartshorn Jelly	145
Almond Custards	ib.	To make Ribband Jelly	ib.
Baked Custards	ib.	Calves Foot Jelly	ib.
To make plain Custards	143	To make Curran Jelly	ib.
To make Orange Butter	ib.	To make Rasberry Giam	ib.
To make Steeple Cream	ib.	To make Hartshorn Flummery	146
Lemon Cream	ib.	A second Way to make Hartshorn Flummery	ib.
A second Lemon Cream	ib.	To make Oatmeal Flummery	ib.
Jelly of Cream	ib.	To make a fine Syllabub from the Cow	ib.
To make Orange Cream	ib.	To make a Hedge-Hog	ib.
To make Gooseberry Cream	ib.	To make French Flummery	147
To make Barley Cream	144	A Buttered Tort	ib.
To make Blanched Cream	ib.	The Flooting Island, a pretty Dish for the Middle of a Table at a second Course, or for Supper	ib.
To make Almond Cream	ib.		
A fine Cream	ib.		

CHAP. XVII.
Of Made Wines, Brewing, French Bread, Muffins, &c.

	Page		Page
To make Raisin Wine	147	Rasberry Wine	149
To make Elder Wine	ib.	Rules for Brewing	ib.
Orange Wine	ib.	The best Thing for Rope Beer	150
To make Orange Wine with Raisins	148	When a Barrel of Beer is turned Sour	ib.
To make Elder Wine very like Fontineac	ib.	To make French Bread	ib.
Gooseberry Wine	ib.	To make Muffins and Oatcakes	151
To make Curran Wine	ib.	Receipt for making Bread without Barm, by the Help of a Leven	ib.
Cherry Wine	ib.		
Birch Wine	ib.	A Method to preserve a large Stock of Yeast, which will keep and be of Use for several Months, either to make Bread or Cakes	ib.
To make Quince Wine	149		
Cowslip or Clary Wine	ib.		
Turnip Wine	ib.		

CHAP. XVIII.
Jarring Cherries and Preserves, &c.

	Page		Page
To jar Cherries Lady North's Way	152	To make Syrup of Citron	153
To dry Cherries	ib.	To make Syrup of Clove Gilliflowers	ib.
Orange Marmalade	ib.	To make Syrup of Peach Blossoms	ib.
White Marmalade	ib.	To make Syrup of Quinces	154
To preserve Oranges whole	ib.	To preserve Apricots	ib.
To make Red Marmalade	ib.	To preserve Damsons whole	ib.
Red Quinces whole	153	To candy any Sort of Flowers	ib.
Jelly for the Quinces	ib.	To preserve Gooseberries whole without stoning	ib.
To make Conserve of Red Roses, or any other Flowers	ib.	To preserve white Wallnuts	ib.
To make Conserve of Hips	ib.	To preserve Wallnuts green	155
To make Syrup of Roses	ib.	A nice Way to preserve Peaches	ib.
		To make Quince Cakes	ib.

CHAP.

CONTENTS.

CHAP. XIX.
To make Anchovies, Vermicella, Ketchup, Vinegar, and to keep Artichokes, French Beans, &c.

	Page		Page
TO make Anchovies	155	To keep Red Gooseberries	157
To pickle Smelts	ib.	To keep Wallnuts all the Year	ib.
To make Vermicella	ib.	Another Way to keep Lemons	ib.
To make Ketchup	156	To keep White Bullice, or Pear-Plumbs, or Damascens, &c. for Tarts, or Pies.	ib.
Another Way to make Ketchup	ib.		
Artichokes to keep all the Year	ib.	To make Vinegar	ib.
To keep French Beans all the Year	ib.	To fry Smelts	158
To keep Green Peas till Christmas	ib.	To roast a Pound of Butter	ib.
To keep Green Gooseberries till Christmas	157	To raise a Sallat in two Hours at the Fire	ib.

CHAP. XX.
Of Distilling.

	Page		Page
TO distil Wallnut-water	158	To distil Red Rose-Buds	159
How to use this ordinary Still	ib.	To make Plague-water	ib.
To make Treacle-water	ib.	To make Surfeit-water	ib.
To make Black Cherry Water	ib.	To make Milk-water	ib.
To make Hysterical Water	ib.		

CHAP. XXI.
How to market, and the Seasons of the Year for Butcher's Meat, Poultry, Fish, Herbs, Roots, &c. and Fruit.

	Page		Page
A Bullock	160	April Fruits which are yet lasting	164
A Sheep	ib.	May, the Product of the Kitchen, and Fruit Garden this Month	ib.
A Calf	ib.		
House Lamb	ib.	June, the Product of the Kitchen, and Fruit Garden this Month	ib.
A Hog	ib.		
A Bacon Hog	ib.	July, the Product of the Kitchen and Fruit Garden	ib.
How to choose Butcher's Meat	ib.		
How to choose Brawn, Venison, Westphalia Hams, &c.	161	August, the Product of the Kitchen and Fruit Garden	ib.
How to choose Poultry	162	September, the Product of the Kitchen and Fruit Garden	ib.
Fish in Season Candlemas Quarter	163		
Midsummer Quarter	ib.	October, the Product of the Kitchen and Fruit Garden	ib.
Michaelmas Quarter	ib.		
Christmas Quarter	ib.	November, the Product of the Kitchen and Fruit Garden	ib.
How to choose Fish	ib.		
January Fruits which are yet lasting	164	December, the Product of the Kitchen and Fruit Garden	ib.
February Fruits which are yet lasting	ib.		
March Fruits which are yet lasting	ib.		

CHAP. XXII.
A certain Cure for the Bite of a Mad Dog.

	Page		Page
A Certain Cure for the Bite of a Mad Dog	166	A Receipt against the Plague	166
Another for the Bite of a Mad Dog	ib.	How to keep clear from Bugs	ib.

CHAP. II.
Of Dusting.

A little Instruction to the House-Maid will not be amiss, to preserve the Furniture, as this BOOK is only designed to INSTRUCT the Young and Ignorant.

ALWAYS when you sweep a *Room*, throw a little wet Sand all over it, and that will gather up all the Flew and Dust, prevents it from rising, cleans the Boards, and saves both Bedding, Pictures, and all other Furniture from Dust and Dirt.

TO THE
READER.

I Believe I have attempted a Branch of Cookery which Nobody has yet thought worth their while to write upon: But as I have both seen, and found by Experience that the Generality of Servants are greatly wanting in that Point, therefore I have taken upon me to instruct them in the best Manner I am capable; and I dare say, that every Servant who can but read will be capable of making a tollerable good Cook; and those who have the least Notion of Cookery can't miss of being very good ones.

If I have not wrote in the high, polite Stile, I hope I shall be forgiven; for my Intention is to instruct the lower Sort, and therefore must treat them in their own Way. For Example; when I bid them lard a Fowl, if I should bid them lard with large Lardoons, they would not know what I meant: But when I say they must lard with little Pieces of Bacon, they know what I mean. So in many other Things in Cookery, the great Cooks have such a high Way of expressing themselves that the poor Girls are a Loss to know what they mean: And in all Receipt Books yet printed there are such an odd Jumble of Things as would quite spoil a good Dish; and indeed some Things so extravagant, that it would be almost a Shame to make Use of them, when a Dish can be made full as good, or better without them. For Example; when you entertain ten or twelve People you shall use for a Cullis a Leg of Veal and a Ham; which, with the other Ingredients, makes it very expensive, and all this only to mix with other Sauce. And again, the Essence of a Ham for Sauce to one Dish; when I will prove it for about three Shillings I will make as rich and high a Sauce as all that will be, when done. For Example; take a large deep Stew-pan, Half a Pound of Bacon, Fat and Lean together, cut the Fat and lay it over the Bottom of the Pan; then take a Pound of Veal, cut it into thin Slices, beat it well with the Back of a Knife, lay it all over the Bacon; then have six Pennyworth of the coarse lean Part of the Beef cut thin and well beat, lay a Layer of it all over, with some Carrot, then the Lean of the Bacon cut thin and laid over that; then cut two Onions and strew over, a Bundle of Sweet Herbs, four or five Blades of Mace, six or seven Cloves, a Spoonful of Whole Pepper, Black and White together, Half a Nutmeg beat, a Pigeon beat all to Pieces, lay that all over, Half an Ounce of Truffles and Morels, then the rest of your Beef, a good Crust of Bread toasted very brown and dry on both Sides: You may add an old Cock beat to Pieces; cover it close, and let it stand over a slow Fire two or three Minutes, then pour in boiling Water enough to fill the Pan, cover it close, let it stew till it is as rich as you would have it; and then strain off all that Sauce. Put all your Ingredients together again, fill the Pan with boiling Water, put in a fresh Onion, a Blade of Mace, and a Piece of Carrot; cover it close, and let it stew till it is as strong as you want it. This will be full as good as the Essence of a Ham for all Sorts of Fowls, or indeed most Made-Dishes, mixed with a Glass of Wine and two or three Spoonfuls of Catchup. When your first Gravy is cool skim off all the Fat, and keep it for Use. This falls far short of the Expence of a Leg of Veal and a Ham; and answers every Purpose you want.

If you go to Market the Ingredients will not come to above Half a Crown; or, for about Eighteen-pence you may make as much good Gravy as will serve twenty People.

A

To the READER.

People. Take twelve Pennyworth of coarse lean Beef, which will be six or seven Pounds, cut it all to Pieces, flour it well; take a Quarter of a Pound of good Butter, put it into a little Pot or large deep Stew-pan, and put in your Beef: Keep stirring it, and when it begins to look a little Brown pour in a Pint of boiling Water; stir it together, put in a large Onion, a Bundle of Sweet Herbs, two or three Blades of Mace, five or six Cloves, a Spoonful of Whole Pepper, a Crust of Bread toasted, and a Piece of Carrot; then pour in four or five Quarts of Water, stir all together, cover close, and let it stew till it is as rich as you would have it; when enough, strain it off, mix with it two or three Spoonfuls of Catchup, and Half a Pint of White Wine; then put all the Ingredients together again, and put in two Quarts of boiling Water, cover it close and let it boil till there is about a Pint; strain it off well, add it to the first, and give it a boil all together. This will make a great deal of rich good Gravy.

You may leave out the Wine, according to what Use you want it for: So that really one might have a genteel Entertainment for the Price the Sauce of one Dish comes to. But if Gentlemen will have *French* Cooks, they must pay for *French* Tricks.

A *Frenchman*, in his own Country, would dress a fine Dinner of twenty Dishes, and all genteel and pretty, for the Expence he will put an *English* Lord to for dressing one Dish. But then there is the little petty Profit. I have heard of a Cook that used six Pounds of Butter to fry twelve Eggs; when every Body knows, that understands Cooking, that Half a Pound is full enough, or more than need be used: But then it would not be *French*. So much is the blind Folly of this Age, that they would rather be impos'd on by a *French* Booby, than give Encouragement to a good *English* Cook!

I doubt I shall not gain the Esteem of those Gentlemen: However, let that be as it will, it little concerns me; but should I be so happy as to gain the good Opinion of my own Sex I desire no more, that will be a full Recompence for all my Trouble: And I only beg the Favour of every Lady to read my Book throughout before they censure me, and then I flatter myself I shall have their Approbation.

I shall not take upon me to meddle in the physical Way farther than two Receipts which will be of Use to the Publick in general: One is for the Bite of a mad Dog; and the other, if a Man should be near where the Plague is, he shall be in no Danger; which, if made Use of, would be found of very great Service to those who go Abroad.

Nor shall I take upon me to direct a Lady in the Oeconomy of her Family, for every Mistress does, or at least ought to know what is most proper to be done there; therefore I shall not fill my Book with a deal of Nonsense of that Kind, which I am very well assur'd none will have Regard to.

I have indeed given some of my Dishes *French* Names to distinguish them, because they are known by those Names: And where there is great Variety of Dishes and a large Table to cover, so there must be Variety of Names for them; and it matters not whether they be call'd by a *French*, *Dutch* or *English* Name, so they are good, and done with as little Expence as the Dish will allow of.

Nor shall I take upon me to direct a Lady how to set out her Table; for that would be impertinent, and lessening her Judgment in the Oeconomy of her Family. I hope she will here find every Thing necessary for her Cook, and her own Judgment will tell her how they are to be placed. Nor indeed do I think it would be pretty, to see a Lady's Table set out after the Directions of a Book.

I shall say no more, only hope my Book will answer the Ends I intend it for; which is to improve the Servants, and save the Ladies a great deal of Trouble.

THE

THE ART OF COOKERY,

MADE

PLAIN and EASY.

CHAP. I.

Of Roasting, Boiling, &c.

THAT profess'd Cooks will find Fault with touching upon a Branch of Cookery which they never thought worth their Notice, is what I expect: However, this I know, it is the most necessary Part of it; and few Servants there are, that know how to Roast and Boil to Perfection.

I don't pretend to teach profess'd Cooks, but my Design is to instruct the Ignorant and Unlearned (which will likewise be of great Use in all private Families) and in so plain and full a Manner, that the most illeterate and ignorant Person, who can but read, will know how to do every Thing in Cookery well.

I shall first begin with Roast and Boil'd of all Sorts, and must desire the Cook to order her Fire according to what she is to dress; if any Thing very little or thin, then a pretty little brisk Fire, that it may be done quick and nice: If a very large Joint, then be sure a good Fire be laid to cake. Let it be clear at the Bottom; and when your Meat is Half done, move the Dripping-pan and Spit a little from the Fire, and stir up a good brisk Fire; for according to the Goodness of your Fire, your Meat will be done sooner or later.

BEEF.

IF Beef, be sure to Paper the Top, and baste it well all the Time it is roasting, and throw a Handful of Salt on it. When you see the Smoke draw to the Fire, it is near enough; then take off the Paper, baste it well, and drudge it with a little Flour to make a fine Froth. (Never salt your roast Meat before you lay it to the Fire, for that draws out all the Gravy. If you would keep it a few Days before you dress it, dry it very well with a clean Cloth, then flour it all over, and hang it where the Air will come to it; but be sure always to mind that there is no damp Place about it, if there is, you must dry it well with a Cloth.) Take up your Meat, and garnish your Dish with nothing but Horse-raddish.

MUTTON.

MUTTON and LAMB.

AS to roasting of Mutton; the Loin, the Saddle of Mutton (which is the two Loins) and the Chine (which is the two Necks) must be done as the Beef above: But all other Sorts of Mutton and Lamb must be roasted with a quick clear Fire, and without Paper; baste it when you lay it down and just before you take it up, and drudge it with a little Flour; but be sure not to use too much, for that takes away all the fine Taste of the Meat. Some chuse to skin a Loin of Mutton, and roast it Brown without Paper: But that you may do just as you please, but be sure always to take the Skin off a Breast of Mutton.

VEAL.

AS to Veal, you must be careful to roast it of a fine Brown; if a large Joint, a very good Fire; if a small Joint, a pretty little brisk Fire; if a Fillet or Loin, be sure to Paper the Fat, that you lose as little of that as possible. Lay it some Distance from the Fire till it is soaked, then lay it near the Fire. When you lay it down, baste it well with good Butter; and when it is near enough baste it again, and drudge it with a little Flour. The Breast you must roast with the Caul on till it is nigh enough; and skewer the Sweetbread on the Back-side of the Breast. When it is nigh enough, take off the Caul, baste it, and drudge it with a little Flour.

PORK.

PORK must be well done, or it is apt to Surfeit. When you roast a Loin, take a sharp Penknife and cut the Skin across, to make the Crackling eat the better. The Chine you must not cut at all. The best Way to roast a Leg, is first to parboil it, then skin it and roast it; baste it with Butter, then take a little Sage, shred it fine, a little Pepper and Salt, a little Nutmeg, and a few Crumbs of Bread; throw these over it all the Time it is roasting, then have a little Drawn Gravy to put in the Dish with the Crumbs that drop from it. Some love the Knuckle stuffed with Onions and Sage shred small, with a little Pepper and Salt, Gravy and Apple-Sauce to it. This they call a Mock-Goose. The Spring, or Hand of Pork, if very young, roasted like a Pig, eats very well, otherwise it is better boiled. The Sparerib should be basted with a little Bit of Butter, a very little Dust of Flour, and some Sage shred small: But we never make any Sauce to it but Apple-Sauce. The best Way to dress Pork Griskins is to roast them, baste them with a little Butter and Crumbs of Bread, Sage, and a little Pepper and Salt. Few eat any Thing with these but Mustard.

To Roast a Pig.

SPIT your Pig and lay it to the Fire, which must be a very good one at each End, or hang a flat Iron in the Middle of the Grate. Before you lay your Pig down, take a little Sage shred small, a Piece of Butter as big as a Walnut, and a little Pepper and Salt; put them into the Pig and sew it up with coarse Thread, then flour it all over very well, and keep flouring it till the Eyes drop out, or you find the Crackling hard. Be sure to save all the Gravy that comes out of it, which you must do by setting Basons or Pans under the Pig in the Dripping-pan, as soon as you find the Gravy begin to run. When the Pig is enough, stir the Fire up brisk; take a coarse Cloth, with about a Quarter of a Pound of Butter in it, and rub the Pig all over till the Crackling is quite crisp, and then take it up. Lay it in your Dish, and with a sharp Knife cut off the Head, and then cut the Pig in two, before you draw out the Spit. Cut the Ears off the Head and lay at each End, and cut the Under-Jaw in two and lay on each Side: Melt some good Butter, take the Gravy you saved and put into it, boil it, and pour it into the Dish with the Brains bruised fine, and the Sage mixed all together, and then send it to Table.

Different Sorts of Sauce for a Pig.

NOW you are to observe there are several Ways of making Sauce for a Pig. Some don't love any Sage in the Pig, only a Crust of Bread; but then you should have a little dried Sage rubbed and mixed with the Gravy and Butter. Some love Bread-Sauce in a Bason; made thus: Take a Pint of Water, put in good Piece of Crumb of Bread, a Blade of Mace, and a little Whole Pepper; boil it for about five or six Minutes, and then pour the Water off: Take out the Spice, and beat up the Bread with a good Piece of Butter. Some love a few Currants boiled in it, a Glass of Wine, and a little Sugar; but that you must do just as you like it. Others take Half a Pint of good Beef Gravy, and the Gravy which comes out of the Pig, with a Piece of Butter rolled in Flour, two Spoonfuls of Catchup, and boil them all together; then take the Brains of the Pig and bruise them fine, with two Eggs boiled hard and chopped: Put all these together, with the Sage in the Pig, and pour into your Dish. It is very good Sauce. When you have not Gravy enough comes out of your Pig with the Butter for Sauce, take about Half a Pint of Veal Gravy and add to it: Or stew the Petty-Toes, and take as much of that Liquor as will do for Sauce mixed with the other.

To Roast the Hind-Quarter of a Pig, Lamb Fashion.

AT the Time of the Year when House-Lamb is very dear, take the Hind-Quarter of a large Pig; take off the Skin and roast it, and it will eat like Lamb with Mint Sauce, or with a Sallad or *Seville* Orange. Half an Hour will roast it.

To Bake a Pig.

IF you should be in a Place where you cannot roast a Pig, lay it in a Dish, flour it all over very well, and rub it over with Butter; Butter the Dish you lay it in, and put it into an Oven. When it is enough, draw it out of the Oven's Mouth, and rub it over with a buttery Cloth; then put it into the Oven again till it is dry, take it out and lay it in a Dish; cut it up, take a little Veal Gravy, and take off the Fat in the Dish it was bak'd in, and there will be some good Gravy at the Bottom; put that to it, with a little Piece of Butter rolled in Flour; boil it up, and put it into the Dish with the Brains and Sage in the Belly. Some love a Pig brought whole to Table, then you are only to put what Sauce you like into the Dish.

To melt Butter.

IN melting of Butter you must be very careful; let your Sauce-pan be well tinn'd, take a Spoonful of cold Water, a little Dust of Flour, and your Butter cut to Pieces: Be sure to keep shaking your Pan one Way for fear it should oil; when it is all melted, let it boil, and it will be smooth and fine. A Silver Pan is best, if you have one.

To Roast Geese, Turkies, &c.

WHEN you roast a Goose, Turky, or Fowls of any Sort, take care to singe them with a Piece of white Paper, and baste them with a Piece of Butter, drudge them with a little Flour, and when the Smoak begins to draw to the Fire, and they look plump, baste them again, and drudge them with a little Flour, and take them up.

Sauce for a Goose.

FOR a Goose make a little good Gravy, and put it in a Bason by itself, and some Apple-sauce in another.

Sauce for a Turky.

FOR a Turky good Gravy in the Dish, and either Bread or Onion Sauce in a Bason.

Sauce for Fowls.

TO Fowls you should put good Gravy in the Dish, and either Bread or Egg Sauce in a Bason.

Sauce for Ducks.

FOR Ducks a little Gravy in the Dish, and Onion in a Cup, if liked.

Sauce for Pheasants and Partridges.

PHEASANTS and Partridges should have Gravy in the Dish, and Bread Sauce in a Cup.

Sauce for Larks.

LARKS, roast them, and for Sauce have Crumbs of Bread done thus: Take a Sauce-pan or Stew-pan and some Butter; when melted, have a good Piece of Crumb of Bread, and rub it in a clean Cloth to Crumbs, then throw it into your Pan; keep stirring them about till they are brown, then throw them into a Sieve to drain, and lay them round your Larks.

To Roast Woodcocks and Snipes.

PUT them on a little Spit; take a Round of a Three-penny Loaf and toast it brown, then lay it in a Dish under the Birds, baste them with a little Butter, and let the Trail drop on the Toast. When they are roasted put the Toast in the Dish, lay the Woodcocks on it, and have about a Quarter of a Pint of Gravy; pour it into the Dish, and set it over a Lamp or Chaffing-dish for three Minutes, and send them to Table. You are to observe, we never take any Thing out of a Woodcock or Snipe.

The Art of Cookery, made Plain and Easy.

To Roast a Pigeon.

TAKE some Parsley shred fine, a Piece of Butter as big as a Wallnut, a little Pepper and Salt; tye the Neck End tight; tye a String round the Legs and Rump, and fasten the other End to the Top of the Chimney-piece: Baste them with Butter, and when they are enough lay them in the Dish, and they will swim with Gravy. You may put them on a little small Spit, and then tye both Ends close.

To Broil a Pigeon.

WHEN you broil them, do them in the same Manner, and take care your Fire is very clear, and set your Gridiron high, that they may not burn, and have a little melted Butter in a Cup. You may split them, and broil them with a little Pepper and Salt; and you may roast them only with a little Parsley and Butter in the Dish.

Directions for Geese and Ducks.

AS to Geese and Ducks, you should have some Sage shred fine, and a little Pepper and Salt, and put them into the Belly; but never put any Thing into Wild Ducks.

To Roast a Hare.

TAKE your Hare when it is cas'd and make a Pudding; take a Quarter of a Pound of Sewet, and as much Crumbs of Bread, a little Parsley shred fine, and about as much Thyme as will lie on a Six-pence, when shred; an Anchovy shred small, a very little Pepper and Salt, some Nutmeg, two Eggs, a little Lemon-peel: Mix all this together, and put it into the Hare. Sew up the Belly, spit it, and lay it to the Fire, which must be a good one. Your Dripping-pan must be very clean and nice. Put two Quarts of Milk and Half a Pound of Butter into the Pan; keep basting it all the while it is roasting with the Butter and Milk till the Whole is used, and your Hare will be enough. You may mix the Liver in the Pudding, if you like it. You must first parboil it, and then chop it fine.

Different Sorts of Sauce for a Hare.

TAKE for Sauce a Pint of Cream and Half a Pound of fresh Butter; put them in a Sauce-pan, and keep stirring it with a Spoon till all the Butter is melted, and the Sauce is thick; then take up the Hare, and pour the Sauce into the Dish. Another Way to make Sauce for a Hare, is to make good Gravy, thicken'd with a little Piece of Butter rolled in Flour, and pour it into your Dish. You may leave the Butter out, if you don't like it, and have some Currant Jelly warm'd in a Cup, or Red Wine and Sugar boil'd to a Syrup: Done thus; take Half a Pint of Red Wine, a Quarter of a Pound of Sugar, and set it over a slow Fire to simmer for about a Quarter of an Hour. You may do Half the Quantity and put it into your Sauce-Boat or Bason.

To Broil Steaks.

FIRST have a very clear brisk Fire; let your Gridiron be very clean; put it on the Fire, and take a Chaffing-dish with a few hot Coals out of the Fire: Put the Dish on it which is to lay your Steaks on, then take fine Rump Steaks about Half an Inch thick; put a little Pepper and Salt on them, lay them on the Gridiron, and (if you like it) take a Shalot or two, or a fine Onion, and cut it fine; put it into your Dish: Don't turn your Steaks till one Side is done, then when you turn the other Side there will soon be a fine Gravy lie on the Top of the Steak, which you must be careful not to lose. When the Steaks are enough take them carefully off into your Dish, that none of the Gravy be lost; then have ready a hot Dish or Cover, and carry them hot to Table, with the Cover on.

Directions concerning the Sauce for Steaks.

IF you love Pickles or Horse-raddish with Steaks, never garnish your Dish; because both the Garnishing will be dry, and the Steaks will be cold, but lay those Things on little Plates, and carry to Table. The great Nicety is to have them hot and full of Gravy.

General Directions concerning Broiling.

AS to Mutton and Pork Steaks, you must keep them turning quick on the Gridiron, and have ready your Dish over a Chaffing-dish of hot Coals, and carry them to Table cover'd hot. When you broil Fowls or Pigeons always take Care your Fire is clear, and never baste any Thing on the Gridiron, for it only makes it smoak'd and burnt.

The Art of Cookery, made Plain and Easy.

General Directions concerning Boiling.

AS to all Sorts of boil'd Meats, allow a Quarter of an Hour to every Pound; be sure the Pot is very clean, and skim it well, for every Thing will have a Scum rise, and if that boils down it makes the Meat black. All Sorts of fresh Meat you are to put in when the Water boils; but salt Meat when the Water is cold.

To Boil a Ham.

WHEN you boil a Ham, put it into a Copper, if you have one; let it be about three or four Hours before it boils, and keep it well skim'd all the Time; then, if it is a small one, one Hour and a Half will boil it, after the Copper begins to boil; and, if a large one, two Hours will do: For you are to consider the Time it has been heating in the Water, which softens the Ham, and makes it boil the sooner.

To Boil a Tongue.

A Tongue, if salt, put it in the Pot over Night, and don't let it boil till about three Hours before Dinner, and then boil all that three Hours; if fresh out of the Pickle, two Hours, and put it in when the Water boils.

To Boil Fowls and House-Lamb.

FOWLS and House-Lamb boil in a Pot by themselves, in a good deal of Water, and if any Scum rises take it off. They will be both sweeter and whiter than if boil'd in a Cloth. A little Chicken will be done in fifteen Minutes, a large Chicken in twenty Minutes, a good Fowl in Half an Hour, a little Turky or Goose in an Hour, and a large Turky an Hour and a Half.

Sauce for a Boil'd Turky.

THE best Sauce to a boil'd Turky is this: Take a little Water, or Mutton Gravy, if you have it, a Blade of Mace, an Onion, a little Bit of Thyme, a little Bit of Lemon-peel, and an Anchovy; boil all these together, strain them through a Sieve, melt some Butter and add to them, and fry a few Sausages and lay round the Dish. Garnish your Dish with Lemon.

Sauce for a Boil'd Goose.

SAUCE for a boil'd Goose must be either Onions or Cabbage, first boil'd, and then stew'd in Butter for five Minutes.

Sauce for Boil'd Ducks or Rabbits.

TO boil'd Ducks or Rabbits, you must pour boil'd Onions over them, which make thus: Take the Onions, peel them, and boil them in a great deal of Water; shift your Water, then let them boil about two Hours, take them up and throw them into a Cullender to drain, then with a Knife chop them on a Board; put them into a Sauce-pan, just shake a little Flour over them, put in a little Milk or Cream, with a good Piece of Butter; set them over the Fire, and when the Butter is all melted they are enough. But if you would have Onion-Sauce in Half an Hour, take your Onions, peel them, and cut them in thin Slices, put them into Milk and Water, and when the Water boils they will be done in twenty Minutes, then throw them into a Cullender to drain, and chop them and put them into a Sauce-pan; shake in a little Flour, with a little Cream, if you have it, and a good Piece of Butter; stir all together over the Fire till the Butter is melted, and they will be very fine. This Sauce is very good with roast Mutton, and it is the best Way of boiling Onions.

To Roast Venison.

TAKE a Haunch of Venison, and spit it; take four Sheets of white Paper, butter them well, and roll about your Venison, then tye the Paper on with a small String, and baste it very well all the Time it is Roasting. If your Fire is very good and brisk, two Hours will do it; and, if a small Haunch, an Hour and a Half. The Neck and Shoulder must be done in the same Manner, which will take an Hour and a Half, and when it is enough take off the Paper, and drudge it with a little Flour just to make a Froth; but you must be very quick, for fear the Fat should melt. You must not put any Sauce in the Dish but what comes out of the Meat, but have some very good Gravy and put into your Sauce-Boat or Bason: You must always have Sweet-Sauce with your Venison in another Bason. If it is a very large Haunch it will take two Hours and a Half.

Different

Different Sorts of Sauce for Venison.

YOU may take either of these Sauces for Venison: Currant Jelly warm'd; or Half a Pint of Red Wine, with a Quarter of a Pound of Sugar, simmer'd over a clear Fire for five or six Minutes; or Half a Pint of Vinegar, and a Quarter of a Pound of Sugar, simmer'd till it is a Syrup.

To Roast Mutton, Venison Fashion.

TAKE a Hind-Quarter of fat Mutton, and cut the Leg like a Haunch; lay it in a Pan with the Back-Side of it down; pour a Bottle of Red Wine over it, and let it lie twenty-four Hours, then spit it, and baste it with the same Liquor and Butter all the Time it is roasting at a good quick Fire, and an Hour and a Half will do it. Have a little good Gravy in a Cup, and Sweet-Sauce in another. A good fat Neck of Mutton eats finely, done thus.

To keep Venison or Hares sweet; or to make them fresh, when they stink.

IF your Venison be very sweet, only dry it with a Cloth, and hang it where the Air comes. If you would keep it any Time, dry it very well with clean Cloths, rub it all over with beaten Ginger, and hang it in an airy Place, and it will keep a great while. If it stinks, or is musty, take some luke-warm Water, and wash it clean; then take fresh Milk and Water luke-warm, and wash it again; then dry it in clean Cloths very well, and rub it all over with beaten Ginger, and hang it in an airy Place. When you roast it, you need only wipe it with a clean Cloth and paper it, as before-mention'd. Never do any Thing else to Venison, for all other Things spoil your Venison, and take away the fine Flavour, and this preserves it better than any Thing you can do. A Hare you may manage just the same Way.

To Roast a Tongue, or Udder.

PArboil it first, then roast it, stick eight or ten Cloves about it; baste it with Butter, and have some Gravy and Sweet-Sauce. An Udder eats very well, done the same Way.

To Roast Rabbits.

BASTE them with good Butter, and drudge them with a little Flour. Half an Hour will do them, at a very quick clear Fire; and, if they are very small, twenty Minutes will do them. Take the Liver, with a little Bunch of Parsley, and boil them, and then chop them very fine together. Melt some good Butter, and put Half the Liver and Parsley into the Butter; pour it into the Dish, and garnish the Dish with the other Half. Let your Rabbits be done of a fine light Brown.

To Roast a Rabbit, Hare Fashion.

LARD a Rabbit with Bacon; roast it as you do a Hare, and it eats very well: But then you must make Gravy-Sauce; but if you don't lard it White-Sauce.

Turkies, Pheasants, &c. may be Larded.

YOU may lard a Turky, or Pheasant, or any Thing, just as you like it.

To Roast a Fowl, Pheasant Fashion.

IF you should have but one Pheasant, and want two in a Dish, take a large full-grown Fowl, keep the Head on, and truss it just as you do a Pheasant; lard it with Bacon, but don't lard the Pheasant, and no Body will know it.

Rules to be observ'd in Roasting.

IN the first Place, take great Care the Spit be very clean; and be sure to clean it with nothing but Sand and Water. Wash it clean, and wipe it with a dry Cloth; for Oil, Brick-dust, and such Things, will spoil your Meat.

BEEF.

TO roast a Piece of Beef of about ten Pounds will take an Hour and a Half, at a good Fire. Twenty Pounds Weight will take three Hours, if it be a thick Piece; but if it be a thin Piece of twenty Pounds Weight, two Hours and a Half will do it; and so on, according to the Weight of your Meat, more or less. *Observe*, In frosty Weather your Beef will take Half an Hour longer.

MUTTON.

The Art of Cookery, made Plain and Easy.

MUTTON.

A Leg of Mutton of six Pounds will take an Hour at a quick Fire; if frosty Weather an Hour and a Quarter; nine Pounds, an Hour and a Half; a Leg of twelve Pounds will take two Hours; if frosty, two Hours and a Half; a large Saddle of Mutton will take three Hours, because of papering it; a small Saddle will take an Hour and a Half, and so on, according to the Size; a Breast will take Half an Hour at a quick Fire; a Neck, if large, an Hour; if very small, little better than Half an Hour; a Shoulder much about the same Time as the Leg.

PORK.

PORK must be well done. To every Pound allow a Quarter of an Hour: For Example; a Joint of twelve Pounds Weight three Hours, and so on; if it be a thin Piece of that Weight two Hours will roast it.

Directions concerning Beef, Mutton and Pork.

THESE three you may baste with fine nice Dripping. Be sure your Fire be very good and brisk; but don't lay your Meat too near the Fire, for fear of burning or scorching.

VEAL.

VEAL takes much the same Time roasting as Pork; but be sure to paper the Fat of a Loin or Fillet, and baste your Veal with good Butter.

HOUSE-LAMB.

IF a large Fore-Quarter an Hour and a Half; if a small one, an Hour. The Out-side must be paper'd, basted with good Butter, and you must have a very quick Fire. If a Leg, about three Quarters of an Hour; a Neck, Breast or Shoulder, three Quarters of an Hour; if very small, Half an Hour will do.

A PIG.

IF just kill'd, an Hour; if kill'd the Day before, an Hour and a Quarter; if a very large one, an Hour and a Half. But the best Way to judge is when the Eyes drop out, and the Skin is grown very hard; then you must rub it with a coarse Cloth, with a good Piece of Butter roll'd in it, till the Crackling is crisp, and of a fine light Brown.

A HARE.

YOU must have a quick Fire. If it be a small Hare, put three Pints of Milk and Half a Pound of fresh Butter in the Dripping-pan, which must be very clean and nice; if a large one, two Quarts of Milk and Half a Pound of fresh Butter. You must baste your Hare well with this all the Time it is roasting, and when the Hare has soak'd up all the Butter and Milk it will be enough.

A TURKY.

A Middling Turky will take an Hour; a very large one, an Hour and a Quarter; a small one, three Quarters of an Hour. You must paper the Breast till it is near done enough, then take the Paper off and froth it up. Your Fire must be very good.

A GOOSE.

OBSERVE the same Rules.

FOWLS.

A Large Fowl, three Quarters of an Hour; a middling one, Half an Hour; very small Chickens, twenty Minutes. Your Fire must be very quick and clear when you lay them down.

TAME DUCKS.

OBSERVE the same Rules.

C   WILD

10   *The Art of Cookery, made Plain and Easy.*

WILD DUCKS.

TEN Minutes at a very quick Fire will do them; but if you love them well done, a Quarter of an Hour.

TEAL, WIGEON, &c.

OBSERVE the same Rules.

WOODCOCKS, SNIPES and PARTRIDGES.

THEY will take twenty Minutes.

PIGEONS and LARKS.

THEY will take fifteen Minutes to do them.

Directions concerning Poultry.

IF your Fire is not very quick and clear when you lay your Poultry down to roast, it will not eat near so sweet, or look so beautiful to the Eye.

To keep Meat hot.

THE best Way to keep Meat hot, if it be done before your Company is ready, is to set the Dish over a Pan of boiling Water; cover the Dish with a deep Cover so as not to touch the Meat, and throw a Cloth over all. Thus you may keep your Meat hot a long Time, and it is better than over roasting and spoiling the Meat. The Steam of the Water keeps the Meat hot, and don't draw the Gravy out, or dry it up: whereas if you set a Dish of Meat any Time over a Chaffing-dish of Coals, it will dry up all the Gravy, and spoil the Meat.

To dress Greens, Roots, &c.

ALWAYS be very careful that your Greens be nicely pick'd and wash'd. You should lay them in a clean Pan for fear of Sand or Dust, which is apt to hang round wooden Vessels. Boil all your Greens in a Copper Sauce-pan by themselves with a great Quantity of Water. Boil no Meat with them, for that discolours them. Use no Iron Pans, &c. for they are not proper; but let them be Copper, Brass or Silver.

To dress Spinach.

PICK it very clean, and wash it in five or six Waters; put it in a Sauce-pan that will just hold it, throw a little Salt over it, and cover the Pan close. Don't put any Water in, but shake the Pan often. You must put your Sauce-pan on a clear quick Fire. As soon as you find the Greens are shrunk and fallen to the Bottom, and that the Liquor which comes out of them boils up, they are enough. Throw them into a clean Sieve to drain, and just give them a little Squeeze. Lay them in a Plate, and never put any Butter on it, but put it in a Cup.

To dress Cabbages, &c.

CAbbage, and all Sorts of young Sprouts must be boiled in a great deal of Water. When the Stalks are tender, or fall to the Bottom, they are enough; then take them off, before they lose their Colour. Always throw Salt into your Water before you put your Greens in. Young Sprouts you send to Table just as they are, but Cabbage is best chop'd and put into a Sauce-pan with a good Piece of Butter, stirring it for about five or six Minutes till the Butter is all melted, and then send it to Table.

To dress Carrots.

LET them be scrap'd very clean, and when they are enough rub them in a clean Cloth, then slice them into a Plate, and pour some melted Butter over them. If they are young Spring Carrots, Half an Hour will boil them; if large, an Hour; but old *Sandwich* Carrots will take two Hours.

To

To dress Turnips.

THEY eat best boil'd in the Pot, and when enough take them out and put them into a Pan and mash them with Butter and a little Salt, and send them to Table. But you may do them thus; pare your Turnips, and cut them into Dice as big as the Top of one's Finger; put them into a clean Sauce-pan and just cover them with Water; when enough throw them into a Sieve to drain, and put them into a Sauce-pan with a good Piece of Butter; stir them over the Fire for five or six Minutes, and send them to Table.

To dress Parsnips.

THEY should be boil'd in a great deal of Water, and when you find they are soft (which you will know by running a Fork into them) take them up, and carefully scrape all the Dirt off them, and then with a Knife scrape them all fine, throwing away all the sticky Parts; then put them into a Sauce-pan with some Milk, and stir them over the Fire till they are thick. Take great Care they don't burn, and add a good Piece of Butter and a little Salt, and when the Butter is melted send them to Table.

To dress Brockala.

STRIP all the little Branches off till you come to the top one, then with a Knife peel off all the hard outside Skin which is on the Stalks and little Branches, and throw them into Water. Have a Stew-pan of Water with some Salt in it: When it boils put in the Brockala, and when the Stalks are tender it is enough, then send it to Table with Butter in a Cup. The *French* eat Oil and Vinegar with it.

To dress Potatoes.

YOU must boil them in as little Water as you can without burning the Sauce-pan. Cover the Sauce-pan close, and when the Skin begins to crack they are enough: Drain all the Water out and let them stand cover'd for a Minute or two; then peel them, lay them in your Plate, and pour some melted Butter over them. The best Way to do them is, when they are peel'd to lay them on a Gridiron till they are of a fine Brown, and send them to Table. Another Way is to put them into a Sauce-pan with some good Beef Dripping; cover them close, and shake the Sauce-pan often for fear of burning to the Bottom: When they are of a fine Brown and crisp, take them up in a Plate, then put them into another for fear of the Fat, and put Butter in a Cup.

To dress Cauliflowers.

TAKE your Flowers, cut off all the green Part, and then cut the Flowers into four, and lay them in Water for an Hour: Then have some Milk and Water boiling, put in the Cauliflowers, and be sure to skim the Sauce-pan well. When the Stalks are tender take them carefully up, and put them into a Cullender to drain; then put a Spoonful of Water into a clean Stew-pan with a little Dust of Flour, about a Quarter of a Pound of Butter, and shake it round till it is all finely melted, with a little Pepper and Salt; then take Half the Cauliflower and cut it as you would for Pickling, lay it into the Stew-pan, turn it, and shake the Pan round. Ten Minutes will do it. Lay the stew'd in the Middle of your Plate, and the boil'd round it: Pour the Butter you did it in over it, and send it to Table.

To dress French Beans.

FIRST string them, then cut them in two, and afterwards across: But if you would do them nice, cut the Bean into four, and then across, which is eight Pieces; lay them into Water and Salt, and when your Pan boils put in some Salt and the Beans: When they are tender they are enough; they will be soon done. Take Care they don't lose their fine Green. Lay them in a Plate, and have Butter in a Cup.

To dress Artichokes.

WRING off the Stalks, and put them into the Water cold with the Tops downwards, that all the Dust and Sand may boil out. When the Water boils, an Hour and a Half will do them.

To dress Asparagus.

SCRAPE all the Stalks very carefully till they look white, then cut all the Stalks even alike, throw them into Water and have ready a Stew-pan boiling: Put in some Salt, and tye the Asparagus in little Bundles. Let the Water keep boiling, and when they are a little tender take them up. If you boil them too much you lose both Colour and Taste. Cut the Round of a small Loaf about Half an Inch thick, toast it Brown on both Sides, dip it in the Asparagus Liquor, and lay it in your Dish: Pour a little Butter over the Toast, then lay your Asparagus on the Toast all round the Dish with the white Tops outward. Don't pour Butter over the Asparagus, for that makes them greesy to the Fingers, but have your Butter in a Bason, and send it to Table.

Directions

Directions concerning Garden Things.

MOST People spoil Garden Things by over boiling them: All Things that are Green should have a little Crispness, for if they are over boil'd they neither have any Sweetness or Beauty.

To dress Beans and Bacon.

WHEN you dress Beans and Bacon, boil the Bacon by itself and the Beans by themselves, for the Bacon will spoil the Colour of the Beans. Always throw some Salt into the Water, and some Parsley nicely pick'd. When the Beans are enough (which you will know by their being tender) throw them into a Cullender to drain: Take up the Bacon and skin it; throw some Raspings of Bread over the Top, and if you have an Iron make it red-hot and hold over it, to brown the Top of the Bacon: If you have not one, set it before the Fire to brown. Lay the Beans in the Dish, and the Bacon in the Middle on the Top, and send them to Table, with Butter in a Bason.

To make Gravy for a Turky, or any Sort of Fowl.

TAKE a Pound of the lean Part of the Beef, hack it with a Knife, flour it very well, have ready a Stew-pan with a Piece of fresh Butter: When the Butter is melted put in the Beef, fry it till it is brown; and then pour in a little boiling Water; shake it round, and then fill up with a Tea-kettle of boiling Water: Stir it all together, and put in two or three Blades of Mace, four or five Cloves, some Whole Pepper, an Onion, a Bundle of Sweet Herbs, a little Crust of Bread baked brown, and a little Piece of Carrot: Cover it close, and let it stew till it is as good as you would have it. This will make a Pint of rich Gravy.

To draw Mutton, Beef, or Veal Gravy.

TAKE a Pound of Meat, cut it very thin, lay a little Piece of Bacon about two Inches long at the Bottom of the Stew-pan or Sauce-pan, and lay the Meat on it: Lay in some Carrot, and cover it close for two or three Minutes, then pour in a Quart of boiling Water, some Spice, Onion, Sweet Herbs, and a little Crust of Bread toasted; let it do over a slow Fire, and thicken it with a little Piece of Butter rolled in Flour. When the Gravy is as good as you would have it season it with Salt, and then strain it off. You may omit the Bacon, if you dislike it.

To burn Butter for thickening of Sauce.

SET your Butter on the Fire and let it boil till it is brown, then shake in some Flour, and stir it all the Time it is on the Fire till it is thick. Put it bye, and keep it for Use. A little Piece is what the Cooks use to thicken and brown their Sauce; but there are few Stomachs it agrees with, therefore seldom make use of it.

To make Gravy.

IF you live in the Country where you can't always have Gravy Meat, when your Meat comes from the Butcher take a Piece of Beef, a Piece of Veal, and a Piece of Mutton; cut them into as small Pieces as you can, and take a large deep Sauce-pan with a Cover, lay your Beef at Bottom, then your Mutton, then a very little Piece of Bacon, a Slice or two of Carrot, some Mace, Cloves, Whole Pepper Black and White, a large Onion cut in Slices, a Bundle of Sweet Herbs, and then lay in your Veal: Cover it close over a very slow Fire for six or seven Minutes, shaking the Sauce-pan now and then; then shake some Flour in, and have ready some boiling Water, pour it in till you cover the Meat and something more: Cover it close, and let it stew till it is quite rich and good; then season it to your Taste with Salt, and strain it off. This will do for most Things.

To make Gravy for Soops, &c.

TAKE a Leg of Beef, cut and hack it, put it into a large earthen Pan; put to it a Bundle of Sweet Herbs, two Onions stuck with a few Cloves, a Blade or two of Mace, a Piece of Carrot, a Spoonful of Whole Pepper Black and White, and a Quart of stale Beer: Cover it with Water, tye the Pot down close with Brown Paper rubbed with Butter, send it to the Oven, and let it be well baked. When it comes Home, strain it through a coarse Sieve; lay the Meat into a clean Dish as you strain it, and keep it for Use. It is a fine Thing in a House, and will serve for Gravy, thicken'd with a Piece of Butter, Red Wine, Catchup, or whatever you have a mind to put in, and is always ready for Soops of most Sorts. If you have Pease ready boil'd, your Soop will soon be made: Or take some of the Broth and some *Vermicelli*, boil it together, fry a *French* Roll and put in the Middle, and you have a good Soop. You may add a few Truffles and Morels, or Sellery stew'd tender, and then you are always ready.

To Bake a Leg of Beef.

DO it just in the same Manner as before directed in the making Gravy for Soops, &c. and when it is baked, strain it through a coarse Sieve: Pick out all the Sinews and Fat, put them into a Sauce-pan with a few Spoonfuls of the Gravy, a little Red Wine, a little Piece of Butter rolled in Flour, and some Mustard; shake your Sauce-pan often, and when the Sauce is hot and thick dish it up and send it to Table. It is a pretty Dish.

To Bake an Ox's Head.

DO it just in the same Manner as the Leg of Beef is directed to be done in the making Gravy for Soops, &c. and it does full as well for the same Uses. If it should be too strong for any Thing you want it for, it is only putting some hot Water to it. Cold Water will spoil it.

To Boil Pickled Pork.

BE sure you put it in when the Water boils. If a middling Piece an Hour will boil it: If a very large Piece, an Hour and a Half, or two Hours. If you boil pickled Pork too long it will go to a Jelly.

CHAP. II.
MADE-DISHES.

To dress Scotch Collops.

TAKE Veal, cut it thin, beat it well with the Back of a Knife or Rolling-pin, and grate some Nutmeg over them; dip them in the Yolk of an Egg, and fry them in a little Butter till they are of a fine Brown; then pour the Butter from them, and have ready Half a Pint of Gravy, a little Piece of Butter rolled in Flour, a few Mushrooms, a Glass of White Wine, the Yolk of an Egg, and a little Cream mixt together. If it wants a little Salt put it in. Stir it all together, and when it is of a fine Thickness dish it up. It does very well without the Cream, if you have none; and very well without Gravy, only put in just as much warm Water, and either Red or White Wine.

To dress White Scotch Collops.

DO not dip them in Egg, but fry them till they are tender, but not Brown. Take your Meat out of the Pan, and pour all out; then put in your Meat again, as above, only you must put in some Cream.

To dress a Fillet of Veal with Collops, &c.

FOR an Alteration, take a small Fillet of Veal, cut what Collops you want, then take the Udder and fill it with Force-Meat, roll it round, tye it with a Packthread across, and roast it; lay your Collops in the Dish, and lay the Udder in the Middle. Garnish your Dishes with Lemon.

To make Force-Meat Balls.

NOW you are to observe, that Force-Meat Balls are a great Addition to all Made-Dishes, made thus: Take Half a Pound of Veal, and Half a Pound of Sewet, cut fine, and beat in a Marble Mortar or Wooden Bowl; have a few Sweet Herbs shred fine, a little Mace dry'd and beat fine, a small Nutmeg grated, or Half a large one, a little Lemon-peel cut very fine, a little Pepper and Salt, and the Yolks of two Eggs; mix all these well together, then roll them in little round Balls, and some in little long Balls; roll them in Flour, and fry them Brown. If they are for any Thing of White Sauce, put a little Water on in a Sauce-pan, and when the Water boils put them in, and let them boil for a few Minutes, but never fry them for White Sauce.

Truffles and Morels, good in Sauces and Soops.

TAKE Half an Ounce of Truffles and Morels, simmer them in two or three Spoonfuls of Water for a few Minutes, then put them with the Liquor into the Sauce. They thicken both Sauce and Soop, and give it a fine Flavour.

14   *The Art of Cookery, made Plain and Easy.*

To Stew Ox-Palates.

STEW them very tender: Which must be done by putting them into cold Water, and let them stew very softly over a slow Fire till they are tender, then cut them into Pieces and put them either into your Made-Dish or Soop; and Cocks-combs and Artichoke-bottoms, cut small, and put into the Made-Dish. Garnish your Dishes with Lemon, Sweetbread stewed for White Dishes, and fry'd for Brown Ones, and cut in little Pieces.

To Ragoo a Leg of Mutton.

TAKE all the Skin and Fat off, cut it very thin the right Way of the Grain, then butter your Stew-pan, and shake some Flour into it; slice Half a Lemon and Half an Onion, cut them very small, a little Bundle of Sweet Herbs, and a Blade of Mace: Put all together with your Meat into the Pan, stir it a Minute or two, then put in six Spoonfuls of Gravy, and have ready an Anchovy minc'd small; mix it with some Butter and Flour, stir it all together for six Minutes, and then dish it up.

To make a Brown Fricasey.

YOU must take your Rabbits or Chickens and skin them, then cut them into small Pieces, and rub them over with Yolks of Eggs: Have ready some grated Bread, a little beaten Mace, and a little grated Nutmeg mixt together, and then roll them in it; put a little Butter into your Stew-pan, and when it is melted put in your Meat; Fry it of a fine Brown, and take Care they don't stick to the Bottom of the Pan, then pour the Butter from them, and pour in Half a Pint of Gravy, a Glass of Red Wine, a few Mushrooms, or two Spoonfuls of the Pickle, a little Salt (if wanted) and a Piece of Butter rolled in Flour. When it is of a fine Thickness dish it up, and send it to Table.

To make a White Fricasey.

YOU may take two Chickens or Rabbits, skin them, and cut them into little Pieces; lay them into warm Water to draw out all the Blood, and then lay them in a clean Cloth to dry: Put them into a Stew-pan with Milk and Water, stew them till they are tender, and then take a clean Pan, put in Half a Pint of Cream and a Quarter of a Pound of Butter; stir it together till the Butter is melted, but you must be sure to keep it stirring all the Time or it will be greasy, and then with a Fork take the Chickens or Rabbits out of the Stew-pan and put into the Sauce-pan to the Butter and Cream: Have ready a little Mace dry'd and beat fine, a very little Nutmeg, a few Mushrooms, shake all together for a Minute or two, and dish it up. If you have no Mushrooms a Spoonful of the Pickle does full as well, and gives it a pretty Tartness. This is a very pretty Sauce for a Breast of Veal roasted.

To Fricasey Chickens, Rabbits, Lamb, Veal, &c.

DO them the same Way.

A second Way to make a White Fricasey.

YOU must take two or three Rabbits or Chickens, skin them, and lay them in warm Water, and dry them with a clean Cloth; put them into a Stew-pan with a Blade or two of Mace, a little Black and a little White Pepper, an Onion, a little Bundle of Sweet Herbs, and do but just cover them with Water; stew them till they are tender, then with a Fork take them out, strain the Liquor, and put them into the Pan again with Half a Pint of the Liquor and Half a Pint of Cream, the Yolks of two Eggs beat well, Half a Nutmeg grated, a Glass of White Wine, a little Piece of Butter rolled in Flour, and a Gill of Mushrooms; keep stirring all together, all the while one Way, till it is smooth and of a fine Thickness, and then dish it up. Add what you please.

A third Way of making a White Fricasey.

TAKE three Chickens, skin them, cut them into small Pieces; that is, every Joint asunder, lay them in warm Water for a Quarter of an Hour, take them out and dry them with a Cloth, then put them into a Stew-pan with Milk and Water, and boil them tender; take a Pint of good Cream, a Quarter of a Pound of Butter, and stir it till it is thick, then let it stand till it is cool, and put to it a little beaten Mace, Half a Nutmeg grated, a little Salt, a Gill of White Wine, and a few Mushrooms; stir all together, then take the Chickens out of the Stew-pan, throw away what they were boil'd in, clean the Pan, and put in the Chickens and Sauce together: Keep the Pan shaking round till they are quite hot, and dish them up. Garnish with Lemon. They will be very good without Wine.

To Fricasey Rabbits, Lamb, Sweetbreads, or Tripe.

DO them the same Way.

Another

Another Way to Fricasey Tripe.

TAKE a Piece of Double Tripe, cut it into Slices two Inches long and Half an Inch broad, put them into your Stew-pan, and sprinkle a little Salt over them; then put in a Bunch of Sweet Herbs, a little Lemon-peel, an Onion, a little Anchovy Pickle, and a Bay Leaf: Put all these to the Tripe, then put in just Water enough to cover them, and let them stew till the Tripe is very tender; then take out your Tripe and strain the Liquor out, shred a Spoonful of Capers, and put to them a Glass of White Wine, and Half a Pint of the Liquor they were stew'd in: Let it boil a little while, then put in your Tripe, and beat the Yolks of three Eggs; put into your Eggs a little Mace, two Cloves, a little Nutmeg dry'd and beat fine, a small Handful of Parsley pick'd and shred fine, a Piece of Butter rolled in Flour, and a Quarter of a Pint of Cream; mix all these well together and put them into your Stew-pan, keep them stirring one Way all the while, and when it is of a fine Thickness and smooth, dish it up, and garnish the Dish with Lemon. You are to observe that all Sauces which have Eggs or Cream in you must keep stirring one Way all the while they are on the Fire, or they will turn to Curds. You may add white Walnut Pickle, or Mushrooms, in the room of Capers, just to make your Sauce a little tart.

To Ragoo Hog's Feet and Ears.

TAKE your Feet and Ears out of the Pickle they are sous'd in, or boil them till they are tender, then cut them into little long thin Bits about two Inches long and about a Quarter of an Inch thick; put them into your Stew-pan with Half a Pint of good Gravy, a Glass of White Wine, a good deal of Mustard, a good Piece of Butter rolled in Flour, and a little Pepper and Salt; stir all together till it is of a fine Thickness, and then dish it up.

Note, They make a very pretty Dish fry'd with Butter and Mustard, and a little good Gravy, if you like it. Then only cut the Feet and Ears in two. You may add Half an Onion, cut small.

To Fry Tripe.

CUT your Tripe into Pieces about three Inches long, dip them in the Yolk of an Egg and a few Crumbs of Bread, fry them of a fine Brown, and then take them out of the Pan and lay them in a Dish to drain; have ready a warm Dish to put them in, and send them to Table, with Butter and Mustard in a Cup.

To Stew Tripe.

CUT it just as you do for frying, and set on some Water in a Sauce-pan, with two or three Onions cut into Slices, and some Salt; when it boils, put in your Tripe. Ten Minutes will boil it. Send it to Table with the Liquor in the Dish, and the Onions; have Butter and Mustard in a Cup, and dish it up. You may put in as many Onions as you like to mix with your Sauce, or leave them quite out, just as you please. Put a little Bundle of Sweet Herbs, and a Piece of Lemon-peel into the Water, when you put in the Tripe.

A Fricasey of Pigeons.

TAKE eight Pigeons, new kill'd, cut them into small Pieces, and put them into a Stew-pan with a Pint of Claret and a Pint of Water; season your Pigeons with Salt and Pepper, a Blade or two of Mace, an Onion, a Bundle of Sweet Herbs, a good Piece of Butter just rolled in a very little Flour; cover it close, and let them stew till there is just enough for Sauce, and then take out the Onion and Sweet Herbs, beat up the Yolks of three Eggs, grate Half a Nutmeg in, and with your Spoon push the Meat all to one Side of the Pan and the Gravy to the other Side, and stir in the Eggs; keep them stirring for fear of turning to Curds, and when the Sauce is fine and thick shake all together, put in Half a Spoonful of Vinegar, and give them a shake; then put the Meat into the Dish, pour the Sauce over it, and have ready some Slices of Bacon toasted, and fry'd Oysters; throw the Oysters all over, and lay the Bacon round. Garnish with Lemon.

A Fricasey of Lambstones and Sweetbreads.

HAVE ready some Lambstones blanched, parboiled and sliced, and flour two or three Sweetbreads; if very thick, cut them in two, the Yolks of six hard Eggs whole, a few Pistaco Nut Kernels, and a few large Oysters: Fry these all of a fine Brown, then pour out all the Butter, and add a Pint of drawn Gravy, the Lambstones, some Asparagus Tops about an Inch long, some grated Nutmeg, a little Pepper and Salt, two Shalots shred small, and a Glass of White Wine; stew all these together for ten Minutes, then add the Yolks of six Eggs beat very fine, with a little White Wine, and a little beaten Mace; stir all together till it is of a fine Thickness, and then dish it up. Garnish with Lemon.

To Hash a Calf's Head.

BOIL the Head almost enough, then take the best Half and with a sharp Knife take it nicely from the Bone, with the two Eyes; lay it in a little deep Dish before a good Fire, and take great Care no Ashes fall into it, and then hack it with a Knife cross and cross; grate some Nutmeg all over, a very little Pepper and Salt, a few Sweet Herbs, some Crumbs of Bread, and a little Lemon-peel chopp'd very fine; baste it with a

little

little Butter, then baste it again and pour over it the Yolks of two Eggs; keep the Dish turning that it may be all Brown alike: Cut the other Half and Tongue into little thin Bits, and set on a Pint of drawn Gravy in a Sauce-pan, a little Bundle of Sweet Herbs, an Onion, a little Pepper and Salt, a Glass of Red Wine, and two Shalots; boil all these together a few Minutes, then strain it through a Sieve, and put it into a clean Stew-pan with the Hash: Flour the Meat before you put it in, and put in a few Mushrooms, a Spoonful of the Pickle, two Spoonfuls of Catchup, and a few Truffles and Morels; stir all these together for a few Minutes, then beat up Half the Brains and stir into the Stew-pan, and a little Piece of Butter rolled in Flour: Take the other Half of the Brains, and beat them up with a little Lemon-peel cut fine, a little Nutmeg grated, a little beaten Mace, a little Thyme shred small, a little Parsley, the Yolk of an Egg, and have some good Dripping boiling in a Stew-pan; then fry the Brains in little Cakes about as big as a Crown-piece: Fry about twenty Oysters dipp'd in the Yolk of an Egg, toast some Slices of Bacon, fry a few Force-Meat Balls, and have ready a hot Dish, if Pewter, over a few clear Coals; if China, over a Pan of hot Water; pour in your Hash, then lay in your toasted Head, throw the Force-Meat Balls over the Hash, and garnish the Dish with fry'd Oysters, the fry'd Brains, and Lemon; throw the rest over the Hash, lay the Bacon round the Dish, and send it to Table.

To Hash a Calf's Head White.

TAKE Half a Pint of Gravy, a large Wine-Glass of White Wine, a little beaten Mace, a little Nutmeg, and a little Salt; throw into your Hash a few Mushrooms, a few Truffles and Morels first parboil'd, a few Artichoke Bottoms and Asparagus Tops, if you have them, a good Piece of Butter rolled in Flour, the Yolks of two Eggs, Half a Pint of Cream, and one Spoonful of Mushroom-Catchup; stir all together very carefully till it is of a fine Thickness, then pour it into your Dish, and lay the other Half of the Head, as before mention'd, in the Middle, and garnish it as before directed, with fry'd Oysters, Brains, Lemon, and Force-Meat Balls fry'd.

To Bake a Calf's Head.

TAKE the Head, pick it and wash it very clean; take an earthen Dish large enough to lay the Head on; rub a little Piece of Butter all over the Dish, then lay some long Iron Skewers across the Top of the Dish, and lay the Head on them; skewer up the Meat in the Middle that it don't lie in the Dish, then grate some Nutmeg all over it, a few Sweet Herbs shred small, some Crumbs of Bread, a little Lemon-peel cut fine, and then flour it all over; stick Pieces of Butter in the Eyes and all over the Head, and flour it again: Let it be well baked, and of a fine Brown; you may throw a little Pepper and Salt over it, and put into the Dish a Piece of Beef cut small, a Bundle of Sweet Herbs, an Onion, some Whole Pepper, a Blade of Mace, two Cloves, a Pint of Water, and boil the Brains with some Sage: When the Head is enough, lay it on a Dish, and set it to the Fire to keep warm, then stir all together in the Dish, and boil it in a Sauce-pan; strain it off, put it into the Sauce-pan again, add a Piece of Butter rolled in Flour, and the Sage in the Brains chopp'd fine, a Spoonful of Catchup, and two Spoonfuls of Red Wine, boil them together, and take the Brains, beat them well, and mix them with the Sauce; pour it into the Dish, and send it to Table. You must bake the Tongue with the Head, and don't cut it out. It will lie the handsomer in the Dish.

To Bake a Sheep's Head.

DO it the same Way, and it eats very well.

To dress a Lamb's Head.

BOIL the Head and Pluck tender, but don't let the Liver be too much done; take the Head up, hack it cross and cross with a Knife, grate some Nutmeg over it, and lay it in a Dish before a good Fire; then grate some Crumbs of Bread, some Sweet Herbs rubb'd, a little Lemon-peel chopp'd fine, a very little Pepper and Salt, and baste it with a little Butter; then throw a little Flour over it, and just before it is done do the same, baste it and drudge it: Take Half the Liver, the Lights, the Heart and Tongue, chop them very small, with six or eight Spoonfuls of Gravy or Water; first shake some Flour over the Meat, and stir it together, then put in the Gravy or Water, a good Piece of Butter rolled in a little Flour, a little Pepper and Salt, and what runs from the Head in the Dish; simmer all together a few Minutes, and add Half a Spoonful of Vinegar, pour it into your Dish, lay the Head in the Middle on the Mince-Meat, have ready the other Half of the Liver cut thin, with some Slices of Bacon broil'd, and lay round the Head. Garnish the Dish with Lemon, and send it to Table.

To Ragoo a Neck of Veal.

CUT a Neck of Veal into Steaks, flatten them with a Rolling-pin, season them with Salt, Pepper, Cloves and Mace, lard them with Bacon, Lemon-peel and Thyme, dip them in the Yolks of Eggs, make a Sheet of strong Cap-Paper up at the four Corners in the Form of a Dripping-pan, pin up the Corners, butter the Paper and also the Gridiron, and set it over a Fire of Charcoal; put in your Meat, let it do leisurely, keep it basting and turning to keep in the Gravy, and when it is enough have ready Half a Pint of strong Gravy, season it high, put in Mushrooms and Pickles, Force-Meat Balls dipp'd in the Yolks of Eggs, Oysters stew'd and fry'd, to lay round and at the Top of your Dish, and then serve it up. If for a Brown Ragoo, put in Red Wine. If for a White One, put in White Wine, with the Yolks of Eggs beat up with two or three Spoonfuls of Cream.

To

The Art of Cookery, made Plain and Easy.

To Ragoo a Breast of Veal.

TAKE your Breast of Veal, put it into a large Stew-pan, put in a Bundle of Sweet Herbs, an Onion, some Black and White Pepper, a Blade or two of Mace, two or three Cloves, a very little Piece of Lemon-peel, and cover it just with Water; when it is tender take it up, bone it, put in the Bones, boil it up till the Gravy is very good, then strain it off, and if you have a little rich Beef Gravy add a Quarter of a Pint, put in Half an Ounce of Truffles and Morels, a Spoonful or two of Catchup, two or three Spoonfuls of White Wine, and let them all boil together; in the mean Time flour the Veal, and fry it in Butter till it is of a fine Brown, then drain out all the Butter and pour the Gravy you are boiling to the Veal, with a few Mushrooms; boil all together till the Sauce is rich and thick, and cut the Sweet-bread into four. A few Force-Meat Balls is proper in it. Lay the Veal in the Dish, and pour the Sauce all over it. Garnish with Lemon.

Another Way to Ragoo a Breast of Veal.

YOU may bone it nicely, flour it, and fry it of a fine Brown, then pour the Fat out of the Pan, and the Ingredients as above, with the Bones; when enough, take it out, and strain the Liquor, then put in your Meat again, with the Ingredients, as before directed.

A Breast of Veal in Hodge-Podge.

TAKE a Breast of Veal, cut the Briscuit into little Pieces, and every Bone asunder, then flour it, and put Half a Pound of good Butter into a Stew-pan; when it is hot, throw in the Veal, fry it all over of a fine light Brown, and then have ready a Tea-Kettle of Water boiling, pour it in the Stew-pan, fill it up and stir it round, throw in a Pint of Green Pease, a fine Lettuce whole, clean wash'd, two or three Blades of Mace, a little Whole Pepper ty'd in a Muslin Rag, a little Bundle of Sweet Herbs, a small Onion stuck with a few Cloves, and a little Salt: Cover it close, and let it stew an Hour, or till it is boil'd to your Palate, if you would have Soop made of it; if you would only have Sauce to eat with the Veal, you must stew it till there is just as much as you would have for Sauce, and season it with Salt to your Palate; take out the Onion, Sweet Herbs and Spice, and pour it all together into your Dish. It is a fine Dish. If you have no Pease, pare three or four Cucumbers, scoop out the Pulp and cut it into little Pieces, and take four or five Heads of Sellery, clean wash'd, and cut the white Part small; when you have no Lettuces, take the little Hearts of Savoys, or the little young Sprouts that grow on the old Cabbage Stalks about as big as the Top of your Thumb.

Note, If you would make a very fine Dish of it, fill the Inside of your Lettuce with Force-Meat, and tye the Top close with a Thread; stew it till there is but just enough for Sauce, set the Lettuce in the Middle, and the Veal round, and pour the Sauce all over it. Garnish your Dish with rasp'd Bread, made into Figures with your Fingers. This is the cheapest Way of dressing a Breast of Veal to be good, and serve a Number of People.

To Collar a Breast of Veal.

TAKE a very sharp Knife and nicely take out all the Bones, but take great Care you do not cut the Meat through, pick all the Fat and Meat off the Bones, then grate some Nutmeg all over the Inside of the Veal, a very little beaten Mace, a little Pepper and Salt, a few Sweet Herbs shred small, some Parsley, a little Lemon-peel shred small, a few Crumbs of Bread and the Bits of Fat pick'd off the Bones, roll it up tight, stick one Skewer in to hold it together, but do it cleaver that it stands upright in the Dish, tye a Packthread across it to hold it together, spit it, then roll the Caul all round it, and roast it. An Hour and a Quarter will do it. When it has been about an Hour at the Fire take off the Caul, drudge it with Flour, baste it well with Fresh Butter, and let it be of a fine Brown. For Sauce take Two Pennyworth of Gravy Beef, cut it and hack it well, then flour it, fry it a little Brown, then pour into your Stew-pan some boiling Water, stir it well together, then fill your Pan two Parts full of Water, put in an Onion, a Bundle of Sweet Herbs, a little Crust of Bread toasted, two or three Blades of Mace, four Cloves, some Whole Pepper, and the Bones of the Veal: Cover it close, and let it stew till it is quite rich and thick, then strain it, boil it up again with Truffles and Morels, a few Mushrooms, a Spoonful of Catchup, two or three Bottoms of Artichokes, if you have them, add a little Salt, just enough to season the Gravy, take the Packthread off the Veal, and set it upright in the Dish; cut the Sweetbread into four, and broil it of a fine Brown, with a few Force-Meat Balls fry'd, lay these round the Dish, and pour in the Sauce. Garnish the Dish with Lemon, and send it to Table.

To Collar a Breast of Mutton.

DO it the same Way, and it eats very well. But you must take off the Skin.

Another good Way to dress a Breast of Mutton.

COLLAR it, as before, roast it, and baste it with Half a Pint of Red Wine, and when that is all soak'd in, baste it well with Butter, have a little good Gravy, set the Mutton upright in the Dish, pour in the Gravy, have Sweet Sauce as for Venison, and send it to Table. Don't garnish the Dish, but be sure to take the Skin off the Mutton.

The Inside of a Surloin of Beef is very good, done this Way.

If you don't like the Wine, a Quart of Milk, and a Quarter of a Pound of Butter, put into the Dripping-pan, does full as well to baste it.

To Force a Leg of Lamb.

WITH a sharp Knife carefully take out all the Meat, and leave the Skin whole and the Fat on it, make the Lean you cut out into Force-Meat thus: To two Pounds of Meat, three Pounds of Beef Sewet cut fine, and beat in a Marble Mortar till it is very fine, and take away all the Skin of the Meat and Sewet, then mix with it four Spoonfuls of grated Bread, eight or ten Cloves, five or six large Blades of Mace dry'd and beat fine, Half a large Nutmeg grated, a little Pepper and Salt, a little Lemon-peel cut fine, a very little Thyme, some Parsley, and four Eggs; mix all together, put it into the Skin again just as it was, in the same Shape, sew it up, roast it, baste it with Butter, cut the Loin into Steaks and fry it nicely, lay the Leg in the Dish and the Loin round it, with stew'd Cauliflower (as in Page 11) all round upon the Loin, pour a Pint of good Gravy into the Dish, and send it to Table. If you don't like the Cauliflower, it may be omitted.

To Boil a Leg of Lamb.

LET the Leg be boil'd very white. An Hour will do it. Cut the Loin into Steaks, dip it into a few Crumbs of Bread and Egg, fry them nice and brown, boil a good deal of Spinach and lay in the Dish, put the Leg in the Middle, lay the Loin round it, cut an Orange in four, and garnish the Dish, and have Butter in a Cup. Some love the Spinach boil'd, then drain'd, put into a Sauce-pan with a good Piece of Butter, and stew'd.

To Force a Large Fowl.

CUT the Skin down the Back, and carefully slip it up so as to take out all the Meat, mix it with one Pound of Beef Sewet, cut it small, and beat them together in a Marble Mortar; take a Pint of large Oysters cut small, two Anchovies cut small, one Shalot cut fine, a few Sweet Herbs, a little Pepper, a little Nutmeg grated, and the Yolks of four Eggs; mix all together and lay this on the Bones, draw over the Skin and sew up the Back, put the Fowl into a Bladder, boil it an Hour and a Quarter, stew some Oysters in good Gravy thicken'd with a Piece of Butter rolled in Flour, take the Fowl out of the Bladder, lay it into your Dish, and pour the Sauce over it. Garnish with Lemon.

It eats much better roasted, with the same Sauce.

To Roast a Turky the genteel Way.

FIRST cut it down the Back, and with a sharp Penknife bone it, then make your Force-Meat thus: Take a large Fowl, or a Pound of Veal, as much grated Bread, Half a Pound of Sewet, cut and beat very fine, a little beaten Mace, two Cloves, Half a Nutmeg grated, about a large Tea Spoonful of Lemon-peel, and the Yolks of two Eggs; mix all together, with a little Pepper and Salt, fill up the Places where the Bones came out, and fill the Body, that it may look just as it did before, sew up the Back, and roast it. You may have Oyster Sauce, Sellery Sauce, or just as you please, but good Gravy in the Dish, and garnish with Lemon, is as good as any Thing. Be sure to leave the Pinions on.

To Stew a Turky or Fowl.

FIRST let your Pot be very clean, lay four clean Skewers at the Bottom, lay your Turky or Fowl upon them, put in a Quart of Gravy, take a Bunch of Sellery, cut it small, and wash it very clean, put it into your Pot, with two or three Blades of Mace, let it stew softly till there is just enough for Sauce, then add a good Piece of Butter rolled in Flour, two Spoonfuls of Red Wine, two of Catchup, and just as much Pepper and Salt as will season it, lay your Fowl or Turky in the Dish, pour the Sauce over it, and send it to Table. If the Fowl or Turky is enough before the Sauce, take it up, and keep it hot till the Sauce is boil'd enough, then put it in, let it boil a Minute or two, and dish it up.

To

The Art of Cookery, made Plain and Easy.   19

To Stew a Knuckle of Veal.

BE sure let the Pot or Sauce-pan be very clean, lay at the Bottom four clean wooden Skewers, wash and clean the Knuckle very well, then lay it in the Pot, with two or three Blades of Mace, a little Whole Pepper, a little Piece of Thyme, a small Onion, a Crust of Bread, and two Quarts of Water; cover it down close, make it boil, then only let it simmer for two Hours, and when it is enough take it up, lay it in a Dish, and strain the Broth over it.

Another Way to Stew a Knuckle of Veal.

CLEAN it as before directed, and boil it till there is just enough for Sauce, add one Spoonful of Catchup, one of Red Wine, and one of Walnut Pickle, some Truffles and Morels, or some dry'd Mushrooms cut small; boil it all together, take up the Knuckle, lay it in a Dish, pour the Sauce over it, and send it to Table.

Note, It eats very well done as the Turky, before directed.

To Ragoo a Piece of Beef.

TAKE a large Piece of the Flank which has Fat at the Top cut square, or any Piece that is all Meat, and has Fat at the Top, but no Bones. The Rump does well. Cut all nicely off the Bone (which makes fine Soop) then take a large Stew-pan and with a good Piece of Butter fry it a little Brown all over, flouring your Meat well before you put it into the Pan, then pour in as much Gravy as will cover it, made thus: Take about a Pound of coarse Beef, a little Piece of Veal cut small, a Bundle of Sweet Herbs, an Onion, some Whole Black Pepper and White Pepper, two or three large Blades of Mace, four or five Cloves, a Piece of Carrot, a little Piece of Bacon steep'd in Vinegar a little while, a Crust of Bread toasted brown; put to this a Quart of Water, and let it boil till Half is wasted. While this is making pour a Quart of boiling Water into the Stew-pan, cover it close, and let it be stewing softly. When the Gravy is done strain it, pour it into the Pan where the Beef is, take an Ounce of Truffles and Morels cut small, some fresh or dry'd Mushrooms cut small, two Spoonfuls of Catchup, and cover it close; let all this stew till the Sauce is rich and thick, then have ready some Artichoke-bottoms cut into four, and a few pickled Mushrooms; give them a Boil or two, and when your Meat is tender and your Sauce quite rich, lay the Meat into a Dish and pour the Sauce over it. You may add a Sweetbread cut in six Pieces, a Palate stew'd tender cut into little Pieces, some Cocks Combs, and a few Force-Meat Balls. These are a great Addition, but it will be good without.

Note, For Variety when the Beef is ready and the Gravy put to it, add a large Bunch of Sellery cut small and wash'd clean, two Spoonfuls of Catchup, and a Glass of Red Wine. Omit all the other Ingredients. When the Meat and Sellery are tender, and the Sauce rich and good, serve it up. It is also very good this Way: Take six large Cucumbers, scoop out the Seeds, pare them, cut them into Slices, and do them just as you do the Sellery.

To Force the Inside of a Surloin of Beef.

TAKE a sharp Knife and carefully lift up the Fat of the Inside, take out all the Meat close to the Bone, chop it small, take a Pound of the Sewet and chop fine, about as many Crumbs of Bread, a little Thyme and Lemon-peel, a little Pepper and Salt, Half a Nutmeg grated, and two Shalots chopp'd fine; mix all together, with a Glass of Red Wine, then put it into the same Place, cover it with the Skin and Fat, skewer it down with fine Skewers, and cover it with Paper; don't take the Paper off till the Meat is in the Dish. Take a Quarter of a Pint of Red Wine, two Shalots shred small, boil them, and pour into the Dish, with the Gravy which comes out of the Meat eats well. Spit your Meat before you take out the Inside.

To Force the Inside of a Rump of Beef.

YOU may do it just in the same Manner, only lift up the outside Skin, take the Middle of the Meat, and do as before directed; put it into the same Place, and with fine Skewers put it down close.

A Roll'd Rump of Beef.

CUT the Meat all off the Bone whole, slit the Inside down from Top to Bottom, but not through the Skin, spread it open, take the Flesh of two Fowls and Beef Sewet, an equal Quantity, and as much cold boil'd Ham, if you have it, a little Pepper, an Anchovy, a Nutmeg grated, a little Thyme, a good deal of Parsley, a few Mushrooms, and chop them all together, beat them in a Mortar, with a Half-Pint Bason full of Crumbs of Bread; mix all these together, with four Yolks of Eggs, lay it into the Meat, cover it up, and roll it round, stick one Skewer in, and tye it with a Packthread cross and cross to hold it together; take a Pot or large Sauce-pan that will just hold it, lay a Layer of Bacon and Layer of Beef cut in thin Slices, a Piece of Carrot, some Whole Pepper, Mace, Sweet Herbs, and a large Onion, lay the roll'd Beef on it, just put Water enough to the Top of the Beef, cover it close, and let it stew very softly on a slow Fire for eight or ten Hours, but not too fast. When you find the Beef tender, which you will know by running a Skewer into the Meat, then take it up, cover it up hot, boil the Gravy till

20 *The Art of Cookery, made Plain and Easy.*

it is good, then strain it off, and add some Mushrooms chopp'd, some Truffles and Morels cut small, two Spoonfuls of Red or White Wine, the Yolks of two Eggs, and a Piece of Butter roll'd in Flour; boil it together, set the Meat before the Fire, baste it with Butter, and throw Crumbs of Bread all over it: When the Sauce is enough, lay the Meat into the Dish, and pour the Sauce over it. Take Care the Eggs don't Curd.

To Boil a Rump of Beef the French Fashion.

TAKE a Rump of Beef, boil it Half an Hour, take it up, lay it into a large deep Pewter Dish or Stew-pan, cut three or four Gashes in it all along the Side, rub the Gashes with Pepper and Salt, and pour into the Dish a Pint of Red Wine, as much hot Water, two or three large Onions cut small, the Hearts of eight or ten Lettuces cut small, and a good Piece of Butter roll'd in a little Flour; lay the fleshy Part of the Meat downwards, cover it close, let it stew an Hour and a Half over a Charcoal Fire, or a very slow Coal Fire. Observe that the Butcher chops the Bone so close that the Meat may lie as flat as you can in the Dish. When it is enough, take the Beef, lay it in the Dish, and pour the Sauce over it.

Note, When you do it in a Pewter Dish, it is best done over a Chaffing-dish of hot Coals, with a Bit or two of Charcoal to keep it alive.

Beef Escarlot.

TAKE a Briscuit of Beef, Half a Pound of coarse Sugar, two Ounces of Bay Salt, a Pound of common Salt, mix all together and rub the Beef, lay it in an earthen Pan, and turn it every Day. It may lie a Fortnight in the Pickle, then boil it, and serve it up either with Savoys, or a Pease Pudding. *Note,* It eats much finer cold, cut into Slices, and sent to Table.

Beef à la Daub.

YOU may take a Buttock or a Rump of Beef, lard it, fry it Brown in some sweet Butter, then put it into a Pot that will just hold it; put in some Broth or Gravy hot, some Pepper, Cloves, Mace, and a Bundle of Sweet Herbs, stew it four Hours, till it is tender, and season it with Salt; take Half a Pint of Gravy, two Sweetbreads cut into eight Pieces, some Truffles and Morels, Palates, Artichoke-bottoms and Mushrooms, boil all together, lay your Beef into the Dish, strain the Liquor into the Sauce, and boil all together. If it is not thick enough roll a Piece of Butter in Flour, and boil in it. Pour this all over the Beef. Take Force-Meat roll'd in Pieces Half as long as one's Finger, dip them into Batter made with Eggs, and fry them Brown, fry some Sippets dipp'd into Batter cut three Corner ways, stick them into the Meat, and garnish with the Force-Meat.

Beef à la Mode in Pieces.

YOU must take a Buttock of Beef, cut it into two Pound Pieces, lard them with Bacon, fry them Brown, put them into a Pot that will just hold them, put in two Quarts of Broth or Gravy, a few Sweet Herbs, an Onion, some Mace, Cloves, Nutmeg, Pepper and Salt; when that is done, cover it close, and stew till it is tender, skim off all the Fat, lay the Meat in the Dish, and strain the Sauce over it. You may serve it up hot or cold.

Beef Olives.

TAKE a Rump of Beef, cut it into Steaks Half a Quarter long, about an Inch thick, let them be square, lay on some good Force-Meat made with Veal, roll them, tye them once round with a hard Knot, dip them in Egg, Crumbs of Bread and grated Nutmeg, and a little Pepper and Salt. The best Way is to roast them, or fry them Brown in Fresh Butter, lay them every one on a Bay-Leaf, and cover them every one with a Piece of Bacon toasted, have some good Gravy, a few Truffles and Morels, and Mushrooms; boil all together, pour into the Dish, and send it to Table.

Veal Olives.

THEY are good done the same Way, only roll them narrow at one End and broad at the other. Fry them of a fine Brown. Omit the Bay-Leaf, but lay little Bits of Bacon about two Inches long on them. The same Sauce. Garnish with Lemon.

Beef Collops.

CUT them into thin Pieces about two Inches long, beat them with a Back of a Knife very well, grate some Nutmeg, flour them a little, lay them in a Stew-pan, put in a Pint of Water, Half an Onion cut small, a little Piece of Lemon-peel cut small, a Bundle of Sweet Herbs, a little Pepper and Salt, a Piece of Butter roll'd in a little Flour: Set them on a slow Fire, when they begin to simmer stir them now and then; when they begin to be hot, ten Minutes will do them, but take Care they don't boil. Take out the Sweet Herbs, pour it into the Dish, and send it to Table.

Note,

Note, You may do the Inside of a Surloin of Beef in the same Manner the Day after it is roasted, only don't beat them, but cut them thin.

N. B. You may do this Dish between two Pewter Dishes, hang them between two Chairs, take six Sheets of White-brown Paper, tare them into Slips, and burn them under the Dish one Piece at a Time.

To Stew Beef Steaks.

TAKE Rump Steaks, pepper and salt them, lay them into a Stew-pan, pour in Half a Pint of Water, a Blade or two of Mace, two or three Cloves, a little Bundle of Sweet Herbs, an Anchovy, a Piece of Butter rolled in Flour, a Glass of White Wine, and an Onion; cover them close, and let them stew softly till they are tender, then take out the Steaks, flour them, fry them in Fresh Butter, and pour away all the Fat, strain the Sauce they were stew'd in, and pour into the Pan; toss it all up together till the Sauce is quite hot and thick. If you add a Quarter of a Pint of Oysters it will make it the better. Lay the Steaks into the Dish, and pour the Sauce over them. Garnish with any Pickle you like.

To Fry Beef Steaks.

TAKE Rump Steaks, beat them very well with a Roller, fry them in Half a Pint of Ale that is not bitter, and whilst they are frying cut a large Onion small, a very little Thyme, some Parsley shred small, some grated Nutmeg, and a little Pepper and Salt; roll all together in a Piece of Butter, and then in a little Flour, put it into the Stew-pan, and shake all together. When the Steaks are tender, and the Sauce of a fine Thickness, dish it up.

A second Way to Fry Beef Steaks.

CUT the Lean by itself, and beat them well with the Back of a Knife, fry them in just as much Butter as will moisten the Pan, pour out the Gravy as it runs out of the Meat, turn them often, do them over a gentle Fire, then fry the Fat by itself and lay upon the Meat, and put to the Gravy a Glass of Red Wine, Half an Anchovy, a little Nutmeg, a little beaten Pepper, and a Shalot cut small; give it two or three little Boils, season it with Salt to your Palate, pour it over the Steaks, and send them to Table.

Another Way to do Beef Steaks.

CUT your Steaks, Half broil them, then lay them into a Stew-pan, season them with Pepper and Salt, just cover them with Gravy, and a Piece of Butter rolled in Flour; let them stew for Half an Hour, beat up the Yolks of two Eggs, stir all together for two or three Minutes, and then serve it up.

A pretty Side-Dish of Beef.

ROAST a tender Piece of Beef, lay fat Bacon all over it and roll it in Paper, baste it, and when it is roasted cut about two Pounds in thin Slices, lay them into a Stew-pan, and take six large Cucumbers, peel them, and chop them small, lay over them a little Pepper and Salt, stew them in Butter for about ten Minutes, then drain out the Butter, and shake some Flour over them; toss them up, pour in Half a Pint of Gravy, let them stew till they are thick, and dish them up.

To dress a Fillet of Beef.

IT is the Inside of the Surloin: You must carefully cut it all out from the Bone, grate some Nutmeg over it, a few Crumbs of Bread, a little Pepper and Salt, a little Lemon-peel, a little Thyme, some Parsley shred small, and roll it up tight; tye it with a Packthread, roast it, put a Quart of Milk and a Quarter of a Pound of Butter into the Dripping-pan and baste it; when it is enough take it up, untye it, leave a little Skewer in it to hold it together, have a little good Gravy in the Dish, and some Sweet Sauce in a Cup. You may baste it with Red Wine and Butter, if you like it better, or it will do very well with Butter only.

Beef Steaks *Rolled*.

TAKE three or four Beef Steaks, flat them with a Cleaver, and make a Force-Meat thus: Take a Pound of Veal beat fine in a Mortar, the Flesh of a large Fowl cut small, Half a Pound of cold Ham chopp'd small, the Kidney-Fat of a Loin of Veal chopp'd small, a Sweetbread cut in little Pieces, an Ounce of Truffles and Morels first stew'd and then cut small, some Parsley, the Yolks of four Eggs, a Nutmeg grated, a very little Thyme, a little Lemon-peel cut fine, a little Pepper and Salt, and Half a Pint of Cream; mix all together, lay it on your Steaks, roll them up firm, of a good Size, and put a little Skewer into them, put them into the Stew-pan, and fry them of a nice Brown; then pour all the Fat quite out, and put in a Pint of good fry'd Gravy (as in *Page* 12) put one Spoonful of Catchup, two Spoonfuls of Red Wine, a few Mushrooms, and let them stew for a Quarter of an Hour. Take up the Steaks, cut them in two, lay the cut Side uppermost, and pour the Sauce over it. Garnish with Lemon.

Note, Before you put the Force-Meat into the Beef, you are to stir it all together over a slow Fire for eight or ten Minutes.

To Stew a Rump of Beef.

HAVING boil'd it till it is little more than Half enough, take it up, and peel off the Skin; take Salt, Pepper, beaten Mace, grated Nutmeg, a Handful of Parsley, a little Thyme, Winter-Savoury, Sweet Marjoram, all chopp'd fine and mixt, and stuff them in great Holes in the Fat and Lean, the rest spread over it, with the Yolks of two Eggs; save the Gravy that runs out, put to it a Pint of Claret, and put the Meat into a deep Pan, pour the Liquor in, cover it close, and let it bake two Hours, then put it into the Dish, pour the Liquor over it, and send it to Table.

Another Way to Stew a Rump of Beef.

YOU must cut the Meat off the Bone, lay it in your Stew-pan, cover it with Water, put in a Spoonful of Whole Pepper, two Onions, a Bundle of Sweet Herbs, some Salt, and a Pint of Red Wine; cover it close, set it over a Stove or slow Fire for four Hours, shaking it sometimes, and turning it four or five Times; make Gravy as for Soop, put in three Quarts, keep it stirring till Dinner is ready: Take ten or twelve Turnips, cut them into Slices the broad Way, then cut them into four, flour them, and fry them Brown in Beef Dripping. Be sure to let your Dripping boil before you put them in, then drain them well from the Fat, lay the Beef into your Soop-dish, toast a little Bread very nice and brown, cut in three Corner Dice, lay them into the Dish, and the Turnips likewise, strain in the Gravy, and send it to Table. If you have the Convenience of a Stove, put the Dish over it for five or six Minutes; it gives the Liquor a fine Flavour of the Turnips, makes the Bread eat better, and is a great Addition. Season it with Salt to your Palate.

Portugal Beef.

TAKE a Rump of Beef, cut off the Bone, cut it across, flour it, fry the thin Part Brown in Butter, the thick End stuff with Sewet, boil'd Chesnuts, an Anchovy, an Onion, and a little Pepper; stew it in a Pan of strong Broth, and when it is tender lay both the Fry'd and Stew'd together into your Dish, cut the Fry'd in two and lay on each Side of the Stew'd, strain the Gravy it was stew'd in, put to it some pickled Gerkins chopp'd and boil'd Chesnuts, thicken it with a Piece of Burnt Butter, give it two or three Boils up, season it with Salt to your Palate, and pour it over the Beef. Garnish with Lemon.

To Stew a Rump of Beef, or the Briscuit, the French Way.

TAKE a Rump of Beef, put it into a little Pot that will hold it, cover it with Water, put on the Cover, let it stew an Hour, but if a Briscuit two Hours; skim it clean, then slash the Meat with a Knife to let out the Gravy, put in a little beaten Pepper, some Salt, four Cloves, with two or three large Blades of Mace beat fine, six Onions sliced, and Half a Pint of Red Wine; cover it close, let it stew an Hour, then put in two Spoonfuls of Capers or Astertion Buds pickled, or Broom Buds, chop them, two Spoonfuls of Vinegar and two of Verjuice; boil six Cabbage Lettuces in Water, then put them in the Pot, put in a Pint of good Gravy, let all stew together for Half an Hour, skim all the Fat off, lay the Meat into the Dish, and pour the rest over it, have ready some Pieces of Bread cut three Corner ways, and fry'd crisp, stick them about the Meat, and garnish with them. When you put in the Cabbage, put with it a good Piece of Butter rolled in Flour.

To Stew Beef Gobbets.

GET any Piece of Beef, except the Leg, cut it in Pieces about the Bigness of a Pullet's Egg, put them in a Stew-pan, cover them with Water, let them stew, skim them clean, and when they have stew'd an Hour take Mace, Cloves, and Whole Pepper ty'd in a Muslin Rag loose, some Sellery cut small, put them into the Pan with some Salt, Turnips and Carrots, par'd and cut in Slices, a little Parsley, a Bundle of Sweet Herbs, and a large Crust of Bread. You may put in an Ounce of Barley or Rice, if you like it. Cover it close, and let it stew till it is tender; take out the Herbs, Spices and Bread, and have ready fry'd a *French* Roll cut in four. Dish up all together, and send to Table.

Beef Royal.

TAKE a Surloin of Beef, or a large Rump, bone it and beat it very well, then lard it with Bacon, season it all over with Salt, Pepper, Mace, Cloves, and Nutmeg, all beat fine, some Lemon-peel cut small, and some Sweet Herbs; in the mean Time make a strong Broth of the Bones, take a Piece of Butter with a little Flour, brown it, put in the Beef, keep it turning often till it is Brown, then strain the Broth, put all together into a Pot, put in a Bay-Leaf, a few Truffles, and some Ox Palates cut small; cover it close, and let it stew till it is tender, take out the Beef, skim off all the Fat, pour in a Pint of Claret, some fry'd Oysters, an Anchovy, and some Gerkins shred small; boil all together, put in the Beef to warm, thicken your Sauce with a Piece of Butter rolled in Flour, or Mushroom Powder, or Burnt Butter. Lay your Meat in the Dish, pour the Sauce over it, and send it to Table. This may be eat either Hot or Cold.

A Tongue

A Tongue and Udder forced.

FIRST parboil your Tongue and Udder, blanch the Tongue and stick it with Cloves; as for the Udder, you must carefully raise it, and fill it with Force-Meat, made with Veal: First wash the Inside with the Yolk of an Egg, then put in the Force-Meat, tye the Ends close and spit them, roast them, and baste them with Butter; when enough, have good Gravy in the Dish, and Sweet Sauce in a Cup.
Note, For Variety you may lard the Udder.

To Fricasey Neats Tongues.

TAKE Neats Tongues, boil them tender, peel them, cut them into thin Slices, and fry them in Fresh Butter, then pour out the Butter, put in as much Gravy as you shall want for Sauce, a Bundle of Sweet Herbs, an Onion, some Pepper and Salt, and a Blade or two of Mace; simmer all together for Half an Hour, then take out your Tongue, strain the Gravy, put it with the Tongue into the Stew-pan again, beat up the Yolks of two Eggs with a Glass of White Wine, a little grated Nutmeg, a Piece of Butter as big as a Walnut rolled in Flour, shake all together for four or five Minutes, dish it up, and send it to Table.

To Force a Tongue.

BOIL it till it is tender, let it stand till it is cold, then cut a Hole at the Root-end of it, take out some of the Meat, chop it with as much Beef Sewet, a few Pippins, some Pepper and Salt, a little Mace beat, some Nutmeg, a few Sweet Herbs, and the Yolks of two Eggs; chop it all together, stuff it, cover the End with a Veal Caul or butter'd Paper, roast it, baste it with Butter, and dish it up. Have for Sauce good Gravy, a little melted Butter, the Juice of an Orange or Lemon, and some grated Nutmeg; boil it up, and pour it into the Dish.

To Stew Neats Tongues Whole.

TAKE two Tongues, let them stew in Water just to cover them for two Hours, then peel them, put them in again with a Pint of strong Gravy, Half a Pint of White Wine, a Bundle of Sweet Herbs, a little Pepper and Salt, some Mace, Cloves, and Whole Pepper ty'd in a Muslin Rag, a Spoonful of Capers chopp'd, Turnips and Carrots sliced, and a Piece of Butter rolled in Flour; let all stew together very softly over a slow Fire for two Hours, then take out the Spice and Sweet Herbs, and send it to Table.

To Fricasey Ox Palates.

AFTER boiling your Palates very tender (which you must do by setting them on in cold Water, and letting them do softly) then blanch them and scrape them clean, take Mace, Nutmeg, Cloves, and Pepper beat fine, rub them all over with those, and with Crumbs of Bread; have ready some Butter in a Stew-pan, and when it is hot put in the Palates, fry them Brown on both Sides, then pour out the Fat, and put to them some Mutton or Beef Gravy, enough for Sauce, an Anchovy, a little Nutmeg, a little Piece of Butter rolled in Flour, and the Juice of a Lemon; let it simmer all together for a Quarter of an Hour, dish it up, and garnish with Lemon.

To Roast Ox Palates.

HAVING boil'd your Palates tender, blanch them, cut them into Slices about two Inches long, lard Half with Bacon, then have ready two or three Pigeons and two or three Chicken-peepers, draw them, truss them, and fill them with Force-Meat, let Half of them be nicely larded, spit them on a Bird-spit, spit them thus; a Bird, a Palate, a Sage-Leaf, and a Piece of Bacon, and so on, a Bird, a Palate, a Sage-Leaf, and a Piece of Bacon. Take Cocks Combs and Lambstones parboil'd and blanch'd, lard them with little Bits of Bacon, large Oysters parboil'd, and each one larded with one Piece of Bacon; put these on a Skewer with a little Piece of Bacon and a Sage-Leaf between them, tye them on to a Spit and roast them, then beat up the Yolks of three Eggs, some Nutmeg, a little Salt and Crumbs of Bread; baste them with these all the Time they are Roasting, and have ready two Sweetbreads each cut in two, some Artichoke-bottoms cut into four and fry'd, and then rub the Dish with Shalots; lay the Birds in the Middle piled upon one another, and lay the other Things all separate by themselves round about in the Dish. Have ready for Sauce a Pint of good Gravy, a Quarter of a Pint of Red Wine, an Anchovy, the Oyster Liquor, a Piece of Butter rolled in Flour; boil all these together and pour into the Dish, with a little Juice of Lemon. Garnish your Dish with Lemon.

To dress a Leg of Mutton à la Royale.

HAVING taken off all the Fat, Skin, and Shank Bone, lard it with Bacon, season it with Pepper and Salt, and a round Piece of about three or four Pounds of Beef or Leg of Veal, lard it; have ready some Hog's-Lard boiling, flour your Meat, and give it a Colour in the Lard, then take the Meat out and put it into a Pot, with a Bundle of Sweet Herbs, some Parsley, an Onion stuck with Cloves, two or three Blades of Mace, some Whole Pepper, and three Quarts of Water; cover it close, and let it boil very softly for two Hours, mean while get ready a Sweetbread split, cut into four, and broil'd, a few Truffles and Morels stew'd in a Quarter of a Pint of strong Gravy, a Glass of Red Wine, a few Mushrooms, two Spoonfuls of Catchup, and some Asparagus Tops; boil all these together, then lay the Mutton in the Middle of the Dish, cut the Beef or Veal into Slices, make a Rim round your Mutton with the Slices, and pour the Ragoo over it; when you have taken the Meat out of the Pot, skim all the Fat off the Gravy, strain it, and add as much to the other as will fill the Dish. Garnish with Lemon.

A Leg of Mutton à la Hautgoût.

LET it hang a Fortnight in an airy Place, then have ready some Cloves of Garlick and stuff it all over, rub it with Pepper and Salt, roast it, have some good Gravy and Red Wine in the Dish, and send it to Table.

To Roast a Leg of Mutton with Oysters.

TAKE a Leg about two or three Days kill'd, stuff it all over with Oysters, and roast it. Garnish with Horse-raddish.

To Roast a Leg of Mutton with Cockles.

STUFF it all over with Cockles, and roast it. Garnish with Horse-raddish.

A Shoulder of Mutton in Epigram.

ROAST it almost enough, then very carefully take off the Skin about the Thickness of a Crown-piece, and the Shank Bone with it at the End, then season that Skin and Shank Bone with Pepper and Salt, a little Lemon-peel cut small, and a few Sweet Herbs and Crumbs of Bread, then lay this on the Gridiron, and let it be of a fine Brown; in the mean Time take the rest of the Meat and cut it like a Hash about the Bigness of a Shilling, save the Gravy and put to it, with a few Spoonfuls of strong Gravy, Half an Onion cut fine, a little Nutmeg, a little Pepper and Salt, a little Bundle of Sweet Herbs, some Gerkins cut very small, a few Mushrooms, two or three Truffles cut small, two Spoonfuls of Wine, either Red or White, and throw a little Flour over the Meat; let all these stew together very softly for five or six Minutes, but be sure it don't boil, take out the Sweet Herbs, and put the Hash into the Dish, lay the Broil'd upon it, and send it to Table.

A Harrico of Mutton.

TAKE a Neck or Loin of Mutton, cut it into six Pieces, flour it, and fry it Brown on both Sides in the Stew-pan, then pour out all the Fat, put in some Turnips and Carrots cut like Dice, two Dozen of Chesnuts blanched, two or three Lettuces cut small, six little round Onions, a Bundle of Sweet Herbs, some Pepper and Salt, and two or three Blades of Mace; cover it close, and let it stew for an Hour, then take off the Fat and dish it up.

To French a Hind Saddle of Mutton.

IT is the two Rumps. Cut off the Rump, and carefully lift up the Skin with a Knife, begin at the broad End, but be sure you don't crack it nor take it quite off, then take some Slices of Ham or Bacon chopp'd fine, a few Truffles, some young Onions, some Parsley, a little Thyme, Sweet Marjoram, Winter Savoury, a little Lemon-peel, all chopp'd fine, a little Mace and two or three Cloves beat fine, Half a Nutmeg, and a little Pepper and Salt; mix all together and throw over the Meat where you took off the Skin, then lay on the Skin again, and fasten it with two fine Skewers at each Side, and roll it in well butter'd Paper. It will take three Hours doing. Then take off the Paper, baste the Meat, strew it all over with Crumbs of Bread, and when it is of a fine Brown take it up. For Sauce take six large Shalots, cut them very fine, put them into a Sauce-pan with two Spoonfuls of Vinegar, and two of White Wine; boil them for a Minute or two, pour it into the Dish, and garnish with Horse-raddish.

The Art of Cookery, made Plain and Easy. 25

Another French Way, call'd, St. Menehout.

TAKE the Hind Saddle of Mutton, take off the Skin, lard it with Bacon, season it with Pepper, Salt, Mace, Cloves beat, and Nutmeg, Sweet Herbs, young Onions, and Parsley, all chopp'd fine; take a large Oval, or a large Gravy-pan, lay Layers of Bacon, and then Layers of Beef all over the Bottom, lay in the Mutton, then lay Layers of Bacon on the Mutton, and then a Layer of Beef, put in a Pint of Wine, and as much good Gravy as will stew it, put in a Bay-Leaf, and two or three Shalots, cover it close, put Fire over and under it, if you have a close Pan, and let it stand stewing for two Hours; when done, take it out, strew Crumbs of Bread all over it, and put it into the Oven to Brown, strain the Gravy it was stew'd in, and boil it till there is just enough for Sauce, lay the Mutton into the Dish, pour the Sauce in, and serve it up. You must Brown it before a Fire, if you have not an Oven.

Cutlets à la Maintenon. A very good Dish.

CUT your Cutlets handsomely, beat them thin with your Cleaver, season them with Pepper and Salt, make a Force-Meat with Veal, Beef Sewet, Spice, and Sweet Herbs, rolled in Yolks of Eggs, roll Force-Meat round each Cutlet within two Inches of the Top of the Bone, then have as many Half Sheets of White Paper as Cutlets, roll each Cutlet in a Piece of Paper, first buttering the Paper well on the Inside, dip the Cutlets in melted Butter and then in Crumbs of Bread, lay each Cutlet on Half a Sheet of Paper cross the Middle of it, leaving about an Inch of the Bone out, then close the two Ends of your Paper as you do a Turnover Tart, and cut off the Paper that is too much; broil your Mutton Cutlets Half an Hour, your Veal Cutlets three Quarters of an Hour, and then take the Paper off and lay them round in the Dish, with the Bone outwards. Let your Sauce be good Gravy thicken'd, and serve it up.

To make a Mutton Hash.

CUT your Mutton in little Bits as thin as you can, strew a little Flour over it, have ready some Gravy (enough for Sauce) wherein Sweet Herbs, Onion, Pepper and Salt have been boil'd; strain it, put in your Meat, with a little Piece of Butter rolled in Flour and a little Salt, a Shalot cut fine, a few Capers and Gerkins chopp'd fine, and a Blade of Mace: Toss all together for a Minuet or two, have ready some Bread toasted thin and cut into Sippets, lay them round the Dish, and pour in your Hash. Garnish your Dish with Pickles and Horse-raddish.

Note, Some love a Glass of Red Wine, or Walnut Pickle; You may put just what you will into a Hash.

To dress Pigs Petty-Toes.

PUT your Petty-Toes into a Sauce-pan with Half a Pint of Water, a Blade of Mace, a little Whole Pepper, a Bundle of Sweet Herbs, and an Onion; let them boil five Minutes, then take out the Liver, Lights, and Heart, mince them very fine, grate a little Nutmeg over them, and shake a little Flour on them; let the Feet do till they are tender, then take them out and strain the Liquor, put all together with a little Salt and a Piece of Butter as big as a Walnut, shake the Sauce-pan often, let it simmer five or six Minutes, then cut some toasted Sippets and lay round the Dish, lay the Mince-Meat and Sauce in the Middle, and the Petty-Toes split round it. You may add the Juice of Half a Lemon, or a very little Vinegar.

A second Way to Roast a Leg of Mutton with Oysters.

STUFF a Leg of Mutton with Mutton Sewet, Salt, Pepper, Nutmeg, and the Yolks of Eggs, then roast it, stick it all over with Cloves, and when it is about Half done cut off some of the Under-side of the fleshy End in little Bits, put these into a Pipkin with a Pint of Oysters, Liquor and all, a little Salt and Mace, and Half a Pint of hot Water; stew them till Half the Liquor is wasted, then put in a Piece of Butter rolled in Flour, shake all together, and when the Mutton is enough take it up, pour this Sauce over it, and send it to Table.

To dress a Leg of Mutton to eat like Venison.

TAKE a Hind Quarter of Mutton and cut the Leg in the Shape of a Haunch of Venison, save the Blood of the Sheep and steep it in for five or six Hours, then take it out and roll it in three or four Sheets of white Paper well butter'd on the Inside, tye it with a Packthread and roast it, basting it with good Beef Dripping or Butter. It will take two Hours at a good Fire, for your Mutton must be fat and thick. About five or six Minutes before you take it up take off the Paper, baste it with a Piece of Butter, and shake a little Flour over it to make it have a fine Froth, and then have a little good drawn Gravy in a Bason, and Sweet Sauce in another. Don't garnish with any Thing.

G

To dress Mutton the Turkish Way.

FIRST cut your Meat into thin Slices, then wash it in Vinegar, and put it into a Pot or Sauce-pan that has a close Cover to it, put in some Rice, Whole Pepper, and three or four whole Onions; let all these stew together, skimming it frequently: When it is enough, take out the Onions, and season it with Salt to your Palate, lay the Mutton in the Dish, and pour the Rice and Liquor over it.

Note, The Neck or Leg are the best Joints to dress this Way. Put into a Leg four Quarts of Water, and a Quarter of a Pound of Rice: To a Neck two Quarts of Water, and two Ounces of Rice. To every Pound of Meat allow a Quarter of an Hour, being close cover'd. If you put in a Blade or two of Mace and a Bundle of Sweet Herbs, it will be a great Addition. When it is just enough, put in a Piece of Butter, and take Care the Rice don't burn to the Pot. In all these Things you should lay Skewers at the Bottom of the Pot to lay your Meat on, that it may not stick.

A Shoulder of Mutton, with a Ragoo of Turnips.

TAKE a Shoulder of Mutton, get the Blade Bone taken out as neat as possible, and in the Place put a Ragoo, done thus: Take one or two Sweetbreads, some Cocks Combs, Half an Ounce of Truffles, some Mushrooms, a Blade or two of Mace, and a little Pepper and Salt; stew all these in a Quarter of a Pint of good Gravy, and thicken it with a Piece of Butter rolled in Flour, or Yolks of Eggs, which you please: Let it be cold before you put it in, and fill up the Place where you took the Bone out just in the Form it was before, and sew it up tight: Take a large deep Stew-pan, or one of the round deep Copper Pans with two Handles, lay at the Bottom thin Slices of Bacon, then Slices of Veal, a Bundle of Parsley, Thyme and Sweet Herbs, some Whole Pepper, a Blade or two of Mace, three or four Cloves, a large Onion, and put in just thin Gravy enough to cover the Meat; cover it close, and let it stew two Hours, then take eight or ten Turnips, pare them, and cut them into what Shape you please, put them into boiling Water, and let them be just enough, throw them into a Sieve to drain over the hot Water that they may keep warm, then take up the Mutton, drain it from the Fat, lay it in a Dish, and keep it hot cover'd; strain the Gravy it was stew'd in, and take off all the Fat, put in a little Salt, a Glass of Red Wine, two Spoonfuls of Catchup, and a Piece of Butter rolled in Flour; boil all together till there is just enough for Sauce, then put in the Turnips, give them a Boil up, pour them over the Meat, and send it to Table. You may fry the Turnips of a light Brown, and toss them up with the Sauce; but that is according to your Palate.

Note, For a Change you may leave out the Turnips, and add a Bunch of Sellery cut and wash'd clean, and stew'd in a very little Water till it is quite tender, and the Water almost boil'd away. Pour the Gravy, as before directed, into it, and boil it up till the Sauce is good. Or you may leave both these out, and add Truffles, Morels, fresh and pickled Mushrooms, and Artichoke-bottoms.

N. B. A Shoulder of Veal, without the Knuckle, first fry'd, and then done just as the Mutton, eats very well. Don't garnish your Mutton, but garnish your Veal with Lemon.

To Stuff a Leg or Shoulder of Mutton.

TAKE a little grated Bread, some Beef Sewet, the Yolks of hard Eggs, three Anchovies, a Bit of an Onion, some Pepper and Salt, a little Thyme and Winter Savoury, twelve Oysters, and some Nutmeg grated; mix all these together, shred them very fine, work them up with raw Eggs like a Paste, stuff your Mutton under the Skin in the thickest Place, or where you please, and roast it: For Sauce, take some of the Oyster Liquor, some Claret, one Anchovy, a little Nutmeg, a Bit of an Onion, and a few Oysters; stew all these together, then take out your Onion, pour your Sauce under your Mutton, and send it to Table. Garnish with Horse-raddish.

Sheeps Rumps with Rice.

TAKE six Rumps, put them into a Stew-pan with some Mutton Gravy, enough to fill it, stew them about Half an Hour, take them up and let them stand to cool, then put into the Liquor a Quarter of a Pound of Rice, an Onion stuck with Cloves, and a Blade or two of Mace; let it boil till the Rice is as thick as a Pudding, but take great Care it don't stick to the Bottom, which you must do by stirring it often: In the mean Time take a clean Stew-pan, put a Piece of Butter into it, dip your Rumps in the Yolks of Eggs beat, and then in Crumbs of Bread with a little Nutmeg, Lemon-peel, and a very little Thyme in it, fry them in the Butter of a fine Brown, then take them out, lay them in a Dish to drain, pour out all the Fat, and toss in the Rice into that Pan; stir it all together for a Minute or two, then lay the Rice into the Dish, lay the Rumps all round upon the Rice, have ready four Eggs boil'd hard, cut them into Quarters, lay them round the Dish with fry'd Parsley between them, and send it to Table.

To Bake Lamb and Rice.

TAKE a Neck and Loin of Lamb, Half roast it, take it up, cut it into Steaks, then take Half a Pound of Rice, put it into a Quart of good Gravy, with two or three Blades of Mace, and a little Nutmeg; do it over a Stove or slow Fire till the Rice begins to be thick, then take it off, stir in a Pound of Butter, and when that is quite melted stir in the Yolks of six Eggs, first beat; then take a Dish and butter it all over, take the Steaks and put a little Pepper and Salt over them, dip them in a little melted

melted Butter, lay them into the Dish, pour the Gravy which comes out of them over them, and then the Rice, beat the Yolks of three Eggs and pour all over; send it to the Oven, and bake it better than Half an Hour.

Baked Mutton Chops.

TAKE a Loin or Neck of Mutton, cut it into Steaks, put some Pepper and Salt over it, butter your Dish and lay in your Steaks, then take a Quart of Milk, six Eggs beat up fine, and four Spoonfuls of Flour; beat your Flour and Eggs in a little Milk first, and then put the rest to it, put in a little beaten Ginger, and a little Salt; pour this over the Steaks, and send it to the Oven. An Hour and a Half will bake it.

A Forced Leg of Lamb.

TAKE a large Leg of Lamb, cut a long Slit on the Back-side, but take great Care you don't deface the other Side, then chop the Meat small with Marrow, Half a Pound of Beef Sewet, some Oysters, an Anchovy unwash'd, an Onion, some Sweet Herbs, a little Lemon-peel, and some beaten Mace and Nutmeg; beat all these together in a Mortar, stuff it up in the Shape it was before, sew it up, and rub it over with the Yolks of Eggs beaten, spit it, flour it all over, lay it to the Fire, and baste it with Butter. An Hour will roast it. You may bake it, if you please, but then you must butter the Dish and lay Butter over it; cut the Loin into Steaks, season them with Pepper, Salt, and Nutmeg, Lemon-peel cut fine, and a few Sweet Herbs, fry them in Fresh Butter of a fine Brown, then pour out all the Butter, put in a Quarter of a Pint of White Wine, shake it about, and put in Half a Pint of strong Gravy wherein good Spice has been boil'd, a Quarter of a Pint of Oysters and the Liquor, some Mushrooms and a Spoonful of the Pickle, a Piece of Butter rolled in Flour, and the Yolk of an Egg beat; stir all these together till it is thick, then lay your Leg of Lamb in the Dish and the Loin round it, pour the Sauce over it, and garnish with Lemon.

To Fry a Loin of Lamb.

CUT the Loin into thin Steaks, put a very little Pepper and Salt, and a little Nutmeg on them, and fry them in Fresh Butter; when enough, take out the Steaks, lay them in a Dish before the Fire to keep hot, then pour out the Butter, shake a little Flour over the Bottom of the Pan, pour in a Quarter of a Pint of boiling Water, and put in a Piece of Butter; shake all together, give it a Boil or two up, pour it over the Steaks, and send it to Table.

Note, You may do Mutton the same Way, and add two Spoonfuls of Walnut Pickle, or a little Vinegar.

Another Way of Frying a Neck or Loin of Lamb.

CUT it into thin Steaks, beat them with a Rolling-pin, fry them in Half a Pint of Ale, season them with a little Salt, and cover them close; when enough, take them out of the Pan, lay them in a Plate before the Fire to keep hot, and pour all out of the Pan into a Bason; then put in Half a Pint of White Wine, a few Capers, the Yolks of two Eggs beat with a little Nutmeg and a little Salt, add to this the Liquor they were fry'd in, and keep stirring it all one Way all the Time till it is thick, then put in the Lamb, keep shaking the Pan for a Minute or two, lay the Steaks into the Dish, pour the Sauce over them, and have some Parsley in a Plate before the Fire a crisping. Garnish your Dish with that and Lemon.

To make a Ragoo of Lamb.

TAKE a Fore-Quarter of Lamb, cut the Knuckle Bone off, lard it with little thin Bits of Bacon, flour it, fry it of a fine Brown, and then put it into an Earthen Pot or Stew-pan; put to it a Quart of Broth or good Gravy, a Bundle of Herbs, a little Mace, two or three Cloves, and a little Whole Pepper; cover it close, and let it stew pretty fast for Half an Hour, pour the Liquor all out, strain it, keep the Lamb hot in the Pot till the Sauce is ready, take Half a Pint of Oysters, flour them, fry them Brown, drain out all the Fat clean that you fry'd them in, skim all the Fat off the Gravy, then pour it into the Oysters, put in an Anchovy, and two Spoonfuls of either Red or White Wine; boil all together till there is just enough for Sauce, add some fresh Mushrooms (if you can get them) and some pickled Ones, with a Spoonful of the Pickle, or the Juice of Half a Lemon; lay your Lamb in the Dish, and pour the Sauce over it. Garnish with Lemon.

To Stew a Lamb's, or Calf's Head.

FIRST wash it, and pick it very clean, lay it in Water for an Hour, take out the Brains, and with a sharp Penknife carefully take out the Bones and the Tongue, but be careful you don't brake the Meat, then take out the two Eyes, and take two Pounds of Veal and two Pounds of Beef Sewet, a very little Thyme, a good Piece of Lemon-peel minced, a Nutmeg grated, and two Anchovies; chop all very well together, grate two stale Rolls, and mix all together with the Yolks of four Eggs: Save enough of this

Meat

Meat to make about twenty Balls, take Half a Pint of fresh Mushrooms clean peel'd and wash'd, the Yolks of six Eggs chopp'd, Half a Pint of Oysters clean wash'd, or pickled Cockles, mix all these together, but first stew your Oysters, and put to it two Quarts of Gravy, with a Blade or two of Mace. It will be proper to tye the Head with a Packthread, cover it close, and let it stew two Hours; in the mean Time beat up the Brains with some Lemon-peel cut fine, a little Parsley chopp'd, Half a Nutmeg grated, and the Yolk of an Egg; have some Dripping boiling, fry Half the Brains in little Cakes, and fry the Balls, keep them both hot by the Fire, take Half an Ounce of Truffles and Morels, then strain the Gravy the Head was stew'd in, put the Truffles and Morels to it with the Liquor, and a few Mushrooms; boil all together, then put in the rest of the Brains that are not fry'd, stew them together for a Minute or two, pour it over the Head, and lay the fry'd Brains and Balls round it. Garnish with Lemon. You may fry about twelve Oysters.

To dress Veal a la Bourgoise.

CUT pretty thick Slices of Veal, lard them with Bacon, and season them with Pepper, Salt, beaten Mace, Cloves, Nutmeg, and chopp'd Parsley, then take your Stew-pan and cover the Bottom with Slices of Fat Bacon, lay the Veal upon them, cover it, and let it over a very slow Fire for eight or ten Minutes just to be hot and no more, then brisk up your Fire and Brown your Veal on both Sides, then shake some Flour over it and Brown it, pour in a Quart of good Broth or Gravy, cover it close, and let it stew gently till it is enough; when enough, take out the Slices of Bacon, and skim all the Fat off clean, and beat up the Yolks of three Eggs with some of the Gravy; mix all together, and keep it stirring one Way till it is smooth and thick, then take it up, lay your Meat in the Dish, and pour the Sauce over it. Garnish with Lemon.

A disguised Leg of Veal and Bacon.

LARD your Veal all over with Slips of Bacon and a little Lemon-peel, and boil it with a Piece of Bacon; when enough, take it up, cut the Bacon into Slices, and have ready some dry'd Sage and Pepper rubb'd fine, rub over the Bacon, lay the Veal in the Dish and the Bacon round it, strew it all over with fry'd Parsley, and have Green Sauce in Cups; made thus: Take two Handfuls of Sorrel, pound it in a Mortar and squeeze out the Juice, put it into a Sauce-pan with some melted Butter, a little Sugar, and the Juice of Lemon. Or you may make it thus: Beat two Handfuls of Sorrel in a Mortar with two Pippins quarter'd, squeeze the Juice out with the Juice of a Lemon or Vinegar, and sweeten it with Sugar.

A Pillaw of Veal.

TAKE a Neck or Breast of Veal, Half roast it, then cut it into six Pieces, season it with Pepper, Salt, and Nutmeg; take a Pound of Rice, put to it a Quart of Broth, some Mace, and a little Salt, do it over a Stove or very slow Fire till it is thick, but butter the Bottom of the Dish or Pan you do it in, beat up the Yolks of six Eggs and stir into it, then take a little round deep Dish, butter it, lay some of the Rice at the Bottom, then lay the Veal on a round Heap and cover it all over with the Rice, wash it over with the Yolks of Eggs and bake it an Hour and a Half, then open the Top and pour in a Pint of rich good Gravy; garnish with *Seville* Orange cut in Quarters, and send it to Table hot.

Bombarded Veal.

YOU must get a Fillet of Veal, cut out of it five lean Pieces as thick as your Hand, round them up a little, then lard them very thick on the round Side with little narrow thin Pieces of Bacon, and lard five Sheeps Tongues (being first boiled and blanched) lard them here and there with very little Bits of Lemon-peel; make a well-season'd Force-Meat of Veal, Bacon, Ham, Beef Sewet, and an Anchovy beat well; make another tender Force-Meat of Veal, Beef Sewet, Mushrooms, Spinach, Parsley, Thyme, Sweet Marjoram, Winter Savoury, and green Onions; season with Pepper, Salt, and Mace, beat it well, make a round Ball of the other Force-Meat and stuff in the Middle of this, roll it up in a Veal Caul, and bake it; what is left tye up like a *Bolognia* Sausage and boil it, but first rub the Caul with the Yolk of an Egg; put the larded Veal into a Stew-pan with some good Gravy, and when it is enough skim off the Fat, put in some Truffles and Morels, and some Mushrooms. Your Force-Meat being baked enough, lay it in the Middle, the Veal round it, and the Tongues fry'd and laid between, the Boil'd cut into Slices and fry'd, and throw all over. Pour on them the Sauce. You may add Artichoke Bottoms, Sweetbreads, and Cocks Combs, if you please. Garnish with Lemon.

Veal Rolls.

TAKE ten or twelve little thin Slices of Veal, lay on them some Force-Meat according to your Fancy, roll them up, and tye them just across the Middle with coarse Thread, put them on a Bird-spit, rub them over with the Yolks of Eggs, flour them, and baste them with Butter. Half an Hour will do them. Lay them into a Dish, and have ready some good Gravy, with a few Truffles and Morels, and some Mushrooms. Garnish with Lemon.

Olives

The Art of Cookery, made Plain and Easy. 29

Olives of Veal, the French *Way.*

TAKE two Pounds of Veal, some Marrow, two Anchovies, the Yolks of two hard Eggs, a few Mushrooms, and some Oysters, a little Thyme, Marjoram, Parsley, Spinach, Lemon-peel, Salt, Pepper, Nutmeg, and Mace, finely beaten; take your Veal Caul, lay a Layer of Bacon and a Layer of the Ingredients, and a Layer of Bacon and a Layer of the Ingredients, roll it in the Veal Caul, and either roast it or bake it. An Hour will do either. When enough, cut it into Slices, lay it into your Dish, and pour good Gravy over it. Garnish with Lemon.

Scotch Collops *a la Francois.*

TAKE a Leg of Veal, cut it very thin, lard it with Bacon, then take Half a Pint of Ale boiling and pour over it till the Blood is out, and then pour the Ale out into a Bason; take a few Sweet Herbs chopp'd small, strew them over the Veal and fry it in Butter, flour it a little till enough, then put it into a Dish and pour the Butter away, toast little thin Pieces of Bacon and lay round, pour the Ale into the Stew-pan with two Anchovies and a Glass of White Wine, then beat up the Yolks of two Eggs and stir in with a little Nutmeg, some Pepper, and a Piece of Butter, shake all together till thick, and then pour it into the Dish. Garnish with Lemon.

To make a savoury Dish of Veal.

CUT large Collops out of a Leg of Veal, spread them abroad on a Dresser, hack them with the Back of a Knife, and dip them in the Yolks of Eggs; season them with Cloves, Mace, Nutmeg, and Pepper, beat fine, make Force-Meat with some of your Veal, Beef Sewet, Oysters chopp'd, Sweet Herbs shred fine, and the aforesaid Spice, strew all these over your Collops, roll and tye them up, put them on Skewers, tye them to a Spit, and roast them; to the rest of your Force-Meat add a raw Egg or two, roll them in Balls and fry them, put them in your Dish with your Meat when roasted, and make the Sauce with strong Broth, an Anchovy, a Shalot, a little White Wine, and some Spice; let it stew, and thicken it with a Piece of Butter rolled in Flour, pour the Sauce into the Dish, lay the Meat in, and garnish with Lemon.

Scotch Collops *Larded.*

PREPARE a Fillet of Veal, cut it into thin Slices, cut off the Skin and Fat, lard them with Bacon, fry them Brown, then take them out and lay them in a Dish, pour out all the Butter, take a Quarter of a Pound of Butter and melt it in the Pan, then strew in a Handful of Flour, stir it till it is Brown, and pour in three Pints of good Gravy, a Bundle of Sweet Herbs, and an Onion, which you must take out soon; let it boil a little, then put in the Collops, let them stew Half a Quarter of an Hour, put in some Force-Meat Balls fry'd, the Yolks of two Eggs, a Piece of Butter, and a few pickled Mushrooms; stir all together for a Minute or two till it is thick, and then dish it up. Garnish with Lemon.

To do *them* White.

AFTER you have cut your Veal in thin Slices lard it with Bacon, season it with Cloves, Mace, Nutmeg, Pepper and Salt, some grated Bread and Sweet Herbs; stew the Knuckle in as little Liquor as you can, a Bunch of Sweet Herbs, some Whole Pepper, a Blade of Mace, and four Cloves; then take a Pint of the Broth, stew the Cutlets in it, and add to it a Quarter of a Pint of White Wine, some Mushrooms, a Piece of Butter rolled in Flour, and the Yolks of two Eggs, stir all together till it is thick, and then dish it up. Garnish with Lemon.

Veal Blanquets.

ROAST a Piece of Veal, cut off the Skin and nervous Parts, cut it into little thin Bits, put some Butter into a Stew-pan over the Fire with some chopp'd Onions, fry them a little, then add a Dust of Flour, stir it together, and put in some good Broth or Gravy, and a Bundle of Sweet Herbs; season it with Spice, make it of a good Taste, and then put in your Veal, the Yolks of two Eggs beat up with Cream and grated Nutmeg, some chopp'd Parsley, a Shalot, some Lemon-peel grated, and a little Juice of Lemon. Keep it stirring one Way; when enough, dish it up.

A Shoulder of Veal *à la Piemontoise.*

TAKE a Shoulder of Veal, cut off the Skin that it may hang at one End, then lard the Meat with Bacon and Ham, and season it with Pepper, Salt, Mace, Sweet Herbs, Parsley, and Lemon-peel, cover it again with the Skin, stew it with Gravy, and when it is just tender take it up; then take Sorrel, some Lettuce chopp'd small, and stew them in some Butter with Parsley, Onions, and Mushrooms; The Herbs being tender put to them some of the Liquor, some Sweetbreads, and some Bits of Ham; let all stew together a little while, then lift up the Skin, lay the stew'd Herbs over and under, cover it

H with

with the Skin again, wet it with melted Butter, strew it over with Crumbs of Bread, and send it to the Oven to Brown; serve it hot, with some good Gravy in the Dish. The *French* strew it over with *Parmesan* before it goes to the Oven.

A Calf's Head Surprise.

YOU must bone it, but not split it, cleanse it well, fill it with a Ragoo (in the Form it was before) made thus: Take two Sweetbreads, each Sweetbread being cut into eight Pieces, an Ox's Palate boil'd tender and cut in little Pieces, some Cocks Combs, Half an Ounce of Truffles and Morels, some Mushrooms, some Artichoke Bottoms and Asparagus Tops; stew all these in Half a Pint of good Gravy, season it with two or three Blades of Mace, four Cloves, Half a Nutmeg, a very little Pepper, and some Salt, pound all these together, and put them into the Ragoo; when it has stew'd about Half an Hour, take the Yolks of three Eggs beat up with two Spoonfuls of Cream and two of White Wine, put it to the Ragoo, keep it stirring one Way for fear of turning, and stir in a Piece of Butter rolled in Flour; when it is very thick and smooth fill the Head, make a Force-Meat with Half a Pound of Veal, Half a Pound of Beef Sewet, as much Crumbs of Bread, a few Sweet Herbs, a little Lemon-peel, and some Pepper, Salt, and Mace, all beat fine together in a Marble Mortar; mix it up with two Eggs, make a few Balls (about twenty) put them into the Ragoo in the Head, then fasten the Head with fine Wooden Skewers, lay the Force-Meat over the Head, do it over with the Yolks of two Eggs, and send it to the Oven to bake. It will take about two Hours baking. You must lay Pieces of Butter all over the Head, and then flour it. When it is baked enough lay it in your Dish, and have a Pint of good fry'd Gravy. If there is any Gravy in the Dish the Head was baked in, put it to the other Gravy, and boil it up; pour it into your Dish, and garnish with Lemon. You may throw some Mushrooms over the Head.

Sweetbreads of Veal a la Dauphine.

TAKE the largest Sweetbreads you can get, open them in such a Manner as you can stuff in Force-Meat, three will make a fine Dish; make your Force-Meat with a large Fowl or young Cock, skin it, and pick off all the Flesh, take Half a Pound of Fat and Lean Bacon, cut these very fine and beat them in a Mortar; season it with an Anchovy, some Nutmeg, a little Lemon-peel, a very little Thyme, and some Parsley: Mix these up with the Yolk of an Egg, fill your Sweetbreads and fasten them with fine Wooden Skewers, take the Stew-pan, lay Layers of Bacon at the Bottom of the Pan, season them with Pepper, Salt, Mace, Cloves, Sweet Herbs, and a large Onion sliced, upon that lay thin Slices of Veal, and then lay on your Sweetbreads; cover it close, let it stand eight or ten Minutes over a slow Fire, and then pour in a Quart of boiling Water or Broth; cover it close, and let it stew two Hours very softly, then take out the Sweetbreads, keep them hot, strain the Gravy, skim all the Fat off, boil it up till there is about Half a Pint, put in the Sweetbreads and give them two or three Minutes stew in the Gravy, then lay them in the Dish, and pour the Gravy over them. Garnish with Lemon.

Another Way to dress Sweetbreads.

DON'T put any Water or Gravy into the Stew-pan, but put the same Veal and Bacon over the Sweetbreads, and season as under directed; cover them close, put Fire over as well as under, and when they are enough take out the Sweetbreads, put in a Ladleful of Gravy, boil it, and strain it, skim off all the Fat, let it boil till it Jellies; and then put in the Sweetbreads to glaze; lay Essence of Ham in the Dish, and lay the Sweetbreads upon it; or make a very rich Gravy with Mushrooms, Truffles and Morels, a Glass of White Wine, and two Spoonfuls of Catchup. Garnish with Cocks Combs forc'd and stew'd in the Gravy.

Note, You may add to the first, Truffles, Morels, Mushrooms, Cocks Combs, Palates, Artichoke Bottoms, two Spoonfuls of White Wine, two of Catchup, or just as you please.

N. B. There are many Ways of dressing Sweetbreads: You may lard them with thin Slips of Bacon, and roast them with what Sauce you please; or you may marinate them, cut them into thin Slices, flour them, and fry them. Serve them up with fry'd Parsley, and either Butter or Gravy. Garnish with Lemon.

Calf's Chitterlings or Andouilles.

TAKE some of the largest Calf's Guts, cleanse them, cut them in Pieces proportionable to the Length of the Puddings you design to make, and tye one End of these Pieces, then take some Bacon, with a Calf's Udder and Chaldron blanched, and cut into Dice or Slices, put them into a Stew-pan and season with fine Spice pounded, a Bay-Leaf, some Salt, Pepper, and Shalot cut small, and about Half a Pint of Cream; toss it up, take off the Pan, and thicken your Mixture with four or five Yolks of Eggs and some Crumbs of Bread, then fill up your Chitterlings with the Stuffing, keep it warm, tye the other Ends with Packthread, blanch and boil them like Hog's Chitterlings, let them grow cold in their own Liquor before you serve them up; boil them over a moderate Fire, and serve them up pretty hot. These Sort of Andouilles, or Puddings, must be made in Summer, when Hogs are seldom kill'd.

To dress Calf's Chitterlings curiously.

CUT a Calf's Nut in Slices of it's Length, and the Thickness of a Finger, together with some Ham, Bacon, and the White of Chickens, cut after the same Manner; put the Whole into a Stew-pan, seasoned with Salt, Pepper, Sweet Herbs and Spice, then take the Guts cleansed, cut and divide them in Parcels, and fill them with your Slices; then lay in the Bottom of a Kettle or Pan some Slices of Bacon and Veal, season them with some Pepper, Salt, a Bay-Leaf and an Onion, and lay some Bacon and Veal over them; then put in a Pint of White Wine, and let it stew softly, close covered, with Fire over and under it, if the Pot or Pan will allow of it; then broil the Puddings on a Sheet of white Paper well butter'd on the Inside.

To dress a Ham à la Braise.

CLEAR the Knuckle, take off the Swerd, and lay it in Water to freshen; then tye it about with a String, take Slices of Bacon and Beef, beat and season them well with Spice and Sweet Herbs; then lay them in the Bottom of a Kettle with Onions, Parsnips, and Carrots sliced, with some Cives and Parsley: Lay in your Ham the Fat Side uppermost, and cover it with Slices of Beef, and over that Slices of Bacon; then lay on some sliced Roots and Herbs, the same as under it: Cover it close, and stop it close with Paste, put Fire both over and under it, and let it stew with a very slow Fire twelve Hours; put it in a Pan, drudge it well with grated Bread, and Brown it with a hot Iron; then serve it up on a clean Napkin, garnished with raw Parsley.

Note, If you eat it hot make a Ragoo thus: Take a Veal Sweetbread, some Livers of Fowls, Cocks Combs, Mushrooms, and Truffles, toss them up in a Pint of good Gravy, season'd with Spice as you like, thicken it with a Piece of Butter roll'd in Flour, and a Glass of Red Wine; then Brown your Ham as above and let it stand a Quarter of an Hour to drain the Fat out; take the Liquor it was stew'd in, strain it, skim all the Fat off, put it to the Gravy and boil it up; it will do as well as the Essence of Ham. Sometimes you may serve it up with a Ragoo of Craw-fish, and sometimes with Carp Sauce.

To Roast a Ham or Gammon.

TAKE off the Swerd, or what we call the Skin, or Rine, and lay it in luke-warm Water for two or three Hours; then lay it in a Pan, pour upon it a Quart of Canary, and let it steep in it for ten or twelve Hours; when you have spitted it, put some Sheets of white Paper over the Fat Side, pour the Canary it was soak'd in into the Dripping-pan, and baste it with it all the Time it is roasting; when it is roasted enough pull off the Paper, and drudge it well with crumb'd Bread and Parsley shred fine; make the Fire brisk, and Brown it well. If you eat it hot, garnish it with Raspings of Bread; if cold, serve it on a clean Napkin, and garnish it with green Parsley, for a Second Course.

To Stuff a Chine of Pork.

MAKE a Stuffing of the fat Leaf of Pork, Parsley, Thyme, Sage, Eggs, and Crumbs of Bread, season it with Pepper, Salt, Shalot, and Nutmeg, and stuff it thick; then roast it gently, and when it is about a Quarter roasted, cut the Skin in Slips, and make your Sauce with Apples, Lemon-peel, two or three Cloves, and a Blade of Mace; sweeten it with Sugar, put some Butter in it, and have Mustard in a Cup.

Various Ways of dressing a Pig.

FIRST skin your Pig up to the Ears whole, then make a good Plumb-pudding Batter, with good Beef Fat, Fruit, Eggs, Milk, and Flour, fill the Skin, and sew it up, it will look like a Pig; but you must bake it, flour it very well, and rub it all over with Butter, and when it is near enough draw it to the Oven's Mouth, rub it dry, and put it in again for a few Minutes; then lay it in the Dish, and let the Sauce be small Gravy and Butter in the Dish: Cut the other Part of the Pig into four Quarters, roast them as you do Lamb, throw Mint and Parsley on it as it roasts; then lay them on Water-cresses, and have Mint-Sauce in a Bason. Any one of these Quarters will make a pretty Side Dish: Or take one Quarter and roast, and cut the other into Steaks, and fry them fine and brown, have stew'd Spinach in the Dish, and lay the Roast upon it, and the Fry'd in the Middle; garnish with hard Eggs and *Seville* Oranges cut into Quarters, and have some Butter in a Cup: Or for Change, you may have good Gravy in the Dish, and garnish with fry'd Parsley and Lemon: Or you may make a Ragoo of Sweetbreads, Artichoke Bottoms, Truffles, Morels, and good Gravy, and pour over them; garnish with Lemon. Either of these will do for a Top Dish of a First Course, or Bottom Dishes at a Second Course; you may fricasey it White for a Second Course at Top, or a Side Dish.

You may take a Pig, skin him, and fill him with Force-Meat made thus: Take two Pounds of young Pork, Fat and all, two Pounds of Veal the same, some Sage, Thyme, Parsley, a little Lemon-peel, Pepper, Salt, Mace, Cloves, and a Nutmeg, mix them, and beat them fine in a Mortar, then fill the Pig, and sew it up; you may either roast or bake it: Have nothing but good Gravy in the Dish: Or you may cut it in Slices, and lay the Head in the Middle: Save the Head whole with the Skin on, and roast it by itself, when it is enough cut it in two, and lay in your Dish; have ready some good Gravy and

dried

dried Sage rubb'd in it, thicken it with a Piece of Butter roll'd in Flour, take out the Brains, beat them up with the Gravy, and pour them into the Dish; you may add a hard Egg chopped, and put into the Sauce.

Note, You may make a very good Pie of it, as you may see in the Directions for Pies, which you may either make a Bottom or Side Dish.

You must observe in your White Fricasey that you take off the Fat: Or you may make a very good Dish thus: Take a Quarter of Pig skinned, cut it into Chops, season them with Spice, and wash them with the Yolks of Eggs, butter the Bottom of a Dish, lay these Steaks on the Dish, and upon every Steak lay some Force-Meat the Thickness of Half a Crown, made thus: Take Half a Pound of Veal, and of Fat Pork the same Quantity, chop them very well together, and beat them in a Mortar fine; add some Sweet Herbs and Sage, a little Lemon-peel, Nutmeg, Pepper and Salt, and a little beaten Mace; upon this lay a Layer of Bacon, or Ham, and then a Bay-Leaf; take a little fine Skewer and stick just in about two Inches long, to hold them together, then pour a little melted Butter over them, and send them to the Oven to bake; when they are enough lay them in your Dish, and pour good Gravy over them, with Mushrooms, and garnish with Lemon.

A Pig *in Jelly.*

CUT it into four Quarters, and lay it in your Stew-pan, put in one Calf's Foot and the Pig's Feet, a Pint of *Rhenish* Wine, the Juice of four Lemons, and one Quart of Water, three or four Blades of Mace, two or three Cloves, some Salt, and a very little Piece of Lemon-peel; stove it, or do it over a slow Fire two Hours; then take it up, lay the Pig into the Dish you intend it for, then strain the Liquor, and when the Jelly is cold, skim off the Fat, and leave the Settling at Bottom; warm the Jelly again, and pour over the Pig, and then serve it up cold in the Jelly.

To dress a Pig *the* French *Way.*

SPIT your Pig, lay it down to the Fire, let it roast till it is thoroughly warm, then cut it off the Spit, and divide it in twenty Pieces; set them to stew in Half a Pint of White Wine, and a Pint of strong Broth, season'd with grated Nutmeg, Pepper, two Onions cut small, and some stripp'd Thyme; let it stew an Hour, then put to it Half a Pint of strong Gravy, a Piece of Butter roll'd in Flour, some Anchovies, and a Spoonful of Vinegar, or Mushroom Pickle; when it is enough lay it in your Dish, and pour the Gravy over it, then garnish with Orange and Lemon.

To dress a Pig *au* Pere-douillet.

CUT off the Head, and divide it into Quarters, lard them with Bacon, season them well with Mace, Cloves, Pepper, Nutmeg and Salt; lay a Layer of Fat Bacon at the Bottom of a Kettle, lay the Head in the Middle, and the Quarters round; then put in a Bay-Leaf, one Rocambole, an Onion sliced, Lemon, Carrots, Parsnips, Parsley, and Cives, cover it again with Bacon, put in a Quart of Broth, stew it over the Fire for an Hour, and then take it up, put your Pig into a Stew-pan or Kettle, pour in a Bottle of White Wine, cover it close, and let it stew for an Hour very softly: If you would serve it cold, let it stand till it is cold, then drain it well, and wipe it, that it may look White, and lay it in a Dish, with the Head in the Middle, and the Quarters round, then throw some green Parsley all over: Or any one of the Quarters is a very pretty little Dish, laid on Water-cresses: If you would have it hot, whilst your Pig is stewing in the Wine, take the first Gravy it was stew'd in and strain it, skim off all the Fat, then take a Sweet-bread cut into five or six Slices, some Truffles, Morels, and Mushrooms; stew all together till they are enough, thicken it with the Yolks of two Eggs, or a Piece of Butter roll'd in Flour, and when your Pig is enough take it out, and lay it in your Dish, and the Wine it was stew'd in to the Ragoo, then pour all over the Pig, and garnish with Lemon.

A Pig Matelote.

GUT and scald your Pig, cut off the Head, and Petty-Toes, then cut your Pig in four Quarters, put them with the Head and Toes into cold Water: Cover the Bottom of a Stew-pan with Slices of Bacon, and place over them the said Quarters, with the Petty-Toes, and the Head cut in two. Season the Whole with Pepper, Salt, Thyme, Bay-Leaf, an Onion, and a Bottle of White Wine; lay over more Slices of Bacon, put over it a Quart of Water, and let it boil. Take two large Eels, skin and gut them, and cut them about five or six Inches long; when your Pig is Half done put in your Eels, then boil a Dozen of large Craw-fish, cut off the Claws, and take off the Shells of the Tails, and when your Pig and Eels are enough, lay first your Pig and the Petty-Toes round it, but don't put in the Head (it will be a pretty Dish cold) then lay your Eels and Craw-fish over them, and take the Liquor they were stew'd in, skim off all the Fat, then add to it Half a Pint of strong Gravy thicken'd with a little Piece of burnt Butter, and pour over it; then garnish with Craw-fish and Lemon. This will do for a First Course, or Remove. Fry the Brains and lay round and all over the Dish.

To

The Art of Cookery, made Plain and Easy. 33

To dress a Pig like a Fat Lamb.

TAKE a fat Pig, cut off his Head, slit and truss him up like a Lamb; when he is slit through the Middle and skinned, parboil him a little, then throw some Parsley over him, roast it and dredge it. Let your Sauce be Half a Pound of Butter and a Pint of Cream, stirred together till it is smooth, then pour it over, and send it to Table.

To roast a Pig with the Hair on.

DRAW your Pig very clean at the Vent, then take out the Guts, Liver, and Lights; cut off his Feet and truss him, prick up his Belly, spit him, lay him down to the Fire, but take care not to scorch him; when the Skin begins to rise up in Blisters, pull off the Skin, Hair and all; when you have clear'd the Pig of both, scotch him down to the Bones, and baste him with Butter and Cream, or Half a Pound of Butter, and a Pint of Milk, put it into the Dripping-pan, and keep basting it well; then throw some Salt over it, and dredge it with Crumbs of Bread, till it is Half an Inch, or an Inch thick: When it is enough, and of a fine Brown, but not scorch'd, take it up, lay it in your Dish, and let your Sauce be good Gravy thicken'd with Butter roll'd in a little Flour; or else make the following Sauce: Take Half a Pound of Butter, and a Pint of Cream, put them on the Fire, and keep them stirring one Way all the Time; when the Butter is melted, and the Sauce thicken'd, pour it into your Dish. Don't garnish with any Thing, unless some Raspings of Bread, and then with your Finger figure it as you fancy.

To roast a Pig with the Skin on.

LET your Pig be newly killed, draw him, flea him, and wipe him very dry with a Cloth, then make a hard Meat, with a Pint of Cream, the Yolks of six Eggs, grated Bread and Beef Sewet, seasoned with Salt, Pepper, Mace, Nutmeg, Thyme, and Lemon-peel; make of this a pretty stiff Pudding, stuff the Belly of the Pig, and sew it up; then spit it, and lay it down to roast: Let your Dripping-pan be very clean, then pour into it a Pint of Red Wine, grate some Nutmeg all over it, then throw a little Salt over, a little Thyme, and some Lemon-peel minced; when it is enough shake a little Flour over, and baste it with Butter, to have a fine Froth. Take it up and lay it in your Dish, cut off the Head, take the Sauce which is in your Dripping-pan, and thicken it with a Piece of Butter; then take the Brains, bruise them, and mix them with the Sauce; rub in a little dried Sage, pour it into your Dish, and serve it up. Garnish with hard Eggs cut into Quarters, and if you have not Sauce enough add Half a Pint of good Gravy.

Note, You must take great Care no Ashes fall into the Dripping-pan, which may be prevented by having a good Fire, which will not want any stirring.

To make a pretty Dish of a Breast of Venison.

TAKE Half a Pound of Butter, flour your Venison, and fry it of a fine Brown on both Sides; then take it up, and keep it hot cover'd in the Dish: Take some Flour and stir it in to the Butter till it is quite thick and brown (but take great Care it don't burn) stir in Half a Pound of Lump Sugar beat fine, and pour in as much Red Wine as will make it of the Thickness of a Ragoo; squeeze in the Juice of a Lemon, give it a boil up, and pour it over the Venison. Don't garnish your Dish, but send it to Table.

To boil a Haunch or Neck of Venison.

LAY it in Salt for a Week, then boil it in a Cloth well flour'd; for every Pound of Venison, allow a Quarter of an Hour for the boiling. For Sauce you must boil some Cauliflowers, pull'd into little Sprigs in Milk and Water, some fine white Cabbage, some Turnips cut into Dice, with some Beet-root cut into long narrow Pieces about an Inch and a Half long, and Half an Inch thick: Lay a Sprig of Cauliflower, and some of the Turnips mashed with some Cream and a little Butter; let your Cabbage be boiled, and then beat in a Sauce-pan with a Piece of Butter and Salt, lay that next the Cauliflower, then the Turnips, then Cabbage, and so on, till the Dish is full; place the Beet-root here and there, just as you fancy; it looks very pretty, and is a fine Dish. Have a little melted Butter in a Cup if wanted.

Note, A Leg of Mutton cut Venison Fashion, and dressed the same Way is a pretty Dish: Or a fine Neck with the Scraig cut off: This eats well broil'd or hash'd, with Gravy and Sweet-sauce the next Day.

I To

The Art of Cookery, made Plain and Easy.

To boil a Leg of Mutton like Venison.

TAKE a Leg of Mutton cut Venison Fashion, boil it in a Cloth well flour'd, and have three or four Cauliflowers boil'd, pulled into Sprigs, stew'd in a Stew-pan with Butter, and a little Pepper and Salt; then have some Spinach pick'd and wash'd clean, put it into a Sauce-pan with a little Salt, cover'd close, and stew'd a little while; then drain the Liquor, and pour in a Quarter of a Pint of good Gravy, a good Piece of Butter roll'd in Flour, and a little Pepper and Salt; when stew'd enough lay the Spinach in the Dish, the Mutton in the Middle, and the Cauliflower over it; then pour the Butter the Cauliflower was stew'd in over it all: But you are to observe in stewing the Cauliflower, to melt your Butter nicely, as for Sauce, before the Cauliflower goes in. This is a genteel Dish for a first Course at Bottom.

To roast Tripe.

CUT your Tripe in two square Pieces, somewhat long, have a Force-Meat made of Crumbs of Bread, Pepper, Salt, Nutmeg, Sweet Herbs, Lemon-peel, and the Yolks of Eggs mixt all together; spread it on the fat Side of the Tripe, and lay the other fat Side next it; then roll it as light as you can, and tye it with a Packthread; spit it, roast it, and baste it with Butter; when roasted lay it in your Dish, and for Sauce melt some Butter, and add what dropped from the Tripe; boil it together, and garnish with Raspings.

To dress POULTRY.

To roast a Turky.

THE best Way to roast a Turky is to loosen the Skin on the Breast of the Turky, and fill it with Force-Meat made thus: Take a Quarter of a Pound of Beef Sewer, as many Crumbs of Bread, a little Lemon-peel, an Anchovy, some Nutmeg, Pepper, Parsley, and a little Thyme; chop and beat them all well together, mix them with the Yolk of an Egg, and stuff up the Breast; when you have no Sewet Butter will do: Or you may make your Force-Meat thus: Spread Bread and Butter thin, and grate some Nutmeg over it; when you have enough roll it up, and stuff the Breast of the Turky; then roast it of a fine Brown, but be sure to pin some white Paper on the Breast till it is near enough. You must have good Gravy in the Dish, and Bread-sauce made thus: Take a good Piece of Crumb, put it into a Pint of Water, with a Blade or two of Mace, two or three Cloves, and some whole Pepper; boil it up five or six Times, then with a Spoon take out the Spice, and pour off the Water (you may boil an Onion in it if you please) then beat up the Bread with a good Piece of Butter and a little Salt; or Onion Sauce made thus: Take some Onions, peel them, and cut them into thin Slices, and boil them Half an Hour in Milk and Water; then drain the Water from them, and beat them up with a good Piece of Butter; shake a little Flour in, and stir it all together with a little Cream, if you have it (or Milk will do) put the Sauce into Boats, and garnish with Lemon.

Another Way to make Sauce: Take Half a Pint of Oysters, strain the Liquor, and put the Oysters with the Liquor into a Sauce-pan, with a Blade or two of Mace; let them just plump, then pour in a Glass of White Wine, let it boil once, and thicken it with a Piece of Butter roll'd in Flour: Serve this up in a Bason by itself, with good Gravy in the Dish, for every Body don't love Oyster Sauce. This makes a pretty Side Dish for Supper, or a Corner Dish of a Table for Dinner. If you chafe it in the Dish, add Half a Pint of Gravy to it, and boil it up together. This Sauce is good either with boiled or roasted Turkies or Fowls; but you may leave the Gravy out, adding as much Butter as will do for Sauce, and garnishing with Lemon.

To make Mock Oyster-Sauce, either for Turkies or Fowls boil'd.

FORCE the Turkies or Fowls as above, and make your Sauce thus: Take a Quarter of a Pint of Water, an Anchovy, a Blade or two of Mace, a Piece of Lemon-peel, and five or six whole Pepper-Corns; boil these together, then strain them, add as much Butter with a little Flour as will do for Sauce; let it boil, and lay Sausages round the Fowl or Turky. Garnish with Lemon.

To make Mushroom-Sauce for White Fowls of all Sorts.

TAKE a Pint of Mushrooms, wash and pick them very clean, and put them into a Sauce-pan, with a little Salt, some Nutmeg, a Blade of Mace, a Pint of Cream, and a good Piece of Butter roll'd in Flour; boil these all together, and keep stirring them; then pour the Sauce into your Dish, and garnish with Lemon.

Mushroom-

The Art of Cookery, made Plain and Easy. 35

Mushroom-Sauce *for* White Fowls *boiled.*

TAKE Half a Pint of Cream, and a Quarter of a Pound of Butter, stir them together one Way, till it is thick; then add a Spoonful of Mushroom Pickle, pickled Mushrooms, or fresh, if you have them. Garnish only with Lemon.

To make Sellery-Sauce *either for roasted or boiled* Fowls, Turkies, Partridges, *or any other Game.*

TAKE a large Bunch of Sellery, wash and pare it very clean, cut it into little Bits, and boil it softly in a little Water till it is tender; then add a little beaten Mace, some Nutmeg, Pepper and Salt, thicken'd with a good Piece of Butter roll'd in Flour; then boil it up, and pour into your Dish.

You may make it with Cream thus: Boil your Sellery as above, and add some Mace, Nutmeg, some Butter as big as a Walnut, roll'd in Flour, and Half a Pint of Cream: Boil them all together, and you may add, if you will, a Glass of White Wine, and a Spoonful of Catchup.

To make Brown Sellery-Sauce.

STEW the Sellery as above, then add Mace, Nutmeg, Pepper, Salt, a Piece of Butter roll'd in Flour, with a Glass of Red Wine, a Spoonful of Catchup, and Half a Pint of good Gravy; boil all these together, and pour into the Dish. Garnish with Lemon.

To Stew a Turky, *or* Fowl, *in* Sellery-Sauce.

YOU must judge according to the Largeness of your Turky or Fowls, what Sellery or Sauce you want. Take a large Fowl, put it into a Sauce-pan or little Pot, and put to it one Quart of good Broth or Gravy, a Bunch of Sellery wash'd clean, and cut small, with some Mace, Cloves, Pepper, and All-Spice, ty'd loose in a Muslin Rag; put in an Onion and a Sprig of Thyme: Let these stew softly till they are enough, then add a Piece of Butter roll'd in Flour; take up your Fowl, and pour the Sauce over it. An Hour will do a large Fowl, or a small Turky; but a very large Turky will take two Hours to do it softly. If it is over done or dry it is spoil'd; but you may be a Judge of that if you look at it now and then. Mind to take out the Onion, Thyme and Spice, before you send it to Table.

Note, A Neck of Veal done this Way is very good, and will take two Hours doing.

To make Egg-Sauce, *proper for roasted* Chickens.

MELT your Butter thick and fine, chop two or three hard-boiled Eggs fine, put them into a Bason, pour the Butter over them, and have good Gravy in the Dish.

Shalot-Sauce *for roasted* Fowls.

TAKE five or six Shalots peel'd and cut small, put them into a Sauce-pan, with two Spoonfuls of White Wine, two of Water, and two of Vinegar; give them a boil up, and pour them into your Dish, with a little Pepper and Salt. Fowls roasted and laid on Water-cresses is very good, without any other Sauce.

Shalot-Sauce *for a* Scraig *of* Mutton *boiled.*

TAKE two Spoonfuls of the Liquor the Mutton is boiled in, two Spoonfuls of Vinegar, two or three Shalots cut fine, with a little Salt; put it into a Sauce-pan, with a Piece of Butter as big as a Walnut roll'd in a little Flour; stir it together, and give it a boil. For those who love Shalot, it is the prettiest Sauce that can be made to a Scraig of Mutton.

To dress Livers *with* Mushroom-Sauce.

TAKE some pickled or fresh Mushrooms, cut small, both if you have them, and let the Livers be bruised fine, with a good deal of Parsley chopped small, a Spoonful or two of Catchup, a Glass of White Wine, and as much good Gravy as will make Sauce enough; thicken it with a Piece of Butter roll'd in Flour. This does either for Roast or Boil'd.

A pretty

A pretty little Sauce.

TAKE the Liver of the Fowl, bruise it with a little of the Liquor, cut a little Lemon-peel fine, melt some good Butter, and mix the Liver by Degrees; give it a boil, and pour it into the Dish.

To make Lemon-Sauce for boiled Fowls.

TAKE a Lemon, pare off the Rind, then cut it into Slices, and cut it small; take all the Kernels out, bruise the Liver with two or three Spoonfuls of good Gravy, then melt some Butter, mix it all together, give them a boil, and cut in a little Lemon-peel very small.

A German Way of dressing Fowls.

TAKE a Turky or Fowl, stuff the Breast with what Force-Meat you like, and fill the Body with roasted Chesnuts peel'd; roast it, and have some more roasted Chesnuts peel'd, put them in Half a Pint of good Gravy, with a little Piece of Butter roll'd in Flour; boil these together, with some small Turnips, and Sausages cut in Slices, and fry'd or boil'd. Garnish with Chesnuts.
Note, You may dress Ducks the same Way.

To dress a Turky or Fowl to Perfection.

BONE them, and make a Force-Meat thus: Take the Flesh of a Fowl, cut it small, then take a Pound of Veal, beat it in a Mortar, with Half a Pound of Beef Sewet, as much Crumbs of Bread, some Mushrooms, Truffles, and Morels cut small, a few Sweet Herbs and Parsley, with some Nutmeg, Pepper, and Salt, a little Mace beaten, some Lemon-peel cut fine; mix all these together, with the Yolk of two Eggs, then fill your Turky, and roast it. This will do for a large Turky, and so in Proportion for a Fowl. Let your Sauce be good Gravy, with Mushrooms, Truffles, and Morels in it; then garnish with Lemon, and for Variety sake you may lard your Fowl or Turky.

To Stew a Turky brown.

TAKE your Turky after it is nicely pick'd and drawn, fill the Skin of the Breast with Force-Meat, and put an Anchovy, a Shalot, and a little Thyme in the Belly, lard the Breast with Bacon, then take a good Piece of Butter in the Stew-pan, flour the Turky, and fry it just of a fine Brown; then take it out, and put it into a deep Stew-pan, or little Pot, that will just hold it, and put in as much Gravy as will barely cover it, a Glass of Red Wine, some whole Pepper, Mace, and two or three Cloves, and a little Bundle of Sweet Herbs; cover it close, and stew it for an Hour, then take up the Turky, and keep it hot cover'd by the Fire, and boil the Sauce to about a Pint, strain it off, add the Yolks of two Eggs, and a Piece of Butter rolled in Flour, stir it till it is thick, and then lay your Turky in the Dish, and pour your Sauce over it. You may have ready some little *French* Loaves about the Bigness of an Egg, cut off the Tops, and take out the Crumb, then fry them of a fine Brown, fill them with stew'd Oysters, lay them round the Dish, and garnish with Lemon.

To Stew a Turky brown the nice Way.

BONE it, and fill it with Force-Meat made thus: Take the Flesh of a Fowl, Half a Pound of Veal, and the Flesh of two Pigeons, with a well pickled or dried Tongue, peel it, and chop it all together, then beat it in a Mortar, with the Marrow of a Beef Bone, or a Pound of the Fat of a Loin of Veal, season it with two or three Blades of Mace, two or three Cloves, and Half a Nutmeg, dried at a good Distance from the Fire, and pounded, with a little Pepper and Salt; mix all this well together, fill your Turky, fry it of a fine Brown, and put it into a little Pot that will just hold it; lay four or five Skewers at the Bottom of the Pot, to keep the Turky from sticking; put in a Quart of good Beef and Veal Gravy, wherein was boiled Spice and Sweet Herbs, cover it close, and let it stew Half an Hour; then put in a Glass of Red Wine, one Spoonful of Catchup, a large Spoonful of pickled Mushrooms, and a few fresh ones, if you have them, a few Truffles and Morels, a Piece of Butter as big as a Walnut, roll'd in Flour; cover it close, and let it stew Half an Hour longer; get the little *French* Rolls ready fry'd, take some Oysters, and strain the Liquor from them, then put the Oysters and Liquor into a Sauce-pan, with a Blade of Mace, a little White Wine, and a Piece of Butter rolled in Flour; let them stew till it is thick, then fill the Loaves, lay the Turky in the Dish, and pour the Sauce over it. If there is any Fat on the Gravy take it off, and lay the Loaves on each Side of the Turky. Garnish with Lemon when you have no Loaves, and take Oysters dipt in Batter and fry'd.
Note, The same will do for any White Fowl.

A Fowl *a la Braise*.

TRUSS your Fowl, with the Legs turned into the Belly, season it both inside and out with beaten Mace, Nutmeg, Pepper, and Salt; lay a Layer of Bacon at the Bottom of a deep Stew-pan, then a Layer of Veal, and afterwards the Fowl; then put in an Onion, two or three Cloves stuck in a little Bundle of Sweet Herbs, with a Piece of Carrot; then put at the Top, a Layer of Bacon, another of Veal, and a third of Beef; cover it close, and let it stand over the Fire for two or three Minutes, then pour in a Pint of Broth, or hot Water, cover it close, and let it stew an Hour; afterwards take up your Fowl, strain the Sauce, and after you have skimm'd off the Fat, thicken it up with a little Piece of Butter: You may add just what you please to the Sauce, a Ragoo of Sweetbreads, Cocks Combs, Truffles and Morels, or Mushrooms, with Force-Meat Balls looks very pretty; or any of the Sauces above.

To Force a Fowl.

TAKE a good Fowl, pick and draw it, slit the Skin down the Back, and take the Flesh from the Bones, mince it very small, and mix it with one Pound of Beef Sewet shred, a Pint of large Oysters chopped, two Anchovies, a Shalot, a little grated Bread, and some Sweet Herbs; shred all this very well, mix them together, and make it up with the Yolks of Eggs; then turn all these Ingredients on the Bones again, and draw the Skin over again, then sew up the Back, and either boil the Fowl in a Bladder an Hour and a Quarter, or roast it; then stew some more Oysters in Gravy, bruise in a little of your Force-Meat, mix it up with a little Fresh Butter, and a very little Flour; then give it a boil, lay your Fowl in the Dish, and pour the Sauce over it, garnishing with Lemon.

To roast a Fowl *with* Chesnuts.

FIRST take some Chesnuts, roast them very carefully, so as not to burn them, take off the Skin, and peel them; take about a Dozen of them cut small, and bruise them in a Mortar, parboil the Liver of the Fowl, bruise it, cut about a Quarter of a Pound of Ham or Bacon, and pound it; then mix them all together, with a good deal of Parsley chopped fine, a little Sweet Herbs, some Mace, Pepper, Salt and Nutmeg; mix these together and put into your Fowl, and roast it. The best Way of doing it is to tye the Neck, and hang it up by the Legs, to roast with a String, and baste it with Butter: For Sauce take the rest of the Chesnuts peel'd and skinned, put them into some good Gravy, with a little White Wine, and thicken it with a Piece of Butter roll'd in Flour; then take up your Fowl, lay it in the Dish, and pour in the Sauce. Garnish with Lemon.

Pullets *a la Sainte* Menehout.

AFTER having truss'd the Legs in the Body, slit them along the Back, spread them open on a Table, take out the Thigh Bone, and beat them with a Rolling-pin; then season them with Pepper, Salt, Mace, Nutmeg, and Sweet Herbs; after that take a Pound and an Half of Veal, cut it into thin Slices, and lay it in a Stew-pan of a convenient Size to stew the Pullets in; cover it, and set it over a Stove, or slow Fire, and when it begins to cleave to the Pan, stir in a little Flour, shake the Pan about till it be a little Brown, then pour in as much Broth as will stew the Fowls, stir it together, put in a little whole Pepper and an Onion, and a little Piece of Bacon or Ham; then lay in your Fowls, cover them close, and let them stew Half an Hour; then take them out, lay them on the Gridiron to Brown on the Inside; then lay them before the Fire to do on the Outside; strew them over with the Yolk of an Egg, some Crumbs of Bread, then baste them with a little Butter: Let them be of a fine Brown, and boil the Gravy till there is about enough for Sauce, strain it, put a few Mushrooms in, and a little Piece of Butter roll'd in Flour; lay the Pullets in the Dish, and pour in the Sauce. Garnish with Lemon.

Note, You may Brown them in an Oven, or fry them, which you please.

Chicken *Surprize*.

IF a small Dish one large Fowl will do, roast it, and take the Lean from the Bone, cut it in thin Slices, about an Inch long, toss it up with six or seven Spoonfuls of Cream, and a Piece of Butter roll'd in Flour, as big as a Walnut; boil it up, and set it to cool; then cut six or seven thin Slices of Bacon round, place them in a Petty-pan, and put some Force-Meat on each Side, work them up into the Form of a *French* Roll, with raw Egg in your Hand, leaving a hollow Place in the Middle; put in your Fowl, and cover them with some of the same Force-Meat, rubbing them smooth with your Hand with a raw Egg; make them of the Height and Bigness of a *French* Roll, and throw a little fine grated Bread over them; bake them three Quarters of an Hour in a gentle Oven, or under a baking Cover, till they come to a fine Brown, and place them on your Mazarine that they may not touch one another, but place them so that they may not fall flat in the baking; or you may form them on your Table with a broad Kitchen Knife, and place them

38   *The Art of Cookery, made Plain and Easy.*

them on the Thing you intend to bake them on: You may put the Leg of a Chicken into one of the Loaves you intend for the Middle: Let your Sauce be Gravy thickened with Butter and a little Juice of Lemon. This is a pretty Side Dish for a first Course, Summer or Winter, if you can get them.

Mutton Chops *in Disguise.*

TAKE as many Mutton Chops as you want, rub them with Pepper, Salt, Nutmeg, and a little Parsley; roll each Chop in Half a Sheet of White Paper, well buttered on the Inside, and rolled at each End close; have some Hog's Lard or Beef Dripping boiling in a Stew-pan, put in the Steaks, fry them of a fine Brown, lay them in your Dish, and garnish with fry'd Parsley; throw some all over, have a little good Gravy in a Cup; but take great Care you don't break the Paper, nor have any Fat in the Dish, but let them be well drained.

Chickens *roasted with Force-Meat and Cucumbers.*

TAKE two Chickens, dress them very neatly, break the Breast Bone, and make a Force-Meat thus: Take the Flesh of a Fowl and of two Pigeons, with some Slices of Ham or Bacon, chop them all well together, take the Crumb of a Penny Loaf soaked in Milk and boiled, then set it to cool; when it is cool mix it all together, season it with beaten Mace, Nutmeg, Pepper, and a little Salt, a very little Thyme, some Parsley, and a little Lemon-peel, with the Yolks of two Eggs; then fill your Fowls, spit them, and tye them at both Ends; after you have pepper'd the Breast, take four Cucumbers, cut them in two, and lay them in Salt and Water two or three Hours before; then dry them, and fill them with some of the Force-Meat (which you must take care to save), and tye them with a Packthread, flour them, and fry them of a fine Brown; when your Chickens are enough, lay them in the Dish, and untye your Cucumbers, but take care the Meat don't come out; then lay them round the Chickens with the flat Side downward, and the narrow End upwards: You must have some rich fry'd Gravy and pour into the Dish; then garnish with Lemon.

Note, One large Fowl done this Way, with the Cucumbers laid round it, looks very pretty, and is a very good Dish.

Chickens *a la Braise.*

YOU must take a Couple of fine Chickens, lard them, and season them with Pepper, Salt, and Mace; then lay a Layer of Veal in the Bottom of a deep Stew-pan, with a Slice or two of Bacon, an Onion cut to Pieces, a Piece of Carrot and a Layer of Beef; then lay in the Chickens with the Breast downward, and a Bundle of Sweet Herbs: After that lay a Layer of Beef, and put in a Quart of Broth or Water, cover it close, let it stew very softly for an Hour after it begins to simmer: In the mean Time, get ready a Ragoo thus: Take a good Veal Sweetbread, or two, cut them small, set them on the Fire, with a very little Broth or Water, a few Cocks Combs, Truffles and Morels, cut small, with an Ox Palate, if you have it, stew them all together till they are enough, and when your Chickens are done, take them up, and keep them hot; then strain the Liquor they were stew'd in, skim the Fat off, and pour into your Ragoo; add a Glass of Red Wine, a Spoonful of Catchup, and a few Mushrooms, then boil all together with a few Artichoke Bottoms cut in four, and Asparagus Tops. If your Sauce is not thick enough, take a little Piece of Butter rolled in Flour, and when enough lay your Chickens in the Dish, and pour your Ragoo over them. Garnish with Lemon.

Or you may make your Sauce thus: Take the Gravy the Fowls were stew'd in, strain it, skim off the Fat, have ready Half a Pint of Oysters, with the Liquor strained, put them to your Gravy with a Glass of White Wine, a good Piece of Butter rolled in Flour, then boil them all together, and pour over your Fowls. Garnish with Lemon.

To marinate Fowls.

TAKE a fine large Fowl or Turky, raise the Skin from the Breast Bone with your Finger, then take a Veal Sweetbread and cut it small, a few Oysters, a few Mushrooms, an Anchovy, some Pepper, a little Nutmeg, some Lemon-peel, and a little Thyme; chop all together small and mix with the Yolk of an Egg, stuff it in between the Skin and the Flesh, but take great Care you don't break the Skin, and then stuff what Oysters you please into the Body of the Fowl. You may lard the Breast of the Fowl with Bacon, if you chuse it. Paper the Breast, and roast it. Make good Gravy, and garnish with Lemon. You may add a few Mushrooms to the Sauce.

To

To broil Chickens.

SLIT them down the Back, and season them with Pepper and Salt, lay them on a very clear Fire, and at a great Distance; let the Inside lie next the Fire till it is above Half done, then turn them, and take great Care the fleshy Side don't burn, throw some fine Raspings of Bread over it, and let them be of a fine Brown, but not burnt. Let your Sauce be good Gravy, with Mushrooms, and garnish with Lemon and the Livers broil'd, the Gizzards cut, slash'd, and broil'd with Pepper and Salt.

Or this Sauce: Take a Handful of Sorrel, dip it in boiling Water, then drain it, and have ready Half a Pint of good Gravy, a Shalot shred small, and some Parsley boil'd very green; thicken it with a Piece of Butter rolled in Flour, and add a Glass of Red Wine, then lay your Sorrel in Heaps round the Fowls, and pour the Sauce over them. Garnish with Lemon.

Note, You may make just what Sauce you fancy.

Pull'd Chickens.

TAKE three Chickens, boil them just fit for eating, but not too much; when they are boiled enough flea all the Skin off, and take the white Flesh off the Bones, pull it into Pieces about as thick as a large Quill, and Half as long as your Finger, have ready a Quarter of a Pint of good Cream and a Piece of Fresh Butter about as big as an Egg, stir them together till the Butter is all melted and then put in your Chickens with the Gravy that came from them, give them two or three Tosses round on the Fire, put them into a Dish, and send them up hot.

Note, The Leg makes a very pretty Dish by itself, broil'd very nicely with some Pepper and Salt: The Livers being broil'd, and the Gizzards broil'd, cut and slash'd, and laid round the Legs, with good Gravy-Sauce in the Dish. Garnish with Lemon.

A pretty Way of stewing Chickens.

TAKE two fine Chickens, Half boil them, then take them up in a Pewter or Silver Dish, if you have one; cut up your Fowls, and separate all the Joint Bones one from another, and then take out the Breast Bones. If there is not Liquor enough from the Fowls add a few Spoonfuls of the Water they were boil'd in, put in a Blade of Mace, and a little Salt; cover it close with another Dish, set it over a Stove or Chaffing-dish of Coals, let it stew till the Chickens are enough, and then send them hot to Table in the same Dish they were stew'd in.

Note, This is a very pretty Dish for any sick Person, or for a lying-in Lady. For Change it is better than Butter; and the Sauce is very agreeable and pretty.

N. B. You may do Rabbits, Partridges, or more Game this Way.

Chickens *Chiringrate*.

CUT off their Feet, break the Breast Bone flat with a Rolling-pin, but take Care you don't break the Skin; flour them, fry them of a fine Brown in Butter, then drain all the Fat out of the Pan, but leave the Chickens in; lay a Pound of Gravy Beef cut very thin over your Chickens, and a Piece of Veal cut very thin, a little Mace, two or three Cloves, some Whole Pepper, an Onion, a little Bundle of Sweet Herbs, and a Piece of Carrot, and then pour in a Quart of boiling Water; cover it close, let it stew for a Quarter of an Hour, then take out the Chickens and keep them hot; let the Gravy boil till it is quite rich and good, then strain it off and put it into your Pan again with two Spoonfuls of Red Wine, and a few Mushrooms; put in your Chickens to heat, then take them up, lay them into your Dish, and pour your Sauce over them. Garnish with Lemon, and a few Slices of cold Ham warm'd in the Gravy.

Note, You may fill your Chickens with Force-Meat and lard them with Bacon, and add Truffles, Morels, and Sweetbreads cut small; but then it will be a very high Dish.

Chickens *boiled with* Bacon *and* Sellery.

BOIL two Chickens very white in a Pot by themselves, and a Piece of Ham, or good thick Bacon; boil two Bunches of Sellery tender, then cut them about two Inches long, all the white Part, put it into a Sauce-pan with Half a Pint of Cream, a Piece of Butter rolled in Flour, and some Pepper and Salt; set it on the Fire, and shake it often: When it is thick and fine, lay your Chickens in the Dish and pour the Sauce in the Middle, that the Sellery may lie between the Fowls, and garnish the Dish all round with Slices of Ham or Bacon.

Note, If you have cold Ham in the House, that cut into Slices and broil'd does full as well, or better, to lay round the Dish.

Chickens

Chickens with Tongues. A good Dish for a great deal of Company.

TAKE six small Chickens boiled very white, six Hogs Tongues boiled and peeled, a Cauliflower boiled very white in Milk and Water whole, and a good deal of Spinach boiled green; then lay your Cauliflower in the Middle, the Chickens close all round, and the Tongues round them with the Roots outwards, and the Spinach in little Heaps between the Tongues. Garnish with little Pieces of Bacon toasted, and lay a little Bit on each of the Tongues.

Scotch Chickens.

FIRST wash your Chickens, dry them in a clean Cloth, and singe them, then cut them into Quarters; put them into a Stew-pan or Sauce-pan, and just cover them with Water, put in a Blade or two of Mace, and a little Bundle of Parsley; cover them close, and let them stew Half an Hour, then chop Half a Handful of clean wash'd Parsley and throw in, and have ready six Eggs, Whites and all, beat fine; let your Liquor boil up, and pour the Egg all over them as it boils, then send all together hot in a deep Dish, but take out the Bundle of Parsley first. You must be sure to skim them well before you put in your Mace, and the Broth will be fine and clear.

Note, This is also a very pretty Dish for sick People, but the *Scotch* Gentlemen are very fond of it.

To marinate Chickens.

CUT two Chickens into Quarters, lay them in Vinegar for three or four Hours with Pepper, Salt, a Bay-Leaf, and a few Cloves, make a very thick Batter, first with Half a Pint of Wine and Flour, then the Yolks of two Eggs, a little melted Butter, some grated Nutmeg, and chopp'd Parsley; beat all very well together, dip your Fowls in the Batter, and fry them in a good deal of Hogs Lard, which must first boil before you put your Chickens in; let them be of a fine Brown, and lay them in your Dish like a Pyramid, with fry'd Parsley all round them. Garnish with Lemon, and have some good Gravy in Boats or Basons.

To stew Chickens.

TAKE two Chickens, cut them into Quarters, wash them clean, and then put them into a Sauce-pan; put to them a Quarter of a Pint of Water, Half a Pint of Red Wine, some Mace, Pepper, a Bundle of Sweet Herbs, an Onion, and a few Raspings; cover them close, let them stew Half an Hour, then take a Piece of Butter about as big as an Egg rolled in Flour, put it in, and cover it close for five or six Minutes, shake the Sauce-pan about, and then take out the Sweet Herbs and Onion. You may take the Yolks of two Eggs, beat and mix'd with them; if you don't like it, leave them out. Garnish with Lemon.

Ducks a la Mode.

TAKE two fine Ducks, cut them into Quarters, fry them in Butter a little Brown, then pour out all the Fat, and throw a little Flour over them; add Half a Pint of good Gravy, a Quarter of a Pint of Red Wine, two Shalots, an Anchovy, and a Bundle of Sweet Herbs; cover them close, and let them stew a Quarter of an Hour; take out the Herbs, skim off the Fat, and let your Sauce be as thick as Cream. Send it to Table, and garnish with Lemon.

To dress a Wild Duck the best Way.

FIRST Half roast it, then lay it in a Dish, carve it, but leave the Joints hanging together, throw a little Pepper and Salt, and squeeze the Juice of a Lemon over it, turn it on the Breast, and press it hard with a Plate, then add to it its own Gravy, and two or three Spoonfuls of good Gravy; cover it close with another Dish, and set it over a Stove for ten Minutes, then send it to Table hot in the Dish it was done in, and garnish with Lemon. You may add a little Red Wine, and a Shalot cut small; if you like it, but it is apt to make the Duck eat hard, unless you first heat the Wine and pour it in just as it is done.

To Boil a Duck or Rabbit with Onions.

BOIL your Duck or Rabbit in a good deal of Water; be sure to skim your Water, for there will always rise a Skim, which if it boil down will difcolour your Fowls, &c. They will take about Half an Hour boiling; for Sauce, your Onions muft be peel'd, and throw them into Water as you peel them, then cut them into thin Slices, boil them in Milk and Water, and skim the Liquor. Half an Hour will boil them. Throw them into a clean Scive to drain them, put them into a Sauce-pan and chop them fmall, fhake in a little Flour, put to them two or three Spoonfuls of Cream, a good Piece of Butter, ftew all together over the Fire till they are thick and fine, lay the Duck or Rabbit in the Difh, and pour the Sauce all over; if a Rabbit you muft cut off the Head and cut it in two, and lay it on each Side the Difh.

Or you may make this Sauce for change: Take one large Onion, cut it fmall, half a Handful of Parfley clean wafhed and picked, chop it fmall, a Lettuce cut fmall, a Quarter of a Pint of good Gravy, a good Piece of Butter rolled in a little Flour; add a little Juice of Lemon, a little Pepper and Salt, let all ftew together for Half an Hour, then add two Spoonfuls of Red Wine; this Sauce is moft proper for a Duck; lay your Duck in the Difh, and pour your Sauce over it.

To drefs a Duck with Green Peas.

PUT a deep Stew-pan over the Fire, with a Piece of frefh Butter, finge your Duck and flour it, turn it in the Pan two or three Minutes, then pour out all the Fat, but let the Duck remain in the Pan; put to it Half a Pint of good Gravy, a Pint of Peas, two Lettuces cut fmall, a fmall Bundle of Sweet Herbs, a little Pepper and Salt, cover them clofe, and let them ftew for Half an Hour, now and then give the Pan a fhake; when they are juft done grate in a little Nutmeg, and put in a very little beaten Mace, and thicken it either with a Piece of Butter rolled in Flour, or the Yolk of an Egg beat up with two or three Spoonfuls of Cream; fhake it all together for three or four Minutes, take out the Sweet Herbs, lay the Duck in the Difh and pour the Sauce over it : You may garnifh with boiled Mint chopped, or let it alone.

To drefs a Duck with Cucumbers.

TAKE three or four Cucumbers, pare them, take out the Seeds, cut them into little Pieces, lay them in Vinegar for two or three Hours before, with two large Onions peeled and fliced, then do your Duck as above; then take the Duck out, and put in the Cucumbers and Onions, firft drain them in a Cloth, let them be a little Brown, fhake a little Flour over them, in the mean time let your Duck be ftewing in the Sauce-pan with Half a Pint of Gravy for a Quarter of an Hour, then add to it the Cucumbers and Onions, with Pepper and Salt to your Palate, a good Piece of Butter rolled in Flour, and two or three Spoonfuls of Red Wine, fhake all together, and let it ftew together for eight or ten Minutes, then take up the Duck and pour the Sauce over it.

Or you may roaft your Duck and make this Sauce and pour over it, but then a Quarter of a Pint of Gravy will be enough.

To drefs a Duck à la Braife.

TAKE a Duck, lard it with little Pieces of Bacon, feafon it infide and out, with Pepper and Salt, lay a Layer of Bacon, cut thin, in the bottom of a Stew-pan, and then a Layer of lean Beef cut thin, then lay on your Duck with fome Carrot, an Onion, a little Bundle of Sweet Herbs, a Blade or two of Mace, and lay a thin Layer of Beef over the Duck, cover it clofe and fet it over a flow Fire for eight or ten Minutes, then take off the Cover and fhake in a little Flour, give the Pan a fhake, pour in a Pint of fmall Broth or boiling Water, give the Pan a fhake or two, cover it clofe again, and let it ftew Half an Hour, then take off the Cover, take out the Duck and keep it hot, let the Sauce boil till there is about a Quarter of a Pint or little better, then ftrain it and put it into the Stew-pan again, with a Glafs of Red Wine; put in your Duck, fhake the Pan and let it ftew four or five Minutes, then lay your Duck into your Difh and pour the Sauce over it and garnifh with Lemon. If you love your Duck very high, you may fill it with the following Ingredients: Take a Veal Sweetbread cut in fix or eight Pieces, a few Truffles, fome Oyfters, a little Sweet Herbs and Parfley chopped fine, a little Pepper, Salt, and beaten Mace; fill your Duck with the above Ingredients, tye both Ends tight, and drefs it as above; or you may fill it with Force-Meat made thus: Take a little Piece of Veal, take all the Skin and Fat off, beat it in a Mortar with as much Sewet, and an equal Quantity of Crumbs of Bread, a few Sweet Herbs, fome Parfley chopped, a little Lemon-peel, Pepper, Salt, beaten Mace, and Nutmeg, mix it up with the Yolk of an Egg.

You may ftew an Ox's Palate tender, and cut it into Pieces, with fome Artichoke Bottoms cut into four, and toffed up in the Sauce; you may lard your Duck or let it alone, juft as you pleafe, for my part I think it beft without.

To Boil Ducks the French Way.

LET your Ducks be larded and half roasted, then take them off the Spit, put them into a large earthen Pipkin, with Half a Pint of Red Wine, and a Pint of good Gravy, some Chesnuts, first roasted and peeled, Half a Pint of large Oysters, the Liquor strained and the Beards taken off, two or three little Onions minced small, a very little stripped Thyme, Mace, Pepper, and a little Ginger beat fine; cover it close and let them stew Half an Hour over a slow Fire, and the Crust of a *French* Roll grated when you put in your Gravy and Wine; when they are enough take them up and pour the Sauce over them.

To dress a Goose with Onions or Cabbage.

TO dress a Goose with Onions or Cabbage, salt the Goose for a Week, then boil it; it will take an Hour; you may either make Onion Sauce as we do for Ducks, or Cabbage boiled, chopped, and stewed in Butter with a little Pepper and Salt; lay the Goose in the Dish, and pour the Sauce over it: It eats very good with either.

Directions for roasting a Goose.

TAKE Sage, wash it, pick it clean, chop it small, with Pepper and Salt; roll them in Butter and put them into the Belly; never put Onion into any thing unless you are sure every body loves it; take Care that your Goose be clean pick'd and wash'd; I think the best way is to scald a Goose, and then you are sure it is clean, and not so strong: Let your Water be scalding hot, and dip in your Goose for a Minute, then all the Feathers will come off clean; when it is quite clean wash it with cold Water, and dry it with a Cloth; roast it and baste it with Butter, and when it is half done throw some Flour over it, that it may have a fine Brown; three Quarters of an Hour will do it at a quick Fire, if it is not too large, otherwise, it will require an Hour; always have good Gravy in a Bason, and Apple-Sauce in another.

A green Goose.

NEVER put any Seasoning into it, unless desired; you must either put good Gravy, or green Sauce in the Dish made thus: Take a Handful of Sorrel, beat it in a Mortar, and squeeze the Juice out, add to it the Juice of an Orange or Lemon, and a little Sugar, heat it in a Pipkin, and pour it into your Dish, but the best way is to put Gravy in the Dish, and green Sauce in a Cup or Boat; or made thus: Take Half a Pint of the Juice of Sorrel, a Spoonful of White Wine, a little grated Nutmeg, a little grated Bread, boil these a Quarter of an Hour softly, then strain it and put it into the Sauce-pan again, and sweeten it with a little Sugar, give it a boil and pour it into a Dish or Bason; some like a little Piece of Butter rolled in Flour and put into it.

To dry a Goose.

GET a fat Goose, take a Handful of common Salt, a Quarter of an Ounce of Salt-Petre, a Quarter of a Pound of coarse Sugar, mix all together, and rub your Goose very well, let it lie in this Pickle a Fortnight, turning and rubbing it every Day, then roll it in Bran and hang it up in a Chimney where Wood-Smoke is for a Week, if you have not that Conveniency send it to the Bakers, the Smoke of the Oven will dry it, or you may hang it in your own Chimney, not too near the Fire, but make a Fire under it, and lay Horse-Dung and Saw-Dust on it, and that will smother and smoke-dry it; when it is well dried keep it in a dry Place, you may keep it two or three Months or more; when you boil it put it in a good deal of Water, and be sure to skim it well.

Note, You may boil Turnips, or Cabbage boiled and stewed in Butter, or Onion Sauce.

To dress a Goose in Ragoo.

FLAT the Breast down with a Cleaver, then press it down with your Hand, skin it, dip it into scalding Water, let it be cold, lard it with Bacon, season it well with Pepper, Salt, and a little beaten Mace, then flour it all over, take a Pound of good Beef Sewet cut small, put it into a deep Stew-pan, let it be melted, then put in your Goose, let it be Brown on both Sides, when it is Brown put in a Pint of boiling Water, an Onion or two, a Bundle of Sweet Herbs, a Bay-Leaf, some whole Pepper, and a few Cloves, cover it close, and let it stew softly, till it is tender; about Half an Hour will do it if small, if a large one three Quarters of an Hour; in the mean time make a Ragoo, boil some Turnips almost enough, some Carrots and Onions quite enough; cut them all into little Pieces, put them into a Sauce-pan with

Half

Half a Pint of good Beef Gravy, a little Pepper and Salt, a Piece of Butter rolled in Flour, let this stew all together for a Quarter of an Hour; take the Goose and drain it well, then lay it in the Dish, and pour the Ragoo over it.

Where the Onion is disliked leave it out.-----You may add Cabbage boiled and chopped small.

A Goose à la Mode.

TAKE a large fine Goose, pick it clean, skin it, and cut it down the Back, Bone it nicely, take the Fat off, then take a dried Tongue, boil it and peel it: Take a Fowl and do it in the same manner as the Goose, season it with Pepper, Salt, and beaten Mace, roll it round the Tongue, season the Goose with the same, put the Tongue and Fowl in the Goose, and sew the Goose up again, in the same Form it was before; put it into a little Pot that will just hold it, put to it two Quarts of Beef Gravy, a Bundle of Sweet Herbs and an Onion; put some Slices of Ham, or good Bacon, between the Fowl and Goose, cover it close, and let it stew an Hour over a good Fire; when it begins to boil let it do very softly, then take up your Goose and skim off all the Fat, strain it, put in a Glass of Red Wine, two Spoonfuls of Catchup, a Veal Sweetbread cut small, some Truffles, Morels, and Mushrooms; a Piece of Butter rolled in Flour, Pepper and Salt if wanted; put in the Goose again, cover it close, and let it stew Half an Hour longer, then take it up and pour the Ragoo over it. Garnish with Lemon.

Note, This is a very fine Dish; you must mind to save the Bones of the Goose and Fowl and put them into the Gravy when it is first set on, and it will be better if you roll some Beef Marrow between the Tongue and Fowl, and between the Fowl and Goose, it will make them mellow and eat fine. You may add six or seven Yolks of hard Eggs whole in the Dish, they are a pretty Addition.

To stew Giblets.

LET them be nicely scalded and picked, break the two Pinion Bones in two, cut the Head in two, and cut off the Nostrils; cut the Liver in two, the Gizzard in four, the Neck in two; slip off the Skin of the Neck, and make a Pudding with two hard Eggs chopped fine, the Crumb of a *French* Roll steeped in hot Milk two or three Hours, then mix it with the hard Egg, a little Nutmeg, Pepper, Salt, and a little Sage chopped fine, a very little melted Butter, stir it together, tie one End of the Skin, and fill it with the Ingredients, tie the other End tight, and put all together into a Sauce-pan, with a Quart of good Mutton-Broth, a Bundle of Sweet Herbs, an Onion, some whole Pepper, Mace, two or three Cloves tied up loose in a Muslin Rag, a very little Piece of Lemon-peel; cover them close and let them stew till quite tender, then take a small *French* Roll toasted Brown on all Sides, and put it into the Sauce-pan, give it a shake, and let it stew till there is just Gravy enough to eat with them, then take out the Onion, Sweet Herbs and Spice; lay the Roll in the middle, the Giblets round, the Pudding cut into Slices and laid round, then pour the Sauce over all.

Another Way.

TAKE the Giblets clean picked and washed, the Feet skinned, and Bill cut off, the Head cut in two, the Pinion Bones broke into two, the Liver cut in two, the Gizzard cut into four, the Pipe pull'd out of the Neck, and the Neck cut in two; put them into a Pipkin with Half a Pint of Water, some whole Pepper, Black and White, a Blade of Mace, a little Sprig of Thyme, a small Onion, a little Crust of Bread, cover them close, and set them on a very slow Fire. Wood Embers is best. Let them stew till they are quite tender, then take out the Herbs and Onion, and pour them into a little Dish. Season them with Salt.

To roast Pigeons.

FILL them with Parsley clean washed and chopped, Pepper and Salt rolled in Butter; fill the Bellies, tie the Neck-End close, so that nothing can run out, put a Skewer through the Legs, and have a little Iron on purpose, with six Hooks to it, on each Hook hang a Pigeon, fasten one End of a String to the Chimney, and the other End to the Iron (this is what we call the poor Man's Spit) flour them, and baste them with Butter, turn them gently for fear of hitting the Bars, they will roast nicely and be full of Gravy: Take Care that you take them off with Care, not to lose any of the Liquor; you may melt a very little Butter and put into the Dish; your Pigeons ought to be quite fresh and not too much done; this is by much the best way of doing them, for then they will swim in their own Gravy, and a very little melted Butter will do.

When you roast them on a Spit all the Gravy runs out, or if you stuff them and broil them whole you cannot save the Gravy so well, though they will be very good with Parsley and Butter in the Dish; or split and broiled with Pepper and Salt.

To boil Pigeons.

BOIL them by themselves, for fifteen Minutes, then boil a handsome square Piece of Bacon and lay in the middle; stew some Spinach to lay round, and lay the Pigeons on the Spinach. Garnish your Dish with Parsley laid in a Plate before the Fire, to crisp. Or you may lay one Pigeon in the middle, and the rest round, and the Spinach between each Pigeon, and a Slice of Bacon on each Pigeon. Garnish with Slices of Bacon and melted Butter in a Cup.

To à la Daube Pigeons.

TAKE a large Sauce-pan, lay a Layer of Bacon, then a Layer of Veal, a Layer of coarse Beef, and another little Layer of Veal, about a Pound of Veal, and a Pound of Beef cut very thin; a Piece of Carrot, a Bundle of Sweet Herbs, an Onion, some black and white Pepper, a Blade or two of Mace, four or five Cloves, and a little Crust of Bread toasted very Brown; cover the Sauce-pan close, set it over a slow Fire for five or six Minutes, shake in a little Flour, then pour in a Quart of boiling Water, shake it round, cover it close, and let it stew till the Gravy is quite rich and good, then strain it off and skim off all the Fat; in the mean time stuff the Bellies of the Pigeons with Force-Meat made thus: Take a Pound of Veal, a Pound of Beef Sewet, beat both in a Mortar fine, an equal Quantity of Crumbs of Bread, some Pepper, Salt, Nutmeg, beaten Mace, a little Lemon-peel cut small, some Parsley cut small, and a very little Thyme stripped, mix all together with the Yolk of an Egg, fill the Pigeons, and flat the Breast down, flour them and fry them in fresh Butter a little Brown; then pour all the Fat clean out of the Pan, and put to the Pigeons the Gravy, cover them close, and let them stew a Quarter of an Hour, or till you think they are quite enough; then take them up, lay them in the Dish, and pour in your Sauce, on each Pigeon lay a Bay Leaf, and on the Leaf a Slice of Bacon. You may garnish with a Lemon notched, or let it alone.

Note, You may leave out the Stuffing, they will be very rich and good without it, and it is the best way of dressing them for a fine made Dish.

Pigeons au Poir.

MAKE a good Force-Meat as above, cut off the Feet quite, stuff them in the Shape of a Pear, roll them in the Yolk of an Egg, and then in Crumbs of Bread; stick a Leg at the Top, and butter a Dish to lay them in; then send them to an Oven to bake, but don't let them touch each other; when they are enough lay them in a Dish and pour good Gravy thicken'd with the Yolk of an Egg, or Butter rolled in Flour; don't pour your Gravy over the Pigeons. You may garnish with Lemon. It is a pretty genteel Dish: Or for Change lay one Pigeon in the middle, the rest round, and stewed Spinach between; poached Eggs on the Spinach. Garnish with notched Lemon and Orange cut into Quarters, melted Butter in Boats.

Pigeons stoved.

TAKE a small Cabbage Lettuce, just cut out the Heart and make a Force-Meat as before, only chop the Heart of the Cabbage and mix with it; fill up the Place you took it out, and tie it across with a Packthread; fry it of a light Brown in fresh Butter, pour out all the Fat, lay the Pigeons round, flat them with your Hand, and season them a little with Pepper, Salt, and beaten Mace (take great Care not to put too much Salt) pour in Half a Pint of *Rhenish* Wine, cover it close, and let it stew about five or six Minutes; then pour in Half a Pint of good Gravy; cover them close and let them stew Half an Hour; take a good Piece of Butter rolled in Flour, shake it in, when it is fine and thick take it up, untie it, lay the Lettuce in the middle, and the Pigeons round; squeeze in a little Lemon-Juice, and pour the Sauce all over them: Stew a little Lettuce and cut it into Pieces for Garnish, with pickled red Cabbage.

Note, Or for Change you may stuff your Pigeons with the same Force-Meat, and cut two Cabbage-Lettuces into Quarters, and stew as above; so lay the Lettuce between each Pigeon, and one in the middle, with Lettuce round it, and pour the Sauce all over them.

Pigeons surtout.

FORCE your Pigeons as above, then lay a Slice of Bacon on the Breast, and a Slice of Veal beat with the Back of a Knife, and season'd with Mace, Pepper and Salt, tie it on with a small Packthread, or two little fine Skewers is better; spit them on a fine Bird-Spit; roast them and baste with a Piece of Butter, then with the Yolk of an Egg, and then baste them again with Crumbs of Bread, a little Nutmeg and Sweet Herbs; when enough lay them in your Dish, have good Gravy ready with Truffles, Morels and Mushrooms, to pour into your Dish. Garnish with Lemon.

Pigeons

Pigeons *in Compôte with white Sauce.*

LET your Pigeons be drawn, pick'd, fcalded, and flea'd; then put them into a Stew-pan with Veal Sweetbreads, Cocks Combs, Mufhrooms, Truffles, Morels, Pepper, Salt, a Pint of thin Gravy, a little Bundle of Sweet Herbs, an Onion, and a Blade or two of Mace; cover them clofe, let them ftew Half an Hour, then take out the Herbs and Onion, then beat up the Yolk of two or three Eggs, and fome chopped Parfley in a Quarter of a Pint of Cream, and a little Nutmeg, mix all together, and ftir it one way till thick; lay the Pigeons in the Difh, and the Sauce all over. Garnifh with Lemon.

A French *Pupton of* Pigeons.

TAKE Savoury Force-Meat rolled out like Pafte, put it in a butter'd Difh, lay a Layer of very thin Bacon, fquab Pigeons fliced, Sweetbread, Afparagus Tops, Mufhrooms, Cocks Combs, a Palate boiled tender and cut into Pieces, and the Yolks of hard Eggs; make another Force-Meat and lay over like a Pie, bake it, and when enough turn it into a Difh, and pour Gravy round it.

Pigeons *boiled with* Rice.

TAKE fix Pigeons, ftuff their Bellies with Parfley, Pepper and Salt, roll in a very little Piece of Butter; put them into a Quart of Mutton-Broth, with a little beaten Mace, a Bundle of Sweet Herbs, and an Onion; cover them clofe, and let them boil a full Quarter of an Hour; then take out the Onion and Sweet Herbs, and take a good Piece of Butter rolled in Flour, put it in and give it a fhake, feafon it with Salt if it wants it, then have ready Half a Pound of Rice boiled tender in Milk; when it begins to be thick (but take great Care it don't burn too) take the Yolks of two or three Eggs, beat up with two or three Spoonfuls of Cream and a little Nutmeg, ftir it together till it is quite thick, then take up the Pigeons and lay them in the Difh; pour the Gravy to the Rice, ftir all together and pour over the Pigeons. Garnifh with hard Eggs cut into Quarters.

Pigeons *tranfmogrified.*

TAKE your Pigeons, feafon them with Pepper and Salt, take a large Piece of Butter, make a Puff Pafte, and roll each Pigeon in a Piece of Pafte; tie them in a Cloth fo that the Pafte don't break; boil them in a good deal of Water. They will take an Hour and Half boiling; untie them carefully that they don't break; lay them in the Difh, and you may pour a little good Gravy into the Difh; they will eat exceeding good and nice, and will yield Sauce enough of a very agreeable Relifh.

Pigeons *in Fricandos.*

AFTER having truffed your Pigeons with their Legs in their Bodies, divide them in two, and lard them with Bacon; then lay them in a Stew-pan with the larded Side downwards, and two whole Leeks cut fmall, a couple of Ladlefuls of Mutton Broth, or Veal Gravy; cover them clofe over a very flow Fire, and when they are enough make your Fire very brisk, to wafte away what Liquor remains; when they are of a fine Brown take them up, and pour out all the Fat that is left in the Pan; then pour in fome Veal Gravy to loofen what fticks to the Pan, and a little Pepper, ftir it about for two or three Minutes and pour it over the Pigeons. This is a pretty little Side Difh.

To roaft Pigeons *with a Farce.*

MAKE a Farce with the Livers minced fmall, as much Sweet Sewet or Marrow, grated Bread, and hard Egg, an equal Quantity of each; feafon with beaten Mace, Nutmeg, a little Pepper, Salt, and a little Sweet Herbs; mix all thefe together with the Yolk of an Egg, then cut the Skin of your Pigeon between the Legs and Body, and very carefully with your Fingers raife the Skin from the Flefh; but take Care you don't break it; then force them with this Farce between the Skin and Flefh; then trufs the Legs clofe to keep it in; fpit them and roaft them, drudge them with a little Flour, and bafte them with a Piece of Butter; fave the Gravy which runs from them, and mix it up with a little Red Wine, a little of the Farce-Meat and fome Nutmeg; let it boil, then thicken it with a Piece of Butter rolled in Flour, and the Yolk of an Egg beat up, and fome minced Lemon; when enough, lay the Pigeons in the Difh and pour in the Sauce. Garnifh with Lemon.

To dress Pigeons à Soleil.

FIRST stew your Pigeons in a very little Gravy till enough, and take different Sorts of Flesh according to your Fancy, &c. both of Butchers Meat and Fowl; chop it small, season it with beaten Mace, Cloves, Pepper and Salt, and beat it in a Mortar till it is like Paste; roll your Pigeons in it, then roll them in the Yolk of an Egg; shake Flour and Crumbs of Bread thick all over; have ready some Beef Dripping or Hogs Lard boiling; fry them Brown, and lay them in your Dish. Garnish with fry'd Parsley.

Pigeons in a Hole.

TAKE your Pigeons, season them with beaten Mace, Pepper and Salt; put a little Piece of Butter in the Belly, lay them in a Dish and pour a light Batter all over them, made with a Quart of Milk and Eggs, and four or five Spoonfuls of Flour; bake it, and send it to Table. It is a good Dish.

Pigeons in Pimlico.

TAKE the Livers with some Fat and Lean of Ham or Bacon, Mushrooms, Truffles, Parsley and Sweet Herbs; season with beaten Mace, Pepper and Salt; beat all this together with two raw Eggs, put it into the Bellies, roll them in a thin Slice of Veal, and over that a thin Slice of Bacon; wrap them up in white Paper, spit them on a small Spit, and roast them; in the mean time, make for them a Ragoo of Truffles, and Mushrooms chopped small, with Parsley cut small; put to it Half a Pint of good Veal Gravy, thicken'd with a Piece of Butter rolled in Flour; an Hour will do your Pigeons; baste them, when enough lay them in your Dish, take off the Paper and pour the Sauce over them. Garnish with Patties made thus: Take Veal and cold Ham, Beef Sewet, an equal Quantity, some Mushrooms, Sweet Herbs and Spice, chop them small, set them on the Fire, and moisten with Milk or Cream; then make a little Puff Paste, roll it, and make little Patties about an Inch deep and two Inches long; fill them with the above Ingredients, cover them close and bake them; lay six of them round a Dish. This makes a fine Dish for a first Course.

To jugg Pigeons.

PULL, crop and draw Pigeons, but don't wash them; save the Livers and put them in scalding Water, and set them on the Fire for a Minute or two; then take them out and mince them small, and bruise them with the Back of a Spoon; mix with them a little Pepper, Salt, grated Nutmeg, and Lemon-peel shred very fine, chopped Parsley, and two Yolks of Eggs very hard; bruise them as you do the Liver, and put as much Sewet as Liver shaved exceeding fine, and as much grated Bread; work these together with raw Eggs and roll it in fresh Butter; put a Piece into the Crops and Bellies, and sew up the Necks and Vents; then dip your Pigeons in Water, and season them with Pepper and Salt as for a Pie; then put them in your Jugg, with a Piece of Sellery, stop them close, and set them in a Kettle of cold Water; first cover them very close and lay a Tile on the Top of the Jugg, and let it boil three Hours; then take them out of the Jugg, and lay them into a Dish, take out the Sellery and put in a Piece of Butter rolled in Flour, shake it about till it is thick, and pour it on your Pigeons. Garnish with Lemon.

To stew Pigeons.

SEASON your Pigeons with Pepper, Salt, Cloves, Mace, and some Sweet Herbs; wrap this Seasoning up in a Piece of Butter, and put it in their Bellies; then tie up the Neck and Vent, and half roast them; then put them into a Stew-pan with a Quart of good Gravy, a little White Wine, some pickled Mushrooms, a few Pepper Corns, three or four Blades of Mace, a Bit of Lemon-peel, a Branch of Sweet Herbs, a Bit of Onion, and some Oysters pickled; let them stew till they are enough, then thicken it up with Butter and Yolks of Eggs. Garnish with Lemon.

Do Ducks the same way; you may put Force-Meat in their Bellies, or into both.

To dress a Calf's Liver in a Caul.

TAKE off the under Skins and shred the Liver very small, then take an Ounce of Truffles and Morels chopped small with Parsley; roast two or three Onions, take off their outermost Coats, pound six Cloves, and a Dozen Coriander Seeds; add them to the Onions, and pound them together in a marble Mortar; then take them out and mix them with the Liver, take a Pint of Cream, Half a Pint of Milk, and seven or eight new laid Eggs, beat them together, boil them, but do not let them curdle, shred a Pound of Sewet as small as you can, half melt it in a Pan, and pour it into your Egg and Cream, then put in your Liver, and mix all well together, season it with Pepper, Salt, Nutmeg, and a little Thyme,

and

and let it stand till it is cold: spread a Caul over the Bottom and Sides of a Stew-pan, and put in your hashed Liver and Cream all together, fold it up in the Caul in the Shape of a Calf's Liver, then turn it up-side down carefully, lay it in a Dish that will bear the Oven, and do it over with beaten Egg, drudge it with grated Bread, and bake it in an Oven. Serve it up hot for a first Course.

To roast a Calf's Liver.

LARD it with Bacon, spit it first, and roast it: Serve it up with good Gravy.

To roast Partridges.

LET them be nicely roasted but not too much, drudge them with a little Flour and baste them moderately, let them have a fine Froth, let there be good Gravy-Sauce in the Dish and Bread-Sauce in Basons made thus: Take a Pint of Water, put in a good thick Piece of Bread, some whole Pepper, a Blade or two of Mace, boil it five or six Minutes till the Bread is soft, then take out all the Spice and pour out all the Water, only just enough to keep it moist, beat it with a Spoon soft, throw in a little Salt, and a good Piece of fresh Butter, stir it well together, set it over the Fire for a Minute or two, then put it into a Boat.

To boil Partridges.

BOIL them in a good deal of Water, let them boil quick, and fifteen Minutes will be sufficient: For Sauce, take a Quarter of a Pint of Cream, and a Piece of fresh Butter, as big as a large Walnut, stir it one way till it is melted and pour it into the Dish.

Or this Sance: Take a Bunch of Sellery clean wash'd, cut all the White very small, wash it again very clean, put it into a Sauce-pan with a Blade of Mace, a little beaten Pepper, and a very little Salt; put to it a Pint of Water, let it boil till the Water is just wasted away, then add a Quarter of a Pint of Cream, and a Piece of Butter rolled in Flour; stir all together, and when it is thick and fine pour it over the Birds.

Or this Sauce: Take the Livers and bruise them fine, some Parsley chopped fine, melt a little nice fresh Butter, then add the Livers and Parsley to it, squeeze in a little Lemon, just give it a boil and pour over your Birds.

Or this Sauce: Take a Quarter of a Pint of Cream, the Yolk of an Egg beat fine, a little Nutmeg grated, a little beaten Mace, a Piece of Butter as big as a Nutmeg rolled in Flour, and one Spoonful of White Wine; stir all together one way, when fine and thick pour it over the Birds; you may add a few Mushrooms.

Or this Sauce: Take a few Mushrooms, fresh peel and wash them clean, put them in a Sauce-pan with a little Salt, put them over a very quick Fire, let them boil up, then put in a Quarter of a Pint of Cream and a little Nutmeg, shake them together with a very little Piece of Butter rolled in Flour, give it two or three shakes over the Fire, three or four Minutes will do it; then pour it over the Birds.

Or this Sauce: Boil Half a Pound of Rice very tender in Beef Gravy, season with Pepper and Salt and pour over your Birds: These Sauces do for boiled Fowls, a Quart of Gravy will be enough, and let it boil till it is quite thick.

To dress Partridges à la Braise.

TAKE two Brace, truss the Legs into the Bodies, lard them, season them with beaten Mace, Pepper and Salt, take a Stew-pan, lay Slices of Bacon at the Bottom, then Slices of Beef, and then Slices of Veal, all cut thin, a Piece of Carrot, an Onion cut small, a Bundle of Sweet Herbs, and some whole Pepper; lay the Partridges with the Breast downwards; lay some thin Slices of Beef and Veal over them, and some Parsley shred fine; cover them and let them stew eight or ten Minutes over a very slow Fire, then give your Pan a shake and pour in a Pint of boiling Water; cover it close and let it stew Half an Hour over a little quicker Fire, then take out your Birds, keep them hot, pour into the Pan a Pint of thin Gravy, let it boil till there is about Half a Pint, then strain it off and skim off all the Fat; in the mean time, have a Veal Sweetbread cut small, Truffles, Morels, Cocks Combs, and Fowls Livers stewed in a Pint of good Gravy Half an Hour, some Artichoke Bottoms, and Asparagus Tops, both blanch'd in warm Water, and a few Mushrooms, then add the other Gravy to this, and put in your Partridges to heat; if it is not thick enough take a Piece of Butter rolled in Flour, and toss up in it; if you will be at the Expence, thicken it with Veal and Ham Cullis, but it will be full as good without.

To

To make Partridges Pains.

TAKE two roasted Partridges and the Flesh of a large Fowl, a little parboiled Bacon, a little Marrow or Sweet Sewet chopped very fine, a few Mushrooms and Morels chopped fine, Truffles and Artichoke Bottoms seasoned with beaten Mace, Pepper, a little Nutmeg, Salt, Sweet Herbs chopped fine, and the Crumb of a two-penny Loaf soaked in hot Gravy; mix all well together with the Yolks of two Eggs, make your Pains on Paper of a round Figure, and of the Thickness of an Egg, at a proper Distance one from another, dip the Point of a Knife in the Yolk of an Egg in order to shape them, bread them neatly, and bake them a Quarter of an Hour in a quick Oven; observe that the Truffles and Morels be boiled tender in the Gravy you soak the Bread in. Serve them up for a Side Dish, or they will serve to Garnish the above Dish, which will be a very fine one for a first Course.

Note, When you have cold Fowls in the House this makes a pretty Addition in an Entertainment.

To roast Pheasants.

PICK and Draw your Pheasants, and singe them, lard one with Bacon but not the other, spit them, roast them fine, and pepper them all over the Breast; when they are just done flour and baste them with a little nice Butter, and let them have a fine white Froth, then take them up and pour good Gravy in the Dish and Bread Sauce in Plates.

Or you may put Water-Cresses nicely picked and washed, and just scalded, with Gravy in the Dish, and lay the Cresses under the Pheasants.

Or you may make Sellery Sauce, stewed tender, strained and mixed with Cream, and poured into the Dish.

If you have but one Pheasant, take a large fine Fowl about the bigness of the Pheasant, pick it nicely with the Head on, draw it and truss it with the Head turned as you do a Pheasant's, lard the Fowl all over the Breast and Legs with a large Piece of Bacon cut in little Pieces; when roasted put them both in a Dish, and no Body will know it: They will take an Hour doing, as the Fire must not be too brisk. A *Frenchman* would order Fish Sauce to them, but then you quite spoil your Pheasants.

A stewed Pheasant.

TAKE your Pheasant and stew it in Veal Gravy, take Artichoke Bottoms parboiled, some Chesnuts roasted and blanched; when your Pheasant is enough (but it must stew till there is just enough for Sauce) then skim it, put in the Chesnuts and Artichoke Bottoms, a little beaten Mace, Pepper and Salt, just enough to season it, and a Glass of White Wine, and if you don't think it thick enough, thicken it with a little Piece of Butter rolled in Flour, and squeeze in a little Lemon; pour the Sauce over the Pheasant, and have some Force-Meat Balls fry'd and put into the Dish.

Note, A good Fowl will do full as well, trussed with the Head on like a Pheasant; you may fry Sausages instead of Force-Meat Balls.

To dress a Pheasant à la Braise.

LAY a Layer of Beef all over your Pan, then a Layer of Veal, a little Piece of Bacon, a Piece of Carrot, an Onion stuck with six Cloves, a Blade or two of Mace, a Spoonful of Pepper, Black and White, and a Bundle of Sweet Herbs; then lay in the Pheasant, lay a Layer of Veal, and then a Layer of Beef to cover it, set it over the Fire five or six Minutes, then pour in two Quarts of boiling Water, cover it close and let it stew very softly an Hour and Half, then take up your Pheasant and keep it hot, and let the Gravy Boil till there is about a Pint, then strain it off, and put it in again, and put in a Veal Sweetbread, first being stewed with the Pheasant, then put in some Truffles and Morels, some Livers of Fowls, Artichoke Bottoms, Asparagus Tops, if you have them, let all these Simmer in the Gravy about five or six Minutes, then add two Spoonfuls of Catchup, two of Red Wine, and a little Piece of Butter rolled in Flour, shake all together, put in your Pheasant, let them stew all together with a few Mushrooms about five or six Minutes more, then take up the Pheasant and pour your Ragoo all over with a few Force-Meat Balls. Garnish with Lemon; you may lard it if you chuse it.

To boil a Pheasant.

TAKE a fine Pheasant, boil it in a good deal of Water, keep your Water boiling, Half an Hour will do a small one, and three Quarters of an Hour a large one; let your Sauce be Sellery stewed and thicken'd with Cream, and a little Piece of Butter rolled in Flour; take up the Pheasant, and pour the Sauce all over. Garnish with Lemon. Observe to stew your Sellery so, that the Liquor will be all wasted away before you put your Cream in; if it wants Salt put in some to your Palate.

To

To roast Snipes or Woodcocks.

SPIT them on a small Bird-Spit, flour them and baste them with a Piece of Butter, then have ready a Slice of Bread toasted Brown, lay it in a Dish, and set it under the Snipes, for the Trail to drop on to know when they are enough; take them up and lay them on the Toast, have ready, for two Snipes, a Quarter of a Pint of good Beef Gravy hot; pour it into the Dish, and set it over a Chaffing-dish two or three Minutes. Garnish with Lemon, and send them hot to Table.

Snipes in a Surtout, or Woodcocks.

TAKE Force-Meat, made with Veal, as much Beef Sewet chopped and beat in a Mortar, with an equal Quantity of Crumbs of Bread; mix in a little beaten Mace, Pepper and Salt, some Parsley, and a little Sweet Herbs, mix it with the Yolk of an Egg, lay some of this Meat round the Dish, then lay in the Snipes, being first drawn and Half roasted; take Care of the Trail, chop it and throw it all over the Dish.

Take some good Gravy, according to the Bigness of your Surtout, some Truffles and Morels, a few Mushrooms, a Sweetbread cut into Pieces, Artichoke Bottoms cut small, let all stew together, shake them, take the Yolks of two or three Eggs, according as you want them, beat them up with a Spoonful or two of White Wine, and stir all together one way, when it is thick take it off, let it cool, and pour it into the Surtout; have the Yolks of a few hard Eggs put in here and there, season with beaten Mace, Pepper, and Salt, to your Taste; cover it with the Force-Meat all over, rub the Yolks of Eggs all over to colour it, then send it to the Oven. Half an Hour does it; send it hot to Table.

To boil Snipes or Woodcocks.

BOIL them in good strong Broth, or Beef Gravy, made thus: Take a Pound of Beef, cut it into little Pieces, put it into two Quarts of Water, an Onion, a Bundle of Sweet Herbs, a Blade or two of Mace, six Cloves, and some whole Pepper; cover it close, let it boil till about Half is wasted, then strain it off, put the Gravy into a Sauce-pan with Salt enough to season it, take the Snipes and gut them clean (but take Care of the Guts) put them into the Gravy and let them boil, cover them close, and ten Minutes will boil them, if they keep boiling; in the mean time, chop the Guts and Liver small, take a little of the Gravy the Snipes are boiling in, and stew the Guts in with a Blade of Mace, take some Crumbs of Bread, and have them ready fry'd in a little fresh Butter crisp, of a fine light Brown; you must take about as much Bread as the inside of a stale Roll, and rub them small into a clean Cloth, when they are done let them stand ready in a Plate before the Fire.

When your Snipes are ready take about Half a Pint of the Liquor they are boiled in, and add to the Guts, two Spoonfuls of Red Wine, and a Piece of Butter, about as big as a Walnut, rolled in a little Flour, set them on the Fire, shake your Sauce-pan often (but don't stir it with a Spoon) till the Butter is all melted, then put in the Crumbs, give your Sauce-pan a shake, take up your Birds, lay them in the Dish, and pour this Sauce over them. Garnish with Lemon.

To dress Ortolans.

SPIT them sideways, with a Bay-Leaf between, baste them with Butter, and have fry'd Crumbs of Bread round the Dish. Dress Quails the same way.

To dress Ruffs and Reifs.

THEY are Lincolnshire Birds, and you may fatten them as you do Chickens, with White Bread, Milk and Sugar; they feed fast and will die in their Fat if not killed in time; truss them cross legg'd as you do a Snipe; spit them the same way, but you must gut them, and you must have good Gravy in the Dish thicken'd with Butter and a Toast under them; serve them up quick.

To dress Larks.

SPIT them on a little Bird-Spit, roast them, and when enough have a good many Crumbs of Bread fry'd and throw all over them, and lay them thick round the Dish.

Or they make a very pretty Ragoo with Fowls Livers; first fry the Larks and Livers very nicely, then put them into some good Gravy to stew, just enough for Sauce, with a little Red Wine. Garnish with Lemon.

To dress Plovers.

TO two Plovers take two Artichoke-Bottoms boiled, some Chesnuts roasted and blanched, some Skirrets boiled, cut all very small, mix it with some Marrow or Beef Sewet, the Yolks of two hard Eggs, chop all together, season with Pepper, Salt, Nutmeg and a little Sweet Herbs, fill the Body of the Plovers, lay them in a Sauce-pan, put to them a Pint of Gravy, a Glass of White Wine, a Blade or two of Mace, some roasted Chesnuts blanched, and Artichoke Bottoms cut into Quarters, two or three Yolks of hard Eggs, and a little Juice of Lemon; cover them close, and let them stew very softly an Hour; if you find the Sauce is not thick enough, take a Piece of Butter rolled in Flour, and put into the Sauce, shake it round, and when it is thick take up your Plover and pour the Sauce over them. Garnish with roasted Chesnuts.

Ducks are very good done this way.

Or you may roast your Plover as you do any other Fowl, and have Gravy Sauce in the Dish.

Or boil them with good Sellery Sauce, either White or Brown, just as you like.

The same way you may dress Wigeons.

To dress Larks Pear fashion.

YOU must truss the Larks close, and cut off the Legs, season them with Salt, Pepper, Cloves and Mace, make a Force-Meat thus: Take a Veal Sweetbread, as much Beef Sewet, a few Morels and Mushrooms, chop all fine together, some Crumbs of Bread, and a few Sweet Herbs, a little Lemon-peel cut small, mix all together with the Yolk of an Egg, wrap up every Lark in Force-Meat, and shape them like a Pear, stick one Leg in the Top like the Stalk of a Pear, rub them over with the Yolk of an Egg and Crumbs of Bread, bake them in a gentle Oven, serve them without Sauce, or they make a good Garnish to a very fine Dish.

You may use Veal if you have not a Sweetbread.

To dress a Hare.

AS to roasting of a Hare I have given full Directions in the Beginning of the Book.

A jugged Hare.

CUT it in little Pieces, lard them here and there with little Slips of Bacon, season them with a very little Pepper and Salt, put them into an earthen Jugg, with a Blade or two of Mace, an Onion stuck with Cloves, and a Bundle of Sweet Herbs; cover the Jugg or Jar you do it in, so close, that nothing can get in, then set it in a Pot of boiling Water, keep the Water boiling, and three Hours will do it; then turn it out into the Dish, and take out the Onion and Sweet Herbs, and send it to Table hot.

To stew a Hare.

CUT it to Pieces, put it into a Stew-pan, with a Blade or two of Mace, some whole Pepper, Black and White, an Onion stuck with Cloves, an Anchovy, a Bundle of Sweet Herbs, and a Nutmeg cut to Pieces, and cover it with Water; cover the Stew-pan close, let it stew till the Hare is tender, but not too much done, then take it up, and with a Fork take out your Hare into a clean Pan, strain the Sauce all through a coarse Sieve, empty all out of the Pan, put in the Hare again with the Sauce, take a Piece of Butter as big as a Walnut rolled in Flour and put in, likewise one Spoonful of Catchup, and one of Red Wine, stew all together (with a few fresh Mushrooms, or pickled ones if you have any) till it is thick and smooth, then dish it up and send it to Table. You may cut a Hare in two, and stew the Fore-Quarters thus, and roast the Hind-Quarters with a Pudding in the Belly.

A Hare Civet.

BONE the Hare and take out all the Sinews, cut one Half in thin Slices, and the other Half in Pieces an Inch thick, flour them and fry them in a little fresh Butter as Collops quick, and have ready some Gravy made good with the Bones of the Hare and Beef, put a Pint of it into the Pan to the Hare, some Mustard and a little Elder Vinegar; cover it close and let it do softly till it is as thick as Cream; then dish it up with the Head in the middle.

Portuguese

Portuguese Rabbits.

I HAVE in the Beginning of my Book given Directions for boiled and roasted. Get some Rabbits, truss them Chicken-fashion, the Head must be cut off, and the Rabbit turned with the Back upwards, and two of the Legs stripped to the Claw End, and so trussed with two Skewers; lard them and roast them with what Sauce you please; if you want Chickens, and they are to appear as such, they must be dressed in this manner, but if otherwise, the Head must be skewer'd back and come to Table on, with Liver, Butter and Parsley, as you have for Rabbits, and they look very pretty boiled and trussed in this manner and smothered with Onions; or if they are to be boiled for Chickens, cut off the Head and cover them with White Sellery Sauce, or Rice Sauce tossed up with Cream.

Rabbits *Surprise.*

ROAST two half grown Rabbits, cut off the Heads close to the Shoulders and the first Joints, then take out all the lean Meat from the Back Bones, cut it small, and toss it up with six or seven Spoonfuls of Cream or Milk, and a Piece of Butter as big as a Walnut rolled in Flour, a little Nutmeg and a little Salt, shake all together till it is as thick as good Cream, and set it to cool; then make a Force-Meat with a Pound of Veal, a Pound of Sewet, as much Crumbs of Bread, two Anchovies, a little Piece of Lemon-peel cut fine, a little Sprig of Thyme, and a Nutmeg grated; let the Veal and Sewet be chopped very fine, and beat in a Mortar, then mix it all together with the Yolks of two raw Eggs, place it all round the Rabbits, leaving a long Trough in the Back Bone open, that you think will hold the Meat you cut out with the Sauce, pour it in and cover it with the Force-Meat, smooth it all over with your Hand as well as you can with a raw Egg, square at both Ends, throw on a little grated Bread, and butter a Mazarine, or Pan, and take them from the Dresser where you formed them, and place them on it very carefully, bake them three Quarters of an Hour till they are of a fine Brown Colour; let your Sauce be Gravy thickened with Butter and the Juice of a Lemon, lay them into the Dish and pour in the Sauce. Garnish with Orange cut into Quarters, and serve it for a first Course.

To *boil* Rabbits.

TRUSS them for boiling, boil them quick and white: For Sauce take the Livers, boil and shred them, and some Parsley shred fine, and pickled Astertion Buds chopped fine, or Capers; mix these with Half a Pint of good Gravy, a Glass of White Wine, a little beaten Mace and Nutmeg, a little Pepper and Salt if wanted, a Piece of Butter as big as a large Walnut rolled in Flour, let it all boil together till it is thick, take up the Rabbits and pour the Sauce over them. Garnish with Lemon. You may lard them with Bacon if it is liked.

To *dress* Rabbits *in Casserole.*

DIVIDE the Rabbits into Quarters, you may lard them or let them alone just as you please; shake some Flour over them, and fry them with Lard or Butter, then put them into an earthen Pipkin with a Quart of good Broth, a Glass of White Wine, a little Pepper, and Salt if wanted, a Bunch of Sweet Herbs, and a Piece of Butter as big as a Walnut rolled in Flour; cover them close and let them stew Half an Hour, then dish them up and pour the Sauce over them. Garnish with *Seville* Orange cut into thin Slices and notched, the Peel that is cut out lay prettily between the Slices.

Mutton *Kebob'd.*

TAKE a Loin of Mutton and joint it between every Bone, season it with Pepper and Salt moderately, grate a small Nutmeg all over, dip them in the Yolks of three Eggs, and have ready Crumbs of Bread and Sweet Herbs, and dip them in and clap them together in the same Shape again, and put it on a small Spit, roast them before a quick Fire, set a Dish under and baste it with a little Piece of Butter, and then keep basting with what comes from it, and throw some Crumbs of Bread all over them as it is a roasting; when it is enough take it up, and lay it in the Dish, and have ready Half a Pint of good Gravy, and what comes from it, take two Spoonfuls of Catchup, and mix a Tea-Spoonful of Flour with it and put to the Gravy, stir it together and give it a boil and pour over the Mutton.

Note, You must observe to take off all the Fat of the inside, and the Skin of the Top of the Meat, and some of the Fat, if there be too much; when you put in what comes from your Meat into the Gravy, observe to pour out all the Fat.

A Neck *of* Mutton, *call'd, The hasty Dish.*

TAKE a large Pewter or Silver Dish, made like a deep Soop Dish, with an Edge about an Inch deep on the inside, on which the Lid fixes (with a Handle at top) so fast that you may lift it up full, by that Handle without falling; this Dish is called a Necromancer. Take a Neck of Mutton about six Pound, take off the Skin, cut it into Chops, not too thick, slice a *French* Roll thin, peel and slice a very large Onion, pare and slice three or four Turnips, lay a Row of Mutton in the Dish, on that a Row of Meat, then a Row of Turnips, and then Onions, a little Salt, then the Meat, and so on; put in a little Bundle of Sweet Herbs, and two or three Blades of Mace; have a Tea-Kettle of Water boiling, fill the Dish and cover it close, hang the Dish on the Back of two Chairs by the Rim, have ready three Sheets of Brown Paper, tare each Sheet into five Pieces, and draw them through your

Hand,

Hand, light one Piece and hold it under the Bottom of the Dish, moving the Paper about; as fast as the Paper burns light another, till all is burnt, and your Meat will be enough; fifteen Minutes just does it; send it to Table hot in the Dish.

Note, This Dish was first contrived by Mr. *Rich*, and is much admired by the Nobility.

To dress a Loin of Pork with Onions.

TAKE a Fore-Loin of Pork and roast it, as at another time, peel a Quarter of a Peck of Onions, and slice them thin, lay them in the Dripping-pan, which must be very clean, under the Pork, let the Fat drop on them; when the Pork is nigh enough, put the Onions into the Sauce-pan, let them simmer over the Fire a Quarter of an Hour, shaking them well, then pour out all the Fat as well as you can, shake in a very little Flour, a Spoonful of Vinegar, and three Tea Spoonfuls of Mustard, shake all well together, and stir in the Mustard, set it over the Fire for four or five Minutes, lay the Pork in a Dish, and the Onions in a Bason. This is an admirable Dish to those who love Onions.

To make a Currey the India way.

TAKE two Fowls or Rabbits, cut them into small Pieces, and three or four small Onions, peeled and cut very small, thirty Pepper Corns, and a large Spoonful of Rice, Brown some Coriander Seeds over the Fire in a clear Shovel, and beat them to Powder, take a Tea Spoonful of Salt, and mix all well together with the Meat, put all together into a Sauce-pan or Stew-pan, with a Pint of Water, let it stew softly till the Meat is enough, then put in a Piece of fresh Butter, about as big as a large Walnut, shake it well together, and when it is smooth and of a fine Thickness, dish it up, and send it to Table; if the Sauce be too thick, add a little more Water before it is done, and more Salt if it wants it. You are to observe the Sauce must be pretty thick.

To make a Pellow the India way.

TAKE a Piece of pickled Pork and better than Half boil it in a Gallon of Water, then take it out and pick out all the Bones; put in two Fowls, and Half a Pound of Rice, a Tea Spoonful of White Pepper, and a Tea Spoonful of Cloves, when beat fine, twelve very small Onions, when you think the Fowls Half boiled put in the Pork and let it do softly over a slow Fire till enough, then lay the Fowls in a Dish, and the Pork on each Side the Rice; if you find it two thin drain it dry, lay it in a Dish and Garnish it with hard Eggs. You must be sure to take great Care the Rice don't burn to the Pot.

Another way to make a Pellow.

TAKE a Leg of Veal, about twelve or fourteen Pounds Weight, an old Cock skinned, chop both to Pieces; put it into a Pot with five or six Blades of Mace, some whole White Pepper, and three Gallons of Water, Half a Pound of Bacon, two Onions and six Cloves; cover it close, and when it boils let it do very softly, till the Meat is good for nothing and above two Thirds is wasted, then strain it, the next Day put this Soop into a Sauce-pan, with a Pound of Rice, set it over a very slow Fire, take great Care it don't burn, when the Rice is very thick and dry turn it into a Dish. Garnish with hard Eggs cut in two, and have roasted Fowls in another Dish.

Note, You are to observe, if your Rice simmers too fast it will burn, when it comes to be thick; it must be very thick and dry, and not the Rice boiled to a Mummy.

To make Essence of Ham.

TAKE off the Fat of a Ham, and cut the Lean in Slices; beat them well and lay them in the Bottom of a Stew-pan, with Slices of Carrots, Parsnips and Onions; cover your Pan, and set it over a gentle Fire; let them stew till they begin to stick, then sprinkle on a little Flour, and turn them; then moisten with Broth and Veal Gravy; season them with three or four Mushrooms, as many Truffles, a whole Leek, Parsley, and Half a Dozen Cloves, or instead of a Leek, a Clove of Garlick, put in some Crusts of Bread, and let them simmer over the Fire for a Quarter of an Hour, strain it and set it away for Use. Any Pork Ham does for this, that is well made.

Rules to be observed in all Made-Dishes.

FIRST, that the Stew-pans, or Sauce-pans and Covers, be very clean, free from Sand, and well tinned; and that all the White Sauces have a little Tartness, and be very smooth, and of a fine Thickness, and all the time any White Sauce is over the Fire keep stirring it one way.

And as to Brown Sauce, take great Care no Fat swims at the Top, but that it be all smooth alike, and about as thick as good Cream, and not to taste of one Thing more than another; as to Pepper and Salt, season to your Palate, but don't put too much of either, for that will take away the fine Flavour of every Thing; and as to most Made-Dishes, you may put in what you think proper to inlarge it, or make it good, as Mushrooms, pickled, dry'd, fresh, or powder'd; Truffles, Morels, Cocks Combs stewed, Ox Palates cut in little Bits, Artichoke Bottoms, either pickled, fresh boiled, or dry'd ones softened in warm Water, each cut in four Pieces, Asparagus Tops, the Yolks of hard Eggs, Force-Meat Balls, &c. The best Things to give Sauce a Tartness are Mushroom Pickle, White Walnut Pickle, or Lemon Juice.

CHAP. III.

Read this CHAPTER, *and you will find how expensive a* French *Cook's Sauce is.*

The French Way of Dressing Partridges.

WHEN they are newly picked and drawn, singe them: You must mince their Livers with a Bit of Butter, some scraped Bacon, green Truffles if you have any, Parsley, Chimbol, Salt, Pepper, Sweet Herbs, and Alspice; the whole being minced together, put it in the Inside of your Partridges; then stop both Ends of them; after which give them a Fry in the Stew-pan, and being done, spit them, and wrap them up in Slices of Bacon and Paper; then take a Stew-pan, and having put in an Onion cut into Slices, a Carrot cut into little Bits, with a little Oil, give them a few Tosses over the Fire; then moisten them with Gravy, Cullis, a little Essence of Ham; put therein half a Lemon cut into Slices, four Cloves of Garlick, a little Sweet Basil, Thyme, a Bay-Leaf, a little Parsley, Chimbol, a Couple of Glasses of White Wine, and four of the Carcasses of the Partridges; let them be pounded, and put them in this Sauce. When the Fat of your Cullis is taken away, be careful to make it relishing; and after your pounded Livers are put into your Cullis, you must strain them through a Sieve. Your Partridges being done, take them off, as also take off the Bacon and Pepper, and lay them in your Dish, with your Sauce over them.

This Dish I do not recommend; for I think it an odd Jumble of Trash, by that time the Cullis, the Essence of Ham, and all other Ingredients are reckoned, the Partridges will come to a fine Penny; but such Receipts as this, is what you have in most Books of Cookery yet printed.

To Make Essence of Ham.

TAKE the Fat off a *Westphalia*-Ham, cut the Lean in Slices, beat them well, and lay them in the Bottom of a Stew-pan, with Slices of Carrots and Parsnips, and Onion: Cover your Pan, and set it over a gentle Fire; let them stew till they begin to stick; then sprinkle on a little Flour, and turn them; then moisten with Broth and Veal-gravy, season with three or four Mushrooms, as many Truffles, a whole Leek, some Basil, Parsley, and half a Dozen Cloves; or instead of the Leek, you may put a Clove of Garlick: Put in some Crust of Bread, and let them simmer over the Fire for three Quarters of an Hour; strain it, and set it by for Use.

A Cullis for all Sorts of Ragoo.

HAVING cut three Pounds of lean Veal, and half a Pound of Ham, into Slices, lay it into the Bottom of a Stew-pan, put in Carrots and Parsnips, and an Onion sliced; cover it, and set it a stewing over a Stove: When it has a good Colour, and begins to stick, put to it a little melted Bacon, and shake in a little Flour, keeping it moving a little while till the Flour is fried; then moisten it with Gravy, and Broth, of each a like Quantity, then put in some Parsley and Basil, a whole Leek, a Bay-leaf, some Mushrooms, and Truffles minced small, three or four Cloves, and the Crust of two *French* Rolls: Let all this simmer together for three Quarters of an Hour; then take out your Slices of Veal; strain it, and keep it for all Sorts of Ragoos. Now compute the Expence, and see if this Dish cannot be dressed full as well without this Expence.

A Cullis for all Sorts of Butcher's Meat.

YOU must take Meat according to your Company. If ten or twelve, you can't take less than a Leg of Veal, and a Ham, with all the Fat, and Skin, and Outside cut off: Cut the Leg of Veal in Pieces, about the Bigness of your Fist, place them in your Stew-pan, and then the Slices of Ham, a Couple of Carrots, an Onion cut in two, cover it close, let it stew softly at first, and as it begins to be brown, take off the Cover, and turn it to colour it on all Sides the same; but take care not to burn the Meat. When it has a pretty brown Colour, moisten your Cullis with Broth made of Beef, or other Meat; season your Cullis with a little sweet Basil, some Cloves with some Garlick; pare a Lemon, cut it into Slices, and put it into your Cullis, with some Mushrooms. Put into a Stew-pan a good Lump of Butter, and set it over a slow Fire; put into it two or three Handfuls of Flour, stir it with a wooden Laden, and let it take a Colour; if your Cullis be pretty brown, you must put in some Flour. Your Flour being brown with your Cullis, then pour it very softly into your Cullis, keeping your Cullis stiring with a wooden Ladle; then let your Cullis stew softly, and skim off the Fat; put in a Couple of Glasses of Champaign, or other White Wine; but take care to keep your Cullis very thin, so that you may take the Fat well off, and clarify it. To clarify it, you must put it on a Stove that draws well, and cover it close, and let it boil without uncovering, till it boils over; then uncover it, and take off the Fat that is round the Stew-pan; then wipe it off the Cover also, and cover it again. When your Cullis is done, take out the Meat, and strain your Cullis through a silk Strainer. This Cullis is for all Sorts of Ragoo, Fowls, Pies, and Terrines.

Cullis the Italian Way.

PUT into a Stew-pan half a Ladleful of Cullis, as much Essence of Ham, half a Ladleful of Gravy, as much of Broth, three or four Onions cut into Slices, four or five Cloves of Garlick, a little beaten Coriander-seed, with a Lemon pared, and cut into Slices, a little sweet Basil, Mushrooms, and good Oil; put all over the Fire, let it stew a good Quarter of an Hour, take the Fat well off, let it be of a good Taste, and you may use it with all Sorts of Meat and Fish, particularly with glazed Fish. This Sauce will do for a Couple of Chickens, six Pidgeons, Quails, or Ducklings, and all Sorts of Tame and Wild Fowl. Now this *Italian* or *French* Sauce, is saucy.

Cullis of Crawfish.

YOU must get the middling Sort of Crawfish, put them over the Fire, seasoned with Salt, Pepper, and Onion cut in Slices: Being done, take them out, pick them, and keep the Tails after they are scaled, pound the rest together in a Mortar; the more they are pounded, the finer your Cullis will be. Take a Bit of Veal, the Bigness of your Fist, with a small Bit of Ham, an Onion cut into four, put it into sweat gently; if it sticks but a very little to the Pan, powder it a little. Moisten it with Broth, put in it some Cloves, sweet Basil in Branches, some Mushrooms, with Lemon pared and cut in Slices. Being done, skim the Fat well; let it be of a good Taste; then take out your Meat with a Skimmer, and go on to thicken it a little, with Essence of Ham; then put in your Crawfish, and strain it off. Being strained, keep it for a first Course of Crawfish.

A White Cullis.

TAKE a Piece of Veal, cut it into small Bits, with some thin Slices of Ham, and two Onions cut into four Pieces; moisten it with Broth, seasoned with Mushrooms, a Bunch of Parsley, green Onions, three Cloves, and so let it stew. Being stewed, taking out all your Meat and Roots with a Skimmer, put in a few Crumbs of Bread, and let it stew softly: Take the White of a Fowl, or of a Couple of Chickens, and pound it in a Mortar. Being well pounded, mix it in your Cullis; but it must not boil, and your Cullis must be very white; but if it is not white enough, you must pound two Dozen of Sweet Almonds blanched, and put into your Cullis; then boil a Glass full of Milk, and put it in your Cullis: Let it be of a good Taste, and strain it off; then put it in a small Kettle, and keep it warm. You may use it for white Loaves, white Crust of Bread, and Bisquets.

Sauce for a Brace of Partridges, Pheasants, or any Thing you please.

ROAST a Partridge, pound it well in a Mortar, with the Pinions of four Turkeys, with a Quart of strong Gravy, and the Livers of the Partridges, and some Truffles; let it simmer till it be pretty thick; let it stand in a Dish for a while; then put a Couple of Glasses of Burgundy into a Stew-pan, with two or three Slices of Onions, a Clove or two of Garlick, and the above Sauce: Let it simmer a few Minutes; then press it through a Hair-bag into a Stew-pan; add the Essence of a Ham; let it all boil for some time; season it with good Spices and Pepper; lay your Partridge, &c. in the Dish, and pour your Sauce in.

They will use as many fine Ingredients to stew a Pigeon, or Fowl, as will make a very fine Dish, which is equal with boiling a Leg of Mutton in Champaign.

It would be needless to name any more; though they have much more expensive Sauce than this.—However, I think here is enough to shew the Folly of these fine *French* Cooks. In their own Country, they will make a grand Entertainment with the Expence of one of these Dishes; but here they want the little petty Profit; and by this Sort of legerdemain Sum, fine Estates are juggled into *France*.

CHAP.

CHAP. IV.

To make a Number of pretty little Dishes, fit for a Supper, or Side-Dish, and little Corner-Dishes for a great Table; and the rest you have in the CHAPTER *for* Lent.

Hog's Ears Forced.

TAKE four Hog's Ears and half boil them, or take them soused; make a Force-meat thus: Take half a Pound of Beef-suet, as much Crumbs of Bread, an Anchovy, some Sage, boil and chop very fine a little Parsley, mix all together with the Yolk of an Egg, a little Pepper, slit your Ears very carefully to make a Place for your Stuffing, fill them, flour them, and fry them in fresh Butter, till they are of a fine light Brown; then pour out all the Fat clean, and put to them half a Pint of Gravy, a Glass of White Wine, three Tea Spoonfuls of Mustard, a Piece of Butter, as big as a Nutmeg rolled in Flour, a little Pepper, a small Onion whole; cover them close, and let them stew softly half an Hour, shaking your Pan now and then. When they are enough, lay them in your Dish, and pour your Sace over them; but first take out the Onion. This makes a very pretty Dish; but if you would make a fine large Dish, take the Feet, and cut all the Meat in small thin Pieces, and stew with the Ears. Season with Salt to your Pallat.

To Force Cock's Combs.

PARBOIL your Cock's Combs, then open them with the Point of a Knife at the Grate-end; take the White of a Fowl, as much Bacon, and Beef-marrow, cut these small, and beat them fine in a Marble Mortar; season them with Salt, Pepper, and grated Nutmeg, and mix it up with an Egg; fill the Combs, and stew them in a little strong Gravy softly for half an Hour; then slice in some fresh Mushrooms, and a few pickled ones; then beat up the Yolk of an Egg in a little Gravy stirring it; season with Salt. When they are enough, dish them up in little Dishes or Plates.

To Preserve Cock's Combs

LET them be well cleaned, then put them into a Pot with some melted Bacon, and boil them a little. About half an Hour after, add a little Bay Salt, some Pepper a little Vinegar, a Lemon sliced, and an Onion stuck with Cloves. When the Bacon begins to stick to the Pot, take them up, put them into the Pan you would keep them in, lay a clean Linnen Cloth over them, and pour melted Butter clarified over them, to keep them close from the Air. These make a pretty Plate at a Supper.

To Preserve or Pickle Pig's Feet and Ears.

TAKE your Feet and Ears single, and wash them well, split the Feet in two, put a Bay-Leaf between every Foot; but in almost as much Water as will cover them. When they are well steemed, add to them Cloves, Mace, whole Pepper and Ginger, Coriander-seed, and Salt, according to your Discretion; put to them a Bottle or two of Rhenish Wine, according to the Quantity you do, half a Score Bay-leaves, and a Bunch of Sweet Herbs: Let them boil softly, till they are very tender; then take them out of the Liquor, lay them in an earthen Pot, then strain the Liquor over them; when they are cold, cover them down close, and keep them for Use.

You should let them stand to be cold; skim off all the Fat, and then put in the Wine and Spice.

Thy eat well cold, or at any time heat them in the Jelly, and thicken it with a little Piece of Butter rolled in Flour, makes a very pretty Dish; or heat the Ears, and take the Feet clean out of the Jelly, and roll it in Yolk of Egg, or melted Butter, and then in Crumbs of Bread, and broil them; or fry them in fresh Butter; lay the Ears in the Middle, and the Feet round, and pour the Sauce over; or you may cut the Ears in long Slips, which is better: And if you chuse it, make a good brown Gravy to mix with them, a Glass of White Wine and some Mustard, thickened with a Piece of Butter rolled in Flour.

To Pickle Ox Palates.

TAKE your Palates and wash them well with Salt and Water, and put them in a Pipkin with Water and some Salt; and when they are ready to boil, skim them well, and put to them Pepper, Cloves, and Mace, as much as will give them a quick Taste. When they are boiled tender, (which will require four or five Hours) peel them and cut them into small Pieces, and let them cool; then make the Pickle of White Wine and Vinegar, an equal Quantity; boil the Pickle, and put in the Spices that were boiled in the Palates: When both the Pickle and Palates are cold, lay your Palates in a

P Jar,

The Art of Cookery made Plain and Easy.

Jar, and put to them a few Bay-leaves, and a little fresh Spice; pour the Pickle over them, cover them close, and keep them for Use.

Of these you may at any time make a pretty little Dish, either with brown Sauce or white, or Butter and Mustard, and a Spoonful of White Wine, or they are ready to put in made Dishes.

To Stew Cucumbers.

PARE twelve Cucumbers, and slice them as thick as a Crown-piece, and put them to drain; and then lay them in a coarse Cloth till they are dry, flour them, and fry them brown in Butter; pour out the Fat, then put to them some Gravy, a little Claret, some Pepper, Cloves, and Mace, and let them stew a little; then roll a Bit of Butter in Flour, and toss them up seasoned with Salt: You may add a very little Mushroom-pickle.

To Ragoo Cucumbers.

TAKE two Cucumbers, two Onions, slice them, and fry them in a little Butter; then drain them in a Sieve, put them into a Sauce-pan, add six Spoonfuls of Gravy, two of White Wine, a Blade of Mace; let them stew for five or six Minutes; then take a Piece of Butter as big as a Wallnut rolled in Flour; shake them altogether; and when it is thick, dish them up.

To make Jumballs.

TAKE a Pound of fine Flour, and a Pound of fine Powder-sugar, make them into a light Paste, with Whites of Eggs beat fine; then add half a Pint of Cream, half a Pound of fresh Butter melted, and a Pound of blanched Almonds well beat. Kneed them all together thoroughly, with a little Rose-water, and cut out your Jumball in what Figures you fancy; and either bake them in a gentle Oven, or fry them in fresh Butter, and they make a pretty Side or Corner Dish. You may melt a little Butter with a Spoonful of Sack, and throw fine Sugar all over the Dish: If you make them in pretty Figures, they make a fine little Dish.

To make a Ragoo of Onions.

TAKE a Pint of little young Onions, peel them, and take four large ones, peal them, and cut them very small; put a Quarter of a Pound of good Butter into a Stew-pan, when it is melted and done making a Noise, throw in your Onions, and fry them till they begin to look a little brown; then shake in a little Flour, and shake them round till they are thick; throw in a little Salt, and a little beaten Pepper, and a Quarter of a Pint of good Gravy, and a Tea Spoonful of Mustard. Stir all together, and when it is well tasted, and of a good Thickness, pour it into your Dish, and garnish it with fry'd Crumbs of Bread or Raspings. They make a pretty little Dish, and are very good. You may strew fine Raspings in the room of Flour, if you please.

A Ragoo of Oysters.

OPEN twenty large Oysters, take them out of their Liquor, save the Liquor, and dip the Oysters in a Batter made thus: Take two Eggs, beat them well, a little Lemon-peel grated, a little Nutmeg grated, a Blade of Mace pounded fine, a little Parsley chopped fine; beat all together with a little Flour, have ready some Butter or Dripping in a Stew-pan, when it boils, dip in your Oysters, one by one, into the Batter, and fry them of a fine brown; then with an Egg-slice take them out, and lay them in a Dish before the Fire. Pour the Fat out of the Pan, and shake a little Flour over the Bottom of the Pan; then rub a little Piece of Butter, as big as a small Walnut, all over with your Knife, whilst it is over the Fire; then pour in three Spoonfuls of the Oyster-liquor strained, one Spoonful of White Wine, and a Quarter of a Pint of Gravy; grate a little Nutmeg, stir all together, throw in the Oysters, give the Pan a-Toss round, and when the Sauce is of a good Thickness, pour all into the Dish, and garnish with Raspings.

A Ragoo of Asparagus.

SCRAPE a hundred of Grass very clean, and throw it into cold Water. When you have scraped all, cut as far as is good and green, about an Inch long, and take two Heads of Endive clean washed and picked, cut it very small, a young Lettice clean washed, and cut small, a large Onion peeled, and cut small, put a Quarter of a Pound of Butter into a Stew-pan, when it is melted, throw in the above Things: Toss them about, and fry them ten Minutes; then season them with a little Pepper and Salt, shake in a little Flour, toss them about, then pour in half a Pint of Gravy. Let them stew, till the Sauce is very thick and good; then pour all into your Dish. Save a few of the little Tops of the Grass to garnish the Dish.

A Ragoo of Livers.

TAKE as many Livers as you would have for your Dish. A Turkey Liver, and six Fowl Livers, will make a pretty Dish. Pick the Galls from them, and throw them into cold Water; take the six Livers, put them into a Sauce-pan with a Quarter of a Pint of Gravy, a Spoonful of Mushrooms, either pickled or fresh, a Spoonful of Ketchup, a little Bit of Butter, as big as a Nutmeg, rolled in Flour, seasoned with Pepper and Salt to your Palate. Let them stew softly ten Minutes; in the mean while broil the Turkey's Liver nicely, lay it in the Middle, and the stewed Livers round; pour the Sauce all over, and garnish with Lemon.

To Ragoo Colliflowers.

LAY a large Colliflower in Water, then pick it to-pieces, as if for pickling, take a Quarter of a Pound of Butter, with a Spoonful of Water, and melt it in a Stew-pan; then throw in your Colliflowers, and shake them about often, till they are quite tender; then shake in a little Flour, and toss the Pan about, season them with a little Pepper and Salt, pour in half a Pint of good Gravy, let them stew till the Sauce is thick, then pour it all into a little Dish. Save a few little Bits of the Colliflowers, when stewed in the Butter, to garnish with.

Stewed Peas and Lettice.

TAKE a Quart of green Peas, two nice Lettices clean washed and picked, cut them small a-cross, put all into a Sauce-pan, with a Quarter of a Pound of Butter, Pepper and Salt to your Palate, cover them close, and let them stew softly, shaking the Pan often. Let them stew ten Minutes, then shake in a little Flour, toss them round, and pour in half a Pint of good Gravy; put in a little Bundle of Sweet Herbs, and an Onion, with three Cloves, and a Blade of Mace stuck in it. Cover it close, and let them stew a Quarter of an Hour; then take out the Onion and Sweet Herbs, and turn it all into a Dish. If you find the Sauce not thick enough, shake in a little more Flour, and let it simmer, then take it up.

Cod-Sounds broiled with Gravy.

SCALD them in hot Water, and rub them with Salt well; blanch them, that is, take off all the black dirty Skin; then set them on in cold Water, and let them simmer till they begin to be tender; take them out and flour them, and broil them on the Gridiron; in the mean time take a little good Gravy, a little Mustard, a little Bit of Butter rolled in Flour, give it a boil, season it with Pepper and Salt, lay the Sounds in your Dish, and pour the Sauce over them.

A Forced Cabbage.

TAKE a fine White-heart Cabbage, about as big as a Quarter of a Peck, lay it in Water two or three Hours, then half boil it, set it in a Cullendar to drain, then very carefully cut out the Heart, but take great Care not to break off any of the outside Leaves, fill it with Force-meat made thus: Take a Pound of Veal, half a Pound of Bacon, Fat and Lean together, cut them small, and beat them fine in a Mortar, with four Eggs boiled hard; season with Pepper and Salt, a little beaten Mace, a very little Lemon-peel cut fine, some Parsley chopped fine, a very little Thyme, two Anchovies; when these are beat fine, take the Crumb of a stale Role, and some Mushrooms, if you have them, either pickled or fresh, the Heart of the Cabbage you cut out chopped fine. Mix all together with the Yolk of an Egg, then fill the hollow Part of the Cabbage, and tye it with a Pack-thread, then lay some Slices of Bacon in the Bottom of a Stew-pan, or Sauce-pan, and on that a Pound of coarse lean Beef, cut thin, put in the Cabbage, cover it close, and let it stew over a slow Fire, till the Bacon begin to stick to the Pan, shake in a little Flour, then pour in a Quart of Broth, an Onion stuck with Cloves, two Blades of Mace, some whole Pepper, a little Bundle of Sweet Herbs, cover it close, and let it stew very softly an Hour and half, put in a Glass of Red Wine, give it a boil, then take it up, and lay it in the Dish, and strain the Gravy and pour over, untye it first. This is a fine Side-dish; and the next Day makes a fine Hash, with a Veal Stake nicely broiled, and laid on it.

Stewed Red Cabbage.

TAKE a red Cabbage, lay it in cold Water an Hour, then cut it into thin Slices a-cross, and cut it into little pieces. Put it into a Stew-pan, with a Pound of Sausages, a Pint of Gravy, a little Bit of Ham or lean Bacon, cover it close, and let it stew half an Hour; then take the Pan off the Fire, and skim off the Fat; shake in a little Flour, and set it on again; let it stew two or three Minutes, then lay the Sausages in your Dish, and pour the rest all over. You may, before you take it up, put in half a Spoonful of Vinegar.

Savoys

Savoys Forced and Stewed.

TAKE two Savoys, fill one with Force-meat, and the other without. Stew them with Gravy, season them with Pepper and Salt, and when they are near enough, take a Piece of Butter, as big as a large Wallnut, rolled in Flour, and put in. Let them stew till they are enough, and the Sauce thick; then lay them in your Dish, and pour the Sauce over them. These Things are best done on a Stove.

To Force Cucumbers.

TAKE three large Cucumbers, scoop out the Pith, fill them with fry'd Onions, seasoned with Pepper and Salt; put on the Piece you cut off again, sew it with a coarse Thread, and fry them in the Butter the Onions was fry'd in; then pour out the Butter, and shake in a little Flour; pour in half a Pint of Gravy, shake it round, and put in the Cucumbers; season it with a little Pepper and Salt; let them stew softly till they are tender; then lay them in a Plate, and pour the Gravy over them; or you may force them with any Sort of Force-meat you fancy, and fry them in Hog's-lard; and then stew them in Gravy and Red Wine.

Fry'd Sausages.

TAKE half a Pound of Sausages, and six Apples; slice four about as thick as a Crown; cut the other two in Quarters, fry them with the Sausages of a fine light-brown; lay the Sausages in the Middle of the Dish, and the Apples round; garnish with the quarter'd Apples.

Stewed Cabbage and Sausages fry'd is a good Dish; then heat cold Peas-pudding in the Pan, lay it in a Dish, and the Sausages round, heap the Pudding in the Middle, and lay the Sausages all round thick, up Edge-ways, and one in the Middle at length.

Collup and Eggs.

CUT either Bacon, pickled Beef, or hung Mutton into thin Slices, broil them nicely, lay them in a Dish before the Fire, have ready a Stew-pan of Water boiling, break as many Eggs as you have Collups, break them one by one in a Cup, and pour them into the Stew-pan. When the White of the Egg begins to harden, and all look of a clear white, take them up one by one in an Egg-slice, and lay them on the Collups.

To Dress Cold Fowl or Pigeon.

CUT them in four Quarters, beat up an Egg or two according to what you dress, grate a little Nutmeg in, a little Salt, some Parsley chopped, a few Crumbs of Bread, beat them well together, dip them in this Batter, and have ready some Dripping hot in a Stew-pan, in which fry them of a fine light brown; have ready a little good Gravy, thickened with a little Flour, mix with a Spoonful of Ketchup, lay the Fry in the Dish, and pour the Sauce over. Garnish with Lemon; a few Mushrooms, if you have any. A Cold Rabit eats well done thus.

To Mince Veal.

CUT your Veal as fine as possible; but don't chop it. Grate a little Nutmeg over it, shread a little Lemon-peel very fine, throw a very little Salt on it, drudge a little Flour over it. To a large Plate of Veal, take four or five Spoonfuls of Water, let it boil, then put in the Veal, with a Piece of Butter, as big as an Egg, stir it well together; when it is all thorough hot, it is enough. Have ready a very thin Piece of Bread toasted brown, cut it into three Corner Sippets, lay it round the Plate, and pour in the Veal. Just before you pour it in, squeeze in half a Lemon, or half a Spoonful of Vinegar; garnish with Lemon. You may put Gravy in the room of Water, if you love it strong; but it is better without.

To Fry Cold Veal.

CUT it in Pieces about as thick as Half a Crown, and as long as you please; dip them in the Yolk of an Egg, and then in Crumbs of Bread, with a few Sweet Herbs, and shread Lemon-peel in it; grate a little Nutmeg over them, and fry them in fresh Butter. The Butter must be hot, just enough to fry them in; in the mean time make a little Gravy of the Bone of the Veal. When the Meat is fry'd, take it out with a Fork, and lay it in a Dish before the Fire; then shake a little Flour into the Pan, and stir it round; then put in the Gravy, squeeze in a little Lemon, and pour it over the Veal. Garnish with Lemon.

To Toss up Cold Veal White.

CUT the Veal into little thin Bits, put Milk enough to it for Sauce, grate in a little Nutmeg, a very little Salt, a little Piece of Butter rolled in Flour: To half a Pint of Milk, the Yolks of two Eggs well beat, a Spoonful of Mushroom-pickle; stir all together till it is thick, then pour it into your Dish, and garnish with Lemon.

Cold Fowl skined, and done this Way, eats well; or the best End of a cold Breast of Veal: First fry it, drain it from the Fat, then pour this Sauce to it.

To Hash Cold Mutton.

CUT your Mutton with a very sharp Knife in very little Bits, as thin as possible; then boil the Bones with an Onion, a little Sweet Herbs, a Blade of Mace, a very little whole Pepper, a little Salt, a Piece of Crust toasted very crisp; let it boil till there is just enough for Sauce, strain it, and put it into a Sauce-pan, with a Piece of Butter rolled in Flour; put in the Meat, when it is thorough hot it is enough. Have ready some thin Bread toasted brown, cut thus △, lay them round the Dish, and pour in the Hash. As to Wallnut-pickle, and all Sorts of Pickles, you must put in according to your Fancy. Garnish with Pickles. Some love a small Onion peeled, and cut very small, and done in the Hash.

To Hash Mutton like Venison.

CUT it very thin, as above; boil the Bones, as above; strain the Liquor, when there is just enough for your Hash. To a Quarter of a Pint of Gravy, put a large Spoonful of Red Wine, a small Onion peeled and chopped fine, a very little Lemon-peel shread fine, a Piece of Butter, as big as a small Walnut, rolled in Flour; put it into a Sauce-pan with the Meat, shake it all together, and when it is thorough hot, pour it into your Dish. Hash Beef the same Way.

To Make Collups of Cold Beef.

IF you have any cold Inside of a Surloin of Beef, take off all the Fat, cut it very thin, in little Bits, cut an Onion very small, boil as much Water as you think will do for Sauce, season it with a little Pepper and Salt, and a Bundle of Sweet Herbs. Let the Water boil, then put in the Meat, with a good Piece of Butter rolled in Flour, shake it round, and stir it. When the Sauce is thick, and the Meat done, take out the Sweet Herbs, and pour it into your Dish. They do better then fresh Meat.

To Make a Florendine of Veal.

TAKE two Kidnies of a Loin of Veal, Fat and all, and mince it very fine, then chop a few Herbs and put to it, and add a few Currants; season it with Cloves, Mace, Nutmeg, and a little Salt, four or five Yolks of Eggs chopped fine, and some Crumbs of Bread, a Pippin or two chopped, some candied Lemon-peel cut small, a little Sack, and Orange Flour-water. Lay a Sheet of Puff-paste at the Bottom of your Dish, and put in the Ingredients, and cover it with another Sheet of Puff-paste. Bake it in a slack Oven, scrape Sugar on the Top, and serve it up hot.

To Make Salamongundy.

TAKE two or three *Roman* or Cabbage Lettice, and when you have washed them clean, swing them pretty dry in a Cloth; then beginning at the open End, cut them cross-ways, as fine as a good big Thread, and lay the Lettices so cut, about an Inch thick all over the Bottom of a Dish. When you have thus garnished your Dish, take a Couple of cold roasted Pullets, or Chickens, and cut the Flesh off the Breasts and Wings into Slices, about three Inches long, a Quarter of an Inch broad, and as thin as a Shilling; lay them upon the Lettice round the End to the Middle of the Dish, and the other towards the Brim; then having boned and cut six Anchovies, each into eight Pieces, lay them all between each Slice of the Fowls, then cut the lean Meat off the Legs into Dice, and cut a Lemon into small Dice; then mince the Yolk of four Eggs, three or four Anchovies, and a little Parsley, and make a round Heap of these in your Dish, piling it up in the Form of a Sugar-loaf, and garnish it with Onions, as big as the Yolk of Eggs, boiled in a good deal of Water very tender and white. Put the largest of the Onions in the Middle on the Top of the Salamongundy, and lay the rest all round the Brim of the Dish, as thick as you can lay them; then beat some Sallat-Oil up with Vinegar, Salt and Pepper, and pour over it all. Garnish with Grapes just scalded, or *French* Beans blanched, or Station Flowers, and serve it up for a first Course.

Another Way.

MINCE a Couple of Chickens, either boiled or roasted, very fine, or Veal, if you please, also mince the Yolks of hard Eggs very small, and mince the Whites very small by themselves, shred the Pulp of two or three Lemons very small, then lay in your Dish a Layer of Mince-meat, and a Layer of Yolk of Eggs, a Layer of Whites, a Layer of Anchovies, a Layer of your shred Lemon-pulp, a Layer of Pickles, a Layer of Sorrel, a Layer of Spinage, and Shalots shred small. When you have filled a Dish with these Ingredients, set an Orange or Lemon on the Top, then garnish with Horse-reddish scraped, Barberries, and sliced Lemon. Beat up some Oil, with the Juice of Lemon, Salt, and Mustard thick, and serve it up for a second Course Side-dish, or Middle-dish, for Supper.

A Third Salamongundy.

MINCE Veal or Fowl very small, a pickle Herring boned and picked small, Cucumber minced small, Apples minced small, and Onion peeled, and minced small, some pickled red Cabbage chopped small, cold Pork minced small, or cold Duck or Pigeons minced small, boiled Parsley chopped fine, Sallery cut small, hard Eggs the Yolks chopped small, and the Whites chopped small, and either lay all the Ingredients by themselves separate on Saucers, or in Heaps in a Dish. Dish them out with what Pickles you have, and sliced Lemon nicely cut; and if you can get Station-flowers lay round it, make a fine Middle-dish for Supper; but you may always make a Salamongundy of such things as you have, according to your Fancy. The other Sorts you have in the Chapter of *Fasts*.

To Make little Pasties.

TAKE the Kidney of a Loin of Veal cut very fine, with as much of the Fat, the Yolk of two hard Eggs, seasoned with a little Salt, and half a small Nutmeg. Mix them well together, and roll it up in a Puff-paste Crust, make three of it, fry them nicely in Hog's-lard or Butter.

They make a pretty little Dish for Change. You may put in some Carrots, and a little Sugar, and Spice, with the Juice of an Orange, and sometimes Apples, first boiled and sweetned, with a little Juice of Lemon, or any Fruit you please.

Petit Patties *for Garnishing of* Dishes.

MAKE a short Crust, roll it thick, make them about as big as the Bowl of a Spoon, and about an Inch deep; take a Piece of Veal, as big as your Fish, as much Bacon and Beef-suet, shread them all very fine, season them with Pepper, Salt, and a little Sweet Herbs; put them into a little Stew-pan, keep turning them about, with a few Mushrooms chopped small, for eight or ten Minutes; then fill your Petit Patties, and cover them with some Crust. Colour them with the Yolk of an Egg, and bake them. Sometimes fill them with Oysters for Fish, or the Melts of the Fish, pounded and seasoned with Pepper and Salt. Fill them with Lobsters, or what you fancy. They make a fine Garnishing, and give a Dish a fine Look: If for a Calve's Head, the Brains seasoned is most proper, and some with Oysters.

Ox Pallat *Baked.*

WHEN you salt a Tongue, cut off the Root, and take an Ox Pallat, wash them clean, cut them into six or seven Pieces, put them into an earthen Pot, just cover them with Water, put in a Blade for two of Mace, twelve whole Pepper, three or four Cloves, a little Bundle of Sweet Herbs, a small Onion, half a Spoonful of Raspings, cover it close with brown Paper, and let it be well baked. When it comes out of the Oven, season it with Salt to your Palate.

CHAP. V.
To DRESS FISH.

AS to Boiled Fish of all Sorts, you have full Directions in the *Lent* Chapter.——But here we can fry Fish much better, because we have Beef-Dripping, or Hog's-Lard.

Observe always in the frying of any Sort of Fish; first, that you dry your Fish very well in a clean Cloth, then flour it. Let your Stew-pan you fry them in be very nice and clean, and put in as much Beef-dripping, or Hog's lard, as will almost cover your Fish; and be sure it boils before you put in your Fish. Let it fry quick; and let it be a fine light-brown, but not too dark a Colour. Have your Fish-slice ready, and if there is Occasion turn it; when it is enough, take it up, and lay a

coarse

coarse Cloth on a Dish, on which lay your Fish to drain all the Grease from it: If you fry Parsley, do it quick, and take great Care to whip it out of the Pan so soon as it is Crisp, or it will lose its fine Colour. Take great Care that your Dripping be very nice and clean. You have Directions in the Eleventh Chapter, how to make it fit for Use, and have it always in Readiness.

Some love Fish in Batter; then you must beat an Egg fine, and dip your Fish in just as you are going to put it in the Pan; or as good a Batter as any, is a little Ale and Flour beat up, just as you are ready for it, and dip the Fish, so fry it.

Fish Sauce *with* Lobster.

FOR Salmon or Turbot, broiled Cod or Haddock, &c. nothing is better than fine Butter melted thick, and take a Lobster, bruise the Body of the Lobster in the Butter, and cut the Flesh into little Pieces, stew it all together, and give it a boil. If you would have your Sauce very rich, let one half be rich Beef Gravy, and the other half melted Butter with the Lobster; but the Gravy, I think, takes away the Sweetness of the Butter and Lobster, and the fine Flavour of the Fish.

To make Shrimp Sauce.

TAKE a Pint of Beef Gravy, and half a Pint of Shrimps, thicken it with a good Piece of Butter rolled in Flour; let the Gravy be well seasoned, and let it boil.

To make Oyster Sauce.

TAKE half a Pint of large Oysters, Liquor and all; put them into a Sauce-pan, with two or three Blades of Mace, and twelve whole Pepper-Corns; let them simmer over a slow Fire, till the Oysters are fine and plump, then carefully with a Fork take out the Oysters from the Liquor and Spice, and let the Liquor boil five or six Minutes; then strain the Liquor, wash out the Sauce-pan clean, and put the Oysters and Liquor in the Sauce-pan again, with half a Pint of Gravy, and half a Pound of Butter just rolled in a little Flour. You may put in two Spoonfuls of White Wine, keep it stiring till the Sauce boils, and all the Butter is melted.

To make Anchovy Sauce.

TAKE a Pint of Gravy, put in an Anchovy, take a Quarter of a Pound of Butter rolled in a little Flour, stir all together till it boils. You may add a little Juice of Lemon, Ketchup, Red Wine, and Wallnut Liquor, just as you please.

Plain Butter melted thick, with a Spoonful of Walnut-pickle, or Ketchup, is good Sauce, or Anchovy: In short, you may put as many Things as you fancy into Sauce; all other Sauces for Fish you have in the *Lent* Chapter.

To Dress a Brace of Carp *with* Gravy.

FIRST, knock the Carp on the Head, save all the Blood you can, scale it, and then gut it: Wash the Carp in a Pint of Red Wine, and the Rows; have some Water boiling with a Handful of Salt, a little Horse-raddish, and a Bundle of Sweet-herbs; put in your Carp, and boil it softly. When it is boiled, drain it well over the hot Water; in the mean time strain the Wine through a Sieve, put it into a Sauce-pan, with a Pint of good Gravy, two or three Blades of Mace, twelve Corns of black and twelve of white Pepper, six Cloves, an Anchovy, an Onion, and a little Bundle of Sweet Herbs; let them simmer very softly a Quarter of an Hour, then strain it, put it into the Sauce-pan again, and add to it two Spoonfuls of Ketchup, and a Quarter of a Pound of Butter rolled in a little Flour, half a Spoonful of Mushroom-pickle, if you have it, if not, the same Quantity of Lemon-juice; stir it all together, and let it boil. Boil one half of the Rows; the other half beat up with an Egg, half a Nutmeg grated, a little Lemon-peel cut fine, and a little Salt. Beat all well together, and have ready some nice Beef Dripping boiling in a Stew-pan, into which drop your Row, and fry them in little Cakes, about as big as a Crown-piece, of a fine light brown, and some Sippets cut thus △, and fry'd crisp, a few Oysters, if you have them, dipped in a little Batter, and fry'd brown, a good Handful of Parsley fry'd green.

Lay the Fish in the Dish, the boiled Rows on each Side, the Sippets standing round the Carp, pour the Sauce boiling hot over the Fish; lay the fry'd Rows and Oysters, with Parsley and scraped Horse-raddish, and Lemon between, all round the Dish; the rest of the Cakes and Oysters lay in the Dish, and send it to Table hot. If you would have the Sauce white, put in White Wine, and good strong Veal Gravy, with the above Ingredients. Dressed as in the *Lent* Chapter, is full as good, if your Beer is not bitter.

As to Dressing of Pike, and all other Fish, you have it in the *Lent* Chapter; only this, when you dress them with a Pudding, you may add a little Beef-suet cut very fine, and good Gravies in the Sauce.

CHAP.

CHAP. VI.

Of SOOPS and BROTHS.

To make Strong Broth for Soops or Gravy.

TAKE a Leg of Beef, chop it to Pieces, set it on the Fire in four Gallons of Water, scum it clean, season it with black and white Pepper three or four Ounces, a few Cloves, and a Bundle of Sweet Herbs: Let it boil till two Parts is wasted, then season it with Salt; let it boil a little while, then strain it off, and keep it for Use.

When you want very strong Gravy, take a Slice of Bacon, lay it in a Stew-pan, take a Pound of Beef, cut it thin, lay it on the Bacon, slice a good Piece of Carrot in, an Onion sliced, a good Crust of Bread, a few Sweet Herbs, a little Mace, Cloves, Nutmeg, and whole Pepper, an Anchovy, cover it, and set it on a slow Fire five or six Minutes, and pour into it a Quart of the above Beef Gravy. Cover it close, and let it boil softly till half is wasted. This will be a rich high brown Sauce for Fish, or Fowl, or Ragoo.

Gravy for White Sauce.

TAKE a Pound of any Part of the Veal, cut it into small Pieces, boil it in a Quart of Water, with an Onion, a Blade of Mace, two Cloves, and a few whole Pepper-Corns. Boil it till it is as rich as you would have it.

Gravy for Turkey, Fowl, or Ragoo.

TAKE a Pound of lean Beef, cut and hack it well; then flour it well, put a Piece of Butter as big as a Hen's Egg, in a Stew-pan; when it is melted, put in your Beef, fry it on all Sides a little brown, then pour in three Pints of boiling Water, and a Bundle of Sweet Herbs, two or three Blades of Mace, three or four Cloves, twelve whole Pepper-corns, a little Bit of Carrot, a little Piece of Crust of Bread toasted brown. Cover it close, and let it boil till there is about a Pint or less; then season it with Salt, and strain it off.

Gravy for a Fowl, when you have no Meat nor Gravy ready.

TAKE the Neck, Liver and Gizard, boil them in half a Pint of Water, with a little Piece of Bread toasted brown, a little Pepper and Salt, and a little Bit of Thyme. Let it boil till there is about a Quarter of a Pint, then pour in half a Glass of Red Wine, boil it and strain it, then bruise the Liver well in, and strain it again; thicken it with a little Piece of Butter rolled in Flour, and it will be very good.

An Ox's Kidney makes good Gravy, cut all to Pieces, and boiled with Spice, &c. as in the forgoing Receipts.

You have a Receipt in the Beginning of the Book, in the Preface, for Gravies.

To Make Mutton or Veal-Gravy.

CUT and hack your Veal well, set it on the Fire with Water, Sweet Herbs, Mace and Pepper. Let it boil till it is as good as you would have it, then strain it off. Your fine Cooks always, if they can, chop a Partridge or two, and put into Gravies.

To Make Strong Fish-Gravy.

TAKE two or three Eels, or any Fish you have, skin or scale them, and gut them, and wash them from Grit. Cut them into little Pieces, put them into a Sauce-pan, cover them with Water, a little Crust of Bread toasted brown, a Blade or two of Mace, and some whole Pepper, a few Sweet Herbs, a very little Bit of Lemon-peel; let it boil till it is rich and good, then have ready a Piece of Butter, according to your Gravy; if a Pint, as big as a Walnut. Melt it in the Sauce-pan, then shake in a little Flour, and toss it about till it is brown, and then strain in the Gravy to it. Let it boil a few Minutes, and it will be good.

Plum-Porridge for Christmas.

TAKE a Leg and Shin of Beef, put to them eight Gallons of Water, and boil them till they are very tender; and when the Broth is strong, strain it out; wipe the Pot, and put in the Broth again; slice six Penny-loaves thin, cutting off the Top and Bottom, put some of the Liquor to it,

cover

cover it up, and let it stand a Quarter of an Hour, boil it and strain it, and then put it in your Pot; let it boil a Quarter of an Hour, then put in five Pounds of Currants, clean washed and picked; let them boil a little, and put in five Pounds of Raisins of the Sun stoned, and two Pound of Pruens, and let them boil till they swell, then put in three Quarters of an Ounce of Mace, half an Ounce of Cloves, two Nutmegs, all of them beat fine, and mix it with a little Liquor cold, and put them in a very little while, and take off the Pot, and put in three Pounds of Sugar, a little Salt, a Quart of Sack, and a Quart of Claret, the Juice of two or three Lemons. You may thicken with Sego, instead of Bread, if you please; pour them into earthen Pans, and keep them for Use. You must boil two Pounds of Pruens in a Quart of Water, till they are tender, and strain them into the Pot, when it is a boiling.

To make Strong Broth to keep for Use.

TAKE Part of a Leg of Beef, and the Scrag-end of a Neck of Mutton, break the Bones in Pieces, and put to it as much Water as will cover it, and a little Salt; and when it boils, skim it clean, and put in to it a whole Onion stuck with Cloves, a Bunch of Sweet Herbs, some Pepper, a Nutmeg quartered; let these boil till the Meat is boiled in Pieces, and the Strength boiled out of it; then put to it three or four Anchovies, and when they are dissolved, strain it out, and keep it for Use.

A Crawfish Soop.

TAKE a Gallon of Water, and set it a boiling; put in it a Bunch of Sweet Herbs, three or four Blades of Mace, an Onion stuck with Cloves, Pepper and Salt; then have about 200 Crayfish, save out about twenty, then pick the rest from the Shells, save the Tails whole, the Body and Shells beat in a Mortar, with a Pint of Peas, green or dry, with half boiled tender in fair Water; put your boiling Water to it, and strain it boiling-hot through a Cloth, till you have all the Goodness out of it; then set it over a slow Fire or Stew-hole, then have ready a French Role, cut very thin, and let it be very dry, put it to your Soop, let it stew till half is wasted, then put a Piece of Butter as big as an Egg into a Sauce-pan, let it simmer till it has done making a Noise, then shake in two Tea Spoonfuls of Flour, stirring it about, and an Onion; put in the Tails of the Fish, give them a Shake round, put to them a Pint of good Gravy, let it boil four or five Minutes softly, take out the Onion, and put to it a Pint of the Soop, stir it well together, and pour it into your Soop, and let it simmer very softly a Quarter of an Hour. Fry a French Role very nice and brown, and the twenty Crawfish, pour your Soop into the Dish, and lay the Role in the Middle, and the Crawfish round the Dish.

Fine Cooks boil a Brace of Carp and Tench, and may be a Lobster or two, and many more rich Things, to make a Craw-fish-soop; but the above is full good, and wants no Addition.

A good Gravy Soop.

TAKE a Pound of Beef, a Pound of Veal, and a Pound of Mutton, cut and hacked all to Pieces, put it into two Gallons of Water, with an old Cock beat to Pieces, a Piece of Carrot, the Upper Crust of a Penny-loaf toasted very crisp, a little Bundle of Sweet Herbs, an Onion, a Tea Spoonful of black Pepper, and one of white Pepper, four or five Blades of Mace, and four Cloves. Cover it, and let it stew over a slow Fire, till half is wasted, then strain it off, and put it into a clean Sauce-pan, with two or three large Spoonfuls of Raspings clean sifted, half an Ounce of Truffles and Morels, three or four Heads of Salary washed very clean, and cut small an Ox's Palate, first boiled tender, and cut into Pieces, a few Cock's Combs, a few of the little Hearts of young Savoys, cover it close, and let it simmer very softly over a slow Fire two Hours; then have ready a French Role fry'd, and a few Forced-meat Balls fry'd, put them into your Dish, and pour in your Soop. You may boil a Leg of Veal, and a Leg of Beef, and as many fine Things as you please; but I believe you will find this rich and high enough.

You may leave out the Cock's Combs, and Pallates, Truffles, &c. If you don't like them, it will be a good Soop without them; and if you would have your Soop very clear, don't put in the Raspings.

Observe, if it be a China-dish not to pour your Soop in boiling-hot off the Fire, but set it down half a Minute, and put a Ladleful in first to warm the Dish, then pour it in; for if it be a Frost, the Bottom of your Dish will fly out. Vermeselly is good in it, an Ounce put in just before you take it up, let it boil four or five Minutes.

You may make this Soop of Beef, or Veal alone, just as you fancy. A Leg of Beef will do without either Veal, Mutton, or Fowl.

A Green Peas Soop.

TAKE a small Nuckle of Veal, about three or four Pounds, chop it all to Pieces, set it on the Fire in six Quarts of Water, a little Piece of lean Bacon, about half an Ounce steeped in Vinegar an Hour, four or five Blades of Mace, three or four Cloves, twelve Pepper-corns of black Pepper, twelve of white, a little Bundle of Sweet Herbs and Parsley, a little Piece of Upper Crust toasted crisp, cover it close, and let it boil softly over a slow Fire, till half is wasted; then strain it off, and put to it a Pint of Green Peas, and a Lettice cut small, four Heads of Salary cut very small, and washed clean.

clean. Cover it close, and let it stew very softly over a slow Fire two Hours; in the mean time boil a Pint of Old Peas in a Pint of Water very tender, and strain them well through a coarse Hair-sieve, and all the Pulp, then pour it into the Soop, and let it boil together. Season with Salt to your Palate; but not too much. Fry a *French* Role crisp, put it in your Dish, and pour your Soop in; be sure there be full two Quarts.

Mutton-Gravy will do, if you have no Veal; or a Shin of Beef chopped to Pieces: A few Asparagus Tops are very good in it.

A White Peas Soop.

TAKE about three Pounds of thick Flank of Beef, or any lean Part of the Leg chopped to Pieces; set it on the Fire in three Gallons of Water, about half a Pound of Bacon, a small Bundle of Sweet Herbs, a good deal of dried Mint; take a Bunch of Salary, wash it very clean, put in the green Tops, and a Quart of Split-peas, cover it close, and let it boil till two Parts is wasted; then strain it off, and put it into a clean Sauce-pan, five or six Heads of Salary cut small, and washed clean, cover it close, and let it boil till there is about three Quarts; then cut some fat and lean Bacon in Dice, some Bread in Dice, and fry them just crisp; throw them into your Dish, season your Soop with Salt, and pour it into your Dish, rub a little dried Mint over it, and send it to Table. You may add Force-meat Balls fry'd, Cock's Combs boiled in it, and an Ox's Palate stewed tender and cut small. Stewed Spinage well drained, and laid round the Dish is very pretty.

Another Way to make it.

WHEN you boil a Leg of Pork, or a good Piece of Beef, save the Liquor. When it is cold, take off the Fat, the next Day boil a Leg of Mutton, save the Liquor, and when it is cold, take off the Fat, set it on the Fire, with two Quarts of Peas; let them boil till they are tender, then put in the Pork or Beef Liquor, with the Ingredients as above, and let it boil till it is as thick as you would have it, allowing for the boiling again; then strain it off, and add the Ingredients as above. You may make your Soop of Veal or Mutton-Gravy if you please, that is according to your Fancy.

A Chesnut Soop.

TAKE half a hundred Chesnuts, pick them, put them in an Earthen Pan, and set them in the Oven half an Hour, or roast them gently over a slow Fire; but take care they don't burn; then peel them, and set them to stew in a Quart of good Beef, Veal, or Mutton-broth, till they are quite tender. In the mean time, take a Slice or two of Ham, or Bacon, a Pound of Veal, and a Pigeon beat to Pieces, a Bundle of Sweet Herbs, an Onion, a little Pepper and Mace, a Piece of Carrot; lay the Bacon at the Bottom of a Stew-pan, and lay the Meat and Ingredients at Top. Set it over a slow Fire, till it begins to stick to the Pan, then put in a Crust of Bread, and pour in two Quarts of Broth; let it boil softly till one Third is wasted; then strain it off, and add it to the Chesnuts. Season it with Salt, and let it boil till it is well tasted, stew two Pigeons in it, and a fry'd *French* Role crisp; lay the Roll in the Middle of the Dish, and the Pigeons on each Side; pour in your Soop, and send it away hot.

A *French* Cook wil beat a Pheasant and a Brace of Partridges to Pieces, and put to it. Garnish your Dish with hot Chesnuts.

To Make Mutton Broth.

TAKE a Neck a Mutton about six Pounds, cut it in two, boil the Scrag, in a Gallon of Water, skim it well, then put in a little Bundle of Sweet Herbs, an Onion, and a good Crust of Bread. Let it boil an Hour, then put in the other Part of the Mutton, a Turnip or two, some dried Merry-golds, a few Clives chopped fine, a little Parsley chopped small; put these in about a Quarter of an Hour before your Broth is enough; season it with Salt, or you may put in a Quarter of a Pound of Barley, or Rice at first. Some love it thickened with Oatmeal, and some with Bread, and some love it seasoned with Mace, instead of Sweet Herbs and Onion. All this is Fancy and different Palates. If you boil Turnips for Sauce, don't boil all in the Pot, it makes the Broth too strong of them, but boil them in a Sauce-pan.

Beef Broth.

TAKE a Leg of Beef, crack the Bone in two or three Parts, wash it clean, put it into a Pot with a Gallon of Water, skim it well, then put in two or three Blades of Mace, a little Bundle of Parsley, and a good Crust of Bread. Let it boil till the Beef is quite tender, and the Sinews. Toast some Bread, and cut it in Dice, and lay in your Dish; lay in the Meat, and pour the Soop in.

To Make Scotch Barley Broth.

TAKE a Leg of Beef, chop it all to Pieces, boil it in three Gallons of Water, with a Piece of Carrot and a Cruft of Bread, till it is half boiled away; then ftrain it off, and put it into the Pot again, with half a Pound of Barley, four or five Heads of Salary wafhed clean and cut fmall, a large Onion, a Bundle of Sweet Herbs, and a little Parfley chopped fmall, and a few Marigolds. Let this boil an Hour; take a Cock, or large Fowl, clean picked and wafhed, and put into the Pot; boil it till the Broth is quite good, then feafon with Salt, and fend it to Table, with the Fowl in the Middle. This Broth is very good without the Fowl; take out the Onion and Sweet Herbs, before you fend it to Table.

Some make this Broth with a Sheep's-Head, inftead of a Leg of Beef, and it is very good; but you muft chop the Head all to Pieces. The thick Flank about fix Pounds to fix Quarts of Water, makes good Broth; but then put the Barley in with the Meat, firft skim it well, boil it an Hour very foftly, then put in the above Ingredients, with Turnips, and Carrots clean fcraped and pared, and cut in little Pieces. Boil all together foftly, till the Broth is very good; then feafon it with Salt, and fend it to Table, with the Beef in the Middle, Turnips and Carrots round, and pour the Broth over all.

To Make Hodge-Podge.

TAKE a Piece of Beef, Fat and Lean together about a Pound, a Pound of Veal, a Pound of Scrag of Mutton, cut all into little Pieces, fet it on the Fire, with two Quarts of Water, an Ounce of Barley, an Onion, a little Bundle of Sweet Herbs, three or four Heads of Salary wafhed clean, and cut fmall, a little Mace, two or three Cloves, fome whole Pepper, tied all in a Muflin Rag, and put to the Meat three Turnips pared and cut in two, a large Carrot fcraped clean, and cut in fix Pieces, a little Lettice cut fmall, put all in the Pot, and cover it clofe. Let it ftew very foftly over a flow Fire five or fix Hours; take out the Spice, Sweet Herbs, and Onion, and pour all into a Soop-difh, and fend it to Table; firft feafon it with Salt. Half a Pint of Green Peas, when it is the Seafon for them, is very good. If you let this boil faft, it will wafte too much; therefore you cannot do it too flow, if it does but fimmer: All other Stews you have in the foregoing Chapter; and *Soops* in the Chapter of *Lent*.

To make Pocket Soop.

TAKE a Leg of Veal, ftrip off all the Skin and Fat, then take all the mufcular or flefhy Parts clean from the Bones. Boil this Flefh in three or four Gallons of Water till it comes to a ftrong Jelly, and that the Meat is good for nothing. Be fure to keep the Pot clofe covered, and not do too faft; take a little out in a Spoon now and then, and when you find it is a good rich Jelly, ftrain it through a Sieve into a clean earthen Pan. When it is cold, take off all the Skim and Fat from the Top, then provide a large deep Stew-pan with Water boiling over a Stove, then take fome deep China-cups, or well glazed Earthen Ware, and fill thefe Cups with the Jelly, which you muft take clear from the Settling at the Bottom, and fet them in the Stew-pan of Water. Take great Care none of the Water gets into the Cups; if it does, it will fpoil it. Keep the Water boiling gently all the time, till the Jelly becomes thick as Glew; then take them out, and let them ftand to cool; then turn the Glew out into fome new coarfe Flannel, which draws out all the Moifture; turn them in fix or eight Hours on frefh Flannel, and fo do till they are quite dry. Keep it in a dry warm Place, and in a little time it will be like a dry hard Piece of Glew, which you may carry in your Pocket, without getting any Harm. The beft Way is to put it into little Tin Boxes. When you ufe it, boil about a Pint of Water, and pour it on a Piece of Glew about as big as a fmall Wallnut, ftirring all the time till it is melted. Seafon with Salt to your Palate; and if you chufe any Herbs, or Spice, boil them in the Water firft, then pour the Water over the Glew.

To make Portable Soop.

TAKE two Legs of Beef, about fifty Pounds Weight, take off all the Skin and Fat as well as you can, then take all the Meat and Sinews clean from the Bones, which Meat put into a large Pot, and put to it eight or nine Gallons of foft Water; firft make it boil, then put in twelve Anchovies, an Ounce of Mace, a Quarter of an Ounce of Cloves, an Ounce of whole Pepper black and white together, fix large Onions peeled, and cut in two, a little Bundle of Thyme, Sweet Margoram, and Winter-favory, the dry hard Cruft of a Two-penny Loaf, ftir it all together, and cover it clofe, lay a Weight on the Cover to keep it clofe down, and let it boil foftly for eight or nine Hours, then uncover it, and ftir it together. Cover it clofe again, and let it boil till it is a very rich good Jelly, which you will know by taking a little out now and then, and let it cool. When you find it is a thick Jelly, take it off and ftrain it through a coarfe Hair-bag, and prefs it hard; then ftrain it through a Hair-fieve into a large Earthen Pan, when it is quite cold, take off all the Skim and Fat, and take the fine Jelly clear from the Settlings at Bottom, and put the Jelly into a large deep well-tinned Stew-pan. Set it over a Stove with a flow Fire,

Fire, keep stirring it often, take great Care it neither sticks to the Pan, or burns; and when you find the Jelly is very stiff and thick, as it will be in Lumps about the Pan, take it out, and put it into large deep China-Cups, or well-glazed Earthen Ware. Fill the Pan two Thirds full with Water, when the Water boils, set in your Cups, be sure no Water gets into the Cups, keep the Water boiling softly all the time, till you find the Jelly is like a stiff Glew; then take out the Cups, and when they are cool, turn out the Glew into coarse new Flannel. Let it lay eight or nine Hours, keeping it in a dry, warm Place, and turn it on fresh Flannel till it is quite dry, and the Glew will be quite hard; then put it into clean new Stone-pots, keep it close coloured from Dust and Dirt, and in a dry Place, where no Damp can come to it.

When you use it, pour boiling Water on it, and stir it all the time till it is melted. Season it with Salt to your Palate; a Piece as big as a large Walnut, will make a Pint of Water very rich; but as to that you are to make it as good as you please; if for Soop, fry a *French* Role and lay in the Middle of the Dish, when the Glew is dissolved in the Water, give it a boil, and pour it into the Dish; if you chuse it for Change, you may boil either Rice, Barley, or Vermecilly, Salary cut small, Truffles or Morels; but let them be very tenderly boiled in the Water before you stir in the Glew, and then give it a boil all together. You may, when you would have it very fine, add Force-meat Balls, Cock's Combs, or a Palate boiled very tender, and cut into little Bits; but it will be very rich and good without any of these Ingredients.

If for Gravy, pour the boiling Water on to what Quantity you think proper; and when it is dissolved, add what Ingredients you please, as in other Sauces. This is only in the room of a rich good Gravy; or you may make your Sauce either weak or strong, by adding more or less.

Rules to be observed in Soops or Broths.

First take great Care the Pots or Sauce-pans, and Covers be very clean, and free from all Grease and Sand, and that they be well tinned, for fear of giving the Broths or Soops any brassy Taste; and if you have time to stew as softly as you can, it will both have a finer Flavour, and the Meat will be tenderer. But then observe, when you make Soops or Broths for present Use, and if it is to be done softly, don't put much more Water than you intend to have Soop or Broth; and if you have the Convenience of an Earthen Pan or Pipkin, and set on Wood Embers till it boils, then skim it, and put in your Seasoning. Cover it close, and set it in Ember, so that it may do very softly for some time, and both the Meat and Broth will be delicious. You must observe in all Broths and Soop, that one thing does not taste more than another; but that the Taste be equal, and have a fine agreeable Relish, according to what you design it for; and be sure, that all the Greens and Herbs you put in be cleaned washed and picked.

CHAP. VI.

Of PUDDINGS.

An Oat Pudding *to* Bake.

OF Oats decoticated take two Pounds, and of new Milk enough to drown it, eight Ounces of Raisins of the Sun stoned, an equal Quantity of Currants neatly picked, a Pound of sweet Suet finely shread, six new-laid Eggs well beat; season with Nutmeg and beaten Ginger and Salt, mix it all well together, it will make a better Pudding than Rice.

To Make Calf's-Foot Pudding.

TAKE of Calves-Feet one Pound minced very fine, the Fat and the Brown to be taken out, Suet a Pound and half, pick off all the Skin, and shread it small, six Eggs, but half the Whites, beat them well, the Crumb of a Halfpenny Role grated, a Pound of Currants clean picked, and washed and rubbed in a Cloth, Milk, as much as will moisten it with the Eggs, a Handful of Flour, a little Salt, Nutmeg, and Sugar to season it to your Taste. Boil it nine Hours with your Meat; when it is done, lay it in your Dish, and pour melted Butter over it. It is very good with White Wine and Sugar in the Butter.

To Make a Pith Pudding.

TAKE the Quantity of the Pith of an Ox, and let it lay all Night in Water to soak out the Blood; the next Morning strip it out of the Skin, and beat it with the Back of a Spoon in Orangewater, till it is as fine as Pap; then take three Pints of thick Cream, and boil in it, two or three Blades of Mace, a Nutmeg quartered, a Stick of Cinnamon; then take half a Pound of the best Jordan

Almonds,

Almonds, blanched in cold Water, then beat them with a little of the Cream, and as it dries put in more Cream, and when they are all beaten, strain the Cream from them to the Pith, then take the Yolks of ten Eggs, the Whites of but two, beat them very well, and put them to the Ingredients: Take a Spoonful of grated Bread, or Naples Biscuit, mingle all these together, with half a Pound of fine Sugar, and the Marrow of four large Bones, and a little Salt; fill them in a small Ox or Hog's Guts, or bake it in a Dish, with a Puff-paste under it and round the Edges.

To make a Marrow-Pudding.

TAKE a Quart of Cream, and three Naples Biskets, a Nutmeg grated, the Yolks of ten Eggs, the Whites of five well beat, and Sugar to your Taste; mix all well together, and put a little Bit of Butter in the Bottom of your Sauce-pan, then put in your Stuff, and set it over the Fire, and stir it till it is pretty thick, then pour it into your Pan, with a Quarter of a Pound of Currants, that have been plumped in hot Water, stir it together, and let it stand all Night. The next Day put some fine Paste and lay at the Bottom of your Dish, and round the Edges; when the Oven is ready, pour in your Stuff, and lay long Pieces of Marrow on the Top. Half an Hour will bake it. You may use the Stuff when cold.

A Boiled Suet-Pudding.

TAKE a Quart of Milk, a Pound of Suet shread small, four Eggs, two Spoonfuls of beaten Ginger, or one of beaten Pepper, a Tea Spoonful of Salt, mix the Eggs and Flower with a Pint of the Milk very thick, and the Seasoning mix in the rest of the Milk and the Suet. Let your Batter be pretty thick, and boil it two Hours.

A Boiled Plumb-Pudding.

TAKE a Pound of Suet cut in little Pieces, not too fine, a Pound of Currants, and a Pound of Raisins stoned, eight Eggs, half the Whites, the Crumb of a Penny-loaf grated fine, half a Nutmeg grated, and a Tea Spoonful of beaten Ginger, a little Salt, a Pound of Flour, a Pint of Milk; beat the Eggs first, then half the Milk, beat them together, and by degrees stir in the Flour and Bread together, then the Suet, Spice and Fruit, and as much Milk as will mix it all well together and very thick; boil it five Hours.

A Yorkshire Pudding.

TAKE a Quart of Milk, four Eggs, and a little Salt, make it up into a thick Batter with Flour, like a Pancake Batter. You must have a good Piece of Meat at the Fire, take a Stew-pan and put some Dripping in, set it on the Fire, when it boils, pour in your Pudding, let it bake on the Fire till you think it is nigh enough; then turn a Plate upside-down in the Dripping-pan, that the Dripping may not be blacked; set your Stew-pan on it under your Meat, and let the Dripping drop on the Pudding, and the Heat of the Fire come to it, to make it of a fine brown. When your Meat is done and set to Table, drain all the Fat from your Pudding, and set it on the Fire again to dry a little; then slide it as dry as you can into a Dish, melt some Butter, and pour into a Cup, and set in the Middle of the Pudding. It is an exceeding good Pudding, the Gravy of the Meat eats well with it.

A Stake-Pudding.

MAKE a good Crust with Suet shread fine with Flour, and mix it up with cold Water. Season it with a little Salt, and make a pretty stiff Crust, about two Pounds of Suet, to a Quarter of a Peck of Flour. Let your Stakes be either Beef or Mutton, well seasoned with Pepper and Salt, make it up as you do an Apple-pudding, tye it in a Cloth, and put it into the Water boiling. If it be a large Pudding, it will take five Hours; if a small one, three Hours. This is the best Crust for a Apple-pudding. Pigeons eat well this Way.

A Vermicella Pudding, with Marrow.

FIRST make your Vermicella, take the Yolks of two Eggs, and mix it up with just as much Flour as will make it to a stiff Paste; roll it out as thin as a Wafer, let it lye to dry till you can roll it up close without breaking, then with a sharp Knife cut it very thin, beginning at the little End. Have ready some Water boiling, into which throw the Vermicella, let it boil a Minute or two at most, then throw it into a Sieve, have ready a Pound of Marrow, lay a Layer of Marrow, and a Layer of Vermicella, and so on till all is laid in the Dish. When it is a little cool, beat it up very well together, take ten Eggs, beat them and mix them with the other, grate the Crumb of a Penny-loaf, and mix with it a Gill of Sack, Brandy, or a little Rose-water, a Tea Spoonful of Salt, a small Nutmeg grated, a little grated Lemon-peel, two large Blades of Mace dried, and beat fine, half a Pound of Currans clean washed and picked, half a Pound of Raisins stoned, mix all well together, and sweeten to your Palate; lay a good thin Crust at the Buttom and Sides of the Dish; pour in the Ingredients, and bake it an Hour and half in an Oven not too hot. You may either put Marrow or Beef-fuet shread fine, or a Pound of Butter, which you please. When it comes out of the Oven, strew some fine Sugar over it, and send it to Table. You may leave out the Fruit if you please, and you may for Change add half an Ounce of Citron, and half an Ounce of candied Orange-peel shread fine.

Suet-Dumplings.

TAKE a Pint of Milk, four Eggs, a Pound of Suet, and a Pound of Currans, two Tea Spoonfuls of Salt, three of Ginger: First take half the Milk, and mix it like a thick Batter, then put the Eggs, and the Salt and Ginger, then the rest of the Milk by degrees, with the Suet and Currans, and Flour to make it like a light Paste. When the Water boils, make them in Rolls as big as a large Turkey's Egg, with a little Flour; then flat them, and throw them into boiling Water. Move them softly, that they don't stick together; keep the Water boiling all the time, and half an Hour will boil them.

An Oxford Pudding.

A Quarter of a Pound of Bisket grated; a Quarter of a Pound of Currans, clean washed and picked; a Quarter of a Pound of Suet, shread small; half a large Spoonful of Powder-sugar; a very little Salt, and some grated Nutmeg; mix all well together, then take two Yolks of Eggs, and make it up in Balls, as big as a Turkey's Egg. Fry them in fresh Butter of a fine light brown; for Sauce have melted Butter and Sugar, with a little Sack or White Wine. You must mind to keep the Pan shaking about, that they may be all of a fine light brown.

All other Puddings you have in the *Lent* Chapter.

Rules to be observed in making Puddings, &c.

In boiled Puddings, take great Care the Bag or Cloth be very clean, and not soapy, and dipped in hot Water, and then well floured. If a Bread-pudding, tye it loose; if a Batter-pudding, tye it close; and be sure the Water boils when you put the Pudding in, and you should move your Puddings in the Pot now and then, for fear they stick. When you make a Batter-pudding, first mix the Flour well with a little Milk, then put in the Ingredients by degrees, and it will be smooth and not have Lumps; but for a plain Batter-pudding, the best way is to strain it through a coarse Hair Sieve, that it may neither have Lumps, nor the Treadles of the Eggs: And all other Puddings, strain the Eggs when they are beat. If you boil them in Wooden-bowls, or China-dishes, butter the Inside before you put in your Batter: And all baked Puddings, butter the Pan or Dish, before the Pudding is put in.

CHAP. VIII.

OF PIES.

To make a very fine Sweet Lamb or Veal Pye.

SEASON your Lamb with Salt, Pepper, Cloves, Mace and Nutmeg, all beat fine, to your Palate. Cut your Lamb, or Veal, into little Pieces, make a good Puff-paste Crust, lay it into your Dish, then lay in your Meat, strew on it some stoned Raisins and Currans clean washed, and some Sugar; then lay on it some Forced-meat Balls made sweet, and in the Summer some Artichoke-bottoms boiled, and scalded Grapes in the Winter. Boil *Spanish* Potatoes cut in Pieces, candied Citron, candied Orange, and Lemon-peel, and three or four large Blades of Mace; put Butter on the Top, close up your Pye, and bake it. Have ready against it comes out of the Oven a Caudle made thus: Take a Pint of White Wine, and mix in the Yolks of three Eggs, stir it well together over the Fire, one way, all the time till it is thick; then take it off, stir in Sugar enough to sweeten it, and squeeze in the Juice of a Lemon; pour it hot into your Pye, and close it up again. Send it hot to Table.

To make pretty Sweet Lamb or Veal Pye.

FIRST make a good Crust, butter the Dish, and lay in your Bottom and Side-crust; then cut your Meat into small Pieces; season with a very little Salt, some Mace and Nutmeg beat fine, and strewed over; then lay a Layer of Meat, and strew according to your Fancy, some Currans, clean washed and picked, and a few Raisins stoned, all over the Meat; lay another Layer of Meat; put a little Butter at the Top, and a little Water, just enough to bake it and no more. Have ready against it comes out of the Oven, a White Wine Caudle made very sweet, and send it to Table hot.

A Savoury Veal Pye.

TAKE a Breast of Veal, cut it into Pieces, season it with Pepper and Salt, lay it all into your Crust, boil six or eight Eggs hard, take only the Yolk, put them into the Pye here and there, fill your Dish almost full of Water, put on the Lid, and bake it well.

To make a Savoury Lamb or Veal Pye.

MAKE a good Puff-paste Crust, cut your Meat into Pieces, season it to your Palate with Pepper, Salt, Mace, Cloves, and Nutmeg finely beat; so lay it into your Crust, with a few Lamb-Stones, and Sweet-Breads seasoned as your Meat; also some Oysters and Force-meat Balls, hard Yolks of Eggs, and the Tops of Asparagus two Inches long, first boiled green; then put Butter all over the Pye, put on the Lid, and set it in a quick Oven an Hour and half; then have ready the Liquor, made thus: Take a Pint of Gravy, and the Oyster-liquor, and a Gill of Red Wine, a little grated Nutmeg, mix all together with the Yolks of two or three Eggs beat, and keep it stirring all one way all the time. When it boils, pour it into your Pye. Put on the Lid again. Send it hot to Table. You must make Liquor according to your Pye.

A Calf's-Foot Pye.

FIRST set four Calves Feet on in a Sauce-pan in three Quarts of Water, with three or four Blades of Mace; let them boil softly, till there is about a Pint and half, then take out your Feet, strain the Liquor, and make a good Crust. Cover your Dish, then pick off the Flesh from the Bones; lay half in the Dish, strew half a Pound of Currans clean washed and picked over, and half a Pound of Raisins stoned; lay on the rest of the Meat, then skim the Liquor, sweeten it to the Palate, and put in half a Pint of White Wine, pour it into the Dish, put on your Lid, and bake it an Hour and half.

To make an Olive-Pye.

MAKE your Crust ready, then take the thin Collops of the But-end of a Leg of Veal, as many as you think will fill your Pye. Hack them with the Back of a Knife, and season them with Salt, Pepper, Cloves and Mace; wash over your Collops with a Bunch of Feathers dipped in Eggs, and have in Readiness a good Handful of Sweet Herbs shread small; the Herbs must be Thyme, Parsley and Spinage, and the Yolks of eight hard Eggs minced, and a few Oysters parboiled and chopped, some Beef-suet shread very fine; mix these together, and strew them over your Collops, and sprinkle a little Orange Flour-water over them, and roll the Collops up very close, and lay them in your Pye; strewing the Seasoning over that is left, put Butter on the Top, and close up your Pye. When it comes out of the Oven, have ready some Gravy hot, and pour into your Pye; one Anchovy dissolved in the Gravy, pour it in boiling-hot; you may put in Artichoke-bottoms and Chesnuts, if you please. You may leave out the Orange-flower Water, if you don't like it.

To Season an Egg-Pye.

BOIL twelve Eggs hard, and shread them, with one Pound of Beef-suet, or Marrow shread fine; season them with a little Cinnamon and Nutmeg, beat fine, one Pound of Currans clean washed and picked, two or three Spoonfuls of Cream, and a little Sack and Rose-water, mix all together, and fill the Pye. When it is baked, stir in half a Pound of fresh Butter, and the Juice of a Lemon.

To make a Mutton-Pye.

TAKE a Loin of Mutton, take off the Skin and Fat of the Inside, cut it into Stakes, season it well with Pepper and Salt to your Palate; lay it into your Crust, fill it, pour in as much Water as will almost fill the Dish; then put on the Crust, and bake it well.

A Beef-Stake-Pye.

TAKE fine Rump-Stakes, beat them with the Rolling-pin, then season them with Pepper and Salt, according to your Palate, make a good Crust, lay in your Stakes, fill your Dish, then pour in as much Water, as will half fill the Dish. Put on the Crust, and bake it well.

A Ham-Pye.

TAKE some cold boiled Ham, and slice it about half an Inch thick, make a good Crust, and thick, cover the Dish, and lay a Layer of Ham, shake a little Pepper over it, then take a large young Fowl clean picked, gutted, washed, and singed; put a little Pepper and Salt in the Belly, and rub a very little Salt on the Outside, lay the Fowl on the Ham, boil some Eggs hard, put in the Yolks, and cover all with Ham; shake some Pepper on the Ham, and put on the Top-crust. Bake it well, have ready when it comes out of the Oven, some very rich Beef-gravy, enough to fill the Pye, lay on the Crust again, and send in to Table hot. A fresh Ham will not be so tender; so that I always

ways boil my Ham one Day, and bring it to Table, and the next Day make a Pye of it. It does better than an unboiled Ham; if you put two large Fowls in, they will make a fine Pye, but that is according to your Company more or less; the larger the Pye, the finer the Meat eats; and the Crust must be the same you make for a Venison-Pasty. You should pour a little small Gravy into the Pye when you make it, just to bake the Meat, and then fill it up when it comes out of the Oven. Boil some Truffles and Morells, and put into the Pye, is a great Addition, and fresh Mushrooms, or dried ones.

A Pigeon-Pye.

MAKE a Puff-paste Crust, cover your Dish, let your Pigeons be very nicely picked and cleaned, season them with Pepper and Salt, and put a good Piece of fine fresh Butter with Pepper and Salt in the Bellies; lay them in your Pan, the Necks, Gizards, Livers, and Pinions, and Hearts lay between, with the Yolk of a hard Egg, a Beef-stake in the Middle; put as much Water as will almost fill the Dish, lay on the Top-Crust, and bake it well. This is the best Way to make a Pigeon-pye; but the *French* fill the Pigeons with a very high Force-meat, and lay Force-meat round the Inside with Ball, Asparagus-tops, and Artichoke-bottoms, and Mushrooms, Truffles and Morells, and season high; but that is according to different Palates.

To make a Gibblet-Pye.

TAKE two Pair of Gibblets nicely cleaned, put all but the Liver into a Sauce-pan, with two Quarts of Water, twenty Corns of whole Pepper, three Blades of Mace, a Bundle of Sweet Herbs, and a large Onion. Cover them close, and let them stew very softly till they are quite tender; then have a good Crust ready, cover your Dish, lay a fine Rump-stake at the Bottom, seasoned with Pepper and Salt; then lay in your Gibblets with the Liver, and strain the Liquor they were stewed in; season it with Salt, and pour into your Pye, put on the Lid, and bake it an Hour and half.

A Duck-Pye.

MAKE a Puff paste Crust, take a Couple of Ducks, scald them, and make them very clean, cut off the Feet, the Pinions, the Neck and Head, all clean picked and scalded, with the Gizard, Liver and Hearts; pick out all the Fat of the Inside, lay a Crust all over the Dish, season the Ducks with Pepper and Salt, inside and out, lay them in your Dish, and the Gibblets at each End seasoned; put in as much Water as will almost fill the Pye, lay on the Crust, and bake it, but not too much.

A Chicken-Pye.

MAKE a Puff-paste Crust, take two young Chickens, cut them to Pieces, season them with Pepper and Salt, a little beaten Mace, lay a Force-meat made thus round the Side of the Dish. Take half a Pound of Veal, half a Pound of Suet, beat them quite fine in a Marble Mortar, with as many Crumbs of Bread; season it with a very little Pepper and Salt, an Anchovy with the Liquor, cut the Anchovy to Pieces, a little Lemon-peel, cut very fine and thread small, a very little Thyme, mix all together with the Yolk of an Egg, make some into round Balls about twelve, the rest lay round the Dish. Lay in one Chicken over the Bottom of the Dish; take two Sweet-breads, cut them into five or six Pieces, lay them all over, season them with Pepper and Salt, strew over them half an Ounce of Truffles and Morells, two or three Artichoke-bottoms cut to Pieces, a few Cock's Combs, if you have them, a Palate boiled tender and cut to Pieces; then lay on the other Part of the Chicken, put half a Pint of Water in, and cover the Pye. Bake it well, and when it comes out of the Oven, fill it with good Gravy, lay on the Crust, and send it to Table.

A Cheshire Pork-Pye.

TAKE a Loin of Pork, skin it, cut it into Stakes, season it with Salt, Nutmeg, and Pepper; make a good Crust, lay a Layer of Pork, and then a large Layer of Pippins pared and cored, a little Sugar, enough to sweeten the Pye, then another Layer of Pork; put in half a Pint of White Wine, lay some Butter on the Top, and close your Pye: If your Pye be large, it will take a Pint of White Wine.

A Devonshire Squab-Pye.

MAKE a good Crust, cover the Dish all over, put at the Bottom a Layer of sliced Pippins, strew over them some Sugar, then a Layer of Mutton-stakes, cut from the Loin, well seasoned with Pepper and Salt, then another Layer of Pippins; peel some Onions and slice them thin, lay a Layer all over the Apples, then a Layer of Mutton, then Pippins and Onions; pour in a Pint of Water, so close your Pye and bake it.

A Shropshire Pye.

FIRST make a good Puff-paste Crust, then cut a Couple of Rabbits to Pieces, with two Pounds of fat Pork cut in little Pieces, season both with Pepper and Salt to your liking, then cover your Dish with Crust, and lay in your Rabbits. Mix the Pork with them, take the Livers of the Rabbits, parboil them, and beat them in a Mortar, with as much fat Bacon, and a little Sweet Herbs, some Oysters if you have them; season with Pepper, and Salt, and Nutmeg; mix it up with Yolk of Egg, and make it into Balls; lay them here and there in your Pye, some Artichoke-bottoms cut in Dice, and Cock's Combs, if you have them; grate a small Nutmeg over the Meat, pour in half a Pint of Red Wine, and half a Pint of Water; close your Pye, and bake it an Hour and half in a quick Oven, but not too fierce an Oven.

A Yorkshire Christmas-Pye.

FIRST make a good Standing Crust, let the Wall and Bottom be very thick, bone a Turkey, a Goose, a Fowl, a Partridge, and a Pigeon, season them all very well, take half an Ounce of Mace, half an Ounce of Nutmegs, a quarter of an Ounce of Cloves, half an Ounce of black Pepper, all beat fine together, two large Spoonfuls of Salt, mix them together. Open the Fowls all down the Back, and bone them; first the Pigeon, then the Partridge, cover them; then the Fowl, then the Goose, and then the Turkey, which must be large; season them all well first, and lay them in the Crust, so as it will look only like a whole Turkey; then have a Hare ready cased, and wiped with a clean Cloth. Cut it to Pieces, that is jointed; season it, and lay it as close as you can on one Side; on the other Side Woodcock, more Game, and what Sort of wild Fowl you can get. Season them well, and lay them close; put at least four Pounds of Butter into the Pye, then lay on your Lid, which must be a very thick one, and let it be well baked. It must have a very hot Oven, and will take at least four Hours.

This Pye will take a Bushel of Flour; in this Chapter, you will see how to make it. These Pies are often sent to *London* in a Box as Presents; therefore the Walls must be well built.

A Goose-Pye.

HALF a Peck of Flower will make the Walls of a Goose-pye, made as in the Receipts for Crust. Raise your Crust just big enough to hold a large Goose; first have a pickled dried Tongue, boiled tender enough to peel, cut off the Root, bone a Goose, and a large Fowl; take half a Quarter of an Ounce of Mace beat fine, a large Tea Spoonful of beaten Pepper, three Tea Spoonfuls of Salt, mix all together, season your Fowl and Goose with it, then lay the Fowl in the Goose, and the Tongue in the Fowl, and the Goose in the same Form as if whole. Put half a Pound of Butter on the Top, and lay on the Lid. This Pye is delicious, either hot or cold, and will keep a great while. A Slice of this Pye, cut down a-cross, makes a pretty little Side-dish for Supper.

To Make a Venison-Pasty.

TAKE a Neck and Breast of Venison, bone it, season it with Pepper and Salt according to your Palate. Cut the Breast in two or three Pieces; but don't cut the Fat off the Neck if you can help it. Lay in the Breast and Neck-end first, and the best End of the Neck on the Top, that the Fat may be whole; make a good rich Puff-paste Crust, let it be very thick on the Sides, a good Bottom-crust, and a thick Top. Cover the Dish, then lay in your Venison, put in half a Pound of Butter, about a quarter of a Pint of Water, close your Pasty, and let it be baked two Hours in a very quick Oven. In the mean time set on the Bones of the Venison in two Quarts of Water, with two or three Blades of Mace, an Onion, a little Piece of Crust baked crisp and brown, a little whole Pepper, cover it close, and let it boil softly over a slow Fire, till above half is wasted, then strain it off. When the Pasty comes out of the Oven, lift up the Lid, and pour in the Gravy.

When your Venison is not fat enough, take the Fat of a Loin of Mutton, steeped in a little rap Vinegar and Red Wine twenty-four Hours, then lay it on the Top of the Venison, and close your Pasty. It is a wrong Notion of some People, to think Venison cannot be baked enough, and will first bake it in a false Crust, and then bake it in the Pasty; by this time the fine Flavour of the Venison is gone. No, if you want it to be very tender, wash it in warm Milk and Water, dry it in clean Cloths till it is very dry, then rub it all over with Vinegar, and hang it in the Air. Keep it as long as you think proper, it will keep thus a Fortnight good; but be sure there be no Moistness about it; if there is, you must dry it well, and throw Ginger over it, and it will keep a long time. When you use it, just dip it in luke-warm Water, and dry it. Bake it in a quick Oven; if it is a large Pasty, it will take three Hours; then your Venison will be tender, and have all the fine Flavour. The Shoulder makes a pretty Pasty boned, and made as above with the Mutton Fat.

A Loyn of Mutton makes a fine Pasty: Take a large fat Loin of Mutton, let it hang four or five Days, then bone it, leaving the Meat as whole as you can; lay the Meat twenty-four Hours in half a Pint of Red Wine, and half a Pint of rap Vinegar; then take it out of the Pickle, and order it as you do a Pasty, and boil the Bones in the same manner to fill the Pasty, when it comes out of the Oven.

A Calf's-Head Pye.

CLEANSE your Head very well, and boil it till it is tender; then carefully take off the Flesh as whole as you can; take out the Eyes, and slice the Tongue; make a good Puff-paste Crust, cover the Dish, lay in your Meat, throw over it the Tongue, lay the Eyes cut in two, at each Corner; season it with a very little Pepper and Salt, pour in half a Pint of the Liquor it was boiled in, lay a thin Top-Crust on, and bake it an Hour in a quick Oven. In the mean time boil the Bones of the Head in two Quarters of the Liquor, with two or three Blades of Mace, half a quarter of an Ounce of whole Pepper, a large Onion, and a Bundle of Sweet Herbs. Let it boil till there is about a Pint, then strain it off, and add two Spoonfuls of Ketchup, three of Red Wine, a Piece of Butter, as big as a Walnut, rolled in Flour, half an Ounce of Truffles and Morells; season with Salt to your Palate; boil it, and have half the Brains boiled with some Sage, beat them, and twelve Leaves of Sage chopped fine: Stir all together, and give it a boil; take the other Part of the Brains, and beat them up with some of the Sage chopped fine, a little Lemon-peel minced fine, and half a small Nutmeg grated. Beat it up with an Egg, and fry it in little Cakes of a fine light-brown, boil six Eggs hard, take only the Yolks; when your Pye comes out of the Oven, take off the Lid, lay the Eggs and Cakes over it, and pour the Sauce all over. Send it to Table hot without the Lid. This is a fine Dish; you may put in it as many fine Things as you please; but it wants no more Addition.

To make a Tart.

FIRST make a fine Puff-paste, cover your Dish with the Crust, make a good Force-meat thus: Take a Pound of Veal, and a Pound of Beef suet, cut them small, and beat them fine in a Mortar; season it with a small Nutmeg grated, a little Lemon-peel shread fine, a few Sweet Herbs, not too much, a little Pepper and Salt, just enough to season it, the Crumb of a Penny-loaf rubbed fine; mix it up with the Yolk of an Egg, make one Third into Balls, and the rest lay round the Sides of the Dish. Get two fine large Veal Sweat-breads, cut each into four Pieces; two Bags of Lamb-stones, cut in two each, twelve Cock's Combs, half an Ounce of Truffles and Morells, four Artichoke-bottoms, cut each into four Pieces, a few Asparagus-tops, some fresh Mushrooms, and some pickled; put all together in your Dish.

Lay first your Sweet-bread, then the Artichoke-bottom, then the Cock's Combs, then the Truffles and Morells, then the Asparagus, then the Mushrooms, then the Force-meat Balls. Season the Sweet-breads with Pepper and Salt; fill your Pye with Water, and put on the Crust. Bake it two Hours.

As to Fruit and Fish-pies, you have them in the Chapter for Lent.

To make Mince-Pies the best Way.

TAKE three Pounds of Suet shread very fine, and chopped as small as possible, two Pounds of Raisins stoned, and chopped as fine as possible, two Pounds of Currans, nicely picked, washed, rubbed, and dried at the Fire, half a hundred of fine Pippins, pared, cored, and chopped small, half a Pound of fine Sugar pounded fine, a quarter of an Ounce of Mace, a quarter of an Ounce of Cloves, two large Nutmegs, all beat fine; put all together into a great Pan, and mix it well together with half a Pint of Brandy, and half a Pint of Sack; put it down close in a Stone-pot, and it will keep good four Months. When you make your Pies, take a little Dish, something bigger than a Soop-plate, lay a very thin Crust all over it, lay a thin Layer of Meat, and then a thin Layer of Citron cut very thin, then a Layer of Mince-meat, and a thin Layer of Orange-peel cut thin, over that a little Meat; squeeze half the Juice of a fine Sevile Orange, or Lemon, and pour in three Spoonfuls of Red Wine; lay on your Crust, and bake it nicely. These Pies eat finely cold. If you make them in little Patties, mix your Meat and Sweet-meats accordingly: If you chuse Meat in your Pies, parboil a Neat's-Tongue, peel it, and chop the Meat as fine as possible, and mix with the rest; or two Pounds of the Inside of a Surloin of Beef boiled.

Tart de Moy.

MAKE Puff-paste, and lay round your Dish, then a Layer of Bisket, and a Layer of Butter and Marrow, and then a Layer of all Sorts of Sweet-meats, or as many as you have, and so do till your Dish is full; then boil a Quart of Cream, and thicken it with four Eggs, and a Spoonful of Orange-flower Water. Sweeten it with Sugar to your Palate, and pour over the rest. Half an Hour will bake it.

To Make Orange or Lemon Tarts.

TAKE six large Lemons, and rub them very well with Salt, and put them in Water for two Days, with a Handful of Salt in it; then change them into fresh Water every Day (without Salt) for a Fortnight, then boil them for two or three Hours till they are tender, then cut them into half Quarters, and then cut them thus △, as thin as you can; then take six Pippins pared, cored, and quartered, and a Pint of fair Water. Let them boil till the Pippins break; put the Liquor to your Orange or Lemon, and half the Pulp of the Pippins well broken, and a Pound of Sugar. Boil these together

gether a quarter of an Hour, then put it in a Gallipot, and squeeze an Orange in it: If it be Lemon-Tart, squeeze a Lemon; two Spoonfuls is enough for a Tart. Your Patty-pans must be small and shallow. Put fine Puff-paste, and very thin; a little while will bake it. Just as your Tarts are going into the Oven, with a Feather, or Brush, do them over with melted Butter, and then sift double-refined Sugar over them; and this is a pretty Iceing on them.

To make different Sorts of Tarts.

IF you bake in tin Patties, butter them, and you must put a little Crust all over, because of the taking them out: If in China, or Glass, no Crust but the top one. Lay fine Sugar at the Bottom, then your Plumbs, Cherries, or any other Sort of Fruit, and Sugar at Top; then put on your Lid, and bake them in a slack Oven. Mince-pies must be baked in Tin-patties, because of taking them out, and Puff-paste is best for them. All Sweet Tarts the beaten Crust is best; but as you fancy. You have the Receipt for the Crusts in this Chapter. Apple, Pear, Apricock, &c. make thus: Apples and Pears, pare them, cut them in Quarters, and core them; cut the Quarters a-cross again, set them on in a Sauce-pan with just as much Water as will barely cover them, let them simmer on a slow Fire just till the Fruit is tender; put a good Piece of Lemon-peel in the Water with the Fruit, then have your Patties ready. Lay fine Sugar at Bottom, then your Fruit, and a little Sugar at Top; that you must put in at your Discretion. Pour over each Tart a Tea Spoonful of Lemon-juice, and three Tea Spoonfuls of the Liquor they were boiled in; put on your Lid, and bake them in a slack Oven. Apricocks do the same Way; only don't use Lemon.

As to Preserved Tarts, only lay in your preserved Fruit, and put a very thin Crust at Top, and let them be baked as little as possible; but if you would make them nice, have a large Patty, the Size you would have your Tart. Make your Sugar-Crust, roll it as thick as a Halfpenny; then butter your Patties, and cover it; shape your Upper-crust on a hollow Thing on purpose, the Size of your Patty, and mark it with a Marking-iron for that purpose, in what Shape you please, to be hollow and open to see the Fruit through; then bake your Crust in a very slack Oven, not to discolour it, but to have it crisp. When the Crust is cold, very carefully take it out, and fill it with what Fruit you please, lay on the Lid, and it is done; therefore if the Tart is not eat, your Sweet-meat is not the worse, and it looks genteel.

Paste for Tarts.

ONE Pound of Flour, three Quarters of a Pound of Butter, mix up together, and beat well with a Rolling-pin.

Another Paste for Tarts.

HALF a Pound of Butter, half a Pound of Flour, and half a Pound of Sugar, mix it well together, and beat it with a Rolling-pin well; then roll it out thin.

Puff-Paste.

TAKE a quarter of a Peck of Flour, rub fine half a Pound of Butter, a little Salt, make it up into a light Paste with cold Water, just stiff enough to work it well up; then roll it out, and stick Pieces of Butter all over, and strew a little Flour; roll it up, and roll it out again; and so do nine or ten times, till you have rolled in a Pound and half of Butter. This Crust is mostly used for all Sorts of Pies.

A Good Crust for Great Pies.

TO a Peck of Flour the Yolk of three Eggs, then boil some Water, and put in half a Pound of try'd Suet, and a Pound and half of Butter. Skim off the Butter and Suet, and as much of the Liquor as will make it a light good Crust; work it up well, and roll it out.

A Standing Crust for Great Pies.

TAKE a Peck of Flour, and six Pounds of Butter, boiled in a Gallon of Water, skim it off into the Flour, and as little of the Liquor as you can; work it well up into a Paste, then pull it into Pieces till it is cold, then make it up in what Form you will have it. This is fit for the Walls of a Goose-pye.

A Cold Crust.

TO three Pounds of Flour, rub in a Pound and half of Butter; break in two Eggs, and make it up with cold Water.

A Dripping Crust.

TAKE a Pound and half of Beef-dripping, boil it in Water, strain it, then let it stand to be cold, and take off the hard Fat; scrape it, boil it so four or five times; then work it well up into three Pounds of Flour, as fine as you can, and make it up into Paste with cold Water, it makes a very fine Crust.

A Crust for Custards.

TAKE half a Pound of Flour, six Ounces of Butter, the Yolks of two Eggs, three Spoonfuls of Cream, mix them together, and let them stand a quarter of an Hour; then work it up and down, and roll it very thin.

Paste for Crackling-Crust.

BLANCH four Handfuls of Almonds, and throw them into Water, then dry them in a Cloth, and pound them in a Mortar very fine, with a little Orange-flower Water, and the White of an Egg. When they are well pounded, pass them through a coarse Hair-sieve, to clear them from all the Lumps or Clods; then spread it on a Dish till it is very pliable; let it stand for a-while, then roll out a Piece for the Under-crust, and dry it in the Oven on the Pye pan, while other Pastry-works are making, as Knots, Cyphers, &c. for garnishing your Pies.

CHAP. IX.

For a Fast-Dinner, a Number of good Dishes, which you may make use of for a Table at any other Time.

A Peas-Soop.

BOIL a Quart of Split-peas in a Gallon of Water; when they are quite soft, put in half a Red Herring, or two Anchovies, a good deal of whole Pepper black and white, two or three Blades of Mace, four or five Cloves, a Bundle of Sweet Herbs, a large Onion, and the green Tops of a Bunch of Salary, a good Bundle of dried Mint, cover them close, and let them boil softly, till there is about two Quarts; then strain it off, and have ready the white Part of the Salary washed clean, and cut small, and stewed tender in a Quart of Water, some Spinage picked and washed clean, put to the Salary; let them stew till the Water is quite wasted, and put it to your Soop.

Take a *French* Role, take out the Crumb, fry the Crust brown in a little fresh Butter, take some Spinage, stew it in a little Butter, after it is boiled, and fill the Role; take the Crumb, cut it to Pieces, beat it in a Mortar with a raw Egg, a little Spinage, and a little Sorrel, a little beaten Mace, and a little Nutmeg, and an Anchovy; then mix it up with your Hand, and roll them into Balls with a little Flour, and cut some Bread into Dice, and fry them crisp. Pour your Soop into your Dish, put in the Balls and Bread, and the Role in the Middle. Garnish your Dish with Spinage: If it wants Salt, you must season it to your Palate, rub in some dried Mint.

A Green Peas-Soop.

TAKE a Quart of old Green Peas, and boil them till they are quite tender as Pap, in a Quart of Water, then strain them through a Sieve, and boil a Quart of young Peas in that Water. In the mean time put the old Peas into a Sieve, pour half a Pound of melted Butter over them, and strain them through the Sieve with the Back of a Spoon, till you have got all the Pulp. When the young Peas are boiled enough, add the Pulp and Butter to the young Peas and Liquor; stir them together till they are smooth, and season with Pepper and Salt. You may fry a *French* Role, and let it swim in the Dish, If you like it, boil a Bundle of Mint in the Peas.

Another Green Peas-Soop.

TAKE a Quart of green Peas, boil them in a Gallon of Water, with a Bundle of Mint, and a few Sweet Herbs, Mace, Cloves and whole Pepper, till they are tender; then strain them, Liquor and all, through a coarse Sieve, till all the Pulp is strained. Put this Liquor into a Sauce-pan, put to it four Heads of Salary clean washed, and cut small, a Handful of Spinage clean washed, and cut small, a Lettice cut small, a fine Leek cut small, a Quart of green Peas, a little Salt; cover them, and let them boil very softly, till there is about two Quarts, and that the Salary is tender. Then send it to Table. If you like it, you may add a Piece of burnt Butter to it, about a quarter of an Hour before the Soop is enough.

Soop Meager.

TAKE half a Pound of Butter, put it into a deep Stew-pan, shake it about, and let it stand till it has done making a Noise; then have ready six middling Onions peeled, and cut small, throw them in, and shake them about. Take a Bunch of Salary clean washed, and picked, cut it in Pieces half as long as your Finger, a large Handful of Spinage clean washed, and picked, a good Lettice clean washed,

if

if you have it, and cut small, a little Bundle of Parsley chopped fine; shake all this well together in the Pan for a quarter of an Hour, then shake in a little Flour, stir all together, and pour into the Stew-pan two Quarts of boiling Water; take a Handful of dry hard Crust, throw in a Tea Spoonful of beaten Pepper, three Blades of Mace beat fine, stir all together, and let it boil softly half an Hour; then take it off the Fire, and beat up the Yolks of two Eggs, and stir in, and one Spoonful of Vinegar. Pour it into the Soop-dish, and send it to Table. If you have any green Peas, boil half a Pint in the Soop for Change.

An Onion Soop.

TAKE half a Pound of Butter, put it into a Stew-pan on the Fire, let it all melt, and boil till it has done making any Noise; then have ready ten or a Dozen middling Onions peeled, and cut small, throw them into the Butter, and let them fry a quarter of an Hour; then shake in a little Flour, and stir them round; shake your Pan, and let them do a few Minutes longer, then pour in a Quart or three Pints of boiling Water, stir them round, take a good Piece of Upper-crust, the stalest Bread you have, about as big as the Top of a Penny-loaf cut small, and throw it in; season with Salt to your Palate; let it boil ten Minutes, stirring it often; then take it off the Fire, and have ready the Yolks of two Eggs beat fine, with half a Spoonful of Vinegar; mix some of the Soop with them, then stir it into your Soop, and mix it well, and pour it into your Dish. This is a delicious Dish.

An Eel Soop.

TAKE Eels, according to the Quantity of Soop you would make, a Pound of Eels will make a Pint of good Soop; so to every Pound of Eels put a Quart of Water, a Crust of Bread, two or three Blades of Mace, a little whole Pepper, an Onion, and a Bundle of Sweet Herbs. Cover them close, and let them boil till half the Liquor is wasted; then strain it, and toast some Bread, and cut it small, lay the Bread into the Dish, and pour in your Soop. If you have a Stew-hole, set the Dish over it for a Minute, and send it to Table. If you find your Soop not rich enough, you must let it boil till it is as strong as you would have it. You may make this Soop as rich and good as if it was Meat: You may add a Piece of Carrot to brown it.

A Crawfish Soop.

TAKE a Carp, a large Eel, half a Thornback, cleanse and wash them clean; put them into a clean Sauce-pan, or little Pot, put to them a Gallon of Water, the Crust of a Penny-loaf, skim them well, season it with Mace, Cloves, whole Pepper black and white, an Onion, a Bundle of Sweet Herbs, some Parsley, a Piece of Ginger; let them boil by themselves close covered, then take the Tails of half a hundred Crawfish, pick out the Bag, and all the woolly Parts that are about them, put them into a Sauce-pan, with two Quarts of Water, a little Salt, a Bundle of Sweet Herbs: Let them stew softly, and when they are ready to boil, take out the Tails, and beat all the other Part of the Craw-fish with the Shells, and boil in the Liquor the Tails come out of, with a Blade of Mace, till it comes to about a Pint; strain it through a clean Sieve, and add to it the Fish a boiling. Let all boil softly, till there is about three Quarts, then strain it off through a coarse Sieve, put it into your Pot again; and if it wants Salt, you must put some in, and the Tails of the Crawfish, and Lobster. Take out all the Meat and Body, and chop it very small, and add to it; take a *French* Role and fry it crisp, and add to it. Let them stew all together for a quarter of an Hour. You may stew a Carp with them; pour your Soop into your Dish, the Role swimming in the Middle.

When you have a Carp, there should be a Role on each Side. Garnish the Dish with Crawfish: If your Crawfish will not lie on the Sides of your Dish, make a little Paste, and lay round the Rim, and lay the Fish on that all round the Dish.

Take care that your Soop be well seasoned, but not too high.

A Muscle Soop.

GET a hundred of Muscles, wash them very clean, put them into a Stew-pan, cover them close, let them stew till they open, then pick them out of the Shells, strain the Liquor through a fine Lawn-sieve to your Muscles, and pick the Beard or Crab out, if any.

Take a Dozen Crawfish, beat them to mash, with a Dozen Almonds blanched, and beat fine, and take a small Parsnip and a Carrot scraped, and cut into thin Slices, fry them brown with a little Butter. Then take two Pounds of any fresh Fish, and boil in a Gallon of Water, with a Bundle of Sweet Herbs, a large Onion stuck with Cloves, whole Pepper black and white, a little Parsley, a little Piece of Horse-reddish, and salt the Muscles liquor, the Crawfish and Almonds. Let them boil till half is wasted, then strain them through a Sieve, put the Soop into a Sauce-pan, put in twenty of the Muscles, a few Mushrooms and Truffles cut small, and a Leek washed, and cut very small. Take two *French* Roles, take out the Crumb, fry it brown, cut it into little Pieces, put it into the Soop, let it boil all together for a quarter of an Hour with the fry'd Carrot and Parsnip; in the mean while, take the Crust of the Roles fry'd crisp, take half a hundred of the Muscles; a quarter of a Pound of Butter, a Spoonful of Water, shake in a little Flour, set them on the Fire, keeping the Sauce-pan shaking all the time till all the Butter is melted. Season it with Pepper and Salt, beat up the Yolks of three

three Eggs put in, stir them all the time for fear of curdling, grate a little Nutmeg; when it is thick and fine, fill the Roles, pour your Soop into the Dish, put in the Roles, and lay the rest of the Muscles round the Rim of the Dish.

A Scate or Thornback Soop.

TAKE two Pound of Scate, or Thornback, skin it and boil it in six Quarts of Water. When it is enough, take it up, pick off the Flesh, and lay it by; put in the Bones again, and about two Pounds of any fresh Fish, a very little Piece of Lemon-peel, a Bundle of Sweet Herbs, whole Pepper, two or three Blades of Mace, a little Piece of Horse-reddish, the Crust of a Penny-loaf, a little Parsley, cover it close, and let it boil till there is about two Quarts; then strain it off, and add an Ounce of Vermicella, set it on the Fire, and let it boil softly. In the mean time take a *French* Role, cut a little Hole in the Top, take out the Crumb, fry the Crust brown in Batter; take the Flesh off the Fish you laid by, cut it into little Pieces, put it into a Sauce-pan, with two or three Spoonfuls of the Soop, shake in a little Flour, put in a Piece of Butter, a little Pepper and Salt; shake them together in the Sauce-pan over the Fire till it is quite thick, then fill the Role with it, pour your Soop into your Dish, let the Role swim in the Middle, and send it to Table.

An Oyster Soop.

YOUR Stock must be made of any Sort of Fish the Place affords; let there be about two Quarts, take a Pint of Oysters, beard them, put them into a Sauce-pan, strain the Liquor, let them stew two or three Minutes in their own Liquor; then take the hard Parts of the Oysters, and beat them in a Mortar, with the Yolks of four hard Eggs, mix them with some of the Soop, put them with the other Part of the Oysters and Liquor into a Sauce-pan, a little Nutmeg, Pepper and Salt; stir them well together, and let it boil a quarter of an Hour, dish it up, and send it to Table.

An Almond Soop.

TAKE a Quart of Almonds, blanch them, and beat them in a Marble Mortar, with the Yolks of twelve hard Eggs, till they are a fine Paste; mix them by degrees with two Quarts of new Milk, a Quart of Cream, a quarter of a Pound of double-refined Sugar beat fine, a Pennyworth of Orange-flower Water; stir all well together; when it is well mixed, set it over a slow Fire, keep it stirring quick all the while, till you find it is thick enough, then pour it into your Dish, and send it to Table. If you don't be very careful it will curdle.

A Rice Soop.

TAKE two Quarts of Water, a Pound of Rice, a little Cinnamon, cover it close, and let it simmer very softly, till the Rice is quite tender. Take out the Cinnamon, and sweeten it to your Palate, grate half a Nutmeg, let it stand till it is cold; then beat up the Yolks of three Eggs, with half a Pint of White Wine, mix them very well, then stir them into the Rice, set them on a slow Fire, keep stirring all the time for fear of curdling. When it is of a good Thickness, and boils, take it up; keep stirring it till you put it into your Dish.

A Barley Soop.

TAKE a Gallon of Water, and half a Pound of Barley, a Blade or two of Mace, a large Crust of Bread, a little Piece of Lemon-peel, let it boil till it comes to two Quarts, then add half a Pint of White Wine, and sweeten to your Palate.

A Turnip Soop.

TAKE a Gallon of Water, and a Bunch of Turnips, pare them, save three or four out, put the rest into the Water, with half an Ounce of whole Pepper, an Onion stuck with Cloves, a Blade of Mace, and half a Nutmeg bruised, a little Bundle of Sweet Herbs, a large Crust of Bread; let these boil an Hour pretty fast, then strain it through a Sieve, squeezing the Turnips through, wash and cut a Bunch of Salary very small, set it on in the Liquor on the Fire, cover it close, and let it stew. In the mean time cut the Turnips you saved into Dice, and two or three small Carrots clear scraped, and cut in little Pieces; put half these Turnips and Carrots into the Pot with the Salary, and the other half fry brown in fresh Butter. You must flour them first, and two or three Onions peeled, and cut in thin Slices, and fry'd brown; then put them all into the Soop, with an Ounce of Vermicella. Let your Soop boil softly till the Salary is quite tender, and your Soop good. Season it with Salt to your Palate.

An Egg Soop.

BEAT the Yolks of two Eggs in your Dish, with a Piece of Butter as big as an Hen's Egg, take a Tea-kettle of boiling Water in one Hand, and a Spoon in the other, pour in about a Quart by degrees, and keep stirring it all the time well, till the Eggs are well mixed, and the Butter melted; then pour it into

into a Sauce-pan, and keep stirring it all the time till it begins to simmer, take it off the Fire, and pour it between two Vessels out of one into the other, till it is quite smooth, and has a great Froth. Set it on the Fire again, keep stirring it till it is quite hot, then pour it into the Soop-dish, and send it to Table hot.

Peas-Porridge.

TAKE a Quart of Green Peas, put to them a Quart of Water, a Bundle of dry'd Mint, and a little Salt. Let them boil till the Peas are quite tender, then put in some beaten Pepper, a Piece of Butter as big as a Wallnut, rolled in Flour; stir it all together, and let it boil a few Minutes. Then add two Quarts of Milk, let it boil a quarter of an Hour, take out the Mint, and serve it up.

A White-Pot.

TAKE two Quarts of new Milk, eight Eggs, and half the Whites beat up, with a little Rose-water, a Nutmeg, a quarter of a Pound of Sugar, cut a Pennyworth in very thin Slices, and pour your Milk and Eggs over; put a little Bit of sweet Butter on the Top; bake it in a slow Oven half an Hour.

A Rice White-Pot.

BOIL a Pound of Rice in two Quarts of new Milk, till it is tender and thick, beat it in a Mortar with a quarter of a Pound of Sweet Almonds blanched; then boil two Quarts of Cream, with a few Crumbs of white Bread, and two or three Blades of Mace; mix all together with eight Eggs, a little Rose-water, and sweeten to your Taste; cut some candied Orange and Citrons-peels thin, and lay it in, when it is in the Oven. It must be put into a slow Oven.

Rice-Milk.

TAKE half a Pound of Rice, boil it in a Quart of Water, with a little Cinnamon, let it boil till the Water is all wasted; take great Care it does not burn, then add three Pints of Milk, and the Yolk of an Egg beat up; keep it stirring; and when it boils take it up. Sweeten to your Palate.

An Orange-Fool.

TAKE the Juice of six Oranges and six Eggs well beaten, a Pint of Cream, a quarter of a Pound of Sugar, a little Cinnamon and Nutmeg; mix all together, and keep stirring over a slow Fire, till it is thick, then put in a little Piece of Butter, and keep stirring till cold, and dish it up.

A Westminster-Fool.

TAKE a Penny-loaf, cut it into thin Slices, wet them with Sack, lay them in the Bottom of a Dish; take a Quart of Cream, beat up six Eggs, two Spoonfuls of Rose-water, a Blade of Mace, some grated Nutmeg, sweeten to your Taste. Put this all into a Sauce-pan, and keep stirring all the time over a slow Fire for fear of curdling. When it begins to be thick, pour it into the Dish over the Bread; let it stand till it is cold, and serve it up.

A Gooseberry-Fool.

TAKE two Quarts of Gooseberries, set them on the Fire in about a Quart of Water; when they begin to simmer, and turn yellow, and begin to plump, throw them into a Culledar to drain the Water out; then with the Back of a Spoon carefully squeeze the Pulp, throw the Sieve into a Dish, make them pretty sweet, and let them stand till they are cold. In the mean time take two Quarts of new Milk, and the Yolks of four Eggs, beat up with a little grated Nutmeg, stir it softly over a slow Fire, when it begins to simmer, take it off, and by degrees stir it into the Gooseberries, let it stand till it is cold, and serve it up. If you make it with Cream, you need not put any Eggs in; and if it is not thick enough, it is only boiling more Gooseberries; but that you must do as you think proper.

Furmity.

TAKE a Quart of ready-boiled Wheat, two Quarts of Milk, a quarter of a Pound of Currans, clean picked and washed; stir these together and boil them, beat up the Yolks of three or four Eggs, a little Nutmeg, with two or three Spoonfuls of Milk, add to the Wheat, stir them together for a few Minutes, then sweeten to your Palate, and send it to Table.

Plumb-Porridge, or Barley-Gruel.

TAKE a Gallon of Water, and half a Pound of Barley, a quarter of a Pound of Raisins clean washed, a quarter of a pound of Currans, clean washed and picked; boil these till above half the Water is wasted, with two or three Blades of Mace; then sweeten it to your Palate, and add half a Pint of White Wine.

Buttered

Buttered-Wheat.

PUT your Wheat into a Sauce-pan, when it is hot, stir in a good Piece of Butter, a little grated Nutmeg, and sweeten to your Palate.

Plumb-Gruel.

TAKE two Quarts of Water, two large Spoonfuls of Oatmeal, stir it together, a Blade or two of Mace, a little Piece of Lemon-peel, boil it for five or six Minutes (take care it don't boil over;) then strain it off, and put it into the Sauce-pan again, with half a Pound of Currans clean washed and picked; let them boil about ten Minutes, add a Glass of White Wine, a little grated Nutmeg, and sweeten to your Palate.

To make a Flour Hasty-Pudding.

TAKE a Quart of Milk, and four Bay-leaves, set it on the Fire to boil, beat up the Yolks of two Eggs, and stir in a little Salt, take two or three Spoonfuls of cold Milk, and beat up with your Eggs, and stir in your Milk; then with a wooden Spoon in one Hand, and the Flower in the other, stir it in till it is of a good Thickness, but not too thick. Let it boil, and keep it stirring, then pour it into a Dish, and stick Pieces of Butter here and there. You may omit the Egg, if you don't like it; but it is a great Addition to the Pudding, and a little Piece of Butter stirred in the Milk, makes it eat short and fine. Take out the Bay-leaves before you put in the Flour.

To make an Oatmeal Hasty-Pudding.

TAKE a Quart of Water, set it on to boil, put in a Piece of Butter, some Salt, when it boils, stir in the Oatmeal as you do the Flour, till it is of a good Thickness; let it boil a few Minutes, pour it in your Dish, and stick Pieces of Butter in it; or eat with Wine and Sugar, or Ale and Sugar, or Cream, or new Milk. This is best made with Scotch Oatmeal.

To make an Excellent Sack-Posset.

BEAT fifteen Eggs, Whites and Yolks very well, and strain them, then put three quarters of a Pound of White Sugar into a Pint of Canary, and mix it with your Eggs in a Bason; set it over a Chaffing-dish of Coals, and keep continually stirring it till it is scalding-hot. In the mean time grate some Nutmeg into a Quart of Milk, and boil it, then pour it into your Eggs and Wine, they being scalding hot. Hold your Hand very high as you pour it, some body stirring it all the time you are pouring in the Milk; then take it off the Chaffing-dish, and set it before the Fire half an Hour, so serve it up.

To make another Sack-Posset.

TAKE a Quart of new Milk, take four Naples Biskets, crumble them, and when the Milk boils, throw them in. Just give it one boil, take it off, grate in some Nutmeg, and sweeten to your Palate; then pour in half a Pint of Sack, stirring it all the time, and serve it up. You may crumble White Bread instead of Biskets.

Or make it thus.

BOIL a Quart of Cream, or new Milk, with the Yolk of two Eggs; first, take a French Role, and cut it as thin as possible you can in little Pieces; lay it in the Dish you intend for the Posset; When the Milk boils (which you must keep stirring all the time) pour it over the Bread, and stir it together. Cover it close, and take a Pint of Canary, a quarter of a Pound of Sugar, grate in some Nutmeg; and when it boils, pour it into the Milk, stirring it all the time, and serve it up.

To make a fine Hasty-Pudding.

BREAK an Egg into fine Flour, and with your Hand work up as much as you can into a stiff Paste as is possible, then mince it as small as Herbs to the Pot, as small as if it were to be sifted; then set a Quart of Milk a boiling, and put it in the Paste so cut; put in a little Salt, a little beaten Cinnamon and Sugar, a Piece of Butter as big as a Wallnut, and stirring all one way. When it is as thick as you would have it, stir in such another Piece of Butter, then pour it into your Dish, and stick Pieces of Butter here and there. Send it to Table hot.

To make Hasty-Fritters.

TAKE a Stew-pan, put in some Butter, let it be hot; in the mean time take half a Pint of all Ale not bitter, stir in some Flour by degrees in a little of the Ale, put in a few Currans, or chopped Apples, beat them up quick, and drop a large Spoonful at a time all over the Pan. Take care they don't stick together, turn them with an Egg-slice, and when of a fine brown, lay them in a Dish, and throw Sugar over them, and garnish with Orange cut into Quarters.

To make Fine Fritters.

PUT to half a Pint of thick Cream four Eggs well beaten, a little Brandy, some Nutmeg, and Ginger; make this into a thick Batter with Flour, and your Apples must be Golden Pippins, pared and chopped with a Knife; mix all together, and fry them in Butter. At any time you may make an Alteration in the Fritters with Currans.

Another Way.

DRY well some of the finest Flour before the Fire, and mix it with a Quart of new Milk, not too thick, six or eight Eggs, a little Nutmeg, a little Mace, a little Salt, a quarter of a Pint of Sack, or Ale, or a Glass of Brandy; beat them well together, make them pretty thick with Pippins; so fry them dry.

Apple Fritters.

BEAT the Yolks of eight Eggs, the Whites of four well together, and strain them into a Pan; then take a Quart of Cream, make it as hot as you can bear your Finger in it, then put to it a quarter of a Pint of Sack, three quarters of a Pint of Ale, and make a Posset of it. When it is cool, put it to your Eggs, beating it well together, then put in Nutmeg, Ginger, Salt, and Flour to your liking. Your Batter should be pretty thick, then put in Pippins sliced or scraped, and fry them in a good deal of Butter, quick.

Curd Fritters.

HAVING a Handful of Curds, and a Handful of Flour, and ten Eggs, well beaten and strained, some Sugar, Cloves, Mace, and Nutmeg beat, a little Saffron; stir all well together, and fry them quick, and of a fine light-brown.

Fritters Royal.

TAKE a Quart of new Milk, put it into a Skellet or Sauce-pan, and as the Milk boils up, pour in a Pint of Sack. Let it boil up, then take it off, and let it stand five or six Minutes, then skim off all the Curd, and put it into a Bason; beat it up well with six Eggs, season it with Nutmeg, then beat it up with a Wisk, add Flour to make it as thick as Batter usually is, put in some fine Sugar, and fry them quick.

Skirret Fritters.

TAKE a Pint of Pulp of Skirrets, and a Spoonful of Flour, the Yolks of four Eggs, Sugar and Spice, make it into a thick Batter, and fry them quick.

White Fritters.

HAVING some Rice, wash it in five or six several Waters, and dry it very well before the Fire, then beat it in a Mortar very fine, and sift it through a Lawn-sieve, that it may be very fine. You must have at least an Ounce of it, then put it into a Sauce-pan, just wet it with Milk, and when it is well incorporated with it, add to it another Pint of Milk. Set the whole over a Stove, or very slow Fire, and take care to keep it always moving; put in a little Sugar, and some candied Lemon-peel grated, keep it over the Fire till it is almost come to the Thickness of a fine Paste, flour a Peal, and pour it on it, and spread it abroad with a Rolling-pin. When it is quite cold, cut it into little Morsels, taking care that they stick not one to the other, flour your Hands and roll up your Fritters handsomely, and fry them. When you serve them up, pour a little Orange-flower Water over them and Sugar. These make a pretty Side-dish; or are very pretty to garnish a fine Dish with.

Water Fritters.

TAKE a Pint of Water put into a Sauce-pan, a Piece of Butter as big as a Wallnut, a little Salt, and some candied Lemon-peel minced very small; make this boil over a Stove, then put in two good Handfuls of Flour, and turn it about by main Strength, till the Water and Flour be well mixed together, and none of the last stick to the Sauce-pan; then take it off the Stove, mix in the Yolks of two Eggs, mix them well together, continuing to put in more, two by two, till you have stirred in ten or twelve, and your Paste be very fine; then drudge a Peel thick with Flour, and dipping your Hand into Flour, take out your Paste, Bit by Bit, and lay it on a Peel. When it has lain a little while, roll it, and cut it into little Pieces, taking care, that they stick not to one another; fry them of a fine brown; put a little Orange-flour Water over them, and Sugar all over.

Syringed

82　　　*The Art of Cookery, made Plain and Easy.*

Syringed Fritters.

TAKE about a Pint of Water, and a Bit of Butter, the Bigness of an Egg, with some Lemon-peel, green if you can get it, rasped, preserved Lemon-peel, and crisped Orange-flowers; put all together in a Stew-pan over the Fire, and when boiling throw in some fine Flour; keep it stirring, put in by degrees more Flour till your Batter be thick enough, take it off the Fire; then take an Ounce of Sweet Almonds, four bitter Ones, pound them in a Mortar, stir in two Naples Biskets crumbled, two Eggs beat; stir all together, and more Egg, till your Batter be thin enough to be syringed. Fill your Syringe, your Butter being hot, syringe your Fritters in it, to make of it a true Lovers-Knot, and being well coloured, serve them up for a dainty Side-dish.

At another time, you may rub a Sheet of Paper with Butter, over which you may syringe your Fritters, and make them in what Shape you please. Your Butter being hot, turn the Paper upside-down over it, and your Fritters will easily drop off. When fry'd, strew them with Sugar, and glaze them.

Vine-Leaves Fritters.

TAKE some of the smallest Vine-leaves you can get, and having cut off the great Stalks, put them in a Dish with some *French* Brandy, green Lemon rasped, and some Sugar; take a good Handful of fine Flour, mixed with White Wine or Ale, let your Butter be hot, and with a Spoon drop in your Batter; take great Care they don't stick one to the other; on each Fritter lay a Leaf; fry them quick, and strew Sugar over them, and glaze them with a red-hot Shovel.

With all Fritter made with Milk and Eggs, you should have beaten Cinnamon and Sugar in a Saucer, and either squeeze an Orange over it, or pour a Glass of White Wine, and so throw Sugar all over the Dish, and they should be fry'd in a good deal of Fat; therefore they are best fried in Beef-dripping, or Hog's-lard, when it can be done.

To make Clarye Fritters.

TAKE your Clarye-leaves, cut off the Stalk, dip them one by one in a Batter made with Milk and Flour, your Butter being hot, fry them quick. This is a pretty heartening Dish for a sick or weak Person; and Camsary-leaves done the same Way.

Apple Frazes.

CUT your Apples in thick Slices, and fry them of a light-brown; take them up, and lay them to drain, keep them as whole as you can, and either pare them, or let it alone; then make a Batter as follows: Take five Eggs, leaving out two Whites, beat them up with Cream and Flour, and a little Sack; make it the Thickness of a Pancake Batter, pour in a little melted Butter and Nutmeg, and a little Sugar. Let your Butter be hot, and drop in your Fritters, and on every one lay a Slice of Apple, and then more Batter on them. Fry them of a fine light-brown; take them up, and strew some double-refined Sugar all over them.

An Almond Fraze.

GET a Pound of Jordan Almonds blanched, steep them in a Pint of sweet Cream, ten Yolks of Eggs, and four Whites, take out the Almonds and pound them in a Mortar fine, then mix them again in the Cream and Eggs, put in Sugar and grated white Bread, stir them well together, put some fresh Butter into the Pan, let it be hot, and pour it in, stirring it in the Pan till they are of a good Thickness; and when it is enough, turn it into a Dish, and throw Sugar over it, and serve it up.

Pancakes.

TAKE a Quart of Milk, beat in six or eight Eggs, leaving half the Whites out, mix it well till your Batter is of a fine Thickness. You must observe to mix your Flour first with a little Milk, then add the rest by degrees; put in two Spoonfuls of beaten Ginger, a Glass of Brandy, a little Salt, stir all together, and take your Stew-pan very clean, put in a Piece of Butter as big as a Wallnut, then pour in a Ladleful of Batter, which will make a Pancake moving the Pan round, that the Batter be all over the Pan; shake the Pan, and when you think that Side is enough, toss it, if you can't, turn it cleaverly; and when both Sides are done, lay it in a Dish before the Fire, and so do the rest. You must take care they are dry; when you send them to Table, strew a little Sugar over them.

To make Fine Pancakes.

TAKE half a Pint of Cream, half a Pint of Sack, the Yolks of eighteen Eggs beat fine, and a little Salt, half a Pound of fine Sugar, a little beaten Cinnamon, Mace, and Nutmeg; then put in as much Flour as will run thin over the Pan, and fry them in fresh Butter. This Sort of Pancake will not be crisp, but very good.

A

A Second Sort of Fine Pancakes.

TAKE a Pint of Cream, and eight Eggs well beat, a Nutmeg grated, a little Salt, half a Pound of good Dish-butter melted; mix all together with as much Flour as will make them into a thin Batter; fry them nice, and turn them on the Back of a Plate.

A Third Sort.

TAKE six new-laid Eggs well beat, mix them with a Pint of Cream, a quarter of a Pound of Sugar, some grated Nutmeg, and as much Flour as will make the Batter of a proper Thickness. Fry these fine Pancakes in small Pans, and let your Pans be hot. You must not put above the Bigness of a Nutmeg of Butter at a time into the Pan.

A Fourth Sort call'd, A Quire of Paper.

TAKE a Pint of Cream, six Eggs, three Spoonfuls of fine Flour, three of Sack, one of Orange-flour-Water, a little Sugar, and half a Nutmeg grated, half a Pound of melted Butter, almost cold; mingle all well together, and butter the Pan for the first Pancake; let them run as thin as possible; when just coloured they are enough: And so do with all the fine Pancakes.

Rice Pancakes.

TAKE a Quart of Cream, and three Spoonfuls of Flour of Rice, set it on a slow Fire, and keep it stirring till it is thick as Pap. Stir in half a Pound of Butter, a Nutmeg grated, then pour it out into an earthen Pan, and when it is cold, stir in three or four Spyonfuls of Flour, a little Salt, some Sugar, nine Eggs well beaten; mix all well together, and fry them nicely. When you have no Cream use new Milk, and one Spoonful more of the Flour of Rice.

To Make a Pupton of Apples.

PARE some Apples, and take out the Cores, put them into a Skellet, to a Quart-Mugful and heaped, of the cut Apples, put in a quarter of a Pound of Sugar, and two Spoonfuls of Water. Do them over a slow Fire; keep them stirring, add a little Cinnamon; when it is quite thick, and like a Marmalade, let it stand till cool. Beat up the Yolks of four or five Eggs, and stir in a Handful of grated Bread, and a quarter of a Pound of fresh Butter; then form it into what Shape you please, and bake it in a slow Oven, and then turn it upside-down on a Plate for a second Course.

To Make Black Caps.

CUT twelve large Apples in Halves, and take out the Cores, place them on a thin Patty-pan, or Mazareen, as close together as they can lye, with the flat Side downwards, squeeze a Lemon in, two Spoonfuls of Orange-flower Water, and pour over them; shread some Lemon-peel fine and throw over them, and grate fine Sugar all over. Set them in a quick Oven, and half an Hour will do them. When you send them to Table, throw fine Sugar all over the Dish.

To Bake Apples Whole

PUT your Apples into an earthen Pan, with a few Cloves, and little Lemon-peel, some coarse Sugar, a Glass of Red Wine; put them into a quick Oven, and they will take an Hour baking.

To Stew Pears.

PARE six Pears, and either quarter them, or do them whole; but makes a pretty Dish with one whole, and the other cut in quarter, and the Cores taken out, lay them in a deep earthen Pot, with a few Cloves, a Piece of Lemon-peel, a Gill of Red Wine, and a quarter of a Pound of fine Sugar: If the Pears are very large, they will take half a Pound of Sugar, and half a Pint of Red Wine. Cover them close with brown Paper, and bake them till they are enough.

Serve them hot or cold, just as you like them, and they will be very good with Water in the place of Wine.

To Stew Pears in a Sauce-Pan.

PUT them into a Sauce-pan with the Ingredients as before. Cover them, and do them over a slow Fire; when they are enough take them off.

To Stew Pears Purple.

PARE four Pears, cut them into Quarters, core them, put them into a Stew-pan, with a quarter of a Pint of Water, a quarter of a Pound of Sugar, cover them with a Pewter-plate, then cover the Pan with the Lid, and do them over a flow Fire. Look at them often, for fear of the Plate melting; when they are enough, and the Liquor looks of a fine Purple, take them off, and lay them in your Dish with the Liquor; when cold, serve them up for a Side-dish as a second Course, or just as you please.

To Stew Pippins Whole.

TAKE twelve Golden Pippins, pare them, put the Parings into a Sauce-pan, with Water enough to cover them, a Blade of Mace, two or three Cloves, a Piece of Lemon-peel, let them simmer till there is just enough to stew the Pippins in, then strain it, and put it into the Sauce-pan again, with Sugar enough to make it like a Syrrup; then put them in a Preserving-pan, or clean Stew-pan, or large Sauce-pan, and pour the Syrrup over them. Let there be enough to stew them in; when they are enough, which you will know by the Pippins being soft, take them up, lay them in a little Dish with the Syrrup; when cold, serve them up; or hot, if you chuse it.

A pretty Made-Dish.

TAKE half a Pound of Almonds blanched, and beat fine, with a little Rose or Orange-flower Water, then take a Quart of sweet thick Cream, and boil it with a Piece of Cinnamon and Mace, sweeten it with Sugar to your Palate, and mix it with your Almonds; stir it well together, and strain it through a Sieve. Let your Cream cool, and thicken it with the Yolks of six Eggs; then garnish a deep Dish, and lay Paste at the Bottom; then put in shread Artichoke-bottoms, being first boiled; upon that a little melted Butter, shread Citron, and candied Orange; so do till your Dish is near full, then pour in your Cream: So bake it without a Lid; when it is baked, scrape Sugar over it, and serve it up hot; half an Hour will bake it.

To make Kickshaws.

MAKE Puff-paste, roll it thin, and if you have any Moulds, work it upon them, make them up with preserved Pippins. You may fill some with Gooseberries, some with Rasberries, or what you please; then close them up, or either bake or fry them; throw grated Sugar over them, and serve them up.

Pain Perdu, or Cream Toasts.

HAVING two French Roles, cut them into Slices, as thick as your Finger, Crumb and Crust together, lay them on a Dish, put to them a Pint of Cream, and half a Pint of Milk; strew them over with beaten Cinnamon, and Sugar, turn them frequently, till they are tender; but take care not to break them, then take them from the Cream with a Slice, break four or five Eggs, turn your Slices of Bread in the Eggs, and fry them in clarified Butter. Make them of a good brown Colour, not black; scrape a little Sugar on them. They may be served for a second Course-dish, but fittest for Supper.

Salamangundy for a Middle Dish at Supper.

IN the top Plate in the Middle, which should stand higher than the rest, take a fine pickled Herring bone it, take off the Head, and mince the rest fine. In the other Plates round, put the following Things; in one, pare a Cucumber, and cut it very thin; in another, Apples pared, and cut small; in another, an Onion peeled, and cut small; in another, two hard Eggs chopped small, the Whites in one, and the Yolks in another; pickled Gerkins in another cut small; in another, Salary cut small; in another pickled red Cabbage chopped fine; take some Water-cresses clean washed, and picked, stick them all about and between every Plate, or Saucer, and throw Stertion-Flowers about the Cresses. You must have Oil and Vinegar, and Lemon to eat with it. If it is prettily set out, it will make a pretty Figure in the Middle of the Table, or you may lay them in Heaps in a Dish. If you have not all these Ingredients, set out your Plates, or Saucers, with just what you fancy; and in the room of a pickled Herring mince Anchovies.

To make a Tansey.

TAKE ten Eggs, break them into a Pan, put to them a little Salt, beat them very well, then put to them eight Ounces of Loaf-Sugar beat fine, and a Pint of the Juice of Spinage. Mix them well together, and strain it into a Quart of Cream; then grate in eight Ounces of Naples Bisket, or white Bread, a Nutmeg grated, a quarter of a Pound of Jordin Almonds, beat in a Mortar, with a little Juice of Tansey to your Taste; mix these all together, put it into a Stew-pan, with a Piece of Butter as large as a Pippin. Set it over a flow Charcoal Fire, keep it stirring till it is hardened very well, then butter a Dish very well, put in your Tansey, bake it, and when it is enough, turn it out on a Pye-plate. Squeeze the Juice of an Orange over it, and throw Sugar all over. Garnish with Orange cut into Quarters, and Sweetmeats cut into little long Bits, and lay all over it.

Another

The Art of Cookery, made Plain and Easy.

Another Way.

TAKE a Pint of Cream, and half a Pound of blanched Almonds beat fine, with Rose and Orange-flower Water, stir them together over a slow Fire; when it boils, take it off, and let it stand till cold. Then beat in ten Eggs, grate in a small Nutmeg, four Naples Biskets, and a little grated Bread, a Grain of Musk. Sweeten to your Taste; and if you think it is too thick, put in some more Cream; the Juice of Spinage to make it green; stir it well together, and either fry it, or bake it. If you fry it, do one Side first, and then with a Dish turn the other Side.

To make Hedge-Hog.

TAKE two Quarts of sweet blanched Almonds, beat them well in a Mortar, with a little Canary and Orange-flower Water, to keep them from oiling. Make them into a stiff Paste, then beat in the Yolks of twelve Eggs, leave out five of the Whites, put to it a Pint of Cream, sweeten it with Sugar, put in half a Pound of sweet Butter melted, set on a Furnace, or slow Fire, and keep it constantly stirring till it is stiff enough to be made into the Form of a Hedge-Hog. Then stick it full of blanched Almonds slit, and stuck up like the Bristels of a Hedge-Hog, then put it into a Dish. Take a Pint of Cream, and the Yolks of four Eggs beat up, and mix with the Cream; sweeten to your Palate, and keep them stirring over a slow Fire all the time till it is hot; then pour it into your Dish round the Hedge-Hog, and let it stand till it is cold, and serve it up.

Or you may make a fine Hartshorn-Jelly, and pour into the Dish, which will look very pretty. You may eat Wine and Sugar with it, or eat it without.

Or cold Cream, sweetned with a Glass of White Wine in it, and the Juice of a Seville Orange, and pour into the Dish. It will be pretty for Change.

This is a pretty Side-dish at a second Course, or in the Middle for Supper, or in a Grand Desert. Plump two Currans for the Eyes.

Or, make it thus for Change.

TAKE two Quarts of sweet Almonds blanched, twelve bitter ones, beat them in a Marble Mortar well together, with Canary and Orange-flower Water, two Spoonfuls of the Tincture of Saffron, two Spoonfuls of the Juice of Sorrel, beat them into a fine Paste, put in half a Pound of melted Butter, mix it up well; a little Nutmeg and beaten Mace, an Ounce of Citron, an Ounce of Orange-peel, both cut fine, mix in; and the Yolk of twelve Eggs, and half the Whites, beat up and mixed in; half a Pint of Cream, half a Pound of double-refined Sugar, work it up all together; and if it is not stiff enough to make up into the Form you would have it, you must have a Mould for it; butter it well, and then put in your Ingredients, and bake it. The Mould must be made in such a manner, as to have the Head peeping out; and when it comes out of the Oven, have ready some Almonds blanched, and slit, and boil up in Sugar till brown. Stick it all over with the Almonds; and for Sauce, have Red Wine made hot and Sugar, with the Juice of an Orange. Send it hot to Table for a first Course.

You may leave out the Saffron and Sorrel, and make it up like Chickens, or any other Shape you please, or alter the Sauce to your Fancy. Butter, Sugar, and White Wine is a pretty Sauce, for either baked or boiled; and you may make the Sauce of what Colour you please; or, put it into a Mould, with half a Pound of Currans added to it, and boil it for a Pudding. You may use Cochineal in the room of Saffron.

The following Liquor you may make to mix with your Sauces: Beat an Ounce of Cochineal very fine, put in a Pint of Water in a Skillet, and a quarter of an Ounce of Roch-Allum, boil it till the Goodness is out; strain it into a Phial, with an Ounce of fine Sugar, it will keep six Months.

To make pretty Almond Puddings.

TAKE a Pound and half of blanched Almonds, beat them fine with a little Rose-water, a Pound of grated Bread, a Pound and quarter of fine Sugar, a quarter of an Ounce of Cinnamon, and a large Nutmeg beat fine, half a Pound of melted Butter, mixed with the Yolks of Eggs, and four Whites beat fine, a Pint of Sack, a Pint and half of Cream, some Rose or Orange-flower Water, boil the Cream, and tye a little Bag of Saffron, and dip in the Cream to colour it. First beat your Eggs very well, and mix with your Batter; beat it up, then the Spice, then the Almonds, then the Rose-water and Wine by degrees, beating it all the time, then the Sugar, and then the Cream by degrees, keeping it stirring, and a quarter of a Pound of Vermicelly. Stir all together, have some Hog's Guts nice and clean; fill them only half full, and as you put in the Ingredients, here and there put in a Bit of Citron, tye both Ends of the Gut tight, and boil them about a quarter of an Hour. You may add Currans for Change.

To make Fry'd Toasts.

TAKE a Penny-loaf, cut it into Slices, a quarter of an Inch thick round ways, toast them, and then take a Pint of Cream, and three Eggs, half a Pint of Sack, some Nutmeg, and sweetened to your Taste. Steep the Toasts in it for three or four Hours, then have ready some Butter hot in a Pan,

put

put in the Toast, and fry them brown, lay them in a Dish, melt a little Butter, and then mix what is left ; if none, put in some Wine and Sugar, and pour over them. They make a pretty Plate or Side-Dish for Supper.

To Dress a Brace of Carp.

SCRAPE them very clean, then gut them, wash them and the Rows in a Pint of good stale Beer, to preserve all the Blood. Boil the Carp with a little Salt in the Water.

In the mean time strain the Beer, and put it into a Sauce-pan, with a Pint of Red Wine, two or three Blades of Mace, some whole Pepper black and white, an Onion stuck with Cloves, half a Nutmeg bruised, a Bundle of Sweet Herbs, a Piece of Lemon-peel as big as a Sixpence, an Anchovy, a little Piece of Horse-reddish ; let these boil together softly for a quarter of an Hour, covered close, then strain it, and add to it half the hard Row beat to Pieces, two or three Spoonfuls of Ketchup, a quarter of a Pound of fresh Butter, a Spoonful of Mushroom-pickle. Let it boil, and keep stirring it, till the Sauce is thick and enough ; if it wants any Salt, you must put some in. Then take the rest of the Row, and beat it up with the Yolk of an Egg, some Nutmeg, a little Lemon-peel cut small ; fry them in fresh Butter, in little Cakes, and some Pieces of Bread cut thus △, and fry'd brown. When the Carp is enough, take them up, pour your Sauce over them, lay the Cakes round the Dish, with Horse-reddish scraped fine, and fry'd Parsley. The rest lay on the Carp, and the Bread stick about them, and lay round them, and sliced Lemon notched, and laid round the Dish ; and two or three Pieces on the Carp. Send it to Table hot.

The boiling of Carp at all times is the best way, they eat fatter and finer. The stewing of them is no Addition to the Sauce, and only hardens the Fish, and spoils it. If you would have your Sauce white, put in good Fish-broth instead of Beer, and White Wine in the room of Red Wine. Make your Broth with any Sort of fresh Fish you have, and season it as you do Gravy.

To Fry Carp.

FIRST scale and gut them, wash them clean, lay them in a Cloth to dry, then flour them, and fry them of a fine light-brown. Fry some Toast cut thus △, and the Rows. When your Fish is done, lay them on a coarse Cloth to drain; let your Sauce be Butter and Anchovy, with the Juice of Lemon. Lay your Carp in the Dish, the Rows on each Side ; and garnish with the fry'd Toast and Lemon.

To Bake a Carp.

SCALE, wash, and clean a Brace of Carp very well ; take an earthen Pan deep enough to lye cleaverly in, butter the Pan a little, lay in your Carp, season it with Mace, Cloves, Nutmeg, and black and white Pepper, a Bundle of Sweet Herbs, an Onion, an Anchovy, pour in a Bottle of White Wine ; cover it close, and let them bake an Hour in a hot Oven if large ; if small, a less Time will do them. When they are enough, carefully take them up, and lay them in a Dish ; set it over hot Water to keep it hot, and cover it close ; then pour all the Liquor they were baked in, into a Sauce-pan, let it boil a Minute or two ; then strain it, and add half a Pound of Butter, rolled in Flour. Let it boil, keep stirring it, squeeze in the Juice of half a Lemon, and put in what Salt you want ; pour the Sauce over the Fish, lay the Rows round, and garnish with Lemon.

To Fry Tench.

SLIME your Tenches, flit the Skin along the Backs, and with the Point of your Knife rise it up from the Bone ; then cut the Skin a-cross at the Head and Tail ; then strip it off, and take out the Bone ; then take another Tench, or a Carp, and mince the Flesh small with Mushrooms, Clives, and Parsley. Season them with Salt, Pepper, beaten Mace, Nutmeg, and a few Savory Herbs minced small. Mingle these all well together ; then pound them in a Mortar, with Crumbs of Bread, as much as two Eggs soaked in Cream, the Yolks of three or four Eggs, and a Piece of Butter. When these have been well pounded, stuff the Tenches with this Farce : Take clarified Butter, put it into a Pan, set it over the Fire, and when it is hot, flour your Tenches, and put them into the Pan, one by one, and fry them brown ; then take them up, lay them in a coarse Cloth before the Fire to keep hot. In the mean time, pour all the Grease and Fat out of the Pan, put in a quarter of a Pound of Butter, shake some Flour all over the Pan, keep stirring with a Spoon till the Butter is a little brown ; then pour in half a Pint of White Wine, stir it together, pour in half a Pint of boiling Water, an Onion stuck with Cloves, a Bundle of Sweet Herbs, and a Blade or two of Mace. Cover them close, and let them stew as softly as you can for a quarter of an Hour, then strain off the Liquor, put it into the Pan again, add two Spoonfuls of Ketchup, have ready an Ounce of Truffles and Morells, boiled in half a Pint of Water tender, pour in Truffles, Water and all, into the Pan, a few Mushrooms, and either half a Pint of Oysters, clean washed in their own Liquor, and the Liquor and all put into the Pan, or some Crawfish ; but then you must put in the Tails, and after clean picking them, boil them in half a Pint of Water, strain the Liquor, and put into the Sauce ; or take some Fish Melts and toss up in your Sauce: All this is just as you fancy.

When

When you find your Sauce is very good, put your Tench into the Pan; make them quite hot, then lay them into your Dish, and pour the Sauce over them. Garnish with Lemon.

Or you may for Change, put in half a Pint of stale Beer, instead of Water. You may dress Tench just as you do Carp.

To Roast a Cod's Head.

WASH it very clean, and score it with a Knife, strew a little Salt on it, and lay it in a Stew-pan before the Fire, with something behind it, that the Fire may roast it. All the Water that comes from it the first half Hour, throw away; then throw on it a little Nutmeg, Cloves, and Mace beat fine, and Salt; flour it, and baste it with Butter. When that has lain some time, turn it, and season, and baste the other Side the same; turn it often, then baste it with Butter and Crumbs of Bread. If it is a large Head, it will take four or five Hours baking; have ready some melted Butter with an Anchovy, some of the Liver of the Fish boiled and bruised fine, mix it well with the Butter, and two Yolks of Eggs beat fine, and mixed with the Butter, then strain them through a Sieve, and put them into the Sauce-pan again, with a few Shrimps, or pickled Cockles, two Spoonfuls of Red Wine, and the Juice of a Lemon. Pour it into the Pan the Head was roasted in, and stir it all together, pour it into the Sauce-pan, keep it stirring, and let it boil; pour it in a Bason. Garnish the Head with fry'd Fish, Lemon, and scraped Horse-reddish. If you have a large Tin Oven it will do better.

To Boil a Cod's Head.

SET a Fish-Kettle on the Fire with Water enough to boil it, a good Handful of Salt, a Pint of Vinegar, a Bundle of Sweet Herbs, and a Piece of Horse-reddish. Let it boil a quarter of an Hour, then put in the Head; and when you are sure it is enough, lift up the Fish-plate, with the Fish on it, set it a-cross the Kettle to drain, then lay it in your Dish, lay the Liver on one Side. Garnish with Lemon and Horse-reddish scraped; melt some Butter, with a little of the Fish-liquor, an Anchovy, Oysters, or Shrimps, or just what you fancy.

To Stew Cod.

CUT your Cod into Slices an Inch thick, lay them in the Bottom of a large Stew-pan, season them with Nutmeg, beaten Pepper and Salt, a Bundle of Sweet Herbs, and an Onion, half a Pint of White Wine, a quarter of a Pint of Water. Cover it close, and let it simmer softly for five or six Minutes, then squeeze in the Juice of a Lemon; put in a few Oysters and the Liquor strained, a Piece of Butter, as big as an Egg rolled in Flour, a Blade or two of Mace; cover it close, and let it stew softly, shaking the Pan often. When it is enough, take out the Sweet Herbs and Onion, and dish it up, pour the Sauce over it, and garnish with Lemon.

To Fricasee Cod.

GET the Sounds, blanch them, and make them very clean, cut them into little Pieces; if they be dried Sounds, you must first boil them tender. Get some of the Rows, blanch them, and wash them clean; cut them into round Pieces about an Inch thick, some of the Livers, an equal Quantity of each, to make a handsome Dish, a Piece of Cod about one Pound in the Middle. Put them into a Stew-pan, season them with a little beaten Mace, and grated Nutmeg and Salt, a little Bundle of Sweet Herbs, an Onion, a quarter of a Pint of Fish-broth, or boiling Water; cover them close, and let them stew a few Minutes; then put in half a Pint of Red Wine, a few Oysters with the Liquor strained, a Piece of Butter rolled in Flour, shake the Pan round, and let them stew softly, till they are enough. Take out the Sweet Herbs and Onion, and dish it up. Garnish with Lemon. Or you may do them white thus: Instead of Red Wine add White, and a quarter of a Pint of Cream.

To Bake a Cod's Head.

BUTTER the Pan you intend to bake it in, make your Head very clean, lay it in the Pan, put in a Bundle of Sweet Herbs, an Onion stuck with Cloves, three or four Blades of Mace, half a large Spoonful of black and white Pepper, a Nutmeg bruised, a quart of Water, a little Piece of Lemon-peel, and a little Piece of Horse-reddish. Flour your Head, grate a little Nutmeg over it, stick Pieces of Butter all over it, and throw Raspings all over that. Send it to the Oven to bake; when it is enough, take it out of that Dish, and lay it carefully into the Dish you intend to serve it up in. Set the Dish over boiling Water, and cover it with a Cover to keep it hot. In the mean time be quick, pour all the Liquor out of the Dish it was baked in, into a Sauce-pan, set on the Fire, to boil for three or four Minutes; then strain it, and put to it a Gill of Red Wine, two Spoonfuls of Ketchup, a Pint of Shrimps, half a Pint of Oysters, or Muscles, Liquor and all; but first strain it, a Spoonful of Mushroom-pickle, a quarter of a Pound of Butter rolled in Flour; stir it all together, till it is thick and boils; then pour it into the Dish, have ready some Toast, cut thus $\triangle$, and fry'd crisp. Stick Pieces about the Head and Mouth; lay the rest round the Head. Garnish with Lemon notched, scraped Horse-reddish, and Parsley crisped in a Plate before the Fire; lay one Slice of Lemon on the Head, and serve it up hot.

88   *The Art of Cookery, made Plain and Easy.*

To Broil Shrimp, Cod, Salmon, Whiting, or Haddocks.

FLOUR it, and have a quick clear Fire, set your Gridiron high, broil it of a fine brown, lay it in your Dish, and for Sauce have good melted Butter, take a Lobster, bruise the Body in the Butter, cut the Meat small, put all together into the melted Butter, make it hot, and pour into your Dish, or into Basons. Garnish with Horse-reddish and Lemon.

Or Oyster Sauce made thus.

TAKE half a Pint of Oysters, put them into a Sauce-pan with their own Liquor, two or three Blades of Mace; let them simmer till they are plump, then with a Fork take out the Oysters, strain the Liquor to them, put them into the Sauce-pan again, with a Gill of White Wine hot, a Pound of Butter rolled in a little Flour; shake the Sauce-pan often, and when the Butter is melted, give it a boil up.

Muscle-Sauce made thus is very good, only you must put them into a Stew-pan, and cover them close, first to open and search, that there be no Crabs under the Tongue.

Or a Spoonful of Wallnut pickle in the Butter, makes the Sauce good, or a Spoonful of either Sort of Ketchup or Horse-reddish Sauce.

Melt your Butter, scrape a good deal of Horse-reddish fine, put it into the melted Butter, grate half a Nutmeg, beat up the Yolk of an Egg, with one Spoonful of Cream, pour it into the Butter, keep it stirring till it boils, then pour it directly into your Bason.

To Dress Little Fish.

AS to all Sorts of little Fish, such as Smelts, Roch, &c. they should be fry'd dry, and of a fine brown, and nothing but plain Butter. Garnish with Lemon.

And to boiled Salmon the same, only garnish with Lemon, and Horse-reddish.

And with all boiled Fish, you should put a good deal of Salt, and Horse-reddish in the Water; except Mackrel, with which put Salt and Mint, Parsley and Fennel, which you must chop to put into the Butter; and some love scalded Gooseberries with them. And be sure to boil your Fish well; but take great Care they don't break.

To Broil Mackrel.

CLEAN them, cut off the Heads, split them, season them with Pepper and Salt, flower them, and broil them of a fine light-brown. Let your Sauce be plain Butter.

To Broil Weavers.

GUT them and wash them clean, dry them in a clean Cloth, flour them, and broil them, and have melted Butter in a Cup. They are a fine Fish, and cut as firm as a Soal; but you must take care not to hurt yourself with the two sharp Bones in the Head.

To Boil a Turbutt.

LAY it in a good deal of Salt and Water an Hour or two; and if it is not quite sweet, shift your Water five or six times; first put in a good deal of Salt in the Mouth and Belly. In the mean time let on your Fish-Kettle with clean Water and Salt, a little Vinegar, and a Piece of Horse-reddish. When the Water boils, lay the Turbutt on a Fish-plate, put it into the Kettle, let it be well boiled; but take great Care it is not too much done; when enough, take off the Fish-Kettle, set it before the Fire, and carefully lift up the Fish-plate, set it a-cross the Kettle to drain; in the mean time melt a good deal of fresh Butter, and bruise in either the Body of one or two Lobsters, and the Meat cut small, and give it a boil, and pour it into Basons. This is the best Sauce; but you may make what you please. Lay the Fish in the Dish; garnish with scraped Horse-reddish and Lemon, and pour a few Spoonfuls of Sauce over it.

To Bake a Turbutt.

TAKE a Dish, the Size of your Turbut, rub Butter all over it thick, throw a little Salt, a little beaten Pepper, and half a large Nutmeg, some Parsley minced fine, and throw all over, pour in a Pint of Wine, cut off the Head and Tail, lay it into the Dish, pour another Pint of White Wine all over it, grate the other half of the Nutmeg over it, and a little Pepper, and some Salt, and chopped Parsley. Lay a Piece of Butter here and there all over, and throw a little Flour all over, and then a good many Crumbs of Bread. Bake it, and be sure that it is of a fine brown, then lay it in your Dish, stir the Sauce in your Dish all together, pour it into a Sauce-pan, shake in a little Flour, stir it well together, let it boil, then stir in a Piece of Butter, and two Spoonfuls of Ketchup, let it boil, and pour it into Basons. Garnish your Dish with Lemon, and you may add what you fancy to the Sauce, as

Shrimps,

Shrimps, Anchovies, Mushrooms, &c. If a small Turbutt, half the Wine will do; it eats finely thus: Lay it in a Dish, skim off all the Fat, and pour the rest over it; let it stand till cold; and it is good with Vinegar, and a fine Dish to set out a cold Table.

To Dress a Jole of Pickled Salmon.

LAY it in fresh Water all Night, then lay it in a Fish-plate, put it into a large Stew-pan, season it with a little whole Pepper, a Blade or two of Mace in a coarse Muslin Rag tied, a whole Onion, a Nutmeg bruised, a Bundle of Sweet Herbs and Parsley, a little Piece of Lemon-peel; put to it three large Spoonfuls of Vinegar, a Pint of White Wine, and a quarter of a Pound of fresh Butter rolled in Flour. Cover it close, and let it simmer over a slow Fire for a quarter of an Hour; then carefully take up your Salmon, and lay it in your Dish, set it over hot Water; and cover it. In the mean time let your Sauce boil, till it is thick and good. Take out the Spice, Onion, and Sweet Herbs, and pour it over the Fish, Garnish with Lemon.

To Broil Salmon.

CUT fresh Salmon into thick Pieces, flour them, and broil them, lay them in your Dish, and have plain melted Butter in a Cup.

Baked Salmon.

TAKE a little Piece cut into Slices, about an Inch thick; butter the Dish that you would serve it to Table on, lay the Slices in the Dish; take off the Skin, make a Force thus: Take the Flesh of an Eel, the Flesh of a Salmon, an equal Quantity, beat it in a Mortar, season it with beaten Pepper, Salt, Nutmeg, two or three Cloves, some Parsley, a few Mushrooms, and a Piece of Butter; ten or a Dozen Coriander-seeds beat fine. Beat all together, boil the Crumb of a Halfpenny Role in Milk, beat up four Eggs, stir it together till it is thick; let it cool, and mix it well together with the rest; then mix all together with four raw Eggs, on every Slice lay this Force-meat all over, pour a very little melted Butter over them, and a few Crumbs of Bread; lay a Crust round the Edge of the Dish, and stick Oysters round upon it. Bake it in an Oven; and when it is of a very fine brown, serve it up; pour a little plain Butter with a little Red Wine in it, into the Dish, and the Juice of a Lemon: Or you may bake it in any Dish, and when it is enough, lay the Slices into another Dish. Pour the Butter and Wine into the Dish it was baked in, give it a Boil, and pour it into the Dish. Garnish with Lemon. This is a fine Dish, squeeze the Juice of a Lemon in.

To Broil Mackrel Whole.

CUT off their Heads, gut them, wash them clean, pull out the Row at the Neck-end, boil it in a little Water, then bruise it with a Spoon, beat up the Yolk of an Egg, with a little Nutmeg, a little Lemon-peel cut fine, a little Thyme, some Parsley boiled and chopped fine, a little Pepper and Salt, a few Crumbs of Bread; mix all well together, and fill the Mackrel; flower it well, and broil it nicely. Let your Sauce be plain Butter, with a little Ketchup or Wallnut-pickle.

To Broil Herrings.

SCALE them, gut them, cut off their Heads, wash them clean, dry them in a Cloath, flower them, and broil them, but with your Knife just notch them a-cross; take the Heads, mash them, boil them in Small Beer or Ale, with a little whole Pepper and Onion. Let it boil a quarter of an Hour; then strain it, thicken it with Butter and Flour, and a good deal of Mustard; lay the Fish in the Dish, and pour the Sauce into a Bason, or plain melted Butter and Mustard.

To Fry Herrings.

CLEAN them as above, fry them in Butter, and have ready a good many Onions peeled, and cut thin. Fry them of a light-brown with the Herrings; lay the Herrings in your Dish, and the Onions round, Butter and Mustard in a Cup. You must do them with a quick Fire.

To Dress Herring and Cabbage.

BOIL your Cabbage tender, then put it into a Sauce-pan, and chop it with a Spoon; put in a good Piece of Butter, let it stew, stirring, least it should burn. Take some Red Herrings and split them open, and toast them before the Fire, till they are hot through. Lay the Cabbage in a Dish, and lay the Herring on it, and send it to Table hot.

Or pick your Herring from the Bones, and throw all over your Cabbage. Have ready a hot Iron, and just hold it over the Herring to make it hot, and send it away quickly.

Z   Water-

Water-Sokey.

TAKE some of the smallest Plaise, or Flounders you can get, wash them clean, cut the Fins close, put them into a Stew-pan, put just Water enough to boil them in, a little Salt, and a Bunch of Parsley. When they are enough, send them to Table in a Soop-dish, with the Liquor to keep them hot, have Parsley and Butter in a Cup.

To Stew Eels.

SKIN, gut, and wash them very clean in six or eight Waters, to wash away all the Sand; then cut them in Pieces about as long as your Finger, put just Water enough for Sauce, put in a small Onion stuck with Cloves, a little Bundle of Sweet Herbs, a Blade or two of Mace, and some whole Pepper in a thin Muslin Rag. Cover it close, and let them stew very softly.

Look at them now and then, and put in a little Piece of Butter rolled in Flour, and a little chopped Parsley. When you find they are quite tender, and well done, take out the Onion, Spice, and Sweet Herbs; put in Salt enough to season it; then dish them up with the Sauce.

To Stew Eels with Broth.

CLEANSE your Eels as above, put them into a Sauce-pan, with a Blade or two of Mace, and a Crust of Bread; put just Water enough to cover them close, let them stew very softly; when they are enough, dish them up with the Broth, and have a little plain melted Butter in a Cup to eat the Eels with. The Broth will be very good, and is fit for weakly and consumptive Constitutions.

To Dress a Pike.

GUT it, cleanse it, and make very clean, then turn it round with the Tail in the Mouth, lay it in a little Dish, cut Toast thus △, fill the Middle with them, flour it, and stick Pieces of Butter all over; then throw a little more Flour, send it to the Oven to bake; or it will do better in a Tin Oven before the Fire, then you can baste it as you will. When it is done, lay it in your Dish, and have ready melted Butter, with an Anchovy dissolved in it, and a few Oysters or Shrimps; and if there is any Liquor in the Dish it was baked in, add it to the Sauce, and put in just what you fancy. Pour your Sauce into the Dish, and garnish it with Toast about the Fish, and Lemon about the Dish. You should have a Pudding in the Belly made thus: Take grated Bread, two hard Eggs chopped fine, half a Nutmeg grated, a little Lemon-peel cut fine, and either the Row or Liver, or both, if any, chopped fine; and if you have none, get either a Piece of the Liver of a Cod, or the Row of any Fish, mix them all together, with a raw Egg and a good Piece of Butter. Role it up, and put it into the Fish's Belly, before you bake it. A Haddock done this Way eats very well.

To Broil Haddocks, when they are in High Season.

SCALE them, gut, and wash them clean, don't rip open the Belly, but take the Guts out with the Gills, dry them in a clean Cloth very well; if there be any Row or Liver, take it out, but put it in again. Flour them well, and have a clear good Fire, let your Gridiron be hot and clean; lay them on, turn them quick two or three times for fear of sticking; then let one Side be enough, and turn the other Side; when that is done, lay them in your Dish, and have plain Butter in a Cup.

They eat finely salted a Day or two before you dress them, and hung up to dry, or boiled with Egg-sauce. *Newcastle* is a famous Place for salted Haddocks; they come in Barrels, and keep a great while.

To Broil Cod-Sounds.

YOU must first lay them in hot Water a few Minutes; take them out and rub them well with Salt, to take off the Skin and black Dirt, then they will look white, then put them in Water, and give them a boil. Take them out and flour them well, Pepper and Salt them, and broil them. When they are enough, lay them in your Dish, and pour melted Butter and Mustard into the Dish. Broil them whole.

To Fricasee Cod-Sounds.

CLEAN them very well as above, then cut them into little pretty Pieces, boil them tender in Milk and Water, then throw them into a Cullendar to drain, put them into a clean Sauce-pan, season them with a little beaten Mace, and grated Nutmeg, and a very little Salt, pour to them just Cream enough for Sauce, and a good Piece of Butter rolled in Flour, keep shaking your Sauce-pan round all the time till it is thick enough; then dish it up, and garnish with Lemon.

To Dress Salmon au Court-Bouillon.

AFTER having washed and made your Salmon very clean, score the Sides pretty deep, that it may take the Season, take a quarter of an Ounce of Mace, a quarter of an Ounce of Cloves, a Nutmeg, dry them, and beat them fine, and a quarter of an Ounce of black Pepper beat fine, and an Ounce of Salt. Lay the Salmon in a Napkin, season it well with this Spice, cut some Lemon-peel fine and Parsley, throw all over, and in the Notches put about a Pound of fresh Butter rolled in Flour, in the Belly of the Fish, a few Bay leaves; roll it up tight in the Napkin, and bind it about with Packthread; put it in a Fish-kettle, just big enough to hold it, pour in a Quart of White Wine, a Quart of Vinegar, and as much Water as will just boil it.

Set it over a quick Fire, cover it close; when it is enough, which you must judge by the Bigness of your Salmon, set it over a Stove to stew till you are ready; then have a clean Napkin folded in the Dish it is to lay it, turn it out of the Napkin it was boiled in, on the other Napkin. Garnish the Dish with a good deal of Parsley, crisped before the Fire.

For Sauce have nothing but plain Butter in a Cup, or Horse-reddish and Vinegar. Serve it up for a first Course.

To Dress Salmon a la Braise.

TAKE a fine large Piece of Salmon, or a large Salmon-Trout, make a Pudding thus: Take a large Eel, make it clean, slit it open, take out the Bone, and take all the Meat clean from the Bone, chop it fine, with two Anchovies, a little Lemon-peel cut fine, a little Pepper, and a grated Nutmeg with Parsley chopped, and a very little Bit of Thyme, a few Crumbs of Bread, the Yolk of an hard Egg chopped fine; roll it up in a Piece of Butter, and put it into the Belly of the Fish, sew it up, lay it in an Oval Stew-pan, or little Kettle, that will just hold it, take half a Pound of fresh Butter, put it into a Sauce-pan, when it is melted, shake in a Handful of Flour, stir it till it is a little brown, then pour to it a Pint of Fish-Broth, stir it together, pour it to the Fish, with a Bottle of White Wine. Season it with Salt to your Palate; put some Mace, Cloves, and whole Pepper into a coarse Muslin Rag, tye it, and put to the Fish an Onion, and a little Bundle of Sweet Herbs. Cover it close, and let it stew very softly over a slow Fire, put in some fresh Mushrooms, or pickled ones cut small, an Ounce of Truffles and Morells cut small, let them all stew together; when it is enough, take up your Salmon carefully, lay it in your Dish, and pour the Sauce all over. Garnish with scraped Horse-reddish and Lemon notched, serve it up hot. This is a fine Dish for a first Course.

Salmon in Cases.

CUT your Salmon into little Pieces, such as will lay rolled in half Sheets of Paper; season it with Pepper, Salt and Nutmeg, butter the Inside of the Paper well, fold the Paper so as nothing can come out; then lay them on a Tin Plate to be baked, pour a little melted Butter over the Papers, and then Crumbs of Bread all over them. Don't let your Oven be too hot, for fear of burning the Paper; a Tin Oven before the Fire does best. When you think they are enough, serve them up; just as they are, there will be Sauce enough in the Papers.

To Dress Flat Fish.

IN Dressing all Sorts of Flat Fish, take great Care in the boiling of them; be sure to have them enough; but don't let them be broke, and mind to put a good deal of Salt in, and Horse-reddish in the Water, and let your Fish be well drained, and mind to cut the Fins off. When you fry them, let them be well dried in a Cloth, and floured, and fry them of a fine light-brown, either in Oil or Butter. If there be any Water in your Dish with the boiled Fish, take it out with a Sponge. As to your fry'd Fish, a coarse Cloth is the best thing to drain it on.

To Dress Salt Fish.

OLD LING, which is the best Sort of Salt Fish, lay it in Water twelve Hours, then lay twelve Hours on a Board, then twelve more in Water. When you boil it, put it into the Water cold; if it is good, it will take about fifteen Minutes boiling softly. Boil Parsnips very tender, scrape them, and put them into a Sauce-pan, put to them some Milk, stir them till thick, then stir in a good Piece of Butter, and a little Salt; when they are enough, lay them in a Plate, the Fish by itself dry, and Butter and Hard Eggs chopped in a Bason.

As to Water-Cod, that need only be boiled and well skimmed.

Scotch-Haddocks you must lay in Water all Night. You may boil or broil them; if you broil, you must split them in two. —— You may garnish your Dishes with hard Eggs and Parsnips.

To Dress Lampreys.

THE best of this Sort of Fish are taken in the River *Severn*; and when they are in Season, the Fishmongers, and others, in *London*, have them from *Gloucester*; but if you are where they are to be had fresh, you may dress them as you please.

To Fry Lampreys.

BLEED them, and save the Blood, then wash them in hot Water to take off the Slime, and cut them to Pieces. Fry them in a little fresh Butter, not quite enough, pour out the Fat, put in a little White Wine, give the Pan a Shake round, season it with whole Pepper, Nutmeg, Salt, and Sweet Herbs, and Bay-leaf, put in a few Capers, a good Piece of Butter rolled in Flour, and the Blood. Give the Pan a Shake round often, cover them close; when you think they are enough, take them out, strain the Sauce, and give them a boil quick, squeeze in a little Lemon, and pour over the Fish. Garnish with Lemon; and dress them just what way you fancy.

To Pitchcock Eels.

YOU must split a large Eel down the Back, and joint the Bones, cut it into two or three Pieces; melt a little Butter, put in a little Vinegar and Salt, let your Eel lay in two or three Minutes, then take the Pieces up, one by one, turn them round with a little fine Skewer, roll them in Crumbs of Bread, and broil them of a fine Brown. Let your Sauce be plain Butter, with the Juice of Lemon.

To Fry Eels.

MAKE them very clean, cut them into Pieces, season them with Pepper and Salt, flour them, and fry them in Butter. Let your Sauce be plain Butter melted, with the Juice of Lemon. Be sure they be well drained from the Fat, before you lay them in the Dish.

To Broil Eels.

TAKE a large Eel, skin it, and make it very clean; open the Belly, cut it into four Pieces, take the Tail-end, strip off the Flesh, beat it in a Mortar; season it with a little beaten Mace, a little grated Nutmeg, Pepper, and Salt, a little Parsley and Thyme, a little Lemon-peel, an equal Quantity of Crumbs of Bread, roll it in a little Piece of Butter, then mix it again with the Yolk of an Egg, roll it up again, and fill the three Pieces of Belly with it. Cut the Skin of the Eel, and wrap the Pieces in, and sew up the Skin. Broil them well, have Butter and an Anchovy for Sauce, with the Juice of Lemon.

To Farce Eels, with White Sauce.

SKIN and clean your Eel well, pick off all the Flesh clean from the Bone, which you must leave whole to the Head. Take the Flesh, cut it small, and beat it in a Mortar; then take half the Quantity of Crumbs of Bread, beat it with the Fish, season it with Nutmeg, and beaten Pepper, an Anchovy, and a good deal of Parsley chopped fine, a few Truffles boiled tender, in a very little Water; chop them fine, and put them into the Mortar with the Liquor, and a few Mushrooms; beat it well together; mix in a little Cream, then take it out, and mix it well together with your Hand, lay it round the Bone in the Shape of the Eel, lay it on a buttered Pan, drudge it well with fine Crumbs of Bread, and bake it. When it is done, lay it carefully in your Dish, and have ready half a Pint of Cream, and a quarter of a Pound of fresh Butter, stir it one way till it is thick, pour it over your Eel, and garnish with Lemon.

To Dress Eels with Brown Sauce.

SKIN and clean a large Eel very well, cut it in Pieces, put it into a Sauce-pan or Stew-pan, put to it a quarter of a Pint of Water, a Bundle of Sweet Herbs, an Onion, some whole Pepper, a Blade of Mace, and a little Salt. Cover it close, and when it begins to simmer, put in a Gill of Red Wine a Spoonful of Mushroom-pickle, a Piece of Butter as big as a Wallnut rolled in Flour, cover it close and let it stew till it is enough, which you will know by the Eel being very tender. Take up your Eel, lay it in a Dish, strain your Sauce, give it a boil quick, and pour it over your Fish. You must make Sauce according to the Largeness of your Eel, more or less. Garnish with Lemon.

To Roast a Piece of Fresh Sturgeon.

GET a Piece of fresh Sturgeon, of about eight or ten Pounds, let it lay in Water and Salt six or eight Hours, with its Scales on; then fasten it on the Spit, and baste it well with Butter for a quarter of an Hour, then with a little Flour, then grate a Nutmeg all over it, a little Mace and Pepper beaten fine, and Salt thrown over it, and a few Sweet Herbs dried and powdered fine; and then Crumbs of Bread, then keep basting a little, and drudging with Crumbs of Bread, and what falls from it, till it is enough. In the mean time prepare this Sauce: Take a Pint of Water, an Anchovy, a little Piece of Lemon-peel, an Onion, a Bundle of Sweet Herbs, Mace, Cloves, whole Pepper black and white, a little Piece of Horse-reddish, cover it close, let it boil a quarter of an Hour, then strain it, put it into the Sauce-pan again, pour in a Pint of White Wine, about a Dozen Oysters and the Liquor, two Spoonfuls of Ketchup, two of Wallnut-pickle, the Inside of a Crab bruised fine, or Lobster, Shrimps

or

or Prawns, a good Piece of Butter rolled in Flour, a Spoonful of Mushroom-pickle, or Juice of Lemon. Boil it all together; when your Fish is enough, lay it in your Dish, and pour the Sauce over it. Garnish with fry'd Toasts and Lemon.

To Roast a Fillet or Collar of Sturgeon.

TAKE a Piece of fresh Sturgeon, scale it, gut it, take out the Bones, and cut in Lengths about seven or eight Inches; then provide some Shrimp-pickle and Oysters, an equal Quantity of Crumbs of Bread, and a little Lemon-peel grated, some Nutmeg, a little beaten Mace, a little Pepper, and chopped Parsley, a few Sweet Herbs, an Anchovy, mix it together; when it is done, butter one Side of your Fish, and strew some of your Mixture upon it; then begin to roll it up as close as possible, and when the first Piece is rolled up, roll upon that another, prepared in the same manner, and bind it round with a narrow Fillet, leaving as much of the Fish apparent as may be; but you must mind that the Roll must not be above four Inches and a half thick, for else one Part will be done before the Inside is warm; therefore we often parboil the inside Roll before we roll it. When it is enough, lay it in your Dish, and prepare Sauce as above. Garnish with Lemon.

To Boil Sturgeon.

CLEAN your Sturgeon, and prepare as much Liquor as will just boil it. To two Quarts of Water a Pint of Vinegar, a Stick of Horse-reddish, two or three Bits of Lemon-peel, some whole Pepper, a Bay-leaf or two, and a small Handful of Salt. Boil your Fish in this, and serve it with the following Sauce: Melt a Pound of Butter, dissolve an Anchovy in it, put in a Blade or two of Mace, bruise the Body of a Crab in the Butter, a few Shrimps or Crawfish, a little Ketchup, a little Lemon-juice, give it a boil, drain your Fish well, and lay it in your Dish. Garnish with fry'd Oysters, sliced Lemon, and scraped Horse-reddish; pour your Sauce into Boats or Basons.——So you may fry it, ragoo it, or bake it.

To Crimp Cod the Dutch Way.

TAKE a Gallon of Pump Water, and a Pound of Salt, and boil it half an Hour, skim it well, cut your Cod into Slices; and when the Salt and Water has boiled half an Hour, put in your Slices, two Minutes is enough to boil them; then take them out, lay them on a Sieve to drain, then flour them, and broil them. Make what Sauce you please.

To Crimp Scate.

IT must be cut into long Slips cross-ways, about an Inch broad; boil Water and Salt as above, then throw in your Scate; let your Water boil quick, and about three Minutes will boil it: Drain it, and send it to Table hot, with Butter and Mustard in one Cup, and Butter and Anchovy in the other Cup.

To Fricasee Scate, or Thornback White.

CUT the Meat clean from the Bone, Fins, &c. and make it very clean, cut it into little Pieces about an Inch broad, and two Inches long; lay it in your Stew-pan. To a Pound of the Flesh, put a quarter of a Pint of Water, a little beaten Mace, and grated Nutmeg, a little Bundle of Sweet Herbs, a little Salt; cover it, and let it boil three Minutes, take out the Sweet Herbs, put in a quarter of a Pint of good Cream, a Piece of Butter as big as a Wallnut rolled in Flour, a Glass of White Wine, keep shaking the Pan all the while one way, till it is thick and smooth, then dish it up, and garnish with Lemon.

To Fricasee it Brown.

TAKE your Fish as above, flour it, and fry it of a fine brown, in fresh Butter; then take it up, lay it before the Fire to keep warm, pour the Fat out of the Pan, shake in a little Flour; and with a Spoon, stir in a Piece of Butter as big as an Egg. Stir it round till it is well mixed in the Pan, then pour in a quarter of a Pint of Water, stir it round, shake in a very little beaten Pepper, a little beaten Mace, put in an Onion, and a little Bundle of Sweet Herbs, an Anchovy; shake it round, and let it boil; then pour in a quarter of a Pint of Red Wine, and a Spoonful of Ketchup, a little Juice of Lemon; stir it all together, and let it boil. When it is enough, take out the Sweet Herbs and Onion, and put in the Fish to heat; then dish it up, and garnish with Lemon.

To Fricasee Soals White.

SKIN, wash, and gut your Soals very clean, cut off their Heads, dry them in a Cloth, then with your Knife very carefully cut the Flesh from the Bones and Fins, on both Sides. Cut the Flesh long-ways, and then a-cross, so that each Soal will be in eight Pieces; take the Heads and Bones, and put them into a Sauce-pan, with a Pint of Water, a Bundle of Sweet Herbs, an Onion, a little whole Pepper, two or three Blades of Mace, a little Salt, a very little Piece of Lemon-peel, and a little

Cruft of Bread. Cover it clofe, let it boil till half is wafted, then ftrain it through a fine Sieve, put it into a Stew-pan, put in the Soals and half a Pint of White Wine, a little Parfley chopped fine, a few Mufhrooms cut fmall, a Piece of Butter as big as a Hen's Egg rolled in Flour, grate in a little Nutmeg, fet all together on the Fire, but keep fhaking the Pan all the while, till your Fifh is enough; then difh it up, and garnifh with Lemon.

To Fricafee Soals Brown.

CLEANSE, and cut your Soals, boil the Water as in the foregoing Receipt; flour your Fifh and fry them in frefh Butter of a fine light-brown; take the Flefh of a fmall Soal, beat it in a Mortar, with a Piece of Bread as big as an Hen's Egg foaked in Cream, the Yolks of two hard Eggs, and a little melted Butter, a little Bit of Thyme, a little Parfley, an Anchovy, feafon it with Nutmeg; mix all together with the Yolk of a raw Egg, and with a little Flour; roll it up into little Balls, and fry them, but not too much; then lay your Fifh and Balls before the Fire, pour out all the Fat of the Pan, pour in the Liquor, which is boiled with the Spice and Herbs; ftir it round in the Pan, then put in half a Pint of Red Wine, a few Truffles and Morells, a few Mufhrooms, and a Spoonful of Ketchup, and the Juice of half a fmall Lemon. Stir it all together, and let it boil, then ftir in a Piece of Butter rolled in Flour; ftir it round, when your Sauce is of a fine Thicknefs, put in your Fifh and Balls, and when it is hot difh it up, put in the Balls, and pour your Sauce over it. Garnifh with Lemon. In the fame manner drefs a fmall Turbut, or any flat Fifh.

To Boil Soals.

TAKE a Pair of Soals, make them clean, lay them in Vinegar, Salt and Water two Hours, then dry them in a Cloth, put them into a Stew-pan, put to them a Pint of White Wine, a Bundle of Sweet Herbs, an Onion ftuck with fix Cloves, fome whole Pepper, and a little Salt. Cover them, and let them boil; when they are enough, take them up lay them in your Difh, ftrain the Liquor, and thicken it up with Butter and Flower, pour the Sauce over, and garnifh with fcraped Horfe-reddifh and Lemon. In this manner drefs a little Turbutt. It is a gentle Difh for Supper. You may add Prawns or Shrimps, or Mufcles to the Sauce.

To make a Collar of Fifh in Ragoo, to look like a Breaft of Veal Collared.

TAKE a large Eel, skin it, wafh it clean, and parboil it, pick off the Flefh, and beat it in a Mortar; feafon it with beaten Mace, Nutmeg, Pepper, Salt, a few Sweet Herbs, Parfley, and a little Lemon-peal chopped fmall; beat all well together with an equal Quantity of Crumbs of Bread; mix it well together, then take a Turbut, Soals, Scate or Thornback, or any flat Fifh, that will roll cleverly; lay the flat Fifh on the Dreffer, take away all the Bones and Fins, and cover your Fifh with the Farce; then roll it up as tight as you can, and open the Skin of your Eel, and bind the Collar with it nicely; fo that it may be flat Top and Bottom, to ftand well in the Difh; then butter an earthen Difh, and fet it in it upright, flour it all over, and ftick a Piece of Butter on the Top, and round the Edges; fo that it may run down on the Fifh, and let it be well baked, but take great Care it is not broke; let there be a quarter of a Pint of Water in the Difh.

In the mean time, take the Water the Eel was boiled in, and all the Bones of the Fifh, fet them on to boil, feafon them with Mace, Cloves, black and white Pepper, Sweet Herbs, and Onion, cover it clofe, and let it boil till there is about a quarter of a Pint; then ftrain it, add to it, a few Truffles and Morels, a few Mufhrooms, two Spoonfuls of Ketchup, a Gill of Red Wine, a Piece of Butter as big as a large Wallnut rolled in Flour. Stir all together, feafon it with Salt to your Palate, fave fome of the Farce you make of the Eel, and mix with the Yolk of an Egg, and roll them up in little Balls with Flour, and fry them, of a light-brown. When your Fifh is enough, lay it in your Difh, skim all the Fat off the Pan, and pour the Gravy to your Sauce. Let it all boil together till it is thick; then pour it over the Roll, and put in your Balls. Garnifh with Lemon.

This does beft in a Tin Oven before the Fire, becaufe then you can bafte it as you pleafe. This is a fine Bottom-difh.

To Butter Crabs, or Lobfters.

TAKE two Crabs, or Lobfters, being boiled, and cold, take all the Meat out of the Shells and Bodies, mince it fmall, and put it all together into a Sauce-pan; add to it a Glafs of White Wine, two Spoonfuls of Vinegar, a Nutmeg grated, then let it boil up till it is thorough hot; then have ready half a Pound of frefh Butter, melted with an Anchovy, and the Yolks of two Eggs beat up and mixed with the Butter; then mix Crab and Butter all together, fhaking the Sauce-pan conftantly round till it is quite hot; then have ready the great Shell, either of the Crab or Lobfter, lay it in the Middle of your Difh, pour fome into the Shell, and the reft in little Saucers round the Shell, fticking three Corner Toafts between the Saucers, and round the Shell. This is a fine Side-difh at a fecond Courfe.

To Butter Lobsters another Way.

PARBOIL your Lobsters, then break the Shells, and pick out all the Meat, cut it small, take the Meat out of the Body, mix it fine with a Spoon in a little White Wine: For example, a small Lobster one Spoonful of Wine, put it into a Sauce-pan with the Meat of the Lobster, and four Spoonfuls of White Wine, a Blade of Mace, a little beaten Pepper, and Salt; let it stew all together a few Minutes. then stir in a Piece of Butter, shake your Sauce-pan round till your Butter is melted, and put in a Spoonful of Vinegar, then strew in as many Crumbs of Bread as will make it thick enough. When it is hot, pour it into your Plate, and garnish with the Chine of a Lobster, cut in four, peppered, salted, and broiled. This makes a pretty Plate, or a fine Dish with two or three Lobsters. You may add one Tea Spoonful of fine Sugar to your Sauce.

To Roast Lobsters.

BOIL your Lobsters, then lay them before the Fire, and baste them with Butter, till they have a fine Froth. Dish them up with plain melted Butter in a Cup. This is as good a Way to the full as roasting them, and not half the Trouble.

To make a Fine Dish of Lobsters.

TAKE three Loosters, boil the largest as above, and froth it before the Fire; take the other two boiled, and butter them as in the foregoing Receipt. Take the two Body-shells, heat them hot, and fill them with the buttered Meat; lay the large Lobster in the Middle, and the two Shells on each Side; and the two great Claws of the middle Lobster at each End; and the four Pieces of Chines of the two Lobsters broiled, and laid on each End. This, if nicely done, makes a pretty Dish.

To Dress a Crab.

HAVING taken out the Meat, and cleansed it from the Skin, put it into a Stew-pan, with half a Pint of White Wine, a little Nutmeg, Pepper, and Salt over a flow Fire; throw in a few Crumbs of Bread, beat up one Yolk of an Egg with one Spoonful of Vinegar, throw it in, and shake the Sauce-pan round a Minute, then serve it up on a Plate.

To Stew Prawns, Shrimps, or Crawfish.

PICK out the Tails, lay them by about two Quarts, take the Bodies, give them a Bruise, put them into a Pint of White Wine, with a Blade of Mace; let them stew a quarter of an Hour, stir them together, and strain them, wash out the Sauce-pan, and put to it the strained Liquor, and the Tails, grate a small Nutmeg in, add a little Salt, and a quarter of a Pound of Butter rolled in Flour, shake it all together, cut a pretty thin Toast round a quarter of a Peck-loaf, toast it brown on both Sides, cut it into six Pieces, lay it close together in the Bottom of your Dish, and pour your Fish and Sauce over it. Send it to Table hot; if it be Crawfish or Prawns, garnish your Dish with some of the bigest Claws, laid thick round. Water will do in the room of Wine, only add a Spoonful of Vinegar.

To make Collups of Oysters.

PUT your Oysters into Scollop-shells for that purpose, set them on your Gridiron over a good clear Fire, let them stew till you think your Oysters are enough, then have ready some Crumbs of Bread rubed in a clean Napkin, fill your Shells, and set them before a good Fire, and baste them well with Butter. Let them be of a fine brown, keeping them turning, to be brown all over alike; but a Tin Oven does them best before the Fire. They eat much the best done this way, though most People stew the Oysters first in a Sauce-pan, with a Blade of Mace, thickened with a Piece of Butter, and fill the Shell, and then cover them with Crumbs, and brown them with a hot Iron.—But the Bread has not the fine Taste of the former.

To Stew Muscles.

WASH them very clean from the Sand in two or three Waters, put them into a Stew-pan, cover them close, and let them stew till all the Shells are opened, then take them out, one by one, pick them out of the Shell, and look under the Tongue to see if there be a Crab; if there is, you must throw away the Muscle; some will only pick out the Crab, and eat the Muscle. When you have picked them all clean, put them into a Sauce-pan, to a Quart of Muscles put half a Pint of the Liquor strained through a Sieve, put in a Blade or two of Mace, a Piece of Butter, as big as a large Wallnut, rolled in Flour, let them stew, toast some Bread brown, and lay them round the Dish, cut thus △, pour in the Cockles, and send them to Table hot.

Another Way to Stew Muscles.

CLEAN, and stew your Muscles, as in the foregoing Receipt, only to a Quart of Muscles, put a Pint of Liquor, and a quarter of a Pound of Butter rolled in, a very little Flour. When they are enough, have some Crumbs of Bread ready, and cover the Bottom of your Dish thick, grate half a Nutmeg over them, and pour the Muscles and Sauce all over the Crumbs, and send them to Table.

A Third Way to Dress Muscles.

STEW them as above, and lay them in your Dish; strew your Crumbs of Bread thick all over them, then set them before a good Fire, turning the Dish round and round, that they may be brown all alike. Keep basting them with Butter, that the Crumbs may be crisp, and it will make a pretty Side-dish. You may do Cockles the same Way.

To Stew Scollops.

BOIL them very well in Salt and Water, take them out and stew them in a little of the Liquor, a little White Wine, and a little Vinegar, two or three Blades of Mace, two or three Cloves, a Piece of Butter rolled in Flour, and the Juice of a Seville Orange. Stew them well and dish them up.

To Ragoo Oysters.

TAKE a Quart of the largest Oysters you can get, open them, save the Liquor, and strain it through a fine Sieve; wash your Oysters in warm Water, make a Batter thus: Take two Yolks of Eggs, beat them well, grate in half a Nutmeg, cut a little Lemon-peel small, a good deal of Parsley, a Spoonful of the Juice of Spinage, two Spoonfuls of Cream or Milk, beat it up with Flour to a thick Batter, have ready some Butter in a Stew-pan, dip your Oysters one by one into the Batter, and have ready Crumbs of Bread, then roll them in it, and fry them quick and brown; some with the Crumbs of Bread, some without. Take them out of the Pan, and set them before the Fire; then have ready a Quart of Chesnuts shelled and skined, fry them in the Butter; when they are enough, take them up, pour the Fat out of the Pan, shake a little Flour all over the Pan, and rub a Piece of Butter as big as a Hen's Egg all over the Pan with your Spoon, till it is melted and thick; then put in the Oyster-liquor, three or four Blades of Mace, stir it round, put in a few Pistachoe-nuts shelled, let them boil, then put in the Chesnuts, and half a Pint of White Wine, have ready the Yolks of two Eggs, beat up with four Spoonfuls of Cream; stir all well together, when it is thick and fine, lay the Oysters in the Dish, and pour the Ragoo over them. Garnish with Chesnuts and Lemon.

You may ragoo Muscles the same way. You may leave out the Pistachoe-nuts if you don't like them; but they give the Sauce a fine Flavour.

To Ragoo Endive.

TAKE some fine White Endive, three Heads, lay them in Salt and Water, two or three Hours, take a hundred of Asparagus, cut off the green Heads, chop the rest as far as is tender small, lay it in Salt and Water, take a Bunch of Salary, wash it, and scrape it clean, cut it in Pieces about three Inches long, put it into a Sauce-pan, with a Pint of Water, three or four Blades of Mace, some whole Pepper tied in a Rag, let it stew till it is quite tender; then put in the Asparagus, shake the Sauce-pan, let it simmer till the Grass is enough. Take the Endive out of the Water, drain it, leave one large Head whole, the other pick Leaf by Leaf, put it into a Stew-pan, put to it a Pint of White Wine, cover the Pan close, let it boil till the Endive is just enough, then put in a quarter of a Pound of Butter rolled in Flour, cover it close, shaking the Pan when the Endive is enough. Take it up, lay the whole Head in the Middle, and with a Spoon take out the Salary and Grass, and lay round, the other Part of the Endive over that, then pour the Liquor off the Sauce-pan into the Stew-pan, stir it together, season it with Salt, and have ready the Yolks of two Eggs, beat up with a quarter of a Pint of Cream, and half a Nutmeg grated in. Mix this with the Sauce, keep it stiring, all one way, till it is thick, then pour it over your Ragoo, and send it to Table hot.

To Ragoo French Beans.

TAKE a few Beans, boil them tender, then take your Stew-pan, put in a Piece of Butter, when it is melted, shake in some Flour, and peel a large Onion, slice it, and fry it brown in that Butter; then put in the Beans, shake in a little Pepper and a little Salt, grate a little Nutmeg in, have ready the Yolk of an Egg and some Cream; stir them all together for a Minute or two, and dish them up.

A Good Brown Gravy.

TAKE half a Pint of Small Beer, or Ale that is not bitter, and half a Pint of Water, an Onion cut small, a little Bit of Lemon-peel cut small, three Cloves, a Blade of Mace, some whole Pepper,

per, a Spoonful of Mushroom-pickle, a Spoonful of Wallnut-pickle, a Spoonful of Ketchup, and Anchovy; first put a Piece of Butter into a Sauce-pan, as big as a Hen's Egg, when it is melted shake in a little Flour, and let it be a little brown; then by degrees stir in the above Ingredients, and let it boil a quarter of an Hour, then strain it, and it is fit for Fish or Roots.

To Fricasee Skirrets.

WASH the Roots very well, and boil them till they are tender; then the Skin of the Roots must be taken off cut in Slices, and have ready a little Cream, a Piece of Butter rolled in Flour, the Yolk of an Egg beat, a little Nutmeg grated, two or three Spoonfuls of White Wine, a very little Salt, and stir all together. Your Roots being in the Dish, pour the Sauce over them. It is a pretty Side-dish. So likewise you may dress Root of Salsify and Scorzonera.

Chardoons *Fry'd and Buttered.*

YOU must cut them about ten Inches, and string them, and tye them up in Bundles like Asparagus, or cut them in small Dice, and boil them like Peas, and toss them up with Pepper, Salt, and melted Butter.

Chardoons à la Framage.

AFTER they are stringed, cut them an Inch long, stew them in a little Red Wine till tender, season with Pepper and Salt, and thicken it with a Piece of Butter rolled in Flour; then pour them into your Dish, squeeze the Juice of Orange over it, and then scrape *Cheshire-Cheese* all over them, then brown it with a Cheese-Iron, and serve it up quick and hot.

To make a Scotch-Rabbit.

TOAST a Piece of Bread very nicely on both Sides, butter it, cut a Slice of Cheese, about as big as the Bread, toast it on both Sides, and lay it on the Bread.

To make a Welch-Rabbit.

TOAST the Bread on both Sides, then toast the Cheese on one Side, and lay it on the Toast, and with a hot Iron brown the other Side. You may rub it over with Mustard.

To make an English-Rabbit.

TOAST a Slice of Bread brown on both Sides, then lay it in a Plate before the Fire, pour a Glass of Red Wine over it, and let it soak the Wine up; then cut some Cheese very thin, and lay it very thick over the Bread; put it in a Tin Oven before the Fire, and it will be toasted and brown presently. Serve it away hot.

Or do it thus.

TOAST the Bread, and soak it in the Wine, set it before the Fire, cut your Cheese in very thin Slices, rub Butter over the Bottom of a Plate, lay the Cheese on, pour in two or three Spoonfuls of White Wine, cover it with another Plate, set it over a Chafindish of hot Coals for two or three Minutes, then stir it till it is done, and well mixed. You may stir in a little Mustard; when it is enough, lay it on the Bread, just brown it with a hot Shovel. Serve it away hot.

Sorrel *with* Eggs.

FIRST your Sorril must be quite boiled, and well strained, then poch three Eggs soft, and three hard, butter your Sorrel well, fry some three-corner Toasts brown, lay the Sorrel in the Dish, and lay three soft Eggs on it, and the hard between; stick the Toast in and about it. Garnish with quartered Orange.

A Fricasee *of* Artichoke-Bottoms.

TAKE them either dried or pickled; if dried, you must lay them in warm Water, for three or four Hours, shifting the Water two or three times; then have ready a little Cream, and a Piece of fresh Butter, stirred together one way over the Fire till it is melted, then put in the Artichokes; and when they are hot dish them up.

To Fry Artichokes.

FIRST blanch them in Water, then flour them, and fry them in fresh Butter, lay them in your Dish, and pour melted Butter over them. Or you may put a little Red Wine into the Butter, and season with Nutmeg, Pepper, and Salt.

98   *The Art of Cookery, made Plain and Easy.*

A White Fricasee of Mushrooms.

TAKE a Quart of fresh Mushrooms, make them clean, put them into a Sauce-pan with three Spoonfuls of Water, and three of Milk, a very little Salt, set them on a quick Fire, and let them boil up three times; then take them off, grate in a little Nutmeg, put in a little beaten Mace, half a Pint of thick Cream, a Piece of butter rolled well in Flour; put it all together into the Sauce-pan, and Mushrooms all together, shake the Sauce-pan well all the time. When it is fine and thick, dish them up; be careful they don't curdle. You may stir the Sauce-pan carefully with a Spoon all the time.

To make Buttered Loaves.

BEAT up the Yolks of a Dozen Eggs with half the Whites, and a quarter of a Pint of Yeast, strain them into a Dish, season with Salt and beaten Ginger, then make it into a high Paste with Flour, lay it in a warm Cloth for a quarter of an Hour, then make it up into little Loaves, and bake them, or boil them with Butter, and put in a Glass of White Wine. Sweeten well with Sugar, lay the Loaves in the Dish, pour the Sauce over them, and throw Sugar over the Dish.

Brockely and Eggs.

BOIL your Brockely tender, saving a large Bunch for the Middle, and six or eight little thick Spriggs to stick round. Take a Toast half an Inch thick, toast it brown, as big as you would have it for your Dish or Buttering-plate; butter some Eggs thus: Take six Eggs more or less, as you have Occasion, beat them well, put them into a Sauce-pan, with a good Piece of Butter, a little Salt, keep beating them with a Spoon, till they are thick enough, then pour them on the Toast. Set the biggest Bunch of Brockely in the Middle, and the other little Piece round and about, and garnish the Dish round with little Spriggs of Brockely. This is a pretty Side-dish, or a Corner-plate.

Asparagus and Eggs.

TOAST a Toast as big as you have Occasion for, butter it and lay it in your Dish, butter some Eggs as above, and lay over it. In the mean time boil some Grass tender, cut it small, and lay it over the Eggs. This makes a pretty Side-dish for a second Course, or a Corner-plate.

Brockely in Sallad.

BROCKELY is a pretty Dish, by way of Sallad, in the Middle of a Table. Boil it like Asparagus (in the Beginning of the Book you have an Account how to clean it) lay it in your Dish, and beat up Oil and Vinegar, and a little Salt. Garnish round with Stertion-buds. Or boil it, and have plain Butter in a Cup. — Or farce *French* Roles with it, and buttered Eggs together for Change. — Or farce your Roles with Muscles done the same way as Oysters, only no Wine.

Potatoe-Cakes.

TAKE Potatoes, boil them, peel them, beat them in a Mortar, mix them with Yolks of Eggs, a little Sack, Sugar, a little beaten Mace, a little Nutmeg, a little Cream, or melted Butter, work it up into a Paste, then make it into Cakes, or just what Shapes you please with Molds, fry them brown in fresh Butter, lay them in Plates or Dishes, melt Butter with Sack and Sugar, and pour over them.

A Pudding made thus.

MIX it as before, make it up in the Shape of a Pudding, and bake it; pour Butter, Sack and Sugar over it.

To make Potatoes like a Collar of Veal or Mutton.

MAKE the Ingredients as before; make it up in the Shape of a Collar of Veal, and with some of it make round Balls; bake it with the Balls, set the Collar in the Middle, lay the Balls round, let your Sauce be half a Pint of Red Wine, Sugar enough to sweeten it, the Yolks of two Eggs, beat up a little Nutmeg, stir all these together, for fear of curdling; when it is thick enough, pour it over the Collar. This is a pretty Dish for a first or second Course.

To Broil Potatoes.

FIRST boil them, peel them, cut them in two, broil them till they are brown on both Sides, then lay them in the Plate or Dish, and pour melted Butter over them.

To

To Fry Potatoes.

CUT them into thin Slices as big as a Crown-piece, fry them brown, lay them in the Plate or Dish, and pour melted Butter, and Sack and Sugar over them. These are a pretty Corner-plate.

Mashed Potatoes.

BOIL your Potatoes, peel them, and put them into a Sauce-pan, mash them well: To two Pounds of Potatoes put a Pint of Milk, a little Salt, stir them well together, take care they don't stick to the Bottom, then take a quarter of a Pound of Butter, stir in and serve it up.

To Grill Shrimps.

SEASON them with Salt and Pepper, and shread Parsley, Butter, Scollups-shells well; add some grated Bread, and let them stew for half an Hour. Brown them with an hot Iron, and serve them up.

Buttered Shrimps.

STEW two Quarts of Shrimps in a Pint of White Wine, with Nutmeg, beat up eight Eggs, with a little White Wine, and half a Pound of Butter, shaking the Sauce-pan one way all the time over the Fire, till they are thick enough, lay toasted Sippets round a Dish, and pour them over it, so serve them up.

To Dress Spinage.

PICK and wash your Spinage well, put it into a Sauce-pan, with a little Salt, cover it close, and let it Stew till it is just tender, then throw it into a Sieve, drain all the Liquor out, and chop it small, as much as the Quantity of a *French* Role, add half a Pint of Cream to it, season with Salt, Pepper, and grated Nutmeg, put in a quarter of a Pound of Butter, and set it a stewing over the Fire for a quarter of an Hour, stirring it often. Cut a *French* Role into long Pieces, about as thick as your Finger, fry them, poach six Eggs, lay them round on the Spinage, stick the Pieces of Role in and about the Eggs. Serve it up either for a Supper, or a Side-dish at a second Course.

Stewed Spinage and Eggs.

PICK and wash your Spinage very clean, put it into a Sauce-pan, with a little Salt, cover it close, shake the Pan often; when it is just tender, and whilst it is green, throw it into a Sieve to drain, lay it into your Dish. In the mean time have a Stew-pan of Water boiling, break as many Eggs into Cups as you would poach. When the Water boils, put in the Eggs, have an Egg-slice ready to take them out with, lay them on the Spinage, and garnish the Dish with Orange cut into Quarters, with melted Butter in a Cup.

To Boil Spinage when you have not Room on the Fire, to do by itself.

HAVE a Tin-box, or any other thing, that shuts very close, put in your Spinage, cover it so close as no Water can get in, and put it into Water, or a Pot of Liquor, or any thing you are boiling. It will take about an Hour, if the Pot or Copper boils. In the same manner you may boil Peas without Water.

Asparagus *Forced in* French *Role.*

TAKE three *French* Roles, take out all the Crumb, by first cutting a Piece of the Top-crust off, but be careful that the Crust fits again the same Place. Fry the Roles brown in fresh Butter, then take a Pint of Cream, the Yolk of six Eggs beat fine, a little Salt and Nutmeg, stir them well together over a slow Fire, till it begins to be thick. Have ready a hundred of small Grass boiled, then save Tops enough to stick the Roles with; the rest, cut small and put into the Cream, fill the Loaves with them. Before you fry the Roles, make Holes thick in the Top-crust to stick the Grass in; then lay on the Piece of Crust, and stick the Grass in, that it may look as if it was growing. It makes a pretty Side-dish at a second Course.

To make Oyster-Loaves.

FRY the *French* Roles as above, take half a Pint of Oysters, stew them in their own Liquor, then take out the Oysters with a Fork, strain the Liquor to them, put them into a Sauce-pan again, with a Glass of White Wine, a little beaten Mace, a little grated Nutmeg, a quarter of a Pound of Butter rolled in Flour, shake them well together, then put them into the Roles; and these make a pretty Side-dish for a first Course. You may rub in the Crumbs of two Roles, and toss up with the Oysters.

To Stew Parsnips.

BOIL them tender, scrape them from the Dust, cut them into Slices, put them into a Sauce-pan, with Cream enough; for Sauce a Piece of Butter rolled in Flour, and a little Salt, shake the Sauce-pan often; when the Cream boils, pour them into a Plate for a Corner-dish, or a Side-dish at Supper.

To Mash Parsnips.

BOIL them tender, scrape them clean, then scrape all the soft into a Sauce-pan, put as much Milk or Cream, as will stew them. Keep them stirring, and when quite thick, stir in a good Piece of Butter, and send them to Table.

To Stew Cucumbers.

PARE twelve Cucumbers, and slice them as thick as a Half-crown, lay them in a coarse Cloth to drain, and when they are dry flour them, and fry them brown in fresh Butter; then take them out with an Egg-slice, lay them in a Plate before the Fire, and have ready one Cucumber whole, cut a long Piece out of the Side, and scoop out all the Pulp; have ready fry'd Onions, peeled and sliced, and fry'd brown with the sliced Cucumber. Fill the whole Cucumber with the fry'd Onion, seasoned with Pepper and Salt; put on the Piece you cut out, and tye it round with a Pack-thread. Fry it brown, first flouring it, then take it out of the Pan, and keep it hot; keep the Pan on the Fire, and with one Hand stir in a little Flour, while with the other you stir it. When it is thick, put in two or three Spoonfuls of Water, and half a Pint of white or Red Wine, two Spoonfuls of Ketchup, stir it together, put in three Blades of Mace, four Cloves, half a Nutmeg, a little Pepper and Salt, all beat fine together; stir it into the Sauce-pan, then throw in your Cucumbers, give them a Toss or two; then lay the whole Cucumbers in the Middle, the rest round, pour the Sauce over all, untye the Cucumber before you lay it into the Dish. Garnish the Dish with fry'd Onions, and send it to Table hot. This is a pretty Side-dish at a first Course.

To Ragoo French Beans.

TAKE a quarter of a Peck of French Beans, string them, don't split them, cut them in three a-cross, lay them in Salt and Water, then take them out, and dry them in a coarse Cloth, fry them brown, then pour out all the Fat, put in a quarter of a Pint of hot Water, stir it into the Pan by degrees, let it boil, then take a quarter of a Pound of fresh Butter, rolled in a very little Flour, two Spoonfuls of Ketchup, one Spoonful of Mushroom-pickle, and four of White Wine, an Onion stuck with six Cloves, two or three Blades of Mace beat, half a Nutmeg grated, a little Pepper and Salt; stir it all together for a few Minutes, then throw in the Beans, shake the Pan for a Minute or two, take out the Onion, and pour them into your Dish. This is a pretty Side-dish, and you may garnish with what you fancy, either pickled French-Beans, Mushrooms, or Sampier, or any thing else.

A Ragoo of Beans with a Force.

RAGOO them as above, take two large Carrots, scrape and boil them tender, then mash them in a Pan, season with Pepper and Salt, mix them with a little Piece of Butter, and the Yolks of two raw Eggs. Make it into what Shape you please, and baking it a quarter of an Hour in a quick Oven will do; but a Tin Oven is the best. Lay it in the Middle of the Dish, and the Ragoo round. Serve it up hot for a first Course.

Or this Way Beans Ragoo'd with a Cabbage.

TAKE a nice little Cabbage, about as big as a Pint Bason; when the outside Leaves, Top, and Stalk are cut off, half-boil it, cut a Hole in the Middle pretty big, take what you cut out and chop it very fine, with a few of the Beans boiled, a Carrot boiled and mashed, a Turnip boiled; mash all together, put them into a Sauce-pan, season them with Pepper, Salt, and Nutmeg, a good Piece of Butter, stew them a few Minutes over the Fire, stirring the Pan often. In the mean time put the Cabbage into a Sauce-pan, but take great care it does not fall to Pieces; put to it four Spoonfuls of Water, two of Wine, and one of Ketchup, have a Spoonful of Mushroom-pickle, a Piece of Butter rolled in a little Flour, a very little Pepper, cover it close, and let it stew softly till it is tender; then take it up carefully, and lay it in the Middle of the Dish, pour your mash Roots in the Middle to fill it up high, and your Ragoo round it; you may add the Liquor the Cabbage was stewed in, send it to Table hot. This will do for a Top, Bottom, Middle, or Side-dish. When Beans are not to be had, you may cut Carrots and Turnips into little Slices and fry them; the Carrots in little round Slices, the Turnips in long Pieces about two Inches long, and as thick as ones Finger, and toss them up in the Ragoo.

Beans

Beans Ragoo'd with Parsnips.

TAKE two large Parsnips, scrape them clean, and boil them in Water; when tender, take them up, scrape all the Soft into a Sauce-pan, add to them four Spoonfuls of Cream, a Piece of Butter as big as a Hen's Egg, chop them in the Sauce-pan well; and when they are quite thick, heap them up in the Middle of the Dish, and the Ragoo round.

Beans Ragoo'd with Potatoes.

BOIL two Pounds of Potatoes soft, then peel them, put them into a Sauce-pan, put to them half a Pint of Milk, stir them about, and a little Salt; then stir in a quarter of a Pound of Butter, keep stirring all the time till it is so thick, that you can't stir the Spoon in it hardly for Stiffness, then put it into a Halfpenny *Welch* Dish, first buttering the Dish. Heap them as high as they will lye, flour them, and pour a little melted Butter over it, and then a few Crumbs of Bread. Set it into a Tin Oven before the Fire, and when brown, lay it in the Middle of the Dish, (take great Care you don't mash it) pour your Ragoo round it, and send it to Table hot.

To Ragoo Salary.

WASH, and make a Bunch of Salary very clean, cut it in Pieces about two Inches long, put them into a Stew-pan, with just as much Water as will cover it, tye three or four Blades of Mace, two or three Cloves, about twenty Corns of whole Pepper in a Muslin Rag loose, put it into the Stew-pan, a little Onion, a little Bundle of Sweet Herbs, cover it close, and let it stew softly till tender; then take out the Spice, Onion, and Sweet Herbs, put in half an Ounce of Truffles and Morells, two Spoonfuls of Ketchup, a Gill of Red Wine, a Piece of Butter as big as an Egg rolled in Flour, six farden *French* Roles, season with Salt to your Palate, stir it all together, cover it close, and let it stew till the Sauce is thick and good. Take care your Roles don't break, shake your Pan often; when it is enough, dish it up, and garnish with Lemon. The Yolks of six hard Eggs, or more, put in with the Roles, will make it a fine Dish; this for a first Course.

If you would have it white, put in White Wine instead of Red, and some Cream, for a second Course.

To Ragoo Mushrooms.

PEEL and scrape the Flaps, put a Quart into a Sauce-pan, a very little Salt, set them on a quick Fire, let them boil up, then take them off, put to them a Gill of Red Wine, a quarter of a Pound of Butter rolled in a little Flour, a little Nutmeg, a little beaten Mace, set it on the Fire, stir it now and then; when it is thick and fine, have ready the Yolks of six Eggs heat, and boiled in a Bladder hard, lay it in the Middle of your Dish, and pour the Ragoo over it. Garnish with broiled Mushrooms.

A Pretty Dish of Eggs.

BOIL six Eggs hard, peel them, and cut them in thin Slices, put a quarter of a Pound of Butter into the Stew-pan, then put in your Eggs, and fry them quick, half a quarter of an Hour will do them. You must be very careful not to break them, throw over them Pepper, Salt, and Nutmeg, lay them in your Dish before the Fire, pour out all the Fat, shake in a little Flour, and have ready two Shallots cut small; throw them into the Pan, pour in a quarter of a Pint of White Wine, a little Juice of Lemon, and a little Piece of Butter rolled in Flour. Stir all together till it is thick; if you have not Sauce enough, put in a little more Wine, toast some thin Slices of Bread cut thus △, and lay round your Dish, pour the Sauce all over, and send it to Table hot. You may put Sweet Oil on the Toast, if it be agreeable.

Eggs a la Tripe.

BOIL your Eggs hard, take off the Shells and cut them long-ways in four Quarters, put a little Butter into a Stew-pan, let it melt, shake in a little Flour, stir it with a Spoon, then put in your Eggs, throw a little grated Nutmeg all over, a little Salt, a good deal of shread Parsley, shake your Pan round, pour in a little Cream, toss the Pan round carefully, that you don't break the Eggs. When your Sauce is thick and fine, take up your Eggs, pour the Sauce all over them, and garnish with Lemon.

A Fricasee of Eggs.

BOIL eight Eggs hard, take off the Shells, cut them into Quarters, have ready half a Pint of Cream, and a quarter of a Pound of fresh Butter; stir it together over the Fire, till it is thick and smooth, lay the Eggs in your Dish, and pour the Sauce all over. Garnish with the hard Yolks of three Eggs cut in two, and lay round the Edge of the Dish.

A Ragoo of Eggs.

BOIL twelve Eggs hard, take off the Shells, and with a little Knife very carefully cut the White a-cross long-ways, so that the White may be in two Halves, and the Yolk whole. Be careful neither to break the Whites, nor Yolks, take a quarter of a Pint of Pickle Mushrooms chopped very fine, half an Ounce of Truffles and Morells, boiled in three or four. Spoonfuls of Water, save the Water, and chop the Truffles and Morells very small, boil a little Parsley, chop it fine, mix them together with the Truffle Water you saved, grate a little Nutmeg in, a little beaten Mace, put it into a Sauce-pan with three Spoonfuls of Water, a Gill of Red Wine, one Spoonful of Ketchup, a Piece of Butter, as big as a large Wallnut, rolled in Flour, stir all together, and let it boil. In the mean time get ready your Eggs, lay the Yolks and Whites in Order in your Dish, the hollow Parts of the Whites uppermost, that they may be filled, take some Crumbs of Bread, and fry them brown and crisp, as you do for Larks, with which fill up the Whites of the Eggs as high as they will lye, then pour in your Sauce all over, and garnish with fry'd Crumbs of Bread. This is a very genteel pretty Dish, if it be well done.

To Broil Eggs.

CUT a Toast round a Quartern Loaf, toast it brown, lay it on your Dish, butter it, and very carefully break six or eight Eggs on the Toast, and take a red-hot Shovel and hold over them. When they are done, squeeze a Seville Orange over them, and grate a little Nutmeg over it, and serve it up for a Side-plate. Or you may poach your Eggs, and lay them on the Toast; or toast your Toasts crisp, and pour a little boiling Water over it, and season it with a little Salt, and then lay your poached Eggs on it.

To Dress Eggs with Bread.

TAKE a Penny-Loaf, soak it in a Quart of hot Milk for two Hours, or till the Bread is soft, then strain it through a coarse Sieve, put to it two Spoonfuls of Orange-flower Water, or Rose Water, sweeten it, grate in a little Nutmeg, take a little Dish, butter the Bottom of it, break in as many Eggs as will cover the Bottom of the Dish, pour in the Bread and Milk, set it in a Tin Oven before the Fire, half an Hour will bake it; or it will do on a Chafindish of Coals. Cover it close before the Fire, or bake it in a slow Oven.

To Farce Eggs.

GET a Couple of Cabbage-lettices, scald them, with a few Mushrooms, Parsley, Sorrel and Chervil; then chop them very small with the Yolks of hard Eggs, seasoned with Salt and Nutmeg, then stew them in Butter; and when they are enough, put in a little Cream, then pour them into the Bottom of a Dish. Take the Whites, and chop them very fine, with Parsley, Nutmeg and Salt, lay this round the Brim of the Dish, and run a red-hot Fire-shovel over it, to brown it.

Eggs with Lettice.

SCALD some Cabbage-lettice in fair Water, squeeze them well, then slice them, and toss them up in a Sauce-pan, with a Piece of Butter, season them with Pepper, Salt, and a little Nutmeg. Let them stew half an Hour, chop them well together, when they are enough, lay them in your Dish, and fry some Eggs nicely in Butter, and lay on them. Garnish with Seville Orange.

To Fry Eggs as round as Balls.

HAVING a deep Frying-pan, and three Pints of clarified Butter, heat it as hot as for Fritters, and stir it with a Stick, till it runs round like a Whirl-pool; then break an Egg into the Middle, and turn it round with your Stick, till it be as hard as a poached Egg, the Whirling round of the Butter will make it as round as a Ball, then take it up with a Slice, and put it in a Dish before the Fire. They will keep hot half an Hour, and yet be soft; so you may do as many as you please. You may serve these with what you please, nothing better than stewed Spinage, and garnish with Orange.

To make an Egg as big as Twenty.

PART the Yolks from the Whites, strain them both separate through a Sieve, tye the Yolks up in a Bladder, in the Form of a Ball; boil them hard, then put this Ball into another Blader, and the Whites round it; tye it up oval Fashion, and boil it. These are used for grand Sallads. This is very pretty for a Ragoo, boil five or six Yolks together, and lay in the Middle of the Ragoo of Eggs; and so you may make them of any Size you please.

A Grand Dish of Eggs

BREAK as many Eggs as the Yolks will fill a Pint Bason, the Whites by themselves, tye the Yolks by themselves in a Bladder round; boil them hard, then have a wooden Bowl that will hold a Quart, made like two Butter-dishes, but in the Shape of an Egg, with a Hole through one at the Top. You are to observe, when you boil the Yolks to run a Pack-thread through it, and a quarter of a Yard hanging out. When the Yolk is boiled hard, put it into the Bowl-dish; but be careful to hang it so as to be in the Middle. The String being drawn through the Hole, then clap the two Bowls together, and tye them tight, and with a fine Tunnel pour in the Whites through the Hole; then stop the Hole close, and boil it hard, it will take an Hour. When it is boiled enough, carefully open it, and cut the String close. In the mean time take twenty Eggs, beat them well, the Yolks by themselves, and the Whites by themselves; divide the Whites into two, and boil them in Bladders the Shape of an Egg. When they are boiled hard, cut one in two long-ways, and one cross-ways, and with a fine sharp Knife cut out some of the White in the Middle, lay the great Egg in the Middle, the two long Halves on each Side, with the hollow Part uppermost, and the two round flat between. Take an Ounce of Truffles and Morells, cut them very small, boil them in half a Pint of Water till they are tender, then chop a Pint of fresh Mushrooms clean picked and washed, chopped small, put into the Truffles and Morells; let them boil, add a little Salt, a little beaten Nutmeg, a little beaten Mace, and add a Gill of pickled Mushrooms chopped fine. Boil fourteen of the Yolks hard in a Bladder, then chop them and mix them with the other Ingredients; thicken it with a Lump of Butter rolled in Flour, shaking your Sauce-pan round till hot and thick, then fill the round with Whites, and turn them down again, and fill the two long ones; what remains, save to put into the Sauce-pan. Take a Pint of Cream, a quarter of a pound of Butter, the other four Yolks beat fine, a Gill of White Wine, a Gill of pickled Mushrooms, a little beaten Mace, a little Nutmeg, put all into the Sauce-pan, to the other Ingredients, stir all well together one way, till it is thick and fine; then pour it over all, and garnish with notched Lemon.

This is a grand Dish at a second Course. Or you may mix it up with Red Wine and Butter, and it will do for a first Course.

A Pretty Dish of Whites of Eggs.

TAKE the Whites of twelve Eggs, beat them up with four Spoonfuls of Rose-water, a little grated Lemon-peel, a little Nutmeg, sweeten with Sugar, mix them well, boil them in four Bladders, tye them in the Shape of an Egg, and boil them hard. They will take half an Hour, lay them in your Dish when cold; mix half a Pint of thick Cream, a Gill of Sack, and half the Juice of a Seville Orange. Mix all together, and sweeten with fine Sugar, and pour over the Eggs. Serve it up for a Side-dish at Supper, or when you please.

To Dress Beans in Ragoo.

BOIL your Beans, so that the Skins will slip off; take about a Quart, season them with Pepper, Salt, and Nutmeg, then flour them, and have ready some Butter in a Stew-pan, throw in your Beans, fry them of a fine brown, then drain them from the Fat, and lay them in your Dish. Have ready a quarter of a Pound of Butter melted, and half a Pint of the blanched Beans boiled, beat in a Mortar, with a very little Pepper, Salt, and Nutmeg; then by degrees mix them into the Butter, and pour over the other Beans. Garnish with a boiled and fry'd Bean, and so on till you fill the Rim of your Dish. They are very good without frying, and only plain Butter melted over them.

An Amulet of Beans.

BLANCH your Beans, and fry them in sweet Butter, with a little Parsley, pour out the Butter, and pour in some Cream. Let it simmer, shaking your Pan; season with Pepper, Salt, and Nutmeg, thicken with three or four Yolks of Eggs, have ready a Pint of Cream, thickened with the Yolks of four Eggs, season with a little Salt, pour it in your Dish, and lay your Beans on the Amulet, and serve it up hot.

The same Way may dress Mushrooms, Truffles, Green Peas, Asparagus, and Artichoke-bottoms, Spinage, Sorrel, &c. all being first cut into small Pieces, or shread fine.

A Bean Tansey.

TAKE two Quarts of Beans, blanch, and beat them very fine in a Mortar; season with Pepper, Salt, and Mace; then put in the Yolks of six Eggs, and a quarter of a Pound of Butter, a Pint of Cream, half a Pint of Sack, and sweeten to your Palates. Soak four Naples Biskets in half a Pint of Milk, mix them with the other Ingredients. Butter a Pan and bake it, then turn it on a Dish, and stick Citron and Orange-peel candied, cut small, and stuck about it. Garnish with Seville Orange.

A Water Tansey.

TAKE twelve Eggs, beat them very well, half a Manchet grated, and sifted through a Cullendar, or half a Penny-Role, half a Pint of fair Water. Colour it with Juice of Spinage, and one small Sprig of Tansey beat together; season it with Sugar to your Palate, a little Salt, a small Nutmeg grated, two or thre Spoonfuls of Rose-water, put it into a Skellet, stir it all one way, and let it thicken like a Hasty-pudding. Then bake it; or you may butter a Stew-pan and put it into. Butter a Dish and lay over it; when one Side is enough, turn it with the Dish, and slip the other Side into the Pan. When that is done, set it into a Massereau, and throw Sugar all over, and garnish with Orange.

Peas Françoise.

TAKE a Quart of shelled Peas, cut a large *Spanish* Onion, or two middling ones small, and two Cabbage or *Silesia* Lettice cut small, put them into a Sauce-pan, with half a Pint of Water, season them with a little Salt, a little beaten Pepper, and a little beaten Mace, and Nutmeg. Cover them close, and let them stew a quarter of an Hour, then put in a quarter of a Pound of fresh Butter rolled in a little Flour, a Spoonful of Ketchup, a little Piece of burnt Butter, as big as a Nutmeg, cover them close, and let it simmer softly an Hour, often shaking the Pan. When it is enough, serve it up for a Side-dish.

For an Alteration, you may stew the Ingredients as above; then take a small Cabbage-lettice, and half boil it, then drain it, cut the Stalk flat at the Bottom, so that it will stand firm in the Dish, and with a Knife very carefully cut out the Middle, leaving the outside Leaves whole. Put what you cut out into a Sauce-pan, chop it, and put a Piece of Butter, a little Pepper, Salt, and Nutmeg, the Yolk of a hard Egg chopped, a few Crumbs of Bread, mix all together, and when it is hot fill your Cabbage, put some Butter into a Stew-pan, tye your Cabbage, and fry it till you think it is enough; then take it up, untye it, and first pour the Ingredients of Peas into your Dish, set the Forced Cabbage in the Middle, and have ready four Artichoke-bottoms fry'd, and cut in two, and laid round the Dish. This will do for a Top Dish.

Green Peas *with* Cream.

TAKE a Quart of fine Green Peas, put them in a Stew-pan with a Piece of Butter as big as an Egg, rolled in a little Flour, season them with a little Salt, and Nutmeg, a Bit of Sugar as big as a Nutmeg, a little Bundle of Sweet Herbs, some Parsley chopped fine, a quarter of a Pint of boiling Water. Cover them close, and let them stew very softly half an Hour, then pour in a quarter of a Pint of good Cream. Give it one boil, and serve it up for a Side-plate.

A Farce Meagre Cabbage.

TAKE a White-heart Cabbage, as big as the Bottom of a Plate, let it boil five Minutes in Water, then drain it, cut the Stalk flat to stand in the Dish, then carefully open the Leaves, and take out the Inside, leaving the outside Leaves whole. Chop what you take out very fine, take the Flesh of two or three Flounders, or Plaise, clean from the Bone; chop it with the Cabbage and the Yolks of four hard Eggs and Whites, a handful of picked Parsley, beat all together in a Mortar, with a quarter of a Pound of melted Butter; mix it up with the Yolk of an Egg, and a few Crumbs of Bread, fill the Cabbage, and tye it together, put it into a deep Stew-pan, or Sauce-pan, put to it half a Pint of Water, a quarter of a Pound of Butter rolled in a little Flour, the Yolks of four hard Eggs, an Onion stuck with six Cloves, whole Pepper, and Mace tied in a Muslin Rag, half an Ounce of Truffles and Morells, a Spoonful of Ketchup, a few pickled Mushrooms, cover it close, and let it simmer an Hour. If you find it is not enough, you must do it longer. When it is done, lay it in your Dish, untye it, and pour the Sauce over.

To Farce Cucumbers.

TAKE six large Cucumbers, cut a Piece off the Top, and scoop out all the Pulp; take a large white Cabbage boiled tender, take only the Heart, chop it fine, cut a large Onion fine, shread some Parsley, and pickled Mushrooms small, two hard Eggs choped very fine, season it with Pepper, Salt, and Nutmeg. Stuff your Cucumbers full, and put on the Pieces, tye them with a Pack-thread, and fry them in Butter of a light-brown; have the following Sauce ready: Take a quarter of a Pint of Red Wine, a quarter of a Pint of boiling Water, a small Onion chopped fine, a little Pepper and Salt, a Piece of Butter as big as a Wallnut rolled in Flour; when the Cucumbers are enough, lay them in your Dish, pour the Fat out of the Pan, and pour in this Sauce, let it boil, and have ready two Yolks of Eggs, beat fine, mixed with two or three Spoonfuls of the Sauce, then turn them into the Pan, let them boil, keeping it stirring all the time, untye the Strings, and pour the Sauce over. Serve it up for a Side-dish. Garnish with the Tops.

To Stew Cucumbers.

TAKE six large Cucumbers, slice them, take six large Onions, peel and cut them in thin Slices, fry them both brown, then drain them, and pour out the Fat, put them into the Pan again, with three Spoonfuls of hot Water, a quarter of a Pound of Butter rolled in Flour, and a Tea Spoonful of Mustard. Season with Pepper and Salt, and let them stew a quarter of an Hour softly, shaking the Pan often; when they are enough, dish them up.

Fry'd Salary.

TAKE six or eight Heads of Salary, cut off the green Tops, and take off the outside Stalks, wash them clean, and pare the Root clean; then have ready half a Pint of White Wine, the Yolks of three Eggs beat fine, a little Salt and Nutmeg, mix all well together with Flour into a Batter, dip every Head into the Batter, and fry them in Butter; when enough, lay them in your Dish, and pour melted Butter over them.

Salary with Cream.

WASH and clean six or eight Heads of Salary, cut them about three Inches long, boil them tender, pour away all the Water, and take the Yolks of four Eggs beat fine, half a Pint of Cream, a little Salt and Nutmeg, pour over, keeping the Pan shaking all the while. When it begins to be thick, dish it up.

Colliflowers Fry'd.

TAKE two fine Colliflowers, boil them in Milk and Water, then leave one whole, and pull the other to Pieces, take half a Pound of Butter, with two Spoonfuls of Water, a little Dust of Flour, and melt the Butter in a Stew-pan; then put in the whole Colliflower cut in two, and the other pull to Pieces, and fry it till it is of a very light-brown, season it with Pepper and Salt. When it is enough, lay the two Halves in the Middle, and pour the rest all over.

An Oatmeal Pudding.

TAKE a Pint of fine Oatmeal, boil it in three Pints of new Milk, stirring it till is as thick as a Hasty Pudding, take it off, and stir in half a Pound of fresh Butter, a little beaten Mace and Nutmeg, a Gill of Sack, then beat up eight Eggs, half the Whites; stir it all well together, lay a Puff-paste all over the Dish, and pour in the Pudding, and bake it half an Hour. Or you may boil it with a few Currans.

A Potatoe Pudding.

TAKE a Quart of Potatoes, boil them soft, peel them, and mash them with the Back of a Spoon, and rub them through a Sieve, to have them fine and smooth; take half a Pound of fresh Butter melted, half a Pound of fine Sugar, so beat them well together, till they are very smooth, beat six Eggs, Whites and all, stir them in, and a Glass of Sack or Brandy. You may add half a Pound of Currans, boil it half an Hour, melt Butter with a Glass of White Wine, and sweeten with Sugar, and pour over it. You may bake it in a Dish, with Puff-paste all round the Dish, and at the Bottom.

A Second Potatoe-Pudding.

BOIL two Pound of Potatoes, boil and beat them in a Mortar fine, beat in half a Pound of melted Butter, boil it half an Hour, pour melted Butter over it, with a Glass of White Wine, or the Juice of Seville Orange, and throw Sugar all over the Pudding and Dish.

A Third Sort of Potatoe Pudding.

TAKE two Pound of white Potatoes, boil them soft, peel and beat them in a Mortar, or strain them through a Sieve, till they are quite fine; then mix in half a Pound of fresh Butter melted, then beat up the Yolks of eight Eggs, and three Whites, stir them in, and half a Pound of white Sugar finely pounded, half a Pint of Sack, stir it well together, grate in half a large Nutmeg, and stir in half a Pint of Cream, make a Puff-past, and lay all over your Dish, and round the Edges, pour in the Pudding, and bake it of a fine light-brown.

For Change put in half a Pound of Currans, or you may strew over the Top, half an Ounce of Citron and Orange-peel cut thin, before you put it into the Oven.

An Orange Pudding.

TAKE the Yolks of sixteen Eggs, beat them well, with half a Pound of melted Butter, grate in the Rind of two fine Seville Oranges, beat in half a Pound of fine Sugar, two Spoonfuls of Orange-flower Water, two of Rose-water, a Gill of Sack, half a Pint of Cream, and two Naples Biskets, or the Crumb of a Halfpenny Role soaked in the Cream, and mix all well together. Make a thin Puff-paste and lay all over the Dish, and round the Rim, pour in the Pudding, and bake it. It will take about as long baking as a Custard.

A Second Sort of Orange Pudding.

TAKE sixteen Yolks of Eggs, beat them fine, mix them with half a Pound of fresh Butter melted, and half a Pound of white Sugar, a little Rose-water, and a little Nutmeg. Cut the Peel of a fine large Seville Orange so thin as none of the White appears, beat it fine in a Mortar, till it is like a Paste, and by degrees mix in the above Ingredients all together, then lay a Puff-paste all over the Dish, pour in the Ingredients, and bake it.

A Third Orange Pudding.

TAKE two large Seville Oranges, and grate off the Rind as far as they are yellow; then put your Oranges in fair Water, and let them boil till they are tender. Shift the Water three or four times to take out the Bitterness; when they are tender, cut them open, and take away the Seeds and Strings, and beat the other Part in a Mortar, with half a Pound of Sugar, till it is a Paste; then put to it the Yolk of six Eggs, three or four Spoonfuls of thick Cream, half a Naples Bisket grated, mix these together, and melt a Pound of fresh Butter very thick, and stir it well in. When it is cold, put a little thin Puff-paste about the Bottom and Rim of your Dish, and pour in the Ingredients, and bake it about three quarters of an Hour.

A Fourth Orange Pudding.

TAKE the outside Rind of three Seville Oranges, boil them in several Waters till they are tender, then pound them in a Mortar, with three quarters of a Pound of Sugar; then blanch half a Pound of Sweet Almonds, beat them very fine with Rose-water to keep them from oiling, then beat sixteen Eggs, but six Whites, and a Pound of fresh Butter, beat all these together till it is light and hollow; then lay a thin Puff-paste all over a Dish, and put in the Ingredients. Bake it with your Tarts.

A Lemon Pudding.

GRATE the outside Rind of two clear Lemons, then grate two Naples Biskets, and mix with the grated Peel, and add to it three quarters of a Pound of white Sugar, twelve Yolks of Eggs, and half the Whites, three quarters of a Pound of melted Butter, half a Pint of thick Cream, mix all well together, lay a Puff-paste all over the Dish, and pour the Ingredients in, and bake it. An Hour will bake it.

An Almond Pudding to bake.

BLANCH half a Pound of Sweet Almonds, and four Bitter Ones, in warm Water, take them and pound them in a Marble Mortar, with two Spoonfuls of Orange-flower Water, and two of Rose-water, a Gill of Sack; mix in four grated Naples Biskets, and three quarters of a Pound of melted Butter, beat eight Eggs, and mix them with a quart of Cream boiled, grate in half a Nutmeg, and a quarter of a Pound of Sugar; mix all well together, make a thin Puff-paste, and lay all over the Dish, pour in the Ingredients, and bake it.

An Almond Pudding to boil.

BEAT a Pound of Sweet Almonds as small as possible, with three Spoonfuls of Rose-water, and a Gill of Sack or White Wine, and mix in half a Pound of fresh Butter melted, with five Yolks of Eggs, and two Whites, a Quart of Cream, a quarter of a Pound of Sugar, half a Nutmeg grated, and one Spoonful of Flour, and three Spoonfuls of Crumbs of white Bread; mix all well together, and boil it. It will take half an Hour's boiling.

A Sagoe Pudding.

LET half a Pound of Sagoe be washed well in three or four hot Waters, then put to it a Quart of new Milk, and let it boil together, till it is thick; stir it carefully, for it is apt to burn, put in a Stick of Cinnamon, when you set it on the Fire; when it is boiled, take it out; before you pour it out, stir in half a Pound of fresh Butter, then pour it into a Pan, and beat up nine Eggs, with five of the Whites, and four Spoonfuls of Sack; stir all together, and sweeten to your Taste. Put in a quarter of a Pound of Currans clean washed and rubbed, and just plump'd in two Spoonfuls of Sack, and two of Rose-water, mix all well together, lay a Puff-paste over a Dish, and pour in the Ingredients, and bake it.

A Millet Pudding.

YOU must get half a Pound of Millet-seed, and after it is washed, and picked clean, put to it half a Pound of Sugar, and a whole Nutmeg grated, three Quarts of Milk; and when you have mixed all well together, break in half a Pound of fresh Butter. Butter your Dish, and pour it in, and bake it.

A Carrot Pudding.

TAKE a raw Carrot, scrape it very clean, then grate it, take half a Pound of the grated Carrot, and a Pound of grated Bread, beat up eight Eggs, leave out half the Whites, mix the Eggs with half a Pint of Cream, then stir in the Bread and Carrot, and half a Pound of fresh Butter melted, half a Pint of Sack, and three Spoonfuls of Orange-flower Water, a Nutmeg grated, sweeten to your Palate. Mix all well together; and if it is not thin enough, stir in a little new Milk or Cream. Let it be of a moderate Thickness, lay a Puff-paste all over the Dish, and pour in the Ingredients. Bake it, it will take an Hour's baking, or you may boil it; but then you must melt Butter, and put in White Wine and Sugar.

A Second Carrot Pudding.

TAKE two Penny-loaves, pare off the Crust, soak them in a Quart of boiling Milk, let it stand till it is cold, then grate in two or three large Carrots; then put in eight Eggs well beat, and three quarters of a Pound of fresh Butter melted, grate in a little Nutmeg, and sweeten to your Taste. Cover your Dish with Puff-paste, and pour in the Ingredients, and bake it an Hour.

A Cowslip Pudding.

HAVING got the Flowers of a Peck of Cowslips, cut them small, and pound them small, with half a Pound of Naples Biskets grated, and three Pints of Cream, boil them a little, then take them off the Fire, and beat up sixteen Eggs, with a little Cream, and a little Rose-water, sweeten to your Palate. Mix it all well together, butter a Dish and pour it in, bake it; and when it is enough, throw fine Sugar over, and serve it up.

New Milk will do in all these Puddings, when you have no Cream.

To make a Quince, Apricot, or White Pear Plumb-Pudding.

SCALD your Quinces very tender, pare them very thin, scrape off the Soft, mix it with Sugar very sweet; put in a little Ginger, and a little Cinnamon. To a Pint of Cream, you must put three or four Yolks of Eggs, stir it into your Quince, till it is of a good Thickness. It must be pretty thick; so you may do Apricocks, or white Pear-Plumbs. Butter your Dish, and pour it in, and bake it.

A Pearl Barley Pudding.

TAKE a Pound of Pearl Barley, wash it clean, put to it three Quarts of new Milk, and half a Pound of double-refined Sugar, a Nutmeg grated, then put it into a deep Pan, and bake it with brown Bread; then take it out of the Oven, beat up six Eggs; mix with half a Pound of melted Butter, and a quarter of a Pound of grated Bread; mix all well together, butter a Dish and pour it in, and bake it again an Hour, and will be excellent.

A French Barley Pudding.

PUT to a Quart of Cream six Eggs well beaten, half the Whites, sweeten to your Palate, a little Orange flower Water or Rose-water, and a Pound of melted Butter; then put in six Handfuls of *French* Barley, that has been boiled tender in Milk, butter a Dish and put it in. It will take as long baking as a Venison-pasty.

To make an Apple Pudding.

TAKE twelve large Pippins, pare them, and take out the Cores; put them into a Sauce-pan, with four or five Spoonfuls of Water, boil them till they are soft and thick; then beat them well, stir in a quarter of a Pound of Butter, a Pound of Loaf-sugar, the Juice of three Lemons, the Peel of two Lemons cut thin, and beat fine in a Mortar, the Yolks of eight Eggs beat; mix all well together, bake it in a slack Oven, when it is near done, throw over a little fine Sugar. You may bake it in Puff-paste, as you do the other Puddings.

An Italian Pudding.

TAKE a Pint of Cream, and slice in some *French* Role, as much as you think will make it thick enough, beat ten Eggs fine, grate a Nutmeg, butter the Bottom of your Dish, slice twelve Pippins into it, and throw some Orange-peel and Sugar over, and half a Pint of Red Wine; then pour your Cream, Bread, and Eggs over it; first lay a Puff-paste at the Bottom of the Dish, and round the Edges, and bake it half an Hour.

A Rice Pudding.

TAKE a quarter of a Pound of Rice, put it into a Sauce-pan, with a Quart of new Milk, a Stick of Cinnamon, stir it often to keep it from sticking to the Sauce-pan. When it is boiled thick, pour it into a Pan, and stir in a quarter of a Pound of fresh Butter, and Sugar to your Palate; grate in half a Nutmeg, and add three or four Spoonfuls of Rose-water, stir all well together; when it is cold, beat up eight Eggs, with half the Whites, beat it all well together, butter a Dish and pour it in, and bake it. You may lay a Puff-paste first all over the Dish; for Change put in a few Currans and Sweetmeats, if you chuse it.

A Second Rice Pudding.

GET half a Pound of Rice, put to it three Quarts of Milk, stir in half a Pound of Sugar, grate a small Nutmeg in, and break in half a Pound of fresh Butter, butter a Dish, and pour it in, and bake. You may add a quarter of a Pound of Currans for Change. If you boil the Rice and Milk, and then stir in the Eggs and Sugar, you may bake it before the Fire, or in a Tin Oven.

A Third Rice Pudding.

TAKE the Flour of Rice six Ounces, put it into a Quart of Milk, and let it boil till it is pretty thick; stiring it all the while; then pour it into a Pan, and stir in half a Pound of fresh Butter, and a quarter of a Pound of Sugar; when it is cold, grate in a Nutmeg, beat six Eggs with a Spoonful or two of Sack, beat and stir all well together, lay a thin Puff-paste at the Bottom of your Dish, and pour it in, and bake it.

A Custard Pudding to boil.

TAKE a Pint of Cream, out of which take two or three Spoonfuls, and mix with a Spoonful of fine Flour, set the rest to boil. When it is boiled, take it off, and stir in the cold Cream and Flour very well; when it is cool, beat up five Yolks and two Whites of Eggs, and stir in a little Salt and some Nutmeg, and two or three Spoonfuls of Sack, sweeten to your Palate, butter a wooden Bole, and pour it in, tye a Cloth over it, and boil it half an Hour. When it is enough, untye the Cloth, turn the Pudding out into your Dish, and pour melted Butter over it.

A Flour Pudding.

TAKE a Quart of Milk, beat up eight Eggs, but four of the Whites, mix with them a quarter of a Pint of the Milk, and stir into that four large Spoonfuls of Flour, beat it well together, boil six bitter Almonds, in two Spoonfuls of Water, pour the Water into the Eggs, blanch the Almonds, and beat them fine in a Mortar; then mix them in with half a large Nutmeg, and a Tea Spoonful of Salt; then mix in the rest of the Milk, flour your Cloth well, and boil it an Hour, pour melted Butter over it, and Sugar, if you like it, thrown all over. Observe always in boiling Puddings, that the Water boils before you put them into the Pot, and have ready, when they are boiled, a Pan of clean cold Water, just give your Pudding one dip in, then untye the Cloth, and it will turn out, without sticking to the Cloth.

A Batter Pudding.

TAKE a Quart of Milk, beat up six Eggs, half the Whites, mix as above six Spoonfuls of Flour, a Tea Spoonful of Salt, and one of beaten Ginger; then mix all together, and boil it an Hour and quarter, pour melted Butter over it. You may put in eight Eggs, if you have Plenty for Change, and half a Pound of Prunes, or Currants.

A Batter Pudding without Eggs.

TAKE a Quart of Milk, mix six Spoonfuls of Flour, with a little of the Milk first, a Tea Spoonful of Salt, two Tea Spoonfuls of beaten Ginger, and two of the Tincture of Saffron; then mix all together, and boil it an Hour. You may add Fruit, as you think proper.

A Grateful Pudding.

TAKE a Pound of fine Flour, and a Pound of white Bread grated, take eight Eggs, but half the Whites, beat them up, and mix with them a Pint of new Milk, then stir in the Bread and Flour, and a Pound of Raisins stoned, and a Pound of Currans, half a Pound of Sugar, a little beaten Ginger, mix all well together, and either bake, or boil it. It will take three Quarters of an Hour's baking. Put Cream instead of Milk, if you have it, it will be an Addition to the Pudding.

A Bread Pudding.

CUT off all the Crust of a Penny white Loaf, and slice it thin into a Quart of new Milk, set it over a Chafindish of Coals, till the Bread has soaked up all the Milk, then put in a Piece of Sweet Butter, stir it round, let it stand till cold, or you may boil your Milk, and pour over your Bread, and cover it up close, does full as well; then take the Yolks of six Eggs, the Whites of three, and beat them up, with a little Rose-water, and Nutmeg, a little Salt, and Sugar, if you chuse it, mix all well together, and boil it half an Hour.

A Fine Bread Pudding.

TAKE all the Crumb of a stale Penny-loaf, cut it thin, a Quart of Cream, set it over a slow Fire till it is scalding hot, then let it stand till it is cold, beat up the Bread and Cream well together, grate in some Nutmeg, take twelve bitter Almonds, boil them in two Spoonfuls of Water, pour the Water to the Cream, and stir it in, with a little Salt, sweeten it to your Palate, blanch the Almonds, and beat them in a Mortar, with two Spoonfuls of Rose or Orange-flower Water, till they are a fine Paste; then mix them by degrees with the Cream, till they are well mixed in the Cream; then take the Yolks of eight Eggs, the Whites of but four, beat them well, and mix them with your Cream; then mix all well together. A Wooden Dish is best to boil it in; but if you boil it in a Cloth, be sure to dip it in the hot Water, and flour it well, tye it loose, and boil it half an Hour. Be sure the Water boils when you put it in, and keeps boiling all the time. When it is enough, turn it into your Dish, melt Butter, and put in two or three Spoonfuls of White Wine or Sack, give it a boil, and pour it over your Pudding; then strew a good deal of fine Sugar all over the Pudding and Dish, and send it to Table hot. New Milk will do, when you cannot get Cream; you may for Change put in a few Currans.

An Ordinary Bread Pudding.

TAKE two Halfpenny Roles, slice them thin, Crust and all, pour over them a Pint of new Milk boiling hot, cover them close, let it stand some Hours to soak; then beat it well with a little melted Butter, and beat up the Yolks and Whites of two Eggs, beat all together well, with a little Salt. Boil it half an Hour; when it is done, turn it into your Dish, pour melted Butter over it and Sugar, some love a little Vinegar in the Butter. If your Roles are stale and grated, they will do better; add a little Ginger. You may bake it with a few Currans.

A Baked Bread Pudding.

TAKE the Crumb of a Penny-loaf, as much Flour, the Yolks of four Eggs and two Whites, a quarter of a Pound of Sugar, a Tea Spoonful of Ginger, half a Pound of Raisins stoned, half a Pound of Currans clean washed and picked, a little Salt; mix first the Bread and Flour, Ginger and Salt and Sugar, then the Eggs, and then as much Milk as will make it like a good Batter, then the Fruit, butter the Dish, and pour it in and bake it.

A Boiled Loaf.

TAKE a Penny-loaf, pour over it half a Pint of Milk boiling hot, cover it close, let it stand till it has soaked up the Milk, then tye it up in a Cloth, and boil it a quarter of an Hour. When it is done, lay it in your Dish, and pour melted Butter over it, and throw Sugar all over, a Spoonful of Wine, or Rose-water, does as well in the Butter, or Juice of Seville Orange. A *French* Manchet does best; but there are little Loaves made on purpose for the Use. A *French* Role, or Oat-cake, does very well boiled thus.

To make a Chesnut Pudding.

PUT a Dozen and half of Chesnuts in a Skillet, or Sauce-pan of Water, boil them a quarter of an Hour, then blanch and peel them, and beat them in a Marble Mortar, with a little Orange-flower or Rose-water, and Sack, till they are a fine thin Paste; then beat up twelve Eggs with half the Whites, and mix them well; grate half a Nutmeg, and a little Salt, mix them with three Pints of Cream, and half a Pound of melted Butter; sweeten it to your Palate, and mix all together. Lay a Puff-paste all over the Dish, and pour in the Mixture, and bake it. When you can't get Cream, take three Pints of Milk, beat up the Yolks of four Eggs, and stir into the Milk, set it over the Fire, stirring it all the time, till it is scalding hot, then mix it in the room of the Cream.

A Fine Plain Baked Pudding.

TAKE a Quart of Milk, and put six Laurel-leaves into it. When it has boiled a little with fine Flour, make it into a Hasty-pudding, with a little Salt, pretty thick; take it off the Fire, and stir in half a Pound of Butter, and a quarter of a Pound of Sugar, and beat up twelve Eggs and half the Whites, stir all well together, lay a Puff-paste all over the Dish, and pour in your Stuff: Half an Hour will bake it.

To make Pretty Little Cheesecurd Pudding.

TAKE a Gallon of Milk, and turn it with Runet, then drain all the Curd from the Whey, put the Curd into a Mortar, and beat it with half a Pound of fresh Butter, till the Butter and Curd are well mixed; then beat six Eggs, half the Whites, and strain them to the Curd, two Naples Biskets, or half a Penny Role grated; mix all these together, and sweeten to your Palate. Butter your Patty-pans, and fill them with the Ingredients. Bake them; but don't let your Oven be too hot; when they are done, turn them out into a Dish, cut Citron and Candied Orange-peel into little narrow Bits, about an Inch long, and blanch Almonds cut in long Slips, stick them here and there on the Tops of the Puddings, just as you fancy; pour melted Butter with a little Sack in it, into the Dish, and throw fine Sugar all over the Puddings and Dish. They make a pretty Side-dish.

An Apricot Pudding.

CODDLE six large Apricots very tender, break them very small, sweeten them to your Taste. When they are cold, add six Eggs, only two Whites well beat, mix them well together with a Pint of good Cream, lay a Puff-paste all over your Dish, and pour in your Ingredients. Bake it half an Hour; don't let the Oven be too hot; when it is enough, throw a little fine Sugar all over it, and send it to Table hot.

The Ipswich Almond Pudding.

STEEP somewhat above three Ounces of the Crumb of white Bread sliced, in a Pint and half of Cream, or grate the Bread, then beat half a Pound of blanched Almonds very fine, till they are like a Paste, with a little Orange-flower Water, beat up the Yolks of eight Eggs, and the Whites of four, mix all well together, put in a quarter of a Pound of white Sugar, and stir in a little melted Butter about a quarter of a Pound, lay a Sheet of Puff-paste at the Bottom of your Dish, and pour in the Ingredients; half an Hour will bake it.

A Vermicella Pudding.

TAKE the Yolks of two Eggs, and mix it up with as much Flour as will make it pretty stiff, so as you can roll it out very thin, like a thin Wafer; and when it is so dry as you can roll it up together without breaking, roll it as close as you can; then, with a sharp Knife, begin at one End, and cut it as thin as you can, have some Water boiling, with a little Salt in it, put in the Paste, and just give it a boil for a Minute or two; then throw it into a Sieve to drain; then take a Pan, lay a Layer of Vermicelly, and a Layer of Butter, and so on. When it is cool, beat it up well together, and melt the rest of the Butter, and pour on it; beat it well (a Pound of Butter is enough, mix half with the Paste, and the other half melt) grate the Crumb of a Penny-loaf, and mix in; beat up ten Eggs, and mix in a small Nutmeg grated, a Gill of Sack, or some Rose-water, a Tea Spoonful of Salt, beat it all well together, and sweeten it to your Palate; grate a little Lemon-peel in, and dry two large Blades of Mace, and beat them fine. You may, for Change, add a Pound of Currans nicely washed and picked clean, butter the Pan or Dish you bake it in, and then pour in your Mixture. It will take an Hour and half baking; but the Oven must not be too hot: If you lay a good thin Crust round the Bottom of the Dish and Sides, it will be better.

Puddings for little Dishes.

TAKE a Pint of Cream, and boil it, and slit a Halfpenny-loaf, and pour the Cream hot over it, and cover it close till it is cold; then beat it fine, and grate in half a large Nutmeg, a quarter of a Pound of Sugar, the Yolks of four Eggs, but two Whites well beat; beat it all well together. With the half of this fill four little wooden Dishes, colour one yellow with Saffron, one red with Cochineal, green with the Juice of Spinage, and blue with Syrrup of Violets; the rest mix, an Ounce of Sweet Almonds blanched and beat fine, and fill a Dish. Your Dishes must be small, and tye your Covers over very close with Pack-thread. When your Pot boils, put them in, an Hour will boil them; when enough, turn them out, in a Dish, the white One in the Middle, and the four coloured ones round. When they are enough, melt some fresh Butter, with a Glass of Sack, and pour over, and throw Sugar all over the Dish. The white Pudding Dish must be of a larger Size than the rest; and be sure to butter your Dishes well before you put them in, and don't fill them too full.

To make a Sweet-meat Pudding.

PUT a thin Puff-paste all over your Dish, then have candied Orange and Lemon-peel, and Citron, of each an Ounce, slice them thin, and lay them all over the Bottom of your Dish, then beat eight Yolks of Eggs, and two Whites, near half a Pound of Sugar, and half a Pound of melted Butter. Beat all well together; when the Oven is ready, pour it on your Sweetmeats; an Hour or less will bake it; the Oven must not be too hot.

To make a fine Plain Pudding.

TAKE a Quart of Milk, put into it six Laurel-leaves, boil it, then take out your Leaves, and stir in as much Flour as will make it a Hasty-pudding pretty thick; take it off, and then stir in half a Pound of Butter, then a quarter of a Pound of Sugar, a small Nutmeg grated, and twelve Yolks and six Whites of Eggs well beaten; mix all well together, butter a Dish, and put in your Stuff: A little more than half an Hour will bake it.

To make a Ratafia Pudding.

TAKE a Quart of Cream, boil it with four or five Laurel-leaves, then take them out, and break in half a Pound of Naples Biskets, half a Pound of Butter, some Sack, Nutmeg, and a little Salt. Take it off the Fire, cover it up, when it is almost cold, put in two Ounces of blanched Almonds beat fine, and the Yolks of five Eggs. Mix all well together, and bake it in a moderate Oven half an Hour; scrape Sugar on it as it goes into the Oven.

A Bread and Butter Pudding.

TAKE a Penny-loaf, and cut it into thin Slices of Bread and Butter, as you do for Tea. Butter your Dish as you cut them, lay Slices all over the Dish, then strew a few Currans, clean washed and picked, then a Row of Bread and Butter, then a few Currans, and so on, till all your Bread and Butter is in; then take a Pint of Milk, beat up four Eggs, a little Salt, half a Nutmeg grated, mix all together with Sugar to your Taste. Pour this over the Bread, and bake it half an Hour. A Puff-paste under does best. You may put in two Spoonfuls of Rose-water.

A Boiled Rice Pudding.

HAVING got a quarter of a Pound of the Flour of Rice, put it over the Fire in a Pint of Milk, and keep it stirring constantly, that it may not clod nor burn. When it is of a good Thickness, take it off, and pour it into an earthen Pan; stir in half a Pound of Butter very smooth, and half a Pint of Cream or new Milk, sweeten it to your Palate, grate in half a Nutmeg, and the outward Rind of a Lemon; beat up the Yolks of six Eggs, and two Whites, beat all well together; boil it either in small China-basons or wooden Bowls. When boiled, turn them in a Dish, and pour melted Butter over them, with a little Sack, and throw Sugar all over.

A Cheap Rice Pudding.

TAKE a quarter of a Pound of Rice, and half a Pound of Raisins stoned, and tye them in a Cloth. Give the Rice a great deal of room to swell, boil it two Hours; when it is enough, turn it into your Dish, and pour melted Butter and Sugar over it, with a little Nutmeg.

A Cheap Plain Rice Pudding.

TAKE a quarter of a Pound of Rice, tye it in a Cloth, but give room for swelling; boil it an Hour, then take it up, untye it, and with a Spoon, stir in a quarter of a Pound of Butter, grate some Nutmeg, and sweeten to your Taste; then tye it up close, and boil it another Hour; then take it up, turn it into your Dish, and pour melted Butter over it.

A Cheap Rice Pudding Baked.

TAKE a quarter of a Pound of Rice, boil it in a Quart of new Milk, stir it that it does not burn; when it begins to be thick, take it off, let it stand till it is a little cool, then stir in well a quarter of a Pound of Butter, and Sugar to your Palate; grate a small Nutmeg, butter your Dish, and pour it in, and bake it.

A Spinage Pudding.

TAKE a quarter of a Peck of Spinage, picked and washed clean, put it into a Sauce-pan, with a little Salt, cover it close, and when it is boiled just tender, throw it into a Sieve to drain; then chop it with a Knife, beat up six Eggs, and mix well with it half a Pint of Cream, and a stale Role grated fine, a little Nutmeg, and a quarter of a Pound of melted Butter; stir all well together, put it into the Sauce-pan you boiled the Spinage in, and keep stirring it all the time till it begins to thicken; then wet and flour your Cloth very well, tye it up, and boil it an Hour. When it is enough, turn it into your Dish, and pour melted Butter over it, and the Juice of a Seville Orange, if you like it; as to Sugar, you must add, or let it alone, just to your Taste. You may bake it; but then you should put in a Quarter of a Pound of Sugar. You may add Bisket in the room of Bread, if you like it better.

A Quaking Pudding.

TAKE a Pint of good Cream, six Eggs, and half the Whites, beat them well, and mix with the Cream; grate a little Nutmeg in, add a little Salt, and a little Rose-water, if it be agreeable, grate in the Crumb of a Halfpenny Role, or a Spoonful of Flour, first mixed with a little of the Cream, or a Spoonful of the Flour of Rice, which you please. Butter a Cloth well, and flour it, then put in your Mixture, tye it, not too close, and boil it half an Hour fast; be sure the Water boils before you put it in.

A Cream Pudding.

TAKE a Quart of Cream, boil it with a Blade of Mace, and half a Nutmeg grated, let it cool; beat up eight Eggs, and three Whites, strain them well, mix a Spoonful of Flour with them, a quarter of a Pound of Almonds blanched, and beat very fine, with a Spoonful of Orange-flower or Rose-water, mix with the Eggs, then by degrees mix in the Cream, beat all well together, take a thick Cloth, wet it, and flour it well, pour in your Stuff, tye it close, and boil it half an Hour. Let the Water boil all the time fast; when it is done, turn it into your Dish, and pour melted Butter over, with a little Sack, and throw fine Sugar all over it.

A Prune Pudding.

TAKE a Quart of Milk, beat six Eggs, half the Whites, with half a Pint of the Milk, and four Spoonfuls of Flour, a little Salt, and two Spoonfuls of beaten Ginger; then by degrees mix in all the Milk, and a Pound of Prunes, tye it in a Cloth, and boil it an Hour, melt Butter and pour over it. Damsons eat well done this way in room of Prunes.

A Spoonful Pudding.

TAKE a Spoonful of Flour, a Spoonful of Cream or Milk, an Egg, a little Nutmeg, Ginger, and Salt, mix all together, and boil it in a little wooden Dish half an Hour. You may add a few Currans.

An Apple Pudding.

MAKE a good Puff-paste, role it out half an Inch thick, pare your Apples, and core them, enough to fill the Crust, and close it up, tye it in a Cloth, and boil it; if a small Pudding, two Hours; if a large one, three or four Hours. When it is enough, turn it into your Dish, cut a Piece of the Crust out of the Top, butter and sugar it to your Palate; lay on the Crust again, and send it to Table hot. A Pear Pudding make the same way. And thus you may make a Damson Pudding, or any Sort of Plumbs, Apricots, Cherries, or Mulberries, and are very fine.

East Dumplings.

FIRST make a light Dough as for Bread, with Flour, Water, Salt, and Yeast, cover with a Cloth, and set it before the Fire for half an Hour; then have a Sauce-pan of Water on the Fire, and when it boils, take the Dough, and make it into little round Balls, as big as a large Hen's Egg; then flat them with your Hand, and put them into the boiling Water, a few Minutes boils them. Take great Care they don't fall to the Bottom of the Pot or Sauce-pan; for then they will be heavy, and be sure to keep the Water boiling all the time. When they are enough, take them up (which they will be in ten Minutes or less) lay them in your Dish, and have melted Butter in a Cup.—As good a way as any to save Trouble, is to send to the Baker's for half a quartern of Dough (which will make a great many) and then you have only the Trouble of boiling it.

Norfolk Dumplings.

MIX a good thick Batter, as for Pancakes, take half a Pint of Milk, two Eggs, a little Salt, and make it into a Batter with Flour. Have ready a clean Sauce-pan of Water boiling, into which drop this Batter. Be sure the Water boils fast, and two or three Minutes will boil them; then throw them into a Sieve to drain the Water away, then turn them into a Dish, and stir a Lump of fresh Butter into them, and eat them hot, they are very good.

Hard Dumplings.

MIX Flour and Water, with a little Salt, like a Paste, roll them in Balls, as big as a Turkey's Egg, roll them in a little Flour, have the Water boiling, and throw them in the Water; half an Hour will boil them. They are best boiled with a good Piece of Beef. You may add for Change a few Currans, have melted Butter in a Cup.

Another

Another Way to make Hard Dumplings.

RUB into your Flour first a good Piece of Butter, then make it like a Crust for a Pye; make them up, and boil them as above.

Apple Dumplings.

MAKE a good Puff-paste, pare some large Apples, cut them in Quarters, and take out the Cores very nicely; take a Piece of Crust, and roll it round, enough for one Apple; if they are big, they will not look pretty, so roll the Crust round each Apple, and make them round like a Ball, with a little Flour in your Hand. Have a Pot of Water boiling, take a clean Cloth, dip it in the Water, and shake Flour over it. Tye each Dumpling by itself, and put them in the Water boiling, which keep boiling all the time; and if your Crust is light and good, and the Apples not too large, half an Hour will boil them; but if the Apples be large, they will take an Hour's boiling. When they are enough, take them up, and lay them in a Dish; throw fine Sugar all over them, and send them to Table. Have good fresh Butter melted in a Cup, and fine beaten Sugar in a Saucer.

Another Way to make Apple Dumplings.

MAKE a good Puff-paste, roll it out a little thicker than a Crown-piece, pare some large Apples, and roll every Apple in a Piece of this Paste, tye them close in a Cloth separate, boil them an Hour, cut a little Piece of the Top off, and take out the Core, take a Tea Spoonful of Lemon-peel, shread as fine as possible, just give it a boil in two Spoonfuls of Rose or Orange-flower Water. In each Dumpling put a Tea Spoonful of this Liquor, and sweeten the Apple with fine Sugar, and pour in some melted Butter, and lay on your Piece of Crust again. Lay them in your Dish, and throw fine Sugar all over them.

To make a Cheesecurd Florendine.

TAKE two Pounds of Cheesecurd, break it all to Pieces with your Hand, a Pound of blanched Almonds finely pounded, with a little Rose-water, half a Pound of Currans, clean washed and picked, a little Sugar to your Palate, some stewed Spinage cut small; mix all well together, lay a Puff-paste in your Dish, put in your Ingredients, cover it with a thin Crust rolled, and laid a-cross, and bake it in a moderate Oven half an Hour. As to the Top-Crust lay it in what Shape you please, either rolled or marked with an Iron on purpose.

A Florendine of Oranges or Apples.

GET half a Dozen Seville Oranges, save the Juice, take out the Pulp, lay them in Water twenty-four Hours, shift them three or four times, then boil them in three or four Waters; then drain them from the Water, put to them a Pound of Sugar, and their Juice, boil them to a Syrup, take great care they don't stick to the Pan you do them in, and set them by for Use. When you use them, lay a Puff-paste all over the Dish, boil ten Pippins pared, quartered, and cored in a little Water and Sugar, and slice two of the Oranges, and mix with the Pippins in the Dish; bake it in a slow Oven with Crust as above. Or just bake the Crust, and then lay in the Ingredients.

An Artichoke Pye.

BOIL twelve Artichokes, take off all the Leaves and Choke, and take the Bottoms clear from the Stalk, make a good Puff-paste Crust, lay a quarter of a Pound of good fresh Butter all over the Bottom of your Pye; then lay a Row of Artichokes, strew a little Pepper, Salt, and beaten Mace over them, then another Row, and strew the rest of your Spice over them, put in a quarter of a Pound more of Butter in little Bits, take half an Ounce of Truffles and Morells, boil them in a quarter of a Pint of Water, pour the Water into the Pye, cut the Truffles and Morells very small, throw all over the Pye; then have ready twelve Eggs boiled hard, take only the hard Yolks, lay them all over the Pye, pour in a Gill of White Wine, cover your Pye and bake it. When the Crust is done, the Pye is enough. Four large Blades of Mace, and twelve Pepper-corns well beat will do, with a Tea Spoonful of Salt.

A Sweet Egg Pye.

MAKE a good Crust, cover your Dish with it, then have ready twelve Eggs boiled hard, cut them in Slices, and lay them in your Pye; throw half a Pound of Currans, clean washed and picked, all over the Eggs; then beat up four Eggs well, and mix with half a Pint of White Wine, grate in a small Nutmeg, make it pretty sweet with Sugar. You are to mind to lay a quarter of a Pound of Butter between the Eggs, then pour in your Wine and Eggs, and cover your Pye. Bake it half an Hour, or till the Crust is done.

A Potatoe Pye.

BOIL three Pounds of Potatoes, and peel them, make a good Crust, and lay in your Dish; lay at the Bottom half a Pound of Butter, then lay in your Potatoes, throw over them three Tea Spoonfuls of Salt, and a small Nutmeg grated all over, six Eggs boiled hard and chopped fine, throw all over, a Tea Spoonful of Pepper strewed all over, then half a Pint of White Wine. Cover your Pye, and bake it half an Hour, or till the Crust is enough.

An Onion Pye.

WASH, and pare some Potatoes, and cut them in Slices, peel some Onions, cut them in Slices, pare some Apples and slice them, make a good Crust, cover your Dish, lay a quarter of a Pound of Butter all over, take a quarter of an Ounce of Mace beat fine, a Nutmeg grated, a Tea Spoonful of beaten Pepper, three Tea Spoonfuls of Salt, mix all together, strew some over the Butter, lay a Layer of Potatoes, a Layer of Onion, a Layer of Apple, and a Layer of Eggs, and so on, till you have filled your Pye, strewing a little of the Seasoning between each Layer, and a quarter of a Pound of Butter in Bits, and six Spoonfuls of Water. Close your Pye, and bake it an Hour and half: A Pound of Potatoes, a Pound of Onion, a Pound of Apples, and twelve Eggs will do.

Orangeado Pye.

MAKE a good Crust, lay it over your Dish, take two Oranges, boil them with two Lemons till tender in four or five Quarts of Water. In the last Water, which there must be about a Pint of, add a Pound of Loaf-sugar, boil it, take them out and slice them into your Pye, then pare twelve Pippins, core them, and give them one boil in the Syrup; lay them all over the Orange and Lemon, pour in the Syrup, and pour on them some Orangeado Syrup. Cover your Pye, and bake it in a slow Oven half an Hour.

A Skirrit Pye.

TAKE your Skirrits and boil them tender, peel them, slice them, fill your Pye, and take to half a Pint of Cream the Yolk of an Egg, beat fine with a little Nutmeg, a little beaten Mace, and a little Salt; beat all together well, with a quarter of a Pound of fresh Butter melted, then pour in as much as your Dish will hold, put on the Top-crust, and bake it half an Hour. You may put in some hard Yolks of Eggs; if you cannot get Cream, put in Milk; but Cream is best. About two Pound of the Root will do.

An Apple Pye.

MAKE a good Puff-paste Crust, lay some round the Sides of the Dish, pare and quarter your Apples, and take out the Cores, lay a Row of Apples thick, throw in half your Sugar you design for your Pye, mince a little Lemon-peel fine, throw over and squeeze a little Lemon over them, then a few Cloves, here and there one, then the rest of your Apples, and the rest of your Sugar. You must sweeten to your Palate, and squeeze a little more Lemon; boil the Peeling of the Apples, and the Cores in some fair Water, with a Blade of Mace, till it is very good; strain it and boil the Syrup with a little Sugar, till there is but very little and good, pour it into your Pye, and put on your Upper-crust, and bake it. You may put in a little Quince and Marmalate, if you please.

Thus make a Pear-pye; but don't put in any Quince. You may butter them when they come out of the Oven; or beat up the Yolks of two Eggs, and half a Pint of Cream, with a little Nutmeg, sweetned with Sugar, and take off the Lid, and pour in the Cream. Cut the Crust in little three-corner Pieces, and stick about the Pye, and send it to Table.

To make a Cherry Pye.

MAKE a good Crust, lay a little round the Sides of your Dish, throw Sugar at the Bottom, and lay in your Fruit and Sugar at Top. A few red Currans does well with them; put on your Lid, and bake in a slack Oven.

Make a Plumb Pye the same way, and a Gooseberry Pye. If you would have it red, let it stand a good while in the Oven, after the Bread is drawn. A Custard is very good with the Gooseberry Pye.

A Salt-Fish Pye.

GET a Side of Salt-Fish, lay it in Water all Night, next Morning put it over the Fire in a Pan of Water till it is tender, drain it, and lay it on the Dresser, take off all the Skin, and pick the Meat clean from the Bones, mince it small, then take the Crumb of two *French* Roles, cut in Slices, and boiled up with a Quart of new Milk, break your Bread very fine with a Spoon, put to it your minced Salt Fish, a Pound of melted Butter, two Spoonfuls of minced Parsley, half a Nutmeg grated, a little beaten Pepper, and three Tea Spoonfuls of Mustard; mix all well together, make a good Crust, and lay all over your Dish, and cover it up. Bake it an Hour.

A Carp Pye.

TAKE a large Carp, fcale, wafh, and gut it clean; take an Eel, boil it juft a little tender, pick off all the Meat, and mince it fine, with an equal Quantity of Crumbs of Bread, a few Sweet Herbs, a little Lemon-peel cut fine, a little Pepper, Salt, and grated Nutmeg, an Anchovy, half a Pint of Oyfters parboiled, and chopped fine, the Yolks of three hard Eggs cut fmall, roll it up with a quarter of a Pound of Butter, and fill the Belly of the Carp. Make a good Cruft, cover the Difh, and lay in your Carp; fave the Liquor you boil your Eel in, and put in the Bones of the Eel, and boil them with a little Mace, whole Pepper, an Onion, fome Sweet Herbs, and an Anchovy. Boil it till there is about half a Pint, ftrain it, and add to it a quarter of a Pint of White Wine, and a Lump of Butter mixed in a very little Flour; boil it up, and pour into your Pye. Put on the Lid, and bake it an Hour in a quick Oven: If there be any Force-meat left after filling the Belly, make Balls of it, and put into the Pye. If you have not Liquor enough, boil a few fmall Eels to make enough to fill your Difh.

A Soal Pye.

MAKE a good Cruft, cover your Difh, boil two Pounds of Eels tender, pick all the Flefh clean from the Bones, throw the Bones into the Liquor you boil the Eel in, with a little Mace, and Salt, till it is very good, and about a quarter of a Pint, then ftrain it. In the mean time cut the Flefh of your Eel fine, with a little Lemon-peel fhread fine, a little Salt, Pepper, and Nutmeg, a few Crumbs of Bread, and chopped Parfley, and an Anchovy; melt a quarter of a Pound of Butter, and mix with it, then lay it in the Difh, cut the Flefh of a Pair of large Soals, or three Pair of very fmall ones clean from the Bones and Fins, lay it on the Force-meat, and pour in the Broth of the Eels you boiled. Put the Lid of the Pye on, and bake it; you fhould boil the Bones of the Soals with the Eel Bones, to make it good. If you boil the Soal Bones with one or two little Eels, without the Force-meat your Pye will be very good. And thus you may do a Turbutt.

An Eel Pye.

MAKE a good Cruft, clean, gut, and wafh your Eels very well, then cut them in Pieces half as long as your Finger; feafon them with Pepper, Salt, and a little beaten Mace to your Palate, either high or low. Fill your Difh with Eels, and put as much Water as the Difh will well hold; put on your Cover, and bake them well.

A Flounder Pye.

GET fome Flounders, wafh them clean, dry them in a Cloth, juft boil them, cut off the Meat clean from the Bones, lay a good Cruft over your Difh, and lay a little frefh Butter at the Bottom, and on that the Fifh; feafon them with Pepper, and Salt to your Mind. Boil the Bones in the Water your Fifh was boiled in, with a little Bit of Horfe-reddifh, a little Parfley, and a very little Bit of Lemon-peel, and a Cruft of Bread. Boil it till there is juft enough Liquor for the Pye; then ftrain it, and put it into your Pye; put on the Top-cruft, and bake it.

A Herring Pye.

SCALE, gut, and wafh them very clean, cut off the Heads, Fins, and Tails. Make a good Cruft, cover your Difh, then feafon your Herrings with beaten Mace, Pepper, and Salt; put a little Butter in the Bottom of your Difh, then a Row of Herrings; pare fome Apples, and cut them in thin Slices all over, then peel fome Onions, and cut them in Slices all over thick, lay a little Butter on the Top, put in a little Water, lay on the Lid, and bake it well.

A Salmon Pye.

MAKE a good Cruft, cleanfe a Piece of Salmon well, feafon it with Salt, Mace, and Nutmeg, lay a little Piece of Butter at the Bottom of the Difh, and lay your Salmon in. Melt Butter according to your Pye; take a Lobfter, boil it, pick out all the Flefh, chop it fmall, bruife the Body, mix it well with the Butter, which muft be very good; pour it over your Salmon, put on the Lid, and bake it well.

A Lobfter Pye.

MAKE a good Cruft, boil two Lobfters, take out the Tails, cut them in two, take out the Gut, cut each Tail in four Pieces, and lay them in the Difh. Take the Bodies, bruife them well with the Claws, and pick out all the reft of the Meat; chop it all together, feafon it with Pepper Salt, and two or three Spoonfuls of Vinegar, melt half a Pound of Butter, ftir all together, with the Crumb of a Halfpenny Role, rubbed in a clean Cloth fmall, lay it over the Tails, put on your Cover, and bake it in a flow Oven.

A Muscle Pye.

MAKE a good Crust, lay it all over the Dish, wash your Muscles clean in several Waters, then put them in a deep Stew-pan, cover them, and let them stew, till they are all open, pick them out, and see there be no Crabs under the Tongue; put them in a Sauce-pan, with two or three Blades of Mace, strain the Liquor just enough to cover them, a good Piece of Butter, and a few Crumbs of Bread; stew them a few Minutes, fill your Pye, and put on the Lid, and bake it half an Hour. So you may make an Oyster Pye.

Lent Mince Pies.

SIX Eggs boiled hard chopped fine, twelve Pippins pared and chopped small, a Pound of Raisins of the Sun stoned, and chopped fine, a Pound of Currans washed, picked, and rubbed clean, a large Spoonful of fine Sugar beat fine, an Ounce of Citron, an Ounce of candied Orange, both cut fine, a quarter of an Ounce of Mace and Cloves, beat fine, and a large Nutmeg beat fine; mix all together with a Gill of Brandy, and a Gill of Sack. Make your Crust good, and bake it in a slack Oven. When you make your Pye, squeeze in the Juice of a Seville Orange, and a Glass of Red Wine.

To Collar Salmon.

TAKE a Side of Salmon, cut off about a Handful of the Tail, wash your large Piece very well, and dry it with a clean Cloth, then wash it over with Yolks of Eggs, then make Force-meat with that you cut off the Tail; but take off the Skin, and put to it a Handful of parboiled Oysters, a Tail or two of Lobsters, the Yolks of three or four Eggs boiled hard, six Anchovies, a Handful of Sweet Herbs chopped small, a little Salt, Cloves, Mace, Nutmeg, Pepper beat fine, and grated Bread; work all these together into a Body, with the Yolks of Eggs, and lay it all over the fleshy Part, and a little more Pepper and Salt over the Salmon; so role it up into a Collar, and bind it with broad Tape, then boil it in Water, Salt, and Vinegar; but let the Liquor boil first, then put in your Collars, a Bunch of Sweet Herbs, sliced Ginger and Nutmeg. Let it boil, but not too fast; it will take near two Hours boiling; and when it is enough, take it up into your Sousing-pan, and when the Pickle is cold, put it to your Salmon, and let it stand in it till used; or otherwise you may pot it. Fill it up with clarified Butter, as you pot Fowls; that Way will keep longest.

To Collar Eels.

TAKE your Eel and cut it open, take out the Bones, and cut off the Head and Tail, and lay the Eel flat on the Dresser, and shread some Sage as fine as possible, and mix it with black Pepper beat, grated Nutmeg and Salt, and lay it all over the Eel, and role it up hard in little Cloths; and tye both Ends tight; then set over the Fire some Water, with Pepper and Salt, five or six Cloves, three or four Blades of Mace, a Bay-leaf or two, boil it Bones, Head, and Tail well together; then take out your Heads and Tails, and put in your Eels, and let them boil till they are tender; then take them out and boil the Liquor longer, till you think there is enough to cover them. Take it off, and when cold, pour it over the Eels, and cover it close; don't take off the Cloths till you use them.

To Pickle or Bake Herrings.

SCALE and wash them clean, cut off the Heads, take out the Rows, or wash them clean, and put them in again just as you like; season them with a little Mace and Cloves beat, a very little beaten Pepper and Salt, lay them in a deep Pan, lay two or three Bay-leaves between each Lay; then put in half Vinegar and half Water, or rap Vinegar. Cover it close with a brown Paper, send it to the Oven to bake; let it stand till cold, then pour off that Pickle, and put fresh Vinegar and Water, and send them to the Oven again to bake. Thus do Sprats; but don't bake them the second time. Some use only All-spice, but that is not so good.

To Pickle or Bake Mackrel, to keep all the Year.

GUT them, cut off their Heads, cut them open, dry them very well with a clean Cloth, take a Pan which they will lye cleverly in, lay a few Bay-leaves at the Bottom, rub the Bone with a little Bay Salt beat fine, take a little beaten Mace, a few Cloves beat fine, black and white Pepper beat fine; mix a little Salt, rub them inside and out with the Spice, lay them in the Pan, and between every Lay of the Mackrel put a few Bay-leaves; then cover them with Vinegar, tye them down close with brown Paper, put them into a slow Oven they will take a good while doing; when they are enough, uncover them, and let them stand till cold, then pour away all that Vinegar, and put as much good Vinegar as will cover them, and put in an Onion stuck with Cloves. Send them to the Oven again, and let them stand two Hours in a very slow Oven, they will keep all the Year; but you must not put in your Hands to take out the Mackrel, if you can avoid it, but take a Slice to take them out with. The great Bones of the Mackrel taken out and broiled, is a pretty little Plate to fill up a Corner of a Table.

The Art of Cookery, made Plain and Easy.

To Souse Mackrel.

YOU must wash them clean, gut them, and boil them in Salt and Water till they are enough; take them out, lay them in a clean Pan, cover them with the Liquor, add a little Vinegar; and when you send them to Table, lay Fennel over them.

To Pot a Lobster.

TAKE a live Lobster, boil it in Salt and Water, peg it that no Water gets in; when it is cold, pick out all the Flesh and Body, take out the Gut, beat it in a Mortar fine, and season it with beaten Mace, grated Nutmeg, Pepper and Salt, mix all together, melt a little Piece of Butter, as big as a large Wallnut, mix it with the Lobster as you are beating it; when it is beat to a Paste, put it into your Potting-pot, and put it down as close and hard as you can, then set some fresh Butter in a deep broad Pan before the Fire, and when it is all melted, take off the Skim at Top, if any, and pour the clear Butter over the Meat as thick as a Crown-piece. The Whey and Churn-milk will settle at the Bottom of the Pan; but take great Care none of that goes in, and always let your Butter be very good, or you will spoil all. Or only put the Tails, laying them as close together as you can, and pour the Butter over them. You must be sure to let the Lobster be well boiled.

To Pot Eels.

TAKE a large Eel, skin it, cleanse it, and wash it very clean, dry it in a Cloth, cut it into Pieces as long as your Finger, season them with a little beaten Mace and Nutmeg, Pepper, Salt, and a little Salprunella beat fine; lay them in a Pan, and pour as much good Butter over them, as will cover them clarified as above. They must be baked half an Hour in a quick Oven; if a slow Oven, longer, till they are enough. With a Fork take them out, and lay them on a coarse Cloth to drain. When they are quite cold, season them again with the same Seasoning, lay them in the Pot close, and take off the Butter they were baked in clear from the Gravy of the Fish, and set in a Dish before the Fire. When it is melted, pour the clear Butter over the Eels, and let them be covered with the Butter. As to the baking, you must judge by the Largeness of the Eel.

In the same manner you may pot what you please. You may bone your Eels, if you chuse it; but then don't put in any Salprunella.

To Pot Lampreys.

SKIN them, and cleanse them with Salt, and then wipe them dry; beat some black Pepper, Mace, and Cloves, mix them with Salt, and season them; lay them in a Pan, and cover them with good clarified Butter; bake them an Hour, order them as the Eels, only let them be well seasoned, and one will be enough for a Pot. You must season them well, and let your Butter be good, they will keep a long time.

To Pot Charrs.

AFTER having cleansed them, cut off the Fins, Tails, and Heads, then lay them in Rows in a long Baking-pan; cover them with Butter, and order them as above.

To Pot a Pike.

YOU must scale it, cut off the Head, split it and take out the Chine-Bone, then strew all over the Inside some Bay-salt and Pepper, roll it up round, and lay it in a Pot. Cover it, and bake it one Hour; then take it out and lay it on a coarse Cloth to drain, when it is cold, put it into your Pot, and cover it with clarified Butter.

To Pot Salmon.

TAKE a Piece of fresh Salmon, scale it, and wipe it clean (let your Piece, or Pieces, be as big as will lye cleverly in your Pot) season it with *Jamaica* Pepper, black Pepper, Mace and Cloves beat fine, mixed with Salt, a little Salprunella beat fine, and rub the Bone with; season with a little of the Spice, pour clarified Butter over it, and bake it well; then take it out carefully, and lay it to drain; when cold, season it well, lay it in your Pot close, and cover it with clarified Butter as above.

Thus you may do Carp, Tench, Trout, and several Sorts of Fish.

Another Way to Pot a Salmon.

SCALE, and clean your Salmon down the Back, and dry it well, and cut it as near the Shape of your Pot as you can, take two Nutmegs, an Ounce of Mace and Cloves beaten, half an Ounce of white Pepper, an Ounce of Salt, take out all the Bones, and cut off the Jole below the Fins, cut off the Tail, season the scaly Side first, and lay that at the Bottom of the Pot, then rub the Seasoning on the other Side, cover it with a Dish, and let it stand all Night. It must be put double, and the scaly Side

Side, Top and Bottom; put Butter Bottom and Top, and cover the Pot with some stiff coarse Paste: Three Hours will bake it, if a large Fish; if a small one, two Hours; and when it comes out of the Oven, let it stand half an Hour; then uncover it, and raise it up at one End, that the Gravy may run out; then put a Trencher and a Weight on it, to press out the Gravy. When the Butter is cold, take it out clear from the Gravy; add some more to it, put it in a Pan before the Fire; when it is melted, pour it over the Salmon; when it is bold, paper it up. As to the seasoning of these things, it must be according to your Palate, more or less.

CHAP. X.

Directions for the SICK.

I don't pretend to meddle here in the *Physical Way*, but a few Directions for the Cook or *Nurse*, I presume will not be improper to make such Diet, *&c.* as the DOCTOR shall order.

To make Mutton Broth.

TAKE a Pound of a Loin of Mutton, take off the Fat, put to it one Quart of Water, let it boil and skim it well, then put in a good Piece of Upper-crust of Bread, and one large Blade of Mace. Cover it close, and let it boil slowly an Hour; don't stir it, but pour the Broth clear off; season it with a little Salt, and the Mutton will be fit to eat. If you boil Turnips, don't boil them in the Broth, but by themselves in another Sauce-pan.

To boil a Scragg of Veal.

SET on the Scragg in a clean Sauce-pan; to each Pound of Veal, put a Quart of Water, skim it very clean, then put in a good Piece of Upper-crust, a Blade of Mace to each Pound, a little Parsley tied with a Thread, cover it close, and let it boil very softly two Hours, and both Broth and Meat will be fit to eat.

Beef or Mutton Broth *for very weak People, who take but little Nourishment.*

TAKE a Pound of Beef, or Mutton, or both together; to a Pound put two Quarts of Water; first skin the Meat, and take off all the Fat, and cut it into little Pieces, boil it till it comes to a quarter of a Pint; season it with a very little Corn of Salt, skim off all the Fat, and give a Spoonful of this Broth at a time; to very weak People half a Spoonful is enough; to some a Tea Spoonful at a time; others a Tea-cup full. There is greater Nourishment from this than any thing else.

To make Beef Drink, *which is ordered for weak People.*

TAKE a Pound of lean Beaf, take off all the Fat and Skin, cut it into Pieces, put it into a Gallon of Water, with the Under-crust of a Penny-loaf, and a very little Salt, let it boil till it comes to two Quarts; then strain it off, and it is a very hearty Drink.

Pork Broth.

TAKE two Pounds of young Pork, take off the Skin and Fat, boil it in a Gallon of Water with a Turnip, and a very little Corn of Salt; let it boil till it comes to two Quarts, then strain it off, and let it stand till cold. Take off the Fat, and leave the Settling at the Bottom of the Pan; and drink half a Pint in the Morning fasting, an Hour before Breakfast; and at Noon, if the Stomach will bear it.

To boil a Chicken.

LET your Sauce-pan be very clean and nice, and when the Water boils, put in your Chicken, which must be very nicely picked and clean, and laid in cold Water a quarter of an Hour before it is boiled; then take it up out of the Water boiling, and lay it in a Pewter-dish. Save all the Liquor that runs from it in the Dish, cut up your Chicken all in Joints in the Dish; then bruise the Liver very fine, add a little boiled Parsley chopped very fine, and a very little Salt, and a very little grated Nutmeg; mix it all well together, with two Spoonfuls of the Liquor of the Fowl, then pour it into the Dish with the rest of the Liquor in the Dish. If there is not Liquor enough, take two or three Spoonfuls of the Liquor it was boiled in; then clap another Dish over it, and set it over a Chafindish of hot Coals five or six Minutes, and carry it to Table hot, with the Cover on. This is better than Butter, and lighter for the Stomach; though some chuse it only with the Liquor, and no Parsley, nor Liver, or any thing else; but that is according to different Palates. If it is for a very weak Person, take

off

off the Skin of the Chicken before you set it on the Chafindish. If you roast it, make nothing but Bread-sauce, and that is lighter than any Sauce you can make for a weak Stomach.

Thus you may dress a Rabbit, only bruise but a little Piece of the Liver.

To boil Pigeons.

LET you Pigeons be cleaned, washed, drawn, and skined, boil them in Milk and Water ten Minutes, and pour over them Sauce made thus: Take the Livers parboiled, and bruise them fine, with as much Parsley boiled and chopped fine; melt some Butter, and mix a little with the Liver and Parsley first, then mix altogether, and pour over the Pigeons.

To boil a Partridge, or any other Wild Fowl.

WHEN your Water boils, put in your Partridge, let it boil ten Minutes, then take it up into a Pewter-plate, and cut it in two, laying the Insides next the Plate, and have ready some Bread-Sauce made thus: Take the Crumb of a Halfpenny Role, or thereabouts, and boil it in half a Pint of Water, with a Blade of Mace; let it boil two or three Minutes, then pour away most of the Water, and beat it up with a little Piece of nice Butter, a little Salt, and pour it over the Partridge. Clap a Cover over it, and set it over a Chafindish of Coals four or five Minutes, and send it away hot covered close.

Thus you may dress any Sort of Wild Fowl, only boiling it more or less according to the Bigness. Ducks, take off the Skins before you pour the Bread-Sauce over them; and if you roast them, lay Bread-Sauce under them. It is lighter than Gravy for weak Stomachs.

To boil a Plaise or Flounder.

LET your Water boil, throw some Salt in, then put in your Fish, boil it till you think it is enough, then take it out of the Water in a Slice to drain, take two Spoonfuls of the Liquor, with a little Salt, and a little grated Nutmeg, and beat up a Yolk of an Egg very well; with the Liquor, and stir in the Egg, beat it well together, with a Knife carefully slice away all the little Bones round the Fish, then pour the Sauce over it, and set it over a Chafindish of Coals for a Minute, then send it hot away. Or in the room of this Sauce, add melted Butter in a Cup.

To mince Veal or Chicken, for the Sick, or Weak People.

MINCE a Chicken or Veal very fine, taking off the Skin; just boil as much Water as will moisten it, and no more, with a very little Salt, grate a very little Nutmeg, throw a little Flour over it, and when the Water boils put in the Meat: Keep shaking it about over the Fire a Minute; then have ready two or three very thin Sippets, toasted nice and brown, laid in the Plate, and pour the Mincemeat over it.

To pull a Chicken for the Sick.

TAKE as much cold Chicken as you think proper, take off the Skin, pull the Meat into little Bits as thick as a Quill; then take the Bones, boil them with a little Salt till they are good, strain it, and take a Spoonful of the Liquor, a Spoonful of Milk, a little Bit of Butter, as big as a large Nutmeg rolled in Flour, a little chopped Parsley, as much as will lye on a Sixpence, a little Salt if wanted: This will be enough for half a small Chicken; put all together into the Sauce-pan, and keep shaking it, till it is thick, then pour it into a hot Plate.

Chicken Broth.

TAKE an old Cock, or large Fowl, flea it, and pick off all the Fat, and break it all to Pieces with a Rolling-pin, put it into two Quarts of Water, with a good Crust of Bread, and a Blade of Mace. Let it boil softly, till it is as good as you would have it. If you do it as it should be done it will take five or six Hours doing, then pour it off, and put a Quart more of boiling Water, and cover it close. Let it boil softly till it is good, then strain it off, season with a very little Salt. When you boil a Chicken, save the Liquor, and when the Meat is eat, take the Bones, break them and put to the Liquor you boiled the Chicken, with a Blade of Mace, and a Crust of Bread; let it boil till it is good, then strain it off.

Chicken Water.

TAKE a Cock, or large Fowl, fle it, and bruise it with a Hammer, put it into a Gallon of Water, with a Crust of Bread. Let it boil half away, then strain it off.

To make White Caudle.

TAKE two Quarts of Water, mix in four Spoonfuls of Oatmeal, a Blade or two of Mace, a Piece of Lemon-peel, let it boil, keep stirring of it often. Let it boil about a quarter of an Hour; but take care it does not boil over; then strain it through a coarse Sieve; when you use it, sweeten it to your Palate, grate in a little Nutmeg; and what Wine is proper; and if it is not for a sick Person, squeeze in the Juice of a Lemon.

To make Brown Caudle.

BOIL the Gruel as above, with six Spoonfuls of Oatmeal, and strain it; then add a Quart of good Ale not bitter, boil it, and sweeten it to your Palate, and add half a Pint of White Wine. When you don't put White Wine, let it be half Ale.

To make Water Gruel.

TAKE a Pint of Water, and a large Spoonful of Oatmeal, stir it together, let it boil up three or four times, stirring it often. Don't let it boil over, then strain it through a Sieve, salt it to your Palate, put in a good Piece of fresh Butter, brue. it with a Spoon till the Butter is all melted, and it will be fine and smooth, and very good. Some love a little Pepper in it.

To make Panado.

TAKE a Quart of Water, in a nice clean Sauce-pan, a Blade of Mace, a large Piece of Crumb of Bread, let it boil two Minutes, then take out the Bread, and bruise it in a Bason very fine, mix as much Water as will make it as thick as you would have it, the rest pour away, and sweeten to your Palate. Put in a Piece of Butter as big as a Wallnut; don't put in any Wine, it spoils it; you may grate in a little Nutmeg. This is hearty and good Diet for sick People.

To boil Sego.

PUT a large Spoonful of Sego into three quarters of a Pint of Water, stir it, and boil it softly, till it is as thick as you would have it, then put in Wine and Sugar, with a little Nutmeg to your Palate.

To boil Salup.

IT is a hard Stone ground to Powder, and generally sold for one Shilling an Ounce, take a large Tea Spoonful of the Powder, and put it into a Pint of boiling Water, keep stirring it till it is like a fine Jelly; then put Wine and Sugar to your Palate, and Lemon if it will agree.

To make Isinglass Jelly.

TAKE a Quart of Water, one Ounce of Isinglass, half an Ounce of Cloves, boil them to a Pint, then strain it upon a Pound of Loaf-sugar, and when cold sweeten your Tea with it. You make the Jelly as above, and leave out the Cloves, and sweeten to your Palate, and add a little Wine. All other Jellies you have in another Chapter.

To make the Pectoral Drink.

TAKE a Gallon of Water, and half a Pound of Pearl-Barley, boil it with a quarter of a Pound of Figs split, and a Pennyworth of Liquorish sliced to Pieces, a quarter of a Pound of Raisins of the Sun stoned; boil all together till half is wasted, then strain it off. This is ordered in the Measels, and several other Disorders, for a Drink.

Buttered Water, or what the Germans call Egg-Soop, and are very fond of it for Supper, you have it in the Chapter for Lent.

TAKE a Pint of Water, beat up the Yolk of an Egg with the Water, and put in a little Piece of Butter as big as a small Wallnut, two or three Nobs of Sugar, keep stirring it all, the time it is on the Fire. When it begins to boil, bruise it between the Sauce-pan and a Mug, till it is smooth, and has a great Froth, then it is fit to drink. This is ordered in a Cold, or where Egg will agree with the Stomach.

Seed Water.

TAKE a Spoonful of Coriander-Seed, half a Spoonful of Caraway-Seed bruised, and boiled in a Pint of Water, then strain it, and bruise it up with the Yolk of an Egg, and so mix it with Sack and double refined Sugar, according to your Palate.

Bread Soop for the Sick.

TAKE a Quart of Water, set it on the Fire in a clean Sauce-pan, and as much dry Crust of Bread cut to Pieces, as the Top of a Penny-loaf, the drier the better, a little Piece of Butter, as

big

big as a Wallnut; let it boil, then beat it with a Spoon, and keep boiling it, till the Bread and Water is well mixed, then season it with a very little Salt, and it is a pretty thing for a weak Stomach.

Artificial Asses Milk.

TAKE two Ounces of Pearl-Barley, two large Spoonfuls of Hartshorn Shavings, one Ounce of Eringo Root, one Ounce of China Root, one Ounce of Preserved Ginger, eighteen Snails bruised with the Shells, to be boiled in three Quarts of Water, till it comes to three Pints, then boil a Pint of new Milk, and mixt it with the rest, and put in two Ounces of Balsam of Tolu. Take half a Pint in the Morning, and half a Pint at Night.

Cows Milk next to Asses Milk done thus.

TAKE a Quart of Milk, set it in a Pan over Night, the next Morning take off all the Cream, then boil it, and set it in the Pan again till Night; then skim it again, and boil it, set it in the Pan again, and the next Morning skim it, and warm it Blood-warm, and drink it as you do Asses Milk. It is very near as good, and with some consumptive People it is better.

A Good Drink.

BOIL a Quart of Milk, and a Quart of Water, with the Top-crust of a Penny-loaf, and one Blade of Mace, a quarter of an Hour very softly, then pour it off, and when you drink it, let it be warm.

Barley Water.

PUT a quarter of a Pound of Pearl-Barley into two Quarts of Water, let it boil, and skim it very clean, boil half away, and strain it off. Sweeten to your Palate, but not too sweet, and put in two Spoonfuls of White Wine; drink it luke-warm.

Sage Drink.

TAKE a little Sage, a little Balm, put it into a Pan, slice a Lemon, Peel and all, a few Nobs of Sugar, one Glass of White Wine, and pour on these two or three Quarts of boiling Water, cover it, and drink when dry. When you think it strong enough of the Herbs, take them out, otherwise it will make it bitter.

For a Child.

A Little Sage, Balm, Rue, Mint, and Pennyroyal, pour boiling Water on, and sweeten to your Palate. Syrup of Cloves, &c. and Black Cherry-water, you have in the Chapter of Preserves.

Liquor for a Child that has the Thrush.

TAKE half a Pint of Spring-water, a Nob of double refined Sugar, and a very little Bit of Allum, beat it well together with the Yolk of an Egg, then beat in a large Spoonful of the Juice of Sage, tye a Rag to the End of a Stick, dip it in this Liquor, and often clean the Mouth. Give the Child over Night one Drop of Laudanum, and the next Day proper Physick, washing the Mouth often with this Liquor.

To boil Camphire Roots.

TAKE a Pound of Camphire Roots, scrape them clean, and cut them into little Pieces, and put them into three Pints of Water. Let them boil till there is about a Pint, then strain it, and when it is cold, put it into a Sauce-pan. If there is any Settling at the Bottom, throw it away, and mix it with Sugar to your Palate, and half a Pint of Mountain Wine, and the Juice of a Lemon. Let it boil, then pour it into a clean earthen Pot, and set it by for Use. Some boil it in Milk, and is very good, where it will agree, and is reckoned a very great Strengthner.

CHAP. XI.

For Captains of Ships.

To make Ketchup to keep twenty Years.

TAKE a Gallon of strong Stale Beer, one Pound of Anchovies washed from the Pickle, a Pound of Shallots peeled, half an Ounce of Mace, half an Ounce of Cloves, a quarter of an Ounce of whole Pepper, three or four large Races of Ginger, two Quarts of the large Mushroom Flaps rubbed to

Pieces,

Pieces. Cover all this close, and let it simmer till it is half wasted, then strain it through a Flannel Bag, let it stand till it is quite cold, then bottle it. You may carry it to the *Indies*; a Spoonful of this to a Pound of fresh Butter melted, makes fine Fish Sauce. Or in the room of Gravy-Sauce, the stronger and staler the Beer is, the Better the Ketchup will be.

Fish Sauce to keep the whole Year.

YOU must take twenty-four Anchovies, chop them, Bones and all, put to them ten Shallots cut small, a Handful of scraped Horse-reddish, a quarter of an Ounce of Mace, a Quart of White Wine, a Pint of Water, one Lemon cut into Slices, half a Pint of Anchovy-liquor, a Pint of Red Wine, twelve Cloves, twelve Pepper Corns; boil them together till it comes to a Quart; strain it off, cover it close, and keep it in a cool dry Place. Two Spoonfuls will be sufficient for a Pound of Butter.

It is a pretty Sauce either for boiled Fowl, Veal, &c. or in the room of Gravy, lowering it with hot Water, and thicken it with a Piece of Butter rolled in Flour.

To pot Dripping to fry Fish, Meat, or Fritters, &c.

TAKE six Pounds of good Beef-dripping, boil it in soft Water, strain it into a Pan, let it stand till cold; then take off the hard Fat, and scrape off the Gravy, which sticks to the Inside. Thus do eight times; when it is cold and hard, take it off clean from the Water, put it into a large Saucepan, with six Bay-leaves, twelve Cloves, half a Pound of Salt, and a quarter of a Pound of whole Pepper. Let the Fat be all melted and just hot; let it stand till it is hot enough to strain through a Sieve into the Pot, and stand till it is quite cold, then cover it up. Thus you may do what Quantity you please. The best Way to keep any Sort of Dripping is to turn the Pot upside-down, and then no Rats can get at it. If it will keep on Ship-board, it will make as fine Puff-paste Crust, as any Butter can do, or Crust for Puddings, &c.

To pickle Mushrooms for the Sea.

WASH them clean with a Piece of Flannel in Salt and Water, put them into a Sauce-pan, and throw a little Salt over them. Let them boil up three times in their own Liquor, then throw them into a Sieve to drain, and spread them on a clean Cloth; let them lye till cold; then put them in wide Mouth'd Bottles, put in with them a good deal of whole Mace, a little Nutmeg sliced, and a few Cloves. Boil the Sugar-Vinegar of your own making, with a good deal of whole Pepper, some Races of Ginger, and two or three Bay-leaves; let it boil a few Minutes, then strain it, and when it is cold pour it on, and fill the Bottle with Mutton Fat fry'd; cork them, and tye a Bladder, and then a Leather over them, and keep it down close, and in as cool a Place as possible. As to all other Pickles, you have them in the Chapter of Pickles.

To make Mushroom Powder.

TAKE half a Peck of fine large thick Mushrooms fresh, wash them clean from Grit and Dirt with a Flannel Rag, scrape out the Inside, and cut out all the Worms, put them into a Kettle over the Fire without any Water, two large Onions stuck with Cloves, a large Handful of Salt, a quarter of an Ounce of Mace, two Tea Spoonfuls of beaten Pepper, let them simmer till all the Liquor is boiled away, take great Care they don't burn; then lay them on Sieves to dry in the Sun, or on Tin-plates, and set them in a slack Oven all Night to dry, till they are well beat to Powder. Press the Powder down hard in a Pot, and keep it for use. You may put what Quantity you please for Sauce.

To keep Mushrooms without Pickle.

TAKE large Mushrooms, peel them, and scrape out the Inside, put them into a Sauce Pan, throw a little Salt over them; let them boil in their own Liquor; then throw them into a Sieve to drain, then lay them on Tin-plates, and set them in a cool Oven. Repeat it often, till they are perfectly dry, put them into a clean Stone-Jar, and tye them down tight, and keep them in a dry Place. They eat deliciously, and look as well as Truffles.

To keep Artichoke Bottoms dry.

BOIL them just so as you can pull off the Leaves and the Choke, cut them from the Stalk, lay them on Tin-plates, and set them in a very cool Oven, and repeat it till they are quite dry; then put them into a Stone-pot, and tye them down. Keep them in a dry Place; and when you use them, lay them in warm Water till they are tender. Shift the Water two or three times. They are fine in almost all Sauces cut to little Pieces, and put in just before your Sauce is enough.

The Art of Cookery, made Plain and Easy. 123

To fry Artichoke Bottoms.

LAY them in Water as above; then have ready some Butter hot in the Pan, flour the Bottoms, and fry them. Lay them in your Dish, and pour melted Butter over them.

To Ragoo Artichoke Bottoms.

TAKE twelve Bottoms, soften them in warm Water, as in the foregoing Receipts, take half a Pint of Water, a Piece of the strong Soop as big as a small Wallnut, half a Spoonful of the Ketchup, five or six of the dried Mushrooms, a Tea Spoonful of the Mushroom-powder, set it on the Fire, shake all together, and let it boil softly two or three Minutes. Let the last Water you put to the Bottoms boil; take them out hot, and lay them in your Dish, pour the Sauce over them, and set them to Table hot.

To fricasee Artichoke Bottoms.

SCALD them, then lay them in boiling Water, till they are quite tender; take half a Pint of Milk, a quarter of a Pound of Butter rolled in Flour, stir it all one way, till it is thick, then stir in a Spoonful of Mushroom-pickle, lay the Bottoms in a Dish, and pour the Sauce over them.

To dress Fish.

AS to frying Fish, first wash it very clean, and then dry it well, and flour it; take some of the Beef-Dripping, make it boil in the Stew-pan, then throw in your Fish, and fry it of a fine light brown. Lay it on the Bottom of a Sieve, or coarse Cloth to drain, and make Sauce according to your fancy.

To bake Fish.

BUTTER the Pan, lay in the Fish, throw a little Salt over it, and Flour, put a very little Water in the Dish, an Onion, and a Bundle of Sweet Herbs; stick some little Bits of Butter, or the fine Dripping, on the Fish. Let it be baked of a fine light-brown; when enough, lay it on a Dish before the Fire, and skim off all the Fat in the Pan; strain the Liquor, and mix it up either with the Fish-Sauce, or Strong Soop, or the Ketchup.

To make a Gravy Soop.

ONLY boil soft Water, and put as much of the strong Soop to it, as will make it to your Palate. Let it boil; and if it wants Salt, you must season it. The Receipt for the Soop, you have in the Chapter for *Soops*.

To make Peas Soop.

TAKE a Quart of Peas, boil them in two Gallons of Water till they are tender, then have ready a Piece of salt Pork, or Beef, which has been laid in Water the Night before; put it into the Pot, with two large Onions peeled, and a Bundle of Sweet Herbs, Salary if you have it, half a quarter of an Ounce of whole Pepper, let it boil till the Meat is enough, then take it up; and if the Soop is not enough, let it boil till the Soop is good; then strain it, and set it on again to boil, and rub in a good deal of dry Mint. Keep the Meat hot, and when the Soop is ready, put in the Meat again for a few Minutes, and let it boil; then serve it away. If you add a Piece of the portable Soop, it will be very good. The Onion Soop you have in the *Lent* Chapter.

To make a Pelow.

TAKE two large Fowls well singed and clean, a Piece of Bacon about two Pounds, skined and pared clean, put them into a Pot with a Pound of Rice, and two Gallons of Water. When the Water boils, let it boil three quarters of an Hour, then take up the Fowls and Bacon, keep them hot, and drain all the Water from the Rice. Set it over a very slow Fire till the Rice is dry, then lay the Rice in your Dish, and the Fowls and Bacon on the Top. When you can have hard Eggs to garnish the Dish, it is proper.

Or boil it this way; set on a large Pot, nice and clean, take a Quart of Rice, tye it loose in a very clean Cloth, put it in the Water cold with the Bacon. Let it boil an Hour, then take up the Rice, untye it, and stir in one Spoonful of the strong Gravy, grate half a Nutmeg, stir it well together, tye it up tight again, put it into the Pot, and the Fowls. When they are enough, take up the Rice, lay it in your Dish, and the Fowls and Bacon on the Top.

To make Pork Pudding, or Beef, &c.

MAKE a good Crust with the Dripping, or Mutton-suet if you have it, shread fine, make a thick Crust, take a Piece of Salt Pork or Beef, which has been four and twenty Hours in soft Water; season it with a little Pepper, and put it into this Crust, and roll it up close, tye it in a Cloth, and boil it; if about four or five Pounds, boil it five Hours.

And

And when you kill Mutton, make a Pudding the same way, only cut the Stakes thin, and season them with Pepper and Salt, and boil it three Hours if large; or two Hours if small, and so according to the Size.

Apple Pudding make with the same Crust, only pare the Apples, and core them, and fill your Pudding; if large 'twill take five Hours boiling. When it is enough, lay it in the Dish, cut a Hole in the Top, and stir in Butter and Sugar; lay the Piece on again, and send it to Table.

A Pruen Pudding eats fine made the same way, only when the Crust is ready, fill it with Prunes, and sweeten it according to your fancy; close it up, and boil it two Hours.

To make a Rice Pudding.

TAKE what Rice you think proper, tye it loose in a Cloth, and boil it an Hour; then take it up, and untye it, grate a good deal of Nutmeg in, stir in a good Piece of Butter, and sweeten to your Palate. Tye it up close, and boil it an Hour more, then take it up, and turn it into your Dish; melt Btter with a little Sugar, and a little White Wine for Sauce.

A Suet Pudding.

TAKE a Pound of Suet shread fine, a Pound of Flour, a Pound of Currans picked clean, and half a Pound of Raisins stoned, two Tea Spoonfuls of beaten Ginger, and a Spoonful of Tincture of Saffron; mix all together with salt Water very thick; then either boil or bake it.

A Liver Pudding boiled.

TAKE the Liver of a Sheep when you kill one, and cut it as thin as you can, and chop it; mix it with as much Suet shread fine, and half as many Crumbs of Bread or Bisket grated, season it with some Sweet Herbs shread fine, and a little Nutmeg grated, a little beaten Pepper, and an Anchovy shread fine; mix all together with a little Salt, or the Anchovy Liquor, with a Piece of Butter; fill the Crust, and close it; boil it three Hours.

An Oatmeal Pudding.

TAKE a Pint of Oatmeal once cut, a Pound of Suet shread fine, a Pound of Currans, and half a Pound of Raisins stoned; mix all together well, with a little Salt, tye it in a Cloth, leaving room for the Swelling.

An Oatmeal Pudding to bake.

BOIL a Quart of Water, season it with a little Salt; when the Water boils, stir in the Oatmeal, till it is as thick you can't easily stir your Spoon, then take it off the Fire, and stir in two Spoonfuls of Brandy, or a Gill of Mountain, and sweeten it to your Palate. Grate in a little Nutmeg, and stir in half a Pound of Currans clean washed and picked; then butter a Pan, and pour it in, and bake it half an Hour.

A Rice Pudding baked.

BOIL a Pound of Rice just till it is tender, then drain all the Water from it as dry as you can, but don't squeeze it; then stir in a good Piece of Butter, and sweeten to your Palate. Grate a small Nutmeg in, stir it well together, butter a Pan, and pour it in and bake it. You may add a few Currans for Change.

A Peas Pudding.

BOIL it till it is quite tender, then take it up, untye it, and stir in a good Piece of Butter, a little Salt, and a good deal of beaten Pepper; then tye it up tight again, and boil it an Hour longer, and it will eat fine. All other Puddings you have in the Chapter of *Puddings*.

A Fowl Pye.

FIRST make a rich thick Crust, cover the Dish with the Paste, then take some very fine Bacon, or cold boiled Ham, slice it, and lay a Layer all over. Season with a little Pepper, then put in the Fowl, after it is picked and cleaned, and singed; shake a very little Pepper and Salt into the Belly, put in a little Water, and cover it with Ham, seasoned with a little beaten Pepper, put on the Lid and bake it two Hours. When it comes out of the Oven, take half a Pint of Water, and boil it, and add to it as much of the strong Soop as will make the Gravy quite rich; pour it boiling hot into the Pan, and lay on the Lid again. Send it to Table hot, or lay a Piece of Beef, or Pork in soft Water twenty-four Hours, slice it in the room of the Ham, and it will eat fine.

A Cheshire Pork Pye for Sea.

TAKE some salt Pork that has been boiled, cut it into thin Slices, an equal Quantity of Potatoes, pared and sliced thin, make a good Crust, cover the Dish, lay a Layer of Meat, seasoned with a little Pepper, and a Layer of Potatoes; then a Layer of Meat, and a Layer of Potatoes, and so on till your Pye is full. Season it with Pepper; when it is full, lay some Butter on the Top, and fill your Dish above half full of soft Water. Close your Pye up, and bake it in a gentle Oven.

To make Sea Venison.

WHEN you kill a Sheep, keep stirring the Blood all the time till it is cold, or at least as cold as it will be, that it may not congeal; then cut up the Sheep, take one Side, cut the Leg like a Hanch, cut off the Shoulder and Loin, the Neck and Breast in two, steep them all in the Blood, as long as the Weather will permit you, then take out the Hanch, and hang it out of the Sun as long as you can to be sweet, and roast it as you do a Hanch of Venison. It will eat very fine, especially if the Heat will give you leave to keep it long. Take off all the Suet before you lay it in the Blood, take the other Joints and lay them in a large Pan, pour over them a Quart of Red Wine, and a Quart of rap Vinegar. Lay the fat Side of the Meat downwards in the Pan on a hollow Tray is best, and pour the Wine and Vinegar over it; let it lay twelve Hours, then take out the Neck, Breast, and Loin of the Pickle, let the Shoulder lay a Week, if the Heat will let you, and rub it with Bay Salt, Salt Petre, and coarse Sugar, of each a quarter of an Ounce, one Handful of common Salt, and let it lay a Week or ten Days. Bone the Neck, Breast, and Loin, season them with Pepper and Salt to your Palate, and make a Pasty as you do Venison. Boil the Bones for Gravy to fill the Pye, when it comes out of the Oven; and the Shoulder boil fresh out of the Pickle, with a Peas Pudding.

And when you cut up the Sheep, take the Heart, Liver and Lights, boil them a quarter of an Hour, then cut them small, and chop them very fine; season them with four large Blades of Mace, twelve Cloves, and a large Nutmeg, all beat to Powder. Chop a Pound of Suet fine, half a Pound of Sugar, two Pound of Currans clean washed, half a Pint of Red Wine, mix all well together, and make a Pye. Bake it an Hour, it is very rich.

To make Dumplings when you have White Bread.

TAKE the Crumb of a Twopenny-loaf grated fine, as much Beef-Suet shread as fine as possible, a little Salt, half a small Nutmeg grated, a large Spoonful of Sugar, beat two Eggs with two Spoonfuls of Sack, mix all well together, and roll them up as big as a Turkey's Egg. Let the Water boil, and throw them in, half an Hour will boil them. For Sauce, melt Butter with a little Sack, lay the Dumplings in a Dish, and pour the Sauce over them, and strew Sugar all over the Dish.

These are very pretty either at Land or Sea. You must observe to rub your Hands with Flour when you make them up.

The Portable Soop to carry abroad, you have in the Sixth Chapter.

CHAP. XII.

Of Hog's Puddings, Sausages, &c.

To make Almond Hog's Puddings.

TAKE two Pounds of Beef-suet, or Marrow, shread very small, and a Pound and half of Almonds blanched, and beaten very fine with Rose-water, one Pound of grated Bread, a Pound and quarter of fine Sugar, a little Salt, half an Ounce of Mace, Nutmeg and Cinnamon together, twelve Yolks of Eggs, four Whites, a Pint of Sack, a Pint and half of thick Cream, some Rose or Orange-flower Water, boil the Cream, and tye the Saffron in a Bag, and dip in the Cream to colour it. First beat your Eggs very well, then stir in your Almonds, then the Spice, the Salt and Suet, and mix all your Ingredients together; fill your Guts but half full, put some Bits of Citron in the Guts as you fill them, tye them up, and boil them a quarter of an Hour.

Another Way.

TAKE a Pound of Beef Marrow chopped fine, half a Pound of sweet Almonds blanched, and beat fine, with a little Orange-flower or Rose-water, half a Pound of white Bread grated fine, half a Pound of Currans clean washed and picked, a quarter of a Pound of fine Sugar, a quarter of an Ounce of Mace, Nutmeg, and Cinnamon together, of each an equal Quantity, and half a Pint of Sack; mix all well together, with half a Pint of good Cream, and the Yolks of four Eggs. Fill your Guts half full,

126   *The Art of Cookery made Plain and Easy.*

full, tye them up, and boil them a quarter of an Hour. You may leave out the Currans for Change; but then you must add a quarter of a Pound more of Sugar.

A Third Way.

HALF a Pint of Cream, a quarter of a Pound of Sugar, a quarter of a Pound of Currans, and the Crumb of a Halfpenny Role grated fine, six large Pippins pared and chopped fine, a Gill of Sack, or two Spoonfuls of Rose-water; six bitter Almonds blanched and beat fine, the Yolks of two Eggs, and one White beat fine; mix all together, and fill the Guts better than half full, and boil them a quarter of an Hour.

To make Hog's Puddings with Currans.

TAKE three Pounds of grated Bread to four Pounds of Beef-suet finely shread, two Pounds of Currans, clean picked and washed; Cloves, Mace, and Cinnamon, of each half an Ounce, finely beaten, a little Salt, a Pound and half of Sugar, a Pint of Sack, a Quart of Cream, a little Rose-water, twenty Eggs well beaten, but half the Whites; mix all these well together, and fill the Guts half full, boil them a little, and prick them as they boil, to keep them from breaking the Guts. Take them up upon clean Cloths, then lay them on your Dish; or when you use them, boil them a few Minutes, or eat them cold.

To make Black Puddings.

FIRST before you kill your Hog, get a Peck of Grits, and boil them half an Hour in Water, then drain them, and put them into a clean Tub or large Pan, then kill your Hog, and save two Quarts of the Blood of the Hog, and keep stirring it till the Blood is quite cold; then mix it with your Grits, and stir them well together. Season with a large Spoonful of Salt, a quarter of an Ounce of Cloves, Mace and Nutmeg together, an equal Quantity of each; dry it, and beat it well, and mix in. Take a little Winter-savoury, Sweet Marjoram, and Thyme, and Pennyroyal striped of the Stalks, and chopped very fine, just enough to season them, and to give them a Flavour, but no more. The next Day, take the Leaf off the Hog, and cut into Dice, scrape and wash the Guts very clean, then tye one End, and begin to fill them; mix in the Fat as you fill them, and be sure to put in a good deal of Fat, fill the Skins three Parts full, tye the other End, and make your Puddings what Length you please; then prick them with a Pin, and put them into a Kettle of boiling Water. Boil them very softly an Hour, then take them out and lay them on clean Straw.

In *Scotland* they make a Pudding with the Blood of a Goose, chop off the Head, and save the Blood; stir it till it is cold, then mix it with Grits, and Spice, Salt, and Sweet Herbs according to their fancy, and some Beef-suet chopped. Take the Skin of the Neck, pull out the Wind-pipe and Fat, and fill the Skin. Tye it at both Ends; so make a Pye of the Giblets, and lay the Pudding in the Middle.

To make Fine Sausages.

TAKE six Pounds of good Pork, free from Skin and Grisles and Fat, cut it very small, and beat it in a Mortar till it is very fine; shread six Pounds of Beef-suet very fine, free from all Skin; shread it as fine as possible; take a good deal of Sage, wash it very clean, pick off the Leaves, and shread it very fine; spread your Meat on a clean Dresser or Table, and shake the Sage all over, about three large Spoonfuls; shread the thin Rind of a middling Lemon very fine, and throw over, with as many Sweet Herbs, when shread fine, as will fill a large Spoon; grate two large Nutmegs over, throw over two Tea Spoonfuls of Pepper, a large Spoonful of Salt, then throw over the Suet, and mix it all well together. Put it down close in a Pot, when you use them, roll them up with as much Egg as will make them roll smooth. Make them the Size of a Sausage, and fry them in Butter, or good Dripping. Be sure it be hot before you put them in, and keep rolling them about. When they are thorough hot, and of a fine light-brown, they are enough. You may chop this Meat very fine, if you don't like it beat: Veal eats well done thus, or Veal and Pork together. You may clean some Guts, and fill them.

To make Common Sausages.

TAKE three Pounds of nice Pork, Fat and Lean together, without Skin or Grisles; chop it as fine as possible, season it with a Tea Spoonful of beaten Pepper, and two of Salt, some Sage shread fine, about three Tea Spoonfuls; mix it well together, have the Guts very nicely cleaned, and fill them, or put them down in a Pot, so roll them of what Size you please, and fry them. Beef makes very good Sausages.

To make Belony Sausages.

TAKE a Pound of Bacon, Fat and Lean together, a Pound of Beef, a Pound of Veal, a Pound of Pork, and one Pound of Beef-suet, cut them small, and chop them fine; take a small Handful of Sage, pick off the Leaves, chop it fine, with a few Sweet Herbs; season pretty high with Pepper and Salt. You must have a large Gut, and fill it; then set on a Sauce-pan of Water, and when it boils, put it in, prick the Gut for fear of bursting. Boil it softly an Hour, then lay it on clean Straw to dry.

CHAP.

The Art of Cookery, made Plain and Easy.

CHAP. XIII.
To Pot and Make Hams, &c.

To pot Pigeons, or Fowls.

CUT off their Legs, draw them, and wipe them with a Cloth; but don't wash them. Season them pretty well with Pepper and Salt, and put them in a Pot, with as much Butter as you think will cover them, when melted, and baked very tender; then drain them very dry from the Gravy; lay them on a Cloth, and that will suck up all the Gravy. Season them again with Salt, Mace, Cloves, and Pepper beaten fine, and put them down close into a Pot. Take the Butter, when cold, clear from the Gravy, set it before the Fire to melt, and pour over the Birds; if you have not enough, clarify some more, and let the Butter be near an Inch thick above the Birds. Thus you may do all Sorts of Fowl.— Only Wild Fowl should be boned.

To pot a Cold Tongue, Beef, or Venison.

CUT it small, and beat it well in a Marble Mortar, with melted Butter, and two Anchovies, till the Meat is mellow and fine; then put it down close in your Pots, and cover it with clarified Butter. Thus you may do cold Wild Fowl; or you may pot any Sort of cold Fowl whole, seasoning them with what Spice you please.

To pot Venison.

TAKE a Piece of Venison, Fat and Lean together, lay it in a Dish, and stick Pieces of Butter all over; tye a brown Paper over it, and bake it. When it comes out of the Oven, take it out of the Liquor hot, drain it, and lay it in a Dish. When cold, take off all the Skin, and beat it in a Marble Mortar, Fat and Lean together. Season it with Mace, Cloves, Nutmeg, black Pepper, and Salt to your Mind. When the Butter is cold, that it was baked in, take a little of it, and beat in with it to moisten it; then put it down close, and cover it with clarified Butter.

You must be sure to beat it, till it is all like a Paste.

To pot Tongues.

TAKE a Neat's Tongue, rub it with a Pound of white Salt, an Ounce of Salt-petre, half a Pound of coarse Sugar, rub it well, turn it every Day in this Pickle for a Fortnight. This Pickle will do several Tongues, only adding a little more white Salt; or we generally do them after our Hams. Take the Tongue out of the Pickle, cut off the Root, and boil it well, till it will peel; then take your Tongues and season them with Salt, Pepper, Cloves, Mace and Nutmeg, all beat fine, rub it well with your Hands whilst it is hot, then put it into a Pot, and melt as much Butter as will cover it all over. Bake it an Hour in the Oven, then take it out, let it stand to cool, rub a little fresh Spice on it; and when it is quite cold, lay it in your Pickling-pot. When your Butter is cold you baked it in, take it off clean from the Gravy, set it in an earthen Pan before the Fire, and when it is melted, pour it over the Tongue. You may lay Pigeons or Chickens on each Side; be sure to let the Butter be about an Inch above the Tongue.

A fine Way to pot a Tongue.

TAKE a dried Tongue, boil it till it is tender, then peel it; take a large Fowl, bone it, and a Goose, bone it; take a quarter of an Ounce of Mace, a quarter of an Ounce of Cloves, a large Nutmeg, a quarter of an Ounce of black Pepper, beat all well together, a Spoonful of Salt, and rub the Inside of the Fowl well, and the Tongue. Put the Tongue into the Fowl, then season the Goose, and fill the Goose with the Fowl and Tongue; and the Goose will look as if it was whole. Lay it in a Pan that will just hold it, melt fresh Butter enough to cover it, send it to the Oven, and bake it an Hour and half; then uncover the Pot, and take out the Meat. Carefully drain it from the Butter, lay it on a coarse Cloth till it is cold; and when the Butter is cold, take off the hard Fat from the Gravy, and lay it before the Fire to melt, put your Meat into the Pot again, and pour the Butter over. If there is not enough, clarify more, and let the Butter be an Inch above the Meat; and this will keep a great while, eats fine, and looks beautiful. When you cut it, it must be cut cross-ways down through, and looks very pretty. It makes a pretty Corner-dish at Table, or Side-dish for Supper. If you cut a Slice down the Middle quite through, lay it in a Plate, and garnish with green Parsley and Stertion-flowers. If you will be at the Expence, bone a Turkey, and put over the Goose. Observe, when you pot it, to save a little of the Spice to throw over it, before the last Butter is put on, or the Meat will not be seasoned enough.

To

To pot Beef like Venison.

CUT the Lean of a Buttock of Beef in Pound Pieces; for eight Pounds of Beef, take four Ounces of Salt-petre, four Ounces of Peter-salt, a Pint of white Salt, and one Ounce of Salprunella, beat the Salts all very fine, mix them well together, rub the Salts all into the Beef, then let it lye four Days, turning it twice a Day; then put it into a Pan, and cover it with Pump-water, and a little of its own Brine; then bake it in an Oven with Houshold Bread, till it is as tender as a Chicken; then drain from the Gravy, and bruise it abroad, and take out all the Skin and Sinews; then pound it in a Marble Mortar, then lay it in a broad Dish, and mix in it an Ounce of Cloves and Mace, and three quarters of an Ounce of Pepper, and one Nutmeg all beat very fine. Mix it all very well with the Meat, then clarify a little fresh Butter, and mix with the Meat, to make it a little moist; mix it very well together, and press it down into Pots very hard, and set it at the Oven's Mouth, just to settle, and cover it two Inches thick with clarified Butter. When cold, cover it with white Paper.

To pot Cheshire-Cheese.

TAKE three Pounds of *Cheshire*-Cheese, and put it into a Mortar, with half a Pound of the best fresh Butter you can get, pound them together, and in the beating, add a Gill of rich Canary Wine, and half an Ounce of Mace finely beat, then sifted fine like a fine Powder. When all is extremely well mixed, press it hard down into a Gallipot, cover it with clarified Butter, and keep it cool. A Slice of this exceeds all the Cream-Cheese that can be made.

To collar a Breast of Veal, or a Pig.

BONE the Pig or Veal, then season it all over the Inside with Cloves, Mace, and Salt beat fine, and a Handful of Sweet Herbs stripped off the Stalks, a little Pennyroyal and Parsley shread very fine, with a little Sage; then roll it up as you do Brawn, bind it with narrow Tape very close, then tye a Cloth round it, and boil it very tender in Vinegar and Water, a like Quantity, with a little Cloves, Mace, and Pepper, and Salt all whole. Make it boil, then put in the Collars; when boiled tender, take them up; and when both are cold, take off the Cloth, lay the Collar in an earthen Pan, and pour the Liquor over. Cover it close, and keep it for Use: If the pickle begins to spoil, strain it through a coarse Cloth, boil it, and skim it; when cold, pour it over. Observe, before you strain the Pickle, to wash the Collar, and wipe it dry, and wipe the Pan clean. Strain it again after it is boiled, and cover it very close.

To collar Beef.

TAKE a thin Piece of Flank Beef, and strip the Skin to the End, and beat it with a Rolling-pin, then dissolve a Quart of Peter-salt in five Quarts of Pump-water, strain it, and put the Beef in, and let it lye five Days, sometimes turning it; then take a quarter of an Ounce of Cloves, a good Nutmeg, a little Mace, a little Pepper, beat very fine, and a Handful of Thyme stripped off the Stalks; mix it with the Spice, strew all over the Beef, lay on the Skin again, then roll it up very close, and tye it hard with Tape, then put it into a Pot, with a Pint of Claret, and bake it in the Oven with the Bread.

Another Way to season a Collar of Beef.

TAKE the Surloin or Flank of Beef, or any Part you think proper, and lay it in as much Pump-water as will cover it; put to it four Ounces of Salt-petre, five or six Handfuls of white Salt, let it lay in it three Days, and then take it out, and take half an Ounce of Cloves and Mace, one Nutmeg, a quarter of an Ounce of Coriander-seeds; beat these well together, and half an Ounce of Pepper, and strew them upon the Inside of the Beef, and roll it up, and bind it up with coarse Tape. Bake it in the same Pickle; and when it is baked, take it out, and hang it in a Net to drain, within the Air of the Fire three Days, and put it into a clean Cloth, and hang it up again, within the Air of the Fire; for it must be kept dry as you do Neat's Tongues.

To collar Salmon.

TAKE a Side of Salmon, and cut off about a Handful of the Tail, wash your large Piece very well, and dry it with a Cloth; then wash it over with the Yolks of Eggs; then make some Forcemeat with that you cut off the Tail, but take care of the Skin, and put to it a Handful of parboiled Oysters, a Tail or two of Lobster, the Yolks of three or four Eggs boiled hard, six Anchovies, a good Handful of Sweet Herbs chopped small, a little Salt, Cloves, Mace, Nutmeg, Pepper, all beat fine, and grated Bread; work all these together into a Body, with the Yolks of Eggs, and lay it all over the Fleshy Part, and a little more Pepper and Salt over the Salmon; so roll it up into a Collar, and bind it with broad Tape; then boil it in Water, Salt and Vinegar; but let the Liquor boil first; then put in your Collars, and a Bunch of Sweet Herbs, sliced Ginger, and Nutmeg. Let it boil, but not too fast; it will take near two Hours boiling; and when it is enough, take it up, put it in your Sousing-pan,

pan, and when the Pickle is cold, put it to your Salmon, and let it stand in it till used. Or you may pot it, after it is boiled, pour clarified Butter over it, it will keep longest so; but either way is good. If you pot it, be sure the Butter be the nicest you can get.

To make Dutch Beef.

TAKE the lean Part of a Buttock of Beef raw, rub it well with brown Sugar all over, and let it lye in a Pan or Tray two or three Hours, turning it two or three times; then salt it well with common Salt, and Salt-petre, and let it lye a Fortnight, turning it every Day; then roll it very strait in a coarse Cloth, and put it in a Cheese-press a Day and a Night, and hang it to dry in a Chimney. When you boil it, you must put it in a Cloth; when it is cold, it will cut in Slvers as *Dutch* Beef.

To make Sham Brawn.

BOIL two Pair of Neat's Feet tender, take a Piece of Pork of the thick Flank, and boil it almost enough, then pick off the Flesh of the Feet, and roll it up in the Pork tight, like a Collar of Brawn; then take a strong Cloth and some coarse Tape, roll it tight round with the Tape, and then tye it up in a Cloth, and boil it till a Straw will run through it; then take it up, and hang it up in a Cloth till it is quite cold; then put it into some Sousing-liquor, and use it at your own pleasure.

To souse a Turkey, in Imitation of Sturgeon.

TAKE a fine large Turkey, dress it very clean, dry and bone it, then tye it up, as you do Sturgeon; put into the Pot you boil it in, one Quart of White Wine, one Quart of Water, and one Quart of good Vinegar, and a very large Handful of Salt, let it boil, and scum it well, and then put in the Turkey. When it is enough, take it out, and tye it tighter. Let the Liquor boil a little longer; and if you think the Pickle wants more Vinegar or Salt, add it when it is cold, pour it upon the Turkey. It will keep some Months, covering it close from the Air, and keeping it in a dry cool Place. Eat it with Oil and Vinegar, and Sugar, just as you like it. Some admire it more than Sturgeon; it looks pretty covered with Fennel for a Side-dish.

To pickle Pork.

BONE your Pork, cut it into Pieces, of a Size fit to lye in the Tub or Pan you design it to lye in, rub your Pieces well with Salt-petre, then take two Parts of common Salt, and two of Bay-salt, and rub every Piece well; lay a Layer of common Salt in the Bottom of your Vessel, cover every Piece over with common Salt, lay them one upon another as close as you can, filling the hollow Places on the Sides with Salt. As your Salt melts on the Top, strew on more, lay a coarse Cloth over the Vessel, and a Board over that, and a Weight on the Board to keep it down. Keep it close covered; it will thus ordered keep the whole Year. Put a Pound of Salt-petre, and two Pounds of Bay-salt to a Hog.

A Pickle for Pork, which is to be eat soon.

TAKE two Gallons of Pump-water, one Pound of Bay-salt, one Pound of coarse Sugar, six Ounces of Salt-petre, boil it all together, and skim it when cold. Cut the Pork in what Pieces you please, lay it down close, and pour the Liquor over it. Lay a Weight on it to keep it close, and cover it close from the Air, will be fit to use in a Week. If you find the Pickle begins to spoil, boil the Pickle again, and skim it; when it is cold, pour it on your Pork again.

To make Veal Hams.

CUT the Leg of Veal like a Ham, then take a Pint of Bay-salt, two Ounces of Salt-petre, and a Pound of common Salt, mix them together, with an Ounce of Juniper-berries beat, rub the Ham well, lay it in a hollow Tray, with the skinny Side downwards. Baste it every Day with the Pickle for a Fortnight; then hang it in the Wood-smoak for a Fortnight. You may boil it, or parboil it, and roast it. In this Pickle, you may do two or three Tongues, or a Piece of Pork.

To make Beef Hams.

TAKE the Leg of a fat, but small Beef, the Fat *Scotch* or *Welch* Cattle is best; cut it Ham-fashion, take an Ounce of Bay-salt, an Ounce of Salt-petre, a Pound of common Salt, and a Pound of coarse Sugar, (this Quantity for about fourteen or fifteen Pounds Weight, and so accordingly, if you pickle the whole Quarter) rub it with the above Ingredients, turn it every Day, and baste it well with the Pickle for a Month; then take it out and roll it in Bran, or Saw-dust, and hang it in Wood-smoke, where there is but little Fire, and a constant Smoke for a Month; then take it down, and hang it in a dry Place, not hot, and keep it for Use. You may cut a Piece off as you have Occasion, and either boil it or cut it in Rashers, and broiled with poached Eggs; or boil a Piece, and it eats fine cold, and will shiver like *Dutch* Beef. After this Beef is done, you may do a thick Brisket of

K k   Beef

Beef in the same Pickle. Let it lay a Month, rubbing it every Day with the Pickle, then boil it till it is tender, hang it in a dry Place, and it eats finely cold, cut in Slices on a Plate. It is a pretty thing for a Side-dish, or for Supper. A Shoulder of Mutton laid in this Pickle a Week, hung in Wood-smoke two or three Days, and then boiled with Cabbage, is very good.

To make Mutton Hams.

TAKE a hind Quarter of Mutton, cut it like a Ham, take one Ounce of Salt-petre, a Pound of coarse Sugar, a Pound of common Salt, mix them, and rub your Ham, lay it in a hollow Tray, with the Skin downwards, baste it every Day for a Fortnight; then roll it in Saw-dust, and hang it in the Wood-smoke a Fortnight; then boil it, and hang it in a dry Place, and cut it out in Rashers. It don't eat well boiled; but eats finely broiled.

To make Pork-Hams.

TAKE a fine fat hind Quarter of Pork, and cut off a fine Ham, take an Ounce of Salt-petre, a Pound of coarse Sugar, and a Pound of common Salt; mix all together, and rub it well; let it lye a Month in this Pickle, turning and basting it every Day; then hang it in Wood-smoke, as you do your Beef, then in a dry Place, so as no Heat comes to it; and if you keep them long, hang them a Month or two in a damp Place, so as they will be mouldy, and it will make them cut fine and short. Never lay these Hams in Water till you boil them, and then boil them in a Copper, if you have one, or the biggest Pot you have. Put them in the cold Water, and let them be four or five Hours before they boil, skim the Pot well often, till it boils; and if it is a very large one, two Hours will boil it; or a small one, an Hour and half will do, provided it be a great while before the Water boils. Take it up half an Hour before Dinner, pull off the Skin, and throw Raspings finely sifted all over, and hold a red hot Fire-shovel over it; and when Dinner is ready, take a few Raspings in a Sieve, and sift all over the Dish; then lay in your Ham, and with your Finger make fine Figures round the Edge of the Dish. But be sure to boil your Ham in as much Water as you can, and to keep it skimming all the time till it boils. It must be at least four Hours before it boils.

This Pickle does finely for Tongues afterwards, to lye in the Pickle a Fortnight, and hang in the Wood-smoke a Fortnight, or boil them out of the Pickle.

Yorkshire is famous for Hams; and the Reason is this: Their Salt is much finer than ours in *London*, it is a large clear Salt, and gives the Meat a fine Flavour. I used to have it in *Essex* from *Malding*, and that Salt will make any Ham as fine as you can desire; it is by much the best Salt for salting Meat. A deep hollow Wood-tray is better than a Pan, because the Pickle swells best about it.

When you broil any of these Hams in Slices or Bacon, have some boiling Water ready, and let the Slices lay a Minute or two in the Water, then broil them, it takes out the Salt, and makes them eat finer.

To make Bacon.

TAKE a Side of Pork, take off all the inside Fat, lay it on a long Board or Dresser, that the Blood may run away, rub it well with good Salt on both Sides, let it lye thus a Week, then take a Pint of Bay-salt, and a quarter of a Pound of Salt-petre, beat them fine, two Pounds of coarse Sugar, and a quarter of a Peck of common Salt. Lay your Pork in something that will hold the Pickle, rub it well with the above Ingredients; lay the skinny Side downwards, and baste it every Day with the Pickle for a Fortnight, then hang it in the Wood-smoke, as you do the Beef; and afterwards hang it in a dry Place, but not hot. You are to observe, that all Hams and Bacon should hang clear from every thing, and not against a Wall.

Observe to wipe off all the old Salt before you put it into this Pickle, and never keep Bacon nor Hams in a hot Kitchen, or in a Room where the Sun comes; it makes them all rusty.

To save Potted Birds, *that begins to be bad.*

I HAVE seen potted Birds, which have come a great way, often smell so bad, that no body could bear the Smell for the Rankness of the Butter, and by managing them in the following manner, have made them as good as ever was eat.

Set a large Sauce-pan of clean Water on the Fire, when it boils, take off the Butter of the Top, and take the Fowls out one by one, throw them into that Sauce-pan of Water half a Minute, whip it out, and dry it in a clean Cloth inside and out; so do all till they are quite done. Scald the Pot clean, and when the Birds are quite cold, season them with Mace, Pepper, and Salt to your Mind, put them down close in the Pot, and pour clarified Butter over them.

To pickle Mackrel, call'd Caveach.

CUT your Mackrel into round Pieces, and divide one into five or six Pieces: To six large Mackrel, you may take one Ounce of beaten Pepper, three large Nutmegs, a little Mace, and a Handful of Salt; mix your Salt and beaten Spice together, and make two or three Holes in each Piece, and thrust

thrust the Seasoning into the Holes with your Finger. Rub the Piece all over with the Seasoning, fry them brown in Oil, and let them stand till they are cold; then put them into Vinegar, and cover them with Oil. They will keep well covered a great while, and are delicious.

CHAP. XIV.

Of PICKLING.

To pickle Wallnuts Green.

TAKE the largest and clearest you can get, pare them as thin as you can, have a Tub of Spring-water stand by you, and throw them in as you do them. Put into the Water a Pound of Bay-salt, let them lye in that Water twenty-four Hours, then take them out of the Water, and put them into a Stone-jar, and between every Layer of Wallnuts, lay a Layer of Vine-leaves, and at Bottom and Top, and fill it up with cold Vinegar. Let them stand all Night, then pour that Vinegar from them into a Copyer or Bell-mettle Skillet, with a Pound of Bay-salt, set it on the Fire, let it boil, and pour it hot on your Nuts, tye them over with a Woollen Cloth, and let them stand a Week; then pour that Pickle away, and rub your Nuts clean with a Piece of Flannel, and put them again in your Jar, with Vine-leaves as above, and boil fresh Vinegar. Put into your Pot to every Gallon of Vinegar, slice a Nutmeg, cut four large Races of Ginger, a quarter of an Ounce of Mace, a quarter of an Ounce of Cloves, a quarter of an Ounce of whole black Pepper, the like of Ordingal Pepper; then pour your Vinegar boiling-hot on your Wallnuts, and cover them with a Woollen Cloth. Let it stand three or four Days; so do two or three times, when cold, put in half a Pint of Mustard-seed, a large Stick of Horse-reddish sliced, tye them down close with a Bladder, and then with a Leather, they will be fit to eat in a Fortnight. Take a large Onion, and stick the Cloves in, and lay in the Middle of the Pot.

To pickle Wallnuts White.

TAKE the largest Nuts you can get, just before the Shell begins to turn, pare them very thin, till the White appears, throw them into Spring-water, with a Handful of Salt as you do them. Let them stand in that Water six Hours, lay on them a thin Board to keep them under the Water; then set a Stew-pan on a Charcoal Fire, with clean Spring-water, take your Nuts out of the other Water, and put them into the Stew-pan. Let them simmer four or five Minutes, but not boil; have ready by you a Pan of Spring-water, with a Handful of white Salt in it, stir it with your Hand till the Salt is melted, then take your Nuts out of the Stew-pan with a wooden Ladle, and put them into the cold Water and Salt. Let them stand a quarter of an Hour, lay the Board on them as before; if they are not kept under the Liquor, they will turn black; then lay them on a Cloth, and cover them with another to dry; then carefully wipe them with a soft Cloth, and put them into your Jar, or Glass, with some Blades of Mace, and Nutmeg sliced thin; mix your Spice between your Nuts, and pour distilled Vinegar over them. First let your Glass be full of Nuts, pour Mutton Fat over them, and tye a Bladder, and then a Leather.

To pickle Wallnuts Black.

TAKE large full-grown Nuts at their full Growth, before they are hard, lay them in Salt and Water, with a little Piece of Allum. Let them lye two Days, then shift them into fresh Water, let them lye two Days longer, then shift them again, and let them lye three Days; then take them out of the Water, and put them into your Pickling-pot. When the Pot is half full, put in a large Onion stuck thick with Cloves; to a hundred of Wallnuts, put in half a Pint of Mustard-seed, a quarter of an Ounce of Mace, half an Ounce of black Pepper, and half an Ounce of All-spice, six Bay-leaves, a Stick of Horse-reddish, then fill your Pot, and pour boiling Vinegar over them. Cover them with a Plate, and when they are cold, tye them down with a Bladder and Leather, and they will be fit to eat in two or three Months. The next Year, if any remains, boil up your Vinegar again, and skim it; when cold, pour it over your Wallnuts. This is by much the best Pickle for Use; therefore you may add more Vinegar to it, what Quantity you please. If you pickle a great many Wallnuts, and eat them fast, make your Pickle for a hundred or two, the rest keep in a strong Brine of Salt and Water boiled till it will bear an Egg; and as your Pot empties, fill them up with those in the Salt and Water. Take care they are covered with Pickle.

In the same manner you may do a smaller Quantity. But if you can get rap Vinegar, use that instead of Salt and Water. Do them thus: Put your Nuts into the Pot you intend to pickle them in, throw in a good Handful of Salt, a little Piece of Allum, and fill the Pot with rap Vinegar, cover it close, and let them stand a Fortnight; then pour them out of the Pot, wipe it clean, and just rub the Nuts with a coarse Cloth, put them in the Jar with the Pickle as above. If you have the best Sugar-

Vinegar

Vinegar of your own making, you need not boil it the first Year, but pour it on cold; and the next Year, if any remain, boil it up again, skim it, and put fresh Spice to it, it will do again.

To pickle Gerkins.

TAKE what Quantity of Cucumbers you think fit, and put them in a Stone-Jar, then take as much Spring-water as you think will cover them: To every Gallon of Water, put as much Salt as will make it bear an Egg, set it on the Fire, and let it boil two or three Minutes; then pour it on the Cucumbers, and cover them with a Pewter-dish, and over that a woollen Cloth, and tye them down close, and let them stand twenty-four Hours; then take them out, and lay them in a Cloth, and another over them to dry them. When they are pretty dry, wipe your Jar out with a dry Cloth, and put your Cucumbers in, and with them a little Dill and Fennel, a very small Quantity. For the Pickle, to every three Quarts of Vinegar, one Quart of Spring-water, till you think you have enough to cover them, put in a little Bay-salt and a little white Salt, not too much. To every Gallon of Pickle, put one Nutmeg cut in Quarters, a quarter of an Ounce of Cloves, a quarter of an Ounce of Mace, a quarter of an Ounce of whole Pepper, a large Race of Ginger sliced; boil all these together in a Bell-mettle or Copper-pot, pour it boiling hot on your Cucumbers, cover them as before. Let them stand two Days, then boil your Pickle again, and pour it on as before, and a third time, when they are cold, cover them with a Bladder, and then a Leather. Mind always to keep your Pickles close covered, and never take them out with any thing but a wooden Spoon, or one for the purpose. This Pickle will do the next Year, only boiling it up again.

You are to observe to put the Spice in the Jar with the Cucumbers, and only boil the Vinegar, Water and Salt, and pour over them. The boiling of your Spice in all Pickles spoils it, and loses ist fine Flavour of the Spice.

To pickle Large Cucumbers in Slices.

TAKE the large Cucumbers before they are too ripe, slice them the Thickness of Crown-pieces into a Pewter-dish: To every Dozen of Cucumbers, slice two large Onions thin, so on till you have filled your Dish; with a Handful of Salt between every Row; then cover them with another Pewter-dish, and let them stand twenty-four Hours; then put them in a Cullender, let them drain very well, then put them into a Jar, and cover them over with White Wine Vinegar, and let them stand four Hours; then pour the Vinegar from them into a Copper Sauce-pan, and boil it with a little Salt. Put to the Cucumbers a little Mace, a little whole Pepper, a large Race of Ginger sliced, and then pour the boiling Vinegar on. Cover them close, and when they are cold, tye them down; they will be fit to eat in two or three Days.

To pickle Asparagus.

TAKE the largest Asparagus you can get, cut off the white End, and wash the green Ends in Spring-water, then put them in another clean Water, and let them lay two or three Hours in it; then have a large broad Stew-pan full of Spring-water, with a good large Handful of Salt, set on the Fire, and when it boils put in the Grass, not tied up but loose, and not too many at a time for fear you break the Heads. Just scald them, and no more, take them out with a broad Skimmer, and lay them on a Cloth to cool. Then for your Pickle: To a Gallon of Vinegar, put one Quart of Spring-water, a Handful of Bay-salt, let them boil, then put your Asparagus in your Jar; to a Gallon of Pickle, two Nutmegs, a quarter of an Ounce of Mace, the same of white Pepper, so pour the Pickle hot over them. Cover them with a Linnen Cloth three or four times double, let them stand a Week, and boil the Pickle. Let them stand a Week longer, and boil the Pickle again, and pour it hot on as before. When they are cold, cover them up close with a Bladder and Leather.

To pickle Peaches.

TAKE your Peaches when they are at the full Growth, just before they turn to be ripe, be sure they are not bruised; then take Spring-water, as much as you think will cover them; make it soft enough to bear an Egg, with Bay and common Salt, an equal Quantity of each; then put in your Peaches, and lay a thin Board over them, to keep them under the Water. Let them stand three Days, and then take them out, and wipe them very carefully with a fine soft Cloth, and lay them in your Glass or Jar; then take as much White Wine Vinegar, as will fill your Gass or Jar: To every Gallon, put one Pint of the best well-made Mustard, two or three Heads of Garlick, a good deal of Ginger sliced, half an Ounce of Cloves, Mace, and Nutmegs; mix your Pickle well together, and pour over your Peaches. Tye them close with a Bladder and Leather, they will be fit to eat in two Months. You may with a fine Penknife cut them a-cross, take out the Stone, and fill them with made Mustard and Garlick, and Horse-reddish and Ginger; tye them together.

To pickle Reddish Pods.

MAKE a strong Pickle with cold Spring-water and Bay-salt, strong enough to bear an Egg, then put your Pods in, and lay a thin Board on them, to keep them under Water. Let them stand ten Days, then drain them in a Sieve, and lay them on a Cloth to dry; then take White Wine Vinegar,

Vinegar, as much as you think will cover them, boil it, and put your Pods in a Jar, with Ginger, Mace, Cloves, and *Jamaica* Pepper. Pour your Vinegar boiling hot on, and cover them with a coarse Cloth, three or four times double, that the Steam may come through a little, and let them stand two Days. Repeat this two or three times; when it is cold, put in a Pint of Mustard-seed, and some Horse-reddish; cover it close.

To pickle French Beans.

PICKLE your Beans as you do the Girkins.

To pickle Colliflowers.

TAKE the largest and finest you can get, cut them in little Pieces, or more properly pull them into little Pieces, pick the small Leaves that grow in the Flowers clean from them; then have a broad Stew-pan on the Fire with Spring-water, and when it boils, put in your Flowers, with a good Handful of white Salt; and just let them boil up very quick; be sure you don't let them boil above one Minute; then take them out with a broad Slice, and lay them on a Cloth, and cover them with another, and let them lye till they are quite cold. Then put them in your wide-mouth'd Bottles, with two or three Blades of Mace in each Bottle, and a Nutmeg sliced in Vinegar thin; then fill up your Bottles with distilled Vinegar, and cover them over with Mutton Fat, and over that a Bladder, and then a Leather. Let them stand a Month before you open them.

If you find the Pickle taste sweet as may be it will, pour off the Vinegar, and put fresh in, the Spice will do again. In a Fortnight, they will be fit to eat. Observe to throw them out of the boiling Water into cold, and then dry them.

To pickle Beat-Root.

SET a Pot of Spring-water on the Fire, when it boils, put in your Beats, and let them boil till they are tender; then peel them with a Cloth, and lay them in a Stone-Jar, take three Quarts of Vinegar, and two of Spring-water, so do till you think you have enough to cover your Beats. Put your Vinegar and Water in a Pan, and salt to your Taste. Stir it well together, till the Salt is all melted, then pour them on the Beats, and cover it with a Bladder. Do not boil the Pickle.

To pickle White Plumbs.

TAKE the large white Plumbs, and if they have Stalks, let them remain on; and do them as you you do your Peaches.

To pickle Nectarines *and* Apricots.

THEY are done the same as the Peaches. All these strong Pickles will waste with the keeping; therefore you must fill them up with cold Vinegar.

To pickle Onions.

TAKE your Onions, when they are dry enough to lye up in your House, such as are about as big as a large Wallnut; or you may do some as small as you please. Take off only the outward dry Coat, then boil them in one Water without shifting, till they begin to grow tender; then drain them through a Cullinder, let them cool, as soon as they are quite cold, slip off two outward Coats or Skins, slip them till they look white from each other, and rub them gently with a fine soft Linnen Cloth, and lay them on a Cloth to cool. When this is done, put them into wide-mouth'd Glasses, with about six or eight Bay-leaves. To a Quarter of Onions, a quarter of an Ounce of Mace, two large Races of Ginger sliced; all these Ingredients must be intersperfed here and there, in the Glasses among the Onions; then boil to each Quart of Vinegar two Ounces of Bay-salt, and skim it well as the Skim rises, and let it stand till it is cold; then pour it into the Glass, and cover it close with a wet Bladder dipped in Vinegar, and tye them down; they will eat well, and look white. As the Pickle wastes, fill them with cold Vinegar.

To pickle Lemons.

TAKE twelve Lemons, scrape them with a Piece of broken Glass, then cut them cross in two, four Parts down right, but not quite through, but that they will hang together; then put in as much Salt as they will hold, and rub them well, and strew them over with Salt. Let them lay in an earthen Dish for three Days, and turn them every Day; then slit an Ounce of Ginger very thin, and salted for three Days, twelve Cloves of Garlick parboiled, and salted three Day, a small Handful of Mustard-seeds bruised, and searched through a Hair-sieve, some red *India* Pepper, one to every Lemon; take your Lemons out of the Salt, and squeeze them very gently, and put them into a Jar, with the Spice and Ingredients, and cover them with the best White Wine Vinegar. Stop them up very close, and in a Month's time they will be fit to eat.

To pickle Mushrooms White.

TAKE small Bottoms, cut and prime them at the Bottom, wash them with a Bit of Flannel through two or three Waters, then set it on the Fire in a Stew-pan with Spring-water, and a small Handful of Salt. When it boils, put your Mushrooms in; let it boil three or four Minutes, then throw them into a Cullinder, and lay them on a Linnen Cloth quick, and cover them with another.

Pickle for Mushrooms.

TAKE a Gallon of the best Vinegar, put it into a cold Still. To every Gallon of Vinegar, put half a Pound of Bay-salt, a quarter of an Ounce of Mace, a quarter of an Ounce of Cloves, a Nutmeg cut into Quarters, keep the Top of the Still covered with a wet Cloth. As the Cloth dries, put on a wet one; don't let the Fire be too large, lest you burn the Bottom of the Still. Draw it as long as you taste the Acid, and no longer. When you fill your Bottles, put in your Mushrooms, and here and there put in a few Blades of Mace, and a Slice of Nutmeg; then fill the Bottle with Pickle, and melt some Mutton-fat, strain it, and pour over it. It will keep them better than Oil.

You must put your Nutmeg over the Fire in a little Vinegar, and give it a boil. While it is hot, you may slice it as you please. When it is cold, it will not cut; for it will crack to Pieces.

To pickle Codlings.

WHEN you have greened them as you do your Pippins, and they are quite cold, with a small Scoope very carefully take off the Eye as whole as you can, and scoope out the Core, put in a Clove of Garlick, and fill it up with Mustard-seed, lay on the Eye again, and put them in your Glasses, with the Eye uppermost. Put the same Pickle as you do to the Pippins, and tye them down close.

To pickle Red Currans.

THEY are done the same Way as Barberries.

To pickle Fennel.

SET Spring-water on the Fire, with a Handful of Salt; when it boils tye your Fennel in Bunches, put them into the Water, just give them a scald, lay them on a Cloth to dry; when cold, put it in a Glass, with a little Mace and Nutmeg, fill it with cold Vinegar, lay a Bit of green Fennel on the Top, and over that a Bladder and Leather.

To pickle Grapes.

TAKE Grapes at the full Growth, but not ripe, cut them in small Bunches fit for garnishing, put them into a Stone-Jar, with Vine-leaves between every Layer of Grapes; then take as much Spring-water as you think will cover them, put in a Pound of Bay-salt, and as much white Salt as will make it bear an Egg. Dry your Bay-salt, and pound it, it will melt the sooner, put it into a Bell-mettle or Copper-pot, boil it and skim it very well; as it boils take all the black Scum off, but not the white Skim. When it has boiled a quarter of an Hour, let it stand to cool and settle; when it is almost cold, pour the clear Liquor on the Grapes, lay Vine-leaves on the Top, tye them down close with a Linnen-cloth, and cover them with a Dish. Let them stand twenty-four Hours, then take them out, and lay them on a Cloth, cover them over with another, let them be dried between the Cloths, then take two Quarts of Vinegar, one Quart of Spring-water, and one Pound of coarse Sugar. Let it boil a little while, skim it as it boils very clean, let it stand till it is quite cold, dry your Jar with a Cloth, put fresh Vine-leaves at the Bottom, and between every Bunch of Grapes, and on the Top; then pour the Clear off the Pickle on the Grapes, fill your Jar, that the Pickle may be above the Grapes, tye a thin Bit of Board in a Piece of Flannel, and lay it in the Top of the Jar, to keep the Grapes under the Pickle, tye them down with a Bladder, and then a Leather. Take them out with a wooden Spoon; be sure to make Pickle enough to cover them.

To pickle Barberies.

TAKE of White Wine Vinegar and Water, of each an equal Quantity: To every Quart of this Liquor put in half a Pound of Sixpenny Sugar; then pick the worst of your Barberries, and put into this Liquor, and the best into Glasses; then boil your Pickle with the worst of your Barberries, and skim it very clean. Boil it till it looks of a fine Colour, then let it stand to be cold before you strain it, then strain it through a Cloth, wringing it to get all the Colour you can from the Barberries. Let it stand to cool and settle, then pour it clear into the Glasses in a little of the Pickle; boil a little Fennel, when cold, put a little Bit at the Top of the Pot or Glass, and cover it close with a Bladder and Leather. To every half Pound of Sugar, put a quarter of a Pound of white Salt.

To pickle Red Cabbage.

SLICE the Cabbage thin, and put to it Vinegar and Salt, and an Ounce of All-spice cold; cover it close, and keep it for Use. It is a Pickle of little Use, but for garnishing of Dishes, Sallats and Pickles, tho' some People are fond of it.

To pickle Golden Pippins.

TAKE the finest Pippins you can get, free from Spots and Bruises, put them into a Preserving-pan of cold Spring water, and set them on a Charcoal Fire. Keep them turning with a wooden Spoon, till they will peel; do not let them boil. When they are boiled, peel them, and put them into the Water again, with a quarter of a Pint of the best Vinegar, and a quarter of an Ounce of Allum. Cover them very close, with a Pewter-dish, and set them on the Charcoal Fire again, a slow Fire not to boil; let them stand, turning them now and then, till they look green; then take them out, and lay them on a Cloth to cool; when cold, make your Pickle as for the Peaches, only instead of made Mustard, this must be Mustard-seed whole. Cover them close, and keep them for Use.

To pickle Stertion Buds and Limes, you pick them off the Lime-trees in the Summer.

TAKE new Stertion-seeds, or Limes, pickle them when large; have ready Vinegar, with what Spice you please, throw them in, and stop the Bottle close.

To pickle Oysters, Cockels and Muscles.

TAKE two hundred of Oysters, the newest and best you can get, be careful to save the Liquor in some Pan as you open them, cut off the black Verge, saving the rest, and put them into their own Liquor, then put all the Liquor and Oysters into a Kettle, and boil them about half an Hour, on a very gentle Fire, and do them very slowly, skimming them as the Scum rises, then take them off the Fire, take out the Oysters, and strain the Liquor through a fine Cloth, then put in the Oysters again; then take out a Pint of the Liquor whilst it is hot, put thereto three Quarters of an Ounce of Mace, half an Ounce of Cloves; just give it one Boil, then put it to the Oysters, and stir up the Spices well among the Oysters; then put in about a Spoonful of Salt, and three Quarters of a Pint of the best white Wine Vinegar, and a quarter of an Ounce of whole Pepper; then let them stand till they be cold, then put the Oysters as many as you well can into a Barrel, and put in as much Liquor as the Barrel will hold, letting them settle a while, they will soon be fit to eat; or you may put them into Stone Jars, and cover them close with a Bladder and Leather, be sure they be quite cold before you cover them up. Thus do Cockels and Muscles, only this, Cockels are small, and to this Spice you must have at least two Quarts; nor is there any Thing to pick off them. Muscles you must have two Quarts, and take great Care to pick the Crab out under the Tongue, and a little Fus which grows at the Root of the Tongue. The two latter, Cockels and Muscles, must be work'd in several Waters, to clean them from the Grit, and put them in a Stew-pan by themselves, cover them close, and when they are open, pick them out of the Shells and strain the Liquor.

To pickle young Suckers, or young Artichoaks before the Leaves are hard.

TAKE young Suckers, pare them very nicely, all the hard Ends of the Leaves and Stalks, just scald them in Salt and Water, and when they are cold put them into little Glass Bottles, with two or three Blades of large Mace and a Nutmeg sliced thin, fill them either with distill'd Vinegar, or the Sugar Vinegar of your own making, with half Spring Water.

To pickle Artichoak-Bottoms.

BOIL Artichoaks till you can pull the Leaves off, then take off the Choaks, and cut them from the Stalk; take great Care you don't let the Knife touch the Top, throw them into Salt and Water for an Hour, then take them out, and lay them on a Cloth to drain, then put them into large wide mouth'd Glasses, put a little Mace and slic'd Nutmeg between, fill them either with distill'd Vinegar, or your Sugar Vinegar and Spring-Water, cover them with Mutton Fat try'd, and tie them down with a Bladder and Leather.

To pickle Samphire.

TAKE the Samphire that is green, lay it in a clean Pan, throw two or three Handfuls of Salt over, and cover it with Spring-water. Let it lye twenty-four Hours, then put it into a clean Brass Saucepan, throw in a Handful of Salt, and cover it with good Vinegar. Cover the Pan close, and set it over a very slow Fire; let it stand till it is just green and crisp, then take it off in a moment; for if it stands to be soft, it is spoiled; put it in your Pickling-pot, and cover it close. When it is cold, tye it down with a Bladder and Leather, and keep it for Use. Or you may keep it all the Year, in a very strong Brine of Salt and Water, and throw it into Vinegar just before you use it.

Elder-Shoots in Imitation of Bamboo.

TAKE the largest and youngest Shoots of Elder, which put out the Middle of *May*, the middle Stalks are most tender and biggest, the small ones not worth doing. Peel off the outward Peel or Skin, and lay them in a strong Brine of Salt and Water for one Night, and then dry them in a Cloth, Piece by Piece. In the mean time make your Pickle of half White Wine, and half Beer-Vinegar: To each Quart of Pickle, you must put an Ounce of white or red Pepper, an Ounce of Ginger sliced, a little Mace, and a few Corns of *Jamaica* Pepper. When the Spice has boiled in the Pickle, pour it hot upon the Shoots, stop them close immediately, and set the Jar two Hours before the Fire, turning it often. It is as good a Way of greening Pickles as often boiling; or you may boil the Pickle two or three times, and pour on boiling hot, just as you please. If you make the Pickle of the Sugar Vinegar, you must let one half be Spring-water. You have the Receipt for this Vinegar in the nineteenth Chapter.

Rules to be observed in Pickling.

Always use Stone-Jars for all Sorts of Pickles that require hot Pickle to them. The first Charge is the least; or these not only lasts longer, but keep the Pickle better; for Vinegar and Salt will penetrate through all earthen Vessels, Stone and Glass is the only thing to keep Pickles in. Be sure never to put your Hands in to take Pickles out, it will soon spoil it. The best Way is to every Pot, tye a wooden Spoon full of little Holes, to take the Pickles out with.

CHAP. XV.

Of Making CAKES, &c.

To make a Rich Cake.

TAKE four Pound of Flower well dried and sifted, seven Pound of Currants washed and rubb'd, six Pound of the best fresh Butter, two Pound of Jordan Almonds blanched, and beaten with Orange Flower Water and Sack till they are fine, then take four Pound of Eggs, put half the Whites away, three Pound of double refin'd Sugar beaten and sifted, a quarter of an Ounce of Mace, the same of Cloves and Cinnamon, three large Nutmegs, all beaten fine, a little Ginger, half a Pint of Sack, half a Pint of right French Brandy, Sweetmeats to your liking, they must be Orange, Lemon, and Citron. Work your Butter to a Cream with your Hands before any of your Ingredients are in, then put in your Sugar, mix it well together; let your Eggs be well beat, and strain'd thro' a Sieve, work in your Almonds first, then put in your Eggs, beat them all together till they look white and thick, then put in your Sack and Brandy and Spices, and shake your Flour in by Degrees, and when your Oven is ready, put in your Currants and Sweetmeats as you put it in your hoop; it will take four Hours baking in a quick Oven, you must keep it beaten with your Hand all the while you are mixing of it, and when your Currants are well wash'd and clean'd, let them be kept before the Fire, so that they may go warm into your Cake. This Quantity will bake best in two Hoops.

To Ice a great Cake another Way.

TAKE two Pound of double refin'd Sugar, beat and sift it very fine, and likewise beat and sift a little Starch and mix with it, then beat six Whites of Eggs to Froth, and put to it some Gum-Water, the Gum must be steep'd in Orange-flower-water, then mix and beat all these together two Hours, and put it on your Cake; when it is baked, set it in the Oven again to harden a quarter of an Hour, take great Care it is not discolour'd. When it is drawn, ice it over the Top and Sides, take two Pound of double refin'd Sugar beat and sifted, and the Whites of three Eggs beat to a Froth, with three or four Spoonfuls of Orange-flower-water, and three Grains of Musk and Ambergreafe together; put all these in a Stone Mortar, and beat these till it is as white as Snow, and with a Brush or Bundle of Feathers, spread it all over the Cake, and put it in the Oven to dry; but take Care the Oven does not discolour it. When it is cold paper it, and it will keep good five or six Weeks.

To make a Pound Cake.

TAKE a Pound of Butter, beat it in an earthen Pan, with your Hand one Way, till it is like a fine thick Cream; then have ready twelve Eggs, but half the Whites, beat them well, and beat them up with the Butter, a Pound of Flour beat in it, and a Pound of Sugar, and a few Carraways, beat it all well together for an Hour with your Hand, or a great wooden Spoon. Butter a Pan, and put it in and bake it an Hour in a quick Oven.

For Change, you may put in a Pound of Currants clean wash'd and pick'd.

A cheap Seed Cake.

TAKE half a Peck of Flour, a Pound and half of Butter, put it in a Sauce-pan, with a Pint of new Milk, set it on the Fire, take a Pound of Sugar and half an Ounce of All-spice beat fine, mix them with the Flour. When the Butter is melted, pour Milk and Butter in the Middle of the Flour, and work it up like Paste. Pour in with the Milk half a Pint of good Ale Yeast, set it before the Fire to rise, just before it goes to the Oven. Either put in some Currants or Carraways-seed, and bake it in a quick Oven. Make it into two Cakes, they will take an Hour and half baking.

To make a Butter Cake.

TAKE a Dish of Butter, and beat it like Cream with your Hands, two Pounds of fine Sugar well beat, three Pounds of Flour well dried, mix them in with the Butter, twenty-four Eggs, leave out half the Whites, then beat all together an Hour. Just as you are going to put it into the Oven, put in a quarter of an Ounce of Mace, a Nutmeg beat, a little Sack or Brandy, and Seeds or Currans, just as you please.

To make Ginger-Bread Cakes.

TAKE three Pounds of Flour, one Pound of Sugar, one Pound of Butter, rubbed in very fine, two Ounces of Ginger beat fine, a large Nutmeg grated; then take a Pound of Treakle, a quarter of a Pint of Cream, make them warm together, and make up the Bread stiff, roll it out, and make it up into thin Cakes, cut them out with a Tea-Cup, or a small Glass, or roll them round like Nuts, bake them on Tin Plates in a slack Oven.

To make a fine Seed or Saffron Cake.

TAKE a quarter of a Peck of fine Flour, a Pound and half of Butter, three Ounces of Carraway Seeds, six Eggs beat well, a quarter of an Ounce of Cloves and Mace beat together very fine, a Pennyworth of Cinnamon, beat a Pound of Sugar, a Pennyworth of Rose-Water, a Pennyworth of Saffron, a Pint and half of Yeast; a Quart of Milk; mix it all together lightly with your Hands thus; first boil your Milk and Butter, then skim off the Butter, and mix it with your Flour, and a little of the Milk, stir the Yeast into the rest and strain it; mix it with the Flour, put in your Seed and Spice, Rose-Water, Tincture of Saffron, and Sugar, and Eggs, beat it all up well with your Hands lightly, and bake it in a Hoop or Pan; but be sure to butter the Pan well. It will take an Hour and half in a quick Oven; you may leave out the Seed if you chuse it, and I think it rather better without it; but that you must do as you like.

A Rich Seed Cake, called the Nun's Cake.

TAKE four Pound of your finest Flour, and three Pound of double refin'd Sugar beaten and sifted, mix them together, and dry them by the Fire till you prepare your other Materials; take four Pound of Butter, beat it with your Hand till it is soft like Cream, then beat thirty-five Eggs, leave out sixteen Whites, and strain off your Eggs from the Treds, and beat them and the Butter together till all appears like Butter. Put in four or five Spoonfuls of Rose or Orange-flower Water, and beat again; then take your Flour and Sugar, with six Ounces of Carraway Seeds, and strew it in by Degrees, beating it up all the Time for two Hours together. You may put in as much Tincture of Cinnamon or Ambergrease as you please, butter your Hoop, and let it stand three Hours in a moderate Oven. You must observe always in beating of Butter to do it with a cool Hand, and beat it always one Way in a deep Earthen Dish.

To make Pepper Cakes.

TAKE half a Gill of Sack, half a quarter of an Ounce of whole white Pepper, put it in and boil it together a quarter of an Hour, then take the Pepper out, and put in as much double refin'd Sugar as will make it like a Paste, then drop it in what Shape you please on Plates, and let it dry itself.

Portugal Cakes.

MIX into a Pound of fine Flour, a Pound of Loaf Sugar beat and sifted, then rub into it a Pound of pure sweet Butter, till it is thick like grated white Bread, then put to it two Spoonfuls of Rose-Water, two of Sack, ten Eggs, whip them very well with a Whisk, then mix into it eight Ounces of Currants, mix'd all well together; butter the Tin Pans, fill them but half full, and bake them; if made without Currants they'll keep half a Year; add a Pound of Almonds blanch'd, and beat with Rose-Water as above, and leave out the Flour. These are another Sort and better.

140   *The Art of Cookery, made Plain and Easy.*

A Pretty Cake.

TAKE five Pounds of Flour well dried, one Pound of Sugar, half an Ounce of Mace, and as much Nutmeg, beat your Spice very fine, mix the Sugar and Spice in the Flour, take twenty-two Eggs, leave out six Whites, beat them, and put a Pint of Ale Yeast and the Eggs in the Flour, take two Pounds and half of fresh Butter, a Pint and half of Cream, set the Cream and Butter over the Fire, till the Butter is melted, let it stand till it is blood warm, before you put it into the Flour, set it an Hour by the Fire to rise, then put in seven Pounds of Currans, which must be plumped in half a Pint of Brandy, and three quarters of a Pound of candied Peels. It must stand an Hour and quarter in the Oven. You must put two Pounds of chopped Raisins in the Flour, and a quarter of a Pint of Sack. When you put the Currans in, bake it in a Hoop.

To make Ginger-Bread.

TAKE three Quarts of fine Flour, two Ounces of beaten Ginger, a quarter of an Ounce of Nutmeg, Cloves, and Mace beat fine, but most of the last; mix all together, three quarters of a Pound of fine Sugar, two Pound of Treacle, set it over the Fire, but don't let it boil; three quarters of a Pound of Butter melted in the Treacle, and some candied Lemon and Orange Peal cut fine, mix all these together well; an Hour will bake it in a quick Oven.

To make little Fine Cakes.

ONE Pound of Butter beat to Cream, a Pound and quarter of Flour, a Pound of fine Sugar beat fine, a Pound of Currans clean wash'd and pick'd, six Eggs, two Whites left out, beat them fine, mix the Flour and Sugar and Eggs by Degrees into the Butter, beat it all well with both Hands, either make it into little Cakes, or bake it in one.

Another Sort of little Cakes.

A Pound of Flour and half a Pound of Sugar, beat half a Pound of Butter with your Hand, and mix them well together; bake it in little Cakes.

To make Drop Biskets.

TAKE eight Eggs and one Pound of double refin'd Sugar, beaten fine, and twelve Ounces of fine Flour well dried, beat your Eggs very well, then put in your Sugar and beat it, and then your Flour by Degrees; beat it all very well together without ceasing, your Oven must be as hot as for Halfpenny Bread, then flower some Sheets of Tin, and drop your Biskets of what Bigness you please, and put them in the Oven as fast as you can; and when you see them rise, watch them, and if they begin to colour take them out, and put in more; and if the first is not enough, put them in again; if they are right done, they will have a white Ice on them. You may, if you chuse it, put in a few Carraways; when they are all baked put them in the Oven again to dry, then keep them in a very dry Place.

To make Common Biskets.

BEAT up six Eggs with a Spoonful of Rose-water, and a Spoonful of Sack; then add a Pound of fine powder'd Sugar, and a Pound of Flour; mix them into the Eggs by degrees, and an Ounce of Coriander-seeds, mix'd all together well, and shape them on white thin Paper, or Tin Moulds in any form you please. Beat the White of an Egg, and with a Feather rub them over, and dust fine Sugar over them. Set them in an Oven moderately heated, till they rise and come to a good Colour; take them out, and when you have done with the Oven, and if you have no Stove to dry them in, put them in the Oven again, and let them stand all Night to dry.

French Biskets.

HAVING a Pair of clean Scales ready, in one Scale, put three new-laid Eggs, in the other Scale put as much dried Flour, an equal Weight with the Eggs, take out the Flour, and as much fine Powder-sugar; first beat the Whites of the Eggs up well with a Whisk till they are of a fine Froth, then whip in half an Ounce of candied Lemon-peel cut very thin and fine, and beat well, then by degrees whip in the Flour and Sugar, then slip in the Yolk, and with a Spoon temper it well together, then shape your Biskets on fine white Paper with your Spoon, and throw powdered Sugar over them. Bake them in a moderate Oven not too hot, giving them a fine Colour on the Top. When they are baked, with a fine Knife cut them off from the Paper, and lay them in Boxes for Use.

To

To make Maccaroons.

TAKE a Pound of Almonds, let them be scal'd, blanch'd and thrown into cold Water, then dry them in a Cloth, and pound them in a Mortar, moisten them with Orange-flower Water, or the White of an Egg, lest they turn to an Oil; afterwards take an equal Quantity of fine powder Sugar, with three or four other Whites of Eggs, and a little Musk, beat all well together, and shape them on Wafer-paper with a Spoon round, bake them in a gentle Oven on Tin Plates.

To make Shrewsbury Cakes.

TAKE two Pound of Flour, a Pound of Sugar finely search'd, mix them together, (take out a quarter of a Pound to roll them in) then take four Eggs beat, four Spoonfuls of Cream, and two Spoonfuls of Rose-water, beat them well together, and mix them with the Flour into a Paste, roll them into thin Cakes, and bake them in a quick Oven.

Madling Cakes.

TO a quarter of a Peck of Flour well dried at the Fire, add two Pound of Mutton Suet tried and strain'd clear of, when it is a little cool, mix it well with the Flour, some Salt, and a very little all Spice beat fine; take half a Pint of good Yeast, and put in half a Pint of Water, stir it well together, and strain it, mix up your Flour into a Paste of a moderate Stiffness; you must add as much cold Water as will make the Paste of a right order; make it into Cakes about the Thickness and Bigness of an Oat-Cake; have ready some Currans clean wash'd and pick'd, strow some just in the middle of your Cakes between your Dough, so that none can be seen till the Cake is broke. You may leave the Currants out if you don't chuse them.

To make light Wigs.

TAKE a Pound and half of Flour, and half a Pint of Milk made warm, mix these together, and cover it up, and let it lie by the Fire half an Hour; then take half a Pound of Sugar, and half a Pound of Butter, then work these in a Paste and make it into Wigs, with as little Flour as possible; let the Oven be pretty quick, and they will rise very much. Mind to mix a quarter of a Pint of good Ale-Yeast in the Milk.

To make very good Wigs.

TAKE a quarter of a Peck of the finest Flour, rub it into three quarters of a Pound of fresh Butter, till it is like grated Bread, something more then half a Pound of Sugar, half a Nutmeg, and half a Race of Ginger grated, three Eggs Yolks and Whites beat very well, and put to them half a Pint of thick Ale-yeast, and three or four Spoonfuls of Sack, make a Hole in the Flour, and pour in your Yeast and Eggs, as much Milk just warm, as will make into a light Paste. Let it stand before the Fire to rise half an Hour, then make it into a Dozen and half of Wigs, wash them over with Egg just as they go into the Oven; a quick Oven and half an Hour will bake them.

To make Buns.

TAKE two Pounds of fine Flour, a Pint of good Ale-yeast, put a little Sack in the Yeast, and three Eggs beaten, knead all these together with a little warm Milk, a little Nutmeg, and a little Salt; then lay it before the Fire till it rise, very light, then knead in a Pound of fresh Butter, and a Pound of rough Carraway-comfits, and bake them in a quick Oven, in what Shape you please on flour'd Papers.

To make little Plumb-Cakes.

TAKE two Pound of Flour dried in the Oven, or at a great Fire, and half a Pound of Sugar finely powder'd, four Yolks of Eggs, two Whites, half a Pound of Butter wash'd with Rose-water, six Spoonfuls of Cream warm'd, a Pound and half of Currans unwash'd, but picked and rubb'd very clean in a Cloth; mix it all well together, then make them up into Cakes, and bake them in an Oven almost as hot as for a Manchet, and let them stand half an Hour till they be colour'd on both Sides, then take down the Oven Lid, and let them stand to soak. You must rub the Butter into the Flour very well, then the Sugar, then the Egg and Cream, and then the Currans.

CHAP.

CHAP. XVI.
Of Cheesecakes, Creams, Jellies, Whip Syllabubs, &c.

To make fine Cheesecakes.

TAKE a Pint of Cream, and warm it, and put it to five Quarts of Milk warm from the Cow, then put Runnet to it, and just give it a stir about; and when it is come, put the Curd in a Linnen Bag, or Cloth, and let it drain well away from the Whey, but do not squeeze it much; then put it in a Mortar, and break the Curd as fine as Butter, then put to your Curd, half a Pound of sweet Almonds blanched, and beat exceeding fine, or half a Pound of Mackeroons beat very fine. If you have Almonds, grate in a Naples Bisket; but if you use Mackeroons, you need not; then add to it the Yolks of nine Eggs beaten, a whole Nutmeg grated, two perfumed Plumbs dissolved in Rose or Orange-flower Water, half a Pound of fine Sugar; mix all well together, then melt a Pound and quarter of Butter, and stir it well in it, and half a Pound of Currans plumped, to let stand to cool till you use it; then make your Puff-paste thus: Take a Pound of fine Flour, and wet it with cold Water, roll it out; and put into it by degrees a Pound of fresh Butter, shake a little Flour on each Coat as you roll it. Make it just as you use it.

You may leave out the Currans, for Change, nor need you put in the perfumed Plumbs, if you dislike them; and for Variety, when you make them of Mackeroons, put in as much Tincture of Saffron as will give them a high Colour, but no Currans. This we call Saffron Cheesecakes; the other without Currans, Almond Cheesecakes; with Currans, fine Cheesecakes; with Mackeroons, Mackeroon Cheesecakes.

To make Lemon Cheesecakes.

TAKE the Peel of two large Lemons, boil it very tender, then pound it well in a Mortar, with a quarter of a Pound or more of Loaf-sugar, the Yolks of six Eggs, and half a Pound of fresh Butter; pound and mix all well together, lay a Puff-paste in your Patty-pans, and fill them half full, and bake them. Orange Cheesecakes are done the same Way, only you boil the Peel in two or three Waters, to take out the Bitterness.

A second Sort of Lemon Cheesecakes.

TAKE two large Lemons, grate off the Peel of both, and squeeze out the Juice of one; add to it half a Pound of double-refined Sugar, twelve Yolks of Eggs, eight Whites well beaten, then melt half a Pound of Butter, in four or five Spoonfuls of Cream, then stir it all together, and set it over the Fire, stirring it till it begins to be pretty thick; then take it off, and when it is cold, fill your Patty-pans little more then half full. Put a Paste very thin at the Bottom of the Patty-pans; half an Hour, with a quick Oven, will bake them.

To make Almond Cheesecakes.

TAKE half a Pound of Jordan Almonds, and lay them in cold Water all Night; the next Morning blanch them into cold Water, then take them out, and dry them in a clean Cloth, and beat them very fine in a little Orange-flower Water, then take six Eggs, leave out four Whites, beat them and strain them, then half a Pound of white Sugar, with a little beaten Mace; beat them well together in a Marble Mortar, take ten Ounces of good fresh Butter, and melt it, a little grated Lemon-peel, and put them in the Mortar, with the other Ingredients; mix all well together, and fill your Patty-pans.

To make Fairy Butter.

TAKE the Yolks of two hard Eggs, and beat them in a Marble-mortar, with a large Spoonful of Orange-flower Water, and two Tea Spoonfuls of fine Sugar beat to Powder; beat this all together till it is a fine Past, then mix it up with about as much fresh Butter out of the Churn, and force it thro' a fine Strainer full of little Holes into a Plate. This is a pretty Thing to set off a Table at Supper.

Almond Custards.

TAKE a Pint of Cream, blanch, and beat a quarter of a Pound of Almonds fine, with two Spoonfuls of Rose-water, sweeten it to your Pallat; beat up the Yolks of four Eggs, stir all together one Way over the Fire till it is thick, then pour it out into Cups, or you may bake it in little China Cups.

Baked Custards.

ONE Pint of Cream, boil with Mace and Cinnamon, when cold take four Eggs, two Whites left out, a little Rose and Orange-flower Water and Sack, Nutmeg and Sugar to your Pallate, mix them well together, and bake them in China Cups.

To make plain Custards.

TAKE a Quart of new Milk, sweeten it to your Palate, grate in a little Nutmeg, beat up eight Eggs, leave out half the Whites, beat them up well, stir them into the Milk, and bake it in China Basons, or put them in a deep China Dish; have a Kettle of Water boiling, set the Cup in, let the Water come above half Way, but don't let it boil too fast for fear of its getting into the Cups. You may add a little Rose-water.

To make Orange Butter.

TAKE the Yolks of ten Eggs beat very well, half a Pint of Rhenish, six Ounces of Sugar, and the Juice of three sweet Oranges; set them over a gentle Fire, stirring them one way till it is thick. When you take it off, stir in a Piece of Butter as big as a large Wallnut.

To make Steeple Cream.

TAKE five Ounces of Hartshorn, and two Ounces of Ivory, and put them into a Stone-Bottle, and fill it up with fair Water to the Neck, and put in a small Quantity of Gum Arabick, and Gum Dragon; then tye up the Bottle very close, and set it into a Pot of Water with Hay at the Bottom. Let it stand six Hours, then take it out, and let it stand an Hour before you open it, left it fly in your Face; then strain it in, and it will be a strong Jelly; then take a Pound of blanched Almonds, and beat them very fine, and mix it with a Pint of thick Cream, and let it stand a little; then strain it out, and mix it with a Pound of Jelly, set it over the Fire till it is scalding hot, sweeten it to your Taste with double refin'd Sugar, then take it of, and put in a little Amber, and pour it into small high Gallipots like a Sugar-loaf at Top; when it is cold turn them out, and lay whipt Cream about them in Heaps; be sure it does not boil when the Cream is in.

Lemon Cream.

TAKE five large Lemons, pare them as thin as possible, steep them all Night in twenty Spoonfuls of Spring-water with the Juice of the Lemons, then strain it through a Jelly-bag into a Silver Sauce-pan if you have one, the Whites of six Eggs beat well, ten Ounces of double refin'd Sugar, set it over a very slow Charcoal Fire, stir it all the Time one Way, skim it, and when it is as hot as you can bear your Fingers in, pour it into Glasses.

A second Lemon Cream.

TAKE the Juice of four large Lemons, and half a Pint of Water, and a Pound of double refin'd Sugar beaten fine, and the Whites of seven Eggs, and the Yolks of one beaten very well; mix all together, and strain it, and set it on a gentle Fire, stirring it all the while, and scum it clean, put into it the Peel of one Lemon, when it is very hot, but not boil, take out the Lemon Peal and pour it into China Dishes. You must observe to keep it stirring one Way all the Time it is over the Fire.

Jelly of Cream.

TAKE four Ounces of Hartshorn, put it on in three Pints of Water, let it boil till it is a stiff Jelly, which you will know by taking a little in a Spoon to cool; then strain it off, and add to it half a Pint of Cream, two Spoonfuls of Rose-water, two Spoonfuls of Sack, and sweeten to your Taste. Then give it a gentle boil, but keep stirring it all the time, or it will curdle; then take it off, and stir it till it is cold; then put it into broad Bottom-cups, let them stand all Night, and turn them out into a Dish; take half a Pint of Cream, two Spoonfuls of Rose-water, and as much Sack; sweeten to your Palate, and pour over them.

To make Orange Cream.

TAKE a Pint of the Juice of Seville Oranges, and put to it the Yolks of six Eggs, the Whites of but four, beat the Eggs very well, and strain them and the Juice together. Add to it a Pound of double-refined Sugar, beaten and sifted; set all those together on a soft Fire, and put the Peel of half an Orange into it, keep it stirring all the while one way. When it is almost ready to boil, take out the Orange-peel, and pour out the Cream into Glasses, or China Dishes.

To make Gooseberry Cream.

TAKE two Quarts of Gooseberries, put to them as much Water as will cover them, let them boil all to mash, then run them through a Sieve with a Spoon: To a Quart of the Pulp, you must have six Eggs well beaten; and when the Pulp is hot, put in an Ounce of fresh Butter, sweeten it to your Taste, and put in your Eggs, and stir them over a gentle Fire till they grow thick; then set it by; and when it is almost cold, put into it two Spoonfuls of Juice of Spinage, and a Spoonful of Orange-flower

flower Water, or Sack; stir it well together, and put it into your Bason; when it is cold, serve it to the Table.

To make Barley Cream.

TAKE a small Quantity of Pearl-Barley, and boil it in Milk and Water till it is tender, then strain the Liquor from it, and put your Barley into a Quart of Cream, and let it boil a little, then take the Whites of five Eggs and the Yolk of one, beaten with a Spoonful of fine Flour, and two Spoonfuls of Orange-flower Water; then take the Cream off the Fire, and mix in the Eggs by Degrees, and set it over the Fire again to thicken, sweeten it to your Taste, pour it into Basons, and when it is cold serve it up.

To make Blanch'd Cream.

TAKE a Quart of the thickest sweet Cream you can get, season it with fine Sugar and Orange-flower Water, then boil it, then beat the Whites of twenty Eggs with a little cold Cream, take out the Treddles, which you must do by straining it after it is beat, and when the Cream is on the Fire and boils, pour in your Eggs, stirring it all the Time one Way till it comes to a thick Curd, then take it up, and pass it through a Hair Sieve, then beat it very well with a Spoon till cold, then put it into Dishes for Use.

To make Almond Cream.

TAKE a Quart of Cream, boil it with half a Nutmeg grated, and a Blade or two of Mace, and a bit of Lemon-peel, and sweeten it to your Taste; then blanch a quarter of a Pound of Almonds, beat them very fine with a Spoonful of Rose or Orange-flower Water, take the Whites of nine Eggs well beat, and strain them to your Almonds, beat them together, and rub them very well through a coarse Hair-sieve, mix all together with your Cream, set it on the Fire; stir it all one Way all the Time till it boils, pour it into your Cups or Dishes, and when it is cold serve it up.

A fine Cream.

TAKE a Pint of Cream, sweeten it to your Palate, grate a little Nutmeg, put in a Spoonful of Orange-flower Water and Rose-water, and two Spoonfuls of Sack, beat up four Eggs, but two Whites; stir all together one Way over the Fire till it is thick, have Cups ready and pour it in.

To make Ratafia Cream.

TAKE six large Laurel-leaves, and boil them in a Quart of thick Cream; when it is boil'd throw away the Leaves, and beat the Yolks of five Eggs with a little cold Cream, and Sugar to your Taste, then thicken the Cream with your Eggs, and set it over the Fire again, but don't let it boil, keep it stirring all the while one Way, and pour it into China Dishes; when it is cold its fit for Use.

To make whipt Cream.

TAKE a Quart of thick Cream, and the Whites of eight Eggs beat well, with half a Pint of Sack, mix it together, and sweeten it to your Taste with double refin'd Sugar.; you may perfume it if you please with a little Musk or Ambergrease tied in a Rag, and steep'd a little in the Cream, whip it up with a Whisk, and some Lemon-peel tied in the middle of the Whisk; take the Froth with a Spoon, and lay it in your Glasses or Basons.

To make Whipt Syllabubs.

TAKE a Quart of thick Cream, and half a Pint of Sack, the Juice of two Seville Oranges, or Lemons, grate in the Peel of two Lemons, half a Pound of double-refined Sugar, pour it into a broad earthen Pan, and whisk it well; but first sweeten some Red Wine, or Sack, and fill your Glasses as full as you chuse; then as the Froth rises, take it off with a Spoon, and lay it carefully into your Glasses, till they are as full as they will hold. Don't make these long before you use them. You may use Cyder sweetned, or any Wine you please, or Lemon, or Orange-whey made thus: Squeeze the Juice of a Lemon or Orange into a quarter of a Pint of Milk, when the Curd is hard, pour the Whey clear off, and sweeten it to your Palate. You may colour some with Juice of Spinage, some with Saffron, and some with Cochineal, just as you fancy.

To make Everlasting Syllabubs.

TAKE five half Pints of thick Cream, half a Pint of Rhenish, and half a Pint of Sack, the Juice of two large Seville Oranges; grate in just the yellow Rind of three Lemons, and a Pound of double-refined Sugar well beat, and sifted. Mix all together with a Spoonful of Orange-flower Water, beat it well together with a Whisk half an Hour, then with a Spoon fill your Glasses. These will keep

above

above a Week, and is better made the Day before. The beft Way to whip Syllabubs is, have a fine large Chocolate-mill, which you muft keep on purpofe, and a large deep Bowl to mill them in; it is both quicker done, and the Froth ftronger. The thin that is left at Bottom, have ready fome Calf's Foot Jelly boiled and clarified; there muft be nothing but the Calf's Foot boiled to a hard Jelly; when cold, take off the Fat, and clear it with the White of Eggs, run it through a Flannel Bag, and mix it with the clear, which you faved of the Syllibubs; fweeten it to your Palate, and give it a boil; then pour it into Bafons, or what you pleafe. When cold, turn it out, and it is a fine Flummery.

To make Hartfhorn Jelly.

BOIL half a Pound of Hartfhorn in three Quarts of Water over a gentle Fire, till it becomes a Jelly. If you take out a little to cool, and it hangs on the Spoon, it is enough. Strain it while it is hot, put it in a well-tinned Sauce-pan, put to it a Pint of Rhenifh Wine, and a quarter of a Pound of Loaf-fugar; beat the Whites of four Eggs or more to a Froth, ftir it all together that the Whites mix well with the Jelly, and pour it in, as if you were cooling it. Let it boil for two or three Minutes, then put in the Juice of three or four Lemons; let it boil a Minute or two longer. When it is finely curdled, and of a pure white Colour, have ready a Swanskin Jelly Bag over a China Bafon, pour in your Jelly, and pour it back again, till it is as clear as Rock-water; then fet a very clean China Bafon under, and have your Glaffes as clean as poffible, and with a clean Spoon fill your Glaffes. Have ready fome thin Rind of the Lemons, and when you have filled half your Glaffes, throw the Peel into the Bafon; and when the Jelly is all run out of the Bag, with a clean Spoon fill the reft of the Glaffes, and they will look of a fine Amber Colour. Now in putting in the Ingredients, there is no certain Rule; you muft put Lemon and Sugar to your Palate. Moft People love them fweet; and indeed they are good for nothing unlefs they are.

To make Ribband Jelly.

TAKE out the great Bones of four Calves Feet, and put the Feet into a Pot with ten Quarts of Water, three Ounces of Hartfhorn, three Ounces of Ifinglafs, a Nutmeg quarter'd, four Blades of Mace; then boil this till it comes to two Quarts, and ftrain it through a Flannel-bag, let it ftand twenty-four Hours, then fcrape off all the Fat from the Top very clean, then flice it, and put to it the Whites of fix Eggs beaten to Froth, boil it a little, and ftrain it again through a Flannel-bag, then run the Jelly into little high Glaffes, run every Colour as thick as your Finger, one Colour muft be thorough cold before you put another on, and that you put on muft not be but Blood-warm, for fear it mix together. You muft colour Red with Cochineal, Green with Spinage, Yellow with Saffron, Blue with Syrup of Violets, White with thick Cream, and fometimes the Jelly by itfelf. You may add Orange-flower Water, or Wine and Sugar, and Lemon if you pleafe; but this is all Fancy.

Calves Foot Jelly.

BOIL two Calves Feet in a Gallon of Water, till it comes to a Quart, then ftrain it, let it ftand till cold, skim off all the Fat clean, and take the Jelly up clean. If there be any Settling in the Bottom, leave it; put the Jelly into a Sauce-pan, with a Pint of Mountain Wine, half a Pound of Loaf-fugar, the Juice of four large Lemons, beat up fix or eight Whites of Eggs with a Whisk, then put them into the Sauce-pan, ftir all together well till it boils. Let it boil a few Minutes; have ready a large Flannel Bag, pour it in, it will run through quick; pour it in again till it runs clear, then have ready a large China Bafon, with the Lemon-peels cut as thin as poffible, let the Jelly run into that Bafon, and the Peels both gives it a fine Amber Colour, and alfo a Flavour; with a clean Silver Spoon fill your Glaffes.

To make Curran Jelly.

STRIP the Currants from the Stalks, put them in a Stone Jar, ftop it clofe, fet it in a Kettle of boiling Water half way the Jar, let it boil half an Hour, take it out and ftrain the Juice thro' a coarfe Hair-fieve. To a Pint of Juice put a Pound of Sugar, fet it over a fine clear, quick Fire, in your Preferving Pan, or a Bell-mettle Skillet, keep ftirring it all the Time till the Sugar is melted, then skim the Scum off as faft as it rifes; when your Jelly is very clear and fine, pour it into Gally-pots, when cold, cut white Paper juft the Bignefs of the Top of the Pot, and lay on the Jelly, then cover the Top clofe with white Paper, and prick it full of Holes, fet it in a dry Place, put fome into Glaffes and paper them.

To make Rasberry Giam.

TAKE a Pint of this Curran-Jelly, and a Quart of Rasberries, bruife them well together, fet them over a flow Fire, keeping them ftirring all the Time till it boils; let it boil five or fix Minutes, pour it into your Gally-pots, and paper as you do the Curran-jelly, and keep it for Ufe. They will keep fo two or three Years, and have the full Flavour of the Rasberry.

To make Hartshorn Flummery.

BOIL half a Pound of the Shavings of Hartshorn in three Pints of Water, till it comes to a Pint, then strain it through a Sieve into a Bason, and set it by to cool; then set it over the Fire, let it just melt, and put to it half a Pint of thick Cream, scalded and grown cold again, a quarter of a Pint of White-wine, and two Spoonfuls of Orange-flower Water, sweeten it with Sugar, and beat it for an Hour and half, or it will not mix well, nor look well; dip your Cups in Water before you put in your Flummery, or else it will not turn out well. It is best when it stands a Day or two before you turn it out; when you serve it up turn it out of the Cups, and stick blanch'd Almonds cut in long narrow Bits on the Top. You may eat them either with Wine or Cream.

A second Way to make Hartshorn Flummery.

TAKE three Ounces of Hartshorn and put it to boil, with two Quarts of Spring-water, let it simmer over the Fire six or seven Hours, till half the Water is consumed, or else put it in a Jug, and set it in the Oven with Houshold Bread, then strain it through a Sieve, and beat half a Pound of Almonds very fine, with some Orange-flower Water in the beating, and when they are beat, mix a little of your Jelly with it, and some fine Sugar, strain it out, and mix it with your other Jelly, stir it together till it is little more then Blood-warm, then pour it into half Pint Basons or Dishes for the Purpose, fill them but half full; but when you use them turn them out of the Dish as you do Flummery; if it does not come out clean, set your Bason a Minute or two in warm Water; you may stick Almonds in it, or not, just as you please. Eat it with Wine and Sugar, or make your Jelly this Way; put six Ounces of Hartshorn in a glazed Jug with a long Neck, and put to it three Pints of soft Water, cover the Top of the Jug close, and put a Weight on it to keep it steady; set it in a Pot or Kettle of Water twenty-four Hours, let it not boil, but be scalding hot; then strain it out, and make your Jelly.

To make Oatmeal Flummery.

TAKE some Oatmeal, put it into a broad deep Pan, then cover it with Water, stir it together, and let it stand twelve Hours, then pour off that Water clear, and put on a good deal of fresh Water, shift it again in twelve Hours, and so in twelve more; then pour off the Water clear, and strain the Oatmeal through a coarse Hair-sieve, and pour it into a Sauce-pan, keeping it stirring all the Time with a Stick till it boils and is very thick, then pour it into Dishes; when cold turn it into Plates, and eat it with what you please, either Wine and Sugar, or Beer and Sugar, or Milk; it eats very pretty with Cyder and Sugar.

You must observe to put a great deal of Water to the Oatmeal, and when you pour off the last Water, pour on just enough fresh as to strain the Oatmeal well. Some let it stand forty-eight Hours, some three Days, shifting the Water every twelve Hours; but that is as you love it for Sweetness or Tartness; Grotes once cut does better than Oatmeal. Mind to stir it together when you put in fresh Water.

To make a fine Syllabub from the Cow.

MAKE your Syllabub of either Cyder or Wine, sweeten it pretty sweet, and grate Nutmeg in, then milk the Milk into the Liquor; when this is done, pour over the Top half a Pint or Pint of Cream, according to the Quantity of Syllabub you make.

You may make this Syllabub at Home, only have new Milk; make it as hot as Milk from the Cow, and out of a Tea-pot or any such Thing, pour it in, holding your Hand very high.

To make a Hedge-Hog.

TAKE two Pounds of blanched Almonds, beat them well in a Mortar with a little Canary and Orange-flower Water, to keep them from oiling. Make them into stiff Paste, then beat in the Yolks of twelve Eggs, leave out five of the Whites, put to it a Pint of Cream, sweeten it with Sugar, put in half a Pound of sweet Butter melted, set it on a Furnace or slow Fire, and keep it constantly stirring, till it is stiff enough to be made into the Form of an Hedge-Hog; then stick it full of blanched Almonds, slit and stuck up like the Bristles of a Hedge-Hog, then put it into a Dish, take a Pint of Cream, and the Yolks of four Eggs beat up, sweetned with Sugar to your Palate. Stir them together over a slow Fire till it is quite hot, then pour it round the Hedge-Hog in the Dish, and let it stand till it is cold, and serve it up.——Or a rich Calf's Foot Jelly made clear and good, pour into the Dish round the Hedge-Hog; and when it is cold, it looks pretty, and makes a pretty Dish; or looks pretty in the Middle of a Table for Supper.

To make French Flummery.

TAKE a Quart of Cream, and half an Ounce of Isinglass; beat it fine, and stir it into the Cream. Let it boil softly over a slow Fire a quarter of an Hour, keep it stirring all the time; then take it off the Fire, sweeten it to your Palate, and put in a Spoonful of Rose-water, and a Spoonful of Orange-flower Water, strain it, and pour it into a Glass or Bason, or just what you please, and when it is cold, turn it out. It makes a fine Side-dish. You may eat it with Cream, Wine, or what you please. Lay it round baked Pears; it both looks very pretty, and eats fine.

A Buttered Tort.

TAKE eight or ten large Codlings and scald them, when cold skin them, take the Pulp and beat it as fine as you can with a Silver Spoon, then mix in the Yolks of six Eggs, and the Whites of four beat all well together, a Seville Orange squeez'd in the Juice, and shread the Rind as fine as possible, some grated Nutmeg and Sugar to your Taste; melt some fine fresh Butter, and beat up with it according as it wants, till it is all like a fine thick Cream, then make a fine Puff-paste, have a large Tin Patty that will just hold it, cover the Patty with the Paste, and pour in the Ingredients, don't put any Cover on, bake it a quarter of an Hour, then slip it out of the Patty on to a Dish, and throw fine Sugar well beat all over it. It is a very pretty Side-dish for a second Course. You may make this of any large Apple you please.

The Flooting Island; a pretty Dish for the Middle of a Table at a second Course, or for Supper.

TAKE a Soop Dish according to the Size and Quantity you would make; but a pretty deep Glass Dish is best, and set it on a China Dish, first take a Quart of the thickest Cream you can get, make it pretty sweet with fine Sugar, pour in a Gill of Sack, grate the yellow Rind of a Lemon in, and mill the Cream till it is all of a thick Froth, then as carefully as you can, pour the thin from the Froth into a Dish; take a French Role, or as many as you want, cut it as thin as you can, lay a Layer of that as light as possible on the Cream, then a Layer of Currant-jelly, then a very thin Layer of Role, and then Hartshorn-jelly, then French Role, and over that whip your Froth, which you saved off the Cream very well milled up, and lay at Top as high as you can heap it; and as for the Rim of the Dish set it round with Fruit or Sweetmeats according to your Fancy, this looks very pretty in the middle of a Table with Candles round it, and you may make it of as many different Colours as you fancy, and according to what Jellies and Giams, or Sweet-meats you have; or at the Bottom of your Dish you may put the thickest Cream you can get; but that is as you fancy.

CHAP. XVII.

Of Made Wines, Brewing, French Bread, Muffins, &c.

To make Raisin Wine.

PUT into a large Vessel, or Mashing-Tub, a Hogshead of Water, and throw into it two hundred of Raisins, let them steep a Fortnight, stirring them every Day; then pour off all the Liquor, and press the Raisins. Put both Liquors together into a very nice clean Vessel, that will just hold it, for it must be full. Let it stand till it has done hissing, or making the least Noise; then stop it close, and let it stand six Months. Peg it, and if you find it quite clear, rack it off into another Vessel, stop it close, and let it stand three Months longer, then bottle it; and when you use it, rack it off into a Decanter.

To make Elder Wine.

PICK the Elderberries when full ripe, put them into a Stone-Jar, and set them in the Oven, or a Kettle of boiling Water, till the Jar is hot through; then take them out and strain them through a coarse Cloth, wringing the Berries, and put the Juice into a clean Kettle: To every Quart of Juice, put a Pound of fine *Lisbon* Sugar, let it boil, and skim it well. When it is clear and fine, pour it into a Jarr; when cold, cover it close, and keep it till you make Raisin Wine; then when you tun your Wine, to every Gallon of Wine, put half a Pint of the Elder-syrup.

Orange Wine.

TAKE twelve Pounds of the best Powder-sugar, with the Whites of eight or ten Eggs well beaten, into six Gallons of Spring-water, and boil it three quarters of an Hour. When it is cold, put it into six Spoonfuls of Yeast, and also the Juice of twelve Lemons, which being pared must stand with two Pounds of white Sugar in a Tankard, and in the Morning skim off the Top, and then put it into the Water. Then add the Juice and Rinds of fifty Oranges, but not the white Part of the Rinds; and so let it work all together two Days and two Nights; then add two Quarts of Rhenish or White Wine, and put it into your Vessel.

To make Orange Wine with Raisins.

TAKE thirty Pounds of new Malaga Raisins pick'd clean, chop them small, you must have twenty large Sevile Oranges, ten of them you must pare as thin as for preserving; boil about eight Gallons of soft Water till a third Part be consumed, let it cool a little, then put five Gallons of it hot upon your Raisins and Orange-peel; stir it well together, cover it up, and when it is cold let it stand five Days, stirring it up once or twice a Day, then pass it through a Hair-sieve, and with a Spoon press it as dry as you can, and put it up in a Runlet fit for it, and put to it the Rinds of the other ten Oranges, cut as thin as the first; then make a Syrrup of the Juices of the twenty Oranges with a Pound of white Sugar. It must be made the Day before you tun it up, stir it well together, and stop it close, let it stand two Months to clear, then bottle it up. It will keep three Years, and is the better for keeping.

To make Elder-Flower Wine very like Fontineac.

TAKE six Gallons of Spring-water, twelve Pounds of white Sugar, six Pounds of Raisins of the Sun chopped, boil these together one Hour, then take the Flower of Elder, when they are falling, and rub them off to the Quantity of half a Peck. When the Liquor is cold, put them in, and the next Day put in the Juice of three Lemons, and four Spoonfuls of good Ale-Yeast. Let it stand covered up two Days, then strain it off, and put it in a Vessel fit for it. To every Gallon of Wine, put a Quart of Rhenish, and put your Bung lightly on a Fortnight, then stop it down close. Let it stand six Months; and if you find it is fine, bottle it off.

Gooseberry Wine.

GATHER your Gooseberries in dry Weather, when they are half ripe, pick them, and bruise a Peck in a Tub, with a wooded Mallet; then take a Horse-hair Cloth, and press them as much as possible, without breaking the Seeds. When you have pressed out all the Juice, to every Gallon of Gooseberry, put three Pounds of fine dry Powder-sugar, stir it together till the Sugar is all dissolved, then put it in a Vessel or Cask, which must be quite full. If ten or twelve Gallons, let it stand a Fortnight; if a twenty Gallon Cask, let it stand five Weeks. Set it in a cool Place, then draw it off from the Lees, clear the Vessel of the Lees, and pour in the clear Liquor again. If it be a ten Gallon Cask, let it stand three Months; if a twenty Gallon, four or five Months, then bottle it off.

To make Curran Wine.

GATHER your Currans of a fine dry Day, when the Fruit is full ripe, strip them, put them in a large Pan, and bruise them with a wooden Pestle, till they are all bruised. Let them stand in a Pan or Tub twenty-four Hours to foment; then run it through a Hair-Sieve, and don't let your Hand touch your Liquor. To every Gallon of this Liquor, put two Pounds and a half of white Sugar, stir it well together, and put it into your Vessel. To every six Gallons, put in a Quart of Brandy, and let it stand six Weeks. If it is fine, bottle it; if it is not, draw it off, as clear as you can, into another Vessel, or large Bottles; and in a Fortnight, bottle it in small Bottles.

To make Cherry Wine.

PULL your Cherries when full ripe, pull off the Stalks, and press them thro' a Hair-sieve; to every Gallon of Liquor put two Pounds of lump Sugar beat fine, stir it together and put it into a Vessel, it must be full; when it has done working and making any Noise, stop it close for three Months, and bottle it off.

Birch Wine.

THE Season for procuring the Liquor from the Birch-Trees is in the Beginning of *March*, while the Sap is rising, and before the Leaves shout out; for when the Sap is come forward, and the Leaves appear, the Juice by being long digested in the Bark, grows thick and colour'd, which before was thin and clear.

The Method of procuring the Juice is by boring Holes in the Body of the Tree, and putting in Fossets, which are commonly made of the Branches of Elder, the Pith being taken out, you may without hurting the Tree, if large, tap it in several Places, four or five at a Time, and by that means save from a good many Trees several Gallons every Day; if you have not enough in one Day, the Bottles in which it drops must be cork'd close, and rosin'd or wax'd; however make Use of it as soon as you can.

Take

Take the Sap and boil it as long as any Scum rises, skimming it all the Time; to every Gallon of Liquor put four Pound of good Sugar, and the thin Peel of a Lemon, boil it afterwards half an Hour scumming it very well, pour it into a clean Tub, and when it is almost cold, set it to work with Yeast spread on a Toast, let it stand five or six Days, stirring it often; then take such a Cask as will hold the Liquor, fire a large Match dipt in Brimstone, and throw it into the Cask, stop it close till the Match is extinguish'd, and tun your Wine, lay the Bung on light till you find it has done working, then stop it close and keep it three Months, then bottle it off.

Quince Wine.

GATHER the Quinces when dry and full ripe, take twenty large Quinces, wipe them clean with a coarse Cloth, and grate them with a large Grater or Rasp, as near the Core as you can, but none of the Core; boil a Gallon of Spring-Water, throw in your Quinces, let it boil softly about a quarter of an Hour, then strain them well into an Earthern Pan on two Pound of double refin'd Sugar, pare the Peel of two large Lemons, throw in and squeeze the Juice in thro' a Sieve, stir it about till it is very cool, then toast a little Bit of Bread very thin and brown, rub a little Yeast on it, let it stand close cover'd twenty-four Hours, then take out the Toast and Lemon, and put it up in a Cag, keep it three Months, then bottle it. If you make a twenty Gallon Cask let it stand six Months before you bottle it; when you strain your Quinces you are to wring them hard in a coarse Cloth.

To make Cowslip or Clary Wine.

TAKE six Gallons of Water, twelve Pounds of Sugar, the Juice of six Lemons, the Whites of four Eggs beat very well, put all together in a Kettle, let it boil half an Hour, scim it very well, take a Peck of Cowslips, if dry ones half a Peck, put them into a Tub with the thin peeling of the six Lemons, then pour on the boiling Liquor, and stir them about; when almost cold, put in a thin Toast baked dry, and rubb'd with Yeast, let it stand two or three Days to work. If you put in before you tun six Ounces of Syrrup of Citron or Lemons, with a Quart of Rhenish Wine, it will be a great Addition; the third Day strain it off, and squeeze the Cowslips thro' a coarse Cloth, then strain it thro' a Flannel-bag and tun it up, lay the bung loose for two or three Days to see if it works, and if it don't bung it down tight, let it stand three Months, then bottle it.

To make Turnep Wine.

TAKE a good many Turnips, pare them, slice them, and put them in a Cyder-press, and press out all the Juice very well. To every Gallon of Juice, have three Pounds of Lump Sugar, have a Vessel ready, just big enough to hold the Juice, put your Sugar into the Vessel; and also to every Gallon of Juice half a Pint of Brandy. Pour in the Juice, and lay something over the Bung for a Week, to see if it works. If it does, you must not bung it down till it has done working, then stop it close for three Months, and draw it off into another Vessel. When it is fine, bottle it off.

Rasberry Wine.

TAKE some fine ripe Rasberries, bruise them with the Back of a Spoon, then strain them through a Flannel Bag into a Stone-Jar. To each Quart of Juice, put a Pound of double refined Sugar, stir it well together, and cover it close; Let it stand three Days, then pour it off clear. To a Quart of Juice put two Quarts of White Wine, bottle it off, it will be fit to drink in a Week. Brandy made thus is a very fine Dram, and a much better Way than steeping the Rasberries.

Rules for Brewing.

CARE must be taken in the first place to have the Malt clean; and after it is grinded, it ought to stand four or five Days.

For strong October, five Quarters of Malt to three Hogsheads, and twenty-four Pounds of Hops. This will afterwards make two Hogsheads of good keeping small Beer, allowing five Pounds of Hops to it.

For good middling Beer, a Quartern of Malt makes a Hogshead of Ale, and one of Small Beer; or it will make three Hogsheads of good Small Beer, allowing eight Pounds of Hops. This will keep all the Year; or it will make twenty Gallons of strong Ale, and two Hogsheads of small Bear, that will keep all the Year.

If you intend your Ale to keep a great while, allow a Pound of Hops to every Bushel; if to keep six Months, five Pounds to a Hogshead; if for present drinking, three Pounds to a Hogshead, the softest and cleanest Water you can get.

Observe the Day before to have all your Vessels very clean, and never use your Tubs for any Use, except to make Wines.

Let your Casks be very clean the Day before with boiling Water; and if your Bung is big enough, scrub them well with a little Birch-Broom or Brush; but if they be very bad, take out the Heads, and

let

let them be ſcrubed clean with a Hand-Bruſh and Sand, and Fuller's Earth. Put on the Head again and ſcald them well, and throw into the Barrel a Piece of unſlacked Lime, and ſtop the Bung cloſe.

The firſt Copper of Water, when it boils, pour into your Maſh-Tub, and let it be cool enough to ſee your Face in; then put in your Malt, and let it be well maſhed, have a Copper of Water boiling in the mean time, and when your Malt is well maſhed, fill your Maſhing-tub; ſtir it well again, and cover it over with the Sacks. Let it ſtand three Hours, then ſet a broad ſhallow Tub under the Cock, let it run very ſoftly, and if it is thick, throw it up again, till it runs fine; then throw a Handful of Hops in the under Tub, and let the Maſh run into it, and fill your Tubs till all is run off. Have Water boiling in the Copper, and lay as much more on as you have Occaſion for, allowing one third for boiling and waſte. Let that ſtand an Hour, boiling more Water to fill the Maſh-tub for ſmall Beer; let the Fire down a little, and put it into Tubs enough to fill your Maſh. Let the ſecond Maſh be run off, and fill your Copper with the firſt Wort; put in Part of your Hops, and make it boil quick. About an Hour is long enough; and when it is half boiled, throw in a Handful of Salt. Have a clean white Wand, and dip it into the Copper, and if the Wort feels clammy, it is boiled enough; then ſlacken your Fire, and take off your Wort. Have ready a large Tub, put two Sticks a-croſs, and ſet your ſtraining Basket over the Tub on the Sticks, and ſtrain your Wort through it. Put your other Wort on to boil with the reſt of the Hops; let your Maſh be ſtill covered again with Water, and thin your Wort that is cooled in as many things as you can; for the thinner it lies, and the quicker it cools, the better. When quite cool, put it into the Tunning-tub; mind to throw a Handful of Salt into every Boil; when the Maſh has ſtood an Hour, draw it off; then fill your Maſh with cold Water, take off the Wort in the Copper, and order it as before. When cool, add to it the firſt in the Tub; ſo ſoon as you empty one Copper, fill the other, ſo boil your ſmall Beer well. Let the laſt Maſh run off; and when both are boiled with freſh Hops, order them as the two firſt Boilings; when cool, empty the Maſh-tub, and put the ſmall Beer to work there. When cool enough, work it, ſet a wooden Bowl of Yeaſt in the Beer, and it will work over with a little of the Beer in the Boil. Stir your Tun up every twelve Hours, let it ſtand two Days, then tun it taking off the Eaſt. Fill your Veſſels full, and ſave ſome to fill your Barrels; let it ſtand till it has done working, then lay on your Bung lightly for a Fortnight, after that ſtop it as cloſe as you can. Mind you have a Vent-peg at the Top of the Veſſel in warm Weather, open it, and if your Drink hiſſes, as it often will, looſen it till it has done, then ſtop it cloſe again. If you can boil your Ale in one boiling it is beſt, if your Copper will allow of it; if not, boil it as Conveniency ſerves. The Strength of your Beer muſt be according to the Malt you allow more or leſs, there is no certain Rule.

When you come to draw your Beer, and find it is not fine, draw off a Gallon, and ſet it on the Fire, with two Ounces of Iſinglaſs cut ſmall and beat. Diſſolve it in the Beer over the Fire; when it is all melted, let it ſtand till it is cold, and pour it in at the Bung, which muſt lay looſe on till it has done fomenting, then ſtop it cloſe for a Month.

Take great Care your Casks are not muſty, or have any ill Taſte; if they have, it is the hardeſt thing in the World to ſweeten them.

You are to waſh your Cask with cold Water before you ſcald them, and they ſhould lye a Day or two ſoaking, and clean them well, then ſcald them.

The beſt Thing for Rope Beer.

MIX two handfuls of Bean-flour, and one handful of Salt, throw this into a Kilderkin of Beer; don't ſtop it cloſe till it has done fomenting, then let it ſtand a Month and draw it off, but ſometimes nothing will do with it.

When a Barrel of Beer is turn'd ſour.

TO a Kilderkin of Beer throw in at the Bung a Quart of Oatmeal, lay the Bung on looſe two or three Days, then ſtop it down cloſe, and let it ſtand a Month; ſome throws in a Piece of Chalk as big as a Turkey's Egg, and when it has done working ſtop it cloſe for a Month, then tap it.

To make French Bread.

TAKE three Quarts of Water and one of Milk, in Winter ſcalding hot, in Summer a little more than Milk warm, ſeaſon it well with Salt, then take a Pint and half of good Ale-yeaſt not bitter, lay it in a Gallon of Water the Night before, pour it off the Water, ſtir in your Yeaſt into the Milk and Water, then with your Hand break in a little more than a Quarter of a Pound of Butter, work it well till it is diſſolv'd, then beat up two Eggs in a Baſon, and ſtir them in, have about a Peck and half of Flour, mix it with your Liquor, in Winter make your Dough pretty ſtiff, in Summer more ſlack; ſo that you may uſe a little more or leſs of Flour, according to the Stiffneſs of your Dough, mix it well, but the leſs you work it the better, make it into Roles, and have a very quick Oven, but not to burn, when they have lain about a quarter of an Hour, turn them on the other ſide, let them lie about a quarter longer, take them out and raſp them, ſtir your Liquor into the Flour as you do for Pye Cruſt; after your Dough is made cover it with a Cloth, and let it lie to riſe while the Oven is heating.

To make Muffings and Oat-Cakes.

TO a Bushel of *Hertfordshire* white Flour, take a Pint and half of good Ale-yeast, from pale Malt if you can get it, because it is whitest; let the Yeast lie in Water all Night, the next Day pour off the Water clear, make two Gallons of Water just Milk warm, not to scald your Yeast, and two Ounces of Salt, mix your Water, Yeast and Salt well together for about a quarter of an Hour, then strain it, and mix up your Dough as light as possible, and let it lie in your Trough an Hour to rise, then with your Hand roll it, and pull it into little Pieces about as big as a large Walnut, roll them with your Hand like a Ball, lay them on your Table, and as fast as you do them lay a Piece of Flannel over them, and be sure to keep your Dough cover'd with Flannel; when you have rolled out all your Dough, begin to bake the first; and by that Time they will be spread out in the right Form; lay them on your Iron, as one Side begins to change Colour turn the other, and take great Care they don't burn, or be too much discolour'd; but that you will be a Judge off in two or three Makings. Take Care the middle of the Iron is not too hot, as it will be, but then you may put a Brick-bat or two in the middle of the Fire to slacken the Heat. The Thing you bake on must be made thus. Build a Place just as if you was going to set a Copper, and in the Stead of a Copper a Piece of Iron all over the Top fix'd in Form, just the same as the Bottom of an Iron Pot, and make your Fire underneath with Coal as in a Copper; observe, Muffings are made the same Way, only this, when you pull them to Pieces roll them in a good deal of Flour, and with a Rolling-pin roll them thin, cover them with a Piece of Flannel, and they will rise to a proper Thickness; and if you find them too big or too little, you must roll Dough accordingly, these must not be the least discolour'd.

And when you eat them, toast them with a Fork crisp on both Sides, then with your Hand pull them open, and they will be like a Honey-Comb; lay in as much Butter as you intend to use, then clap them together again, and set it by the Fire, when you think the Butter is melted turn them, that both Sides may be butter'd alike, but don't touch them with a Knife, either to spread or cut them open, if you do they will be as heavy as Lead, only when they are quite butter'd and done, you may cut them across with a Knife.

Note, Some Flour will soak up a Quart or three Pints more Water then other Flour, then you must add more Water, or shake in more Flour in the making up, for the Dough must be as light as possible.

Receipt for making Bread without Barm, by the Help of a Leaven.

TAKE a Lump of Dough, about two Pounds of your last making, which has been raised by Barm, keep it by you in a wooden Vessel, and cover it well with Flour. This is your Leaven; then the Night before you intend to bake, put the said Leaven to a Peck of Flour, and work them well together with warm Water. Let it lye in a dry wooden Vessel, well covered with a Linnen Cloth and a Blanket, and keep it in a warm Place. This Dough kept warm will rise against next Morning, and will be sufficient to mix with two or three Bushels of Flour, being worked up with warm Water and a little Salt. When it is well worked up, and thoroughly mixed with all the Flour, let it be well covered with the Linen and Blanket, until you find it rise; then knead it well, and work it up into Bricks, or Loaves, making the Loaves broad, and not so thick and high as is frequently done, by which means the Bread will be better baked: Then bake your Bread.

Always keep by you two or more Pounds of the Dough of your last baking, well cover'd with Flour to make Leaven to serve from one baking Day to another; the more Leaven is put to the Flour the lighter and spongier the Bread will be, the fresher the Leaven, the Bread will be less sour.

From the Dublin *Society.*

A Method to preserve a large Stock of Yeast, which will keep and be of Use for several Months, either to make Bread or Cakes.

WHEN you have Yeast in Plenty, take a Quantity of it, stir and work it well with a Whisk until it becomes liquid and thin, then get a large wooden Platter, Cooler or Tub, clean and dry, and with a soft Brush lay a thin Layer of the Yeast on the Tub, and turn the Mouth downwards that no Dust may fall upon it, but so that the Air may get under to dry it. When that Coat is very dry, then lay on another Coat, and let it dry, and so go on to put one Coat upon another, till you have a sufficient Quantity, even to two or three Inches thick, to serve for several Months, always taking Care the Yeast in the Tub be very dry before you lay more on; when you have occasion to make Use of this Yeast, cut a Piece off, and lay it in warm Water, stir it together, and it will be fit for Use; if it is for Brewing, take a large handful of Birch tied together, and dip it into the Yeast and hang it up to dry, take great Care no Dust comes to it, and so you may do as many as you please, and when your Beer is fit to set to work, throw in one of these, and it will make it work as well as if you had fresh Yeast; you must whip it about in the Wort and then let it lie, when the Fat works well take out the Broome and dry it again, it will do for the next Brewing.

CHAP.

CHAP. XVIII.

Jarring Cherries, and Preserves, &c.

To jar Cherries Lady North's Way.

TAKE twelve Pounds of Cherries, then stone them, put them in your Preserving-pan, with three Pounds of double-refined Sugar, and a Quart of Water, then set them on the Fire, till they are scalding hot; take them off a little while, and set them on the Fire again, and boil them till they are tender, then sprinkle them with half a Pound of double-refined Sugar pounded, and skim them clean. Put them all together in a China Bowl, let them stand in the Syrup three Days, then drain them through a Sieve, and take them one by one, with the Holes downwards on a Wicker-Sieve, and set them in a Stove to dry, and as they dry, turn them upon clean Sieves. When they are dry enough, put a clean white Sheet of Paper in a Preserving-pan, and then put all the Cherries in, with another clean white Sheet of Paper on the Top of them; then cover them close with a Cloth, and set them over a cool Fire till they sweat; then take them off the Fire, and let them stand till they are cold, then put them in Boxes or Jars to keep.

To dry Cherries.

TO four Pounds of Cherries, put one Pound of Sugar, put just as much Water to the Sugar as will wet it. When it is melted, make it boil; stone your Cherries, put them in, and make them boil. Skim them two or three times, take them off, and let them stand in the Syrup two or three Day, then boil your Syrup, and put to them again; but don't boil your Cherries any more. Let them stand three or four Days longer, then take them out and lay them in Sieves to dry; lay them in the Sun, or in a slow Oven to dry. When dry, lay them in Rows in Papers, and so a Row of Cherries, and a Row of white Paper in Boxes.

Orange Marmalade.

TAKE the best Seville Oranges, cut them in Quarters, grate them to take out the Bitterness, put them in Water, which you must shift twice or thrice a Day for three Days; then boil them, shifting the Water till they are tender, then shread them very small, then pick out the Skins and Seeds from the Meat which you pulled out, and put it to the Peel that is shread; and to a Pound of that Pulp take a Pound of double-refined Sugar. Wet your Sugar with Water, and boil it up to a candy Height, (with a very quick Fire) which you may know by the dropping of it; for it hangs like a Hair; then take off the Fire, put in your Pulp, stir it well together, then set it on the Embers, and stir it till it is thick, but let it not boil. If you would have it cut like Marmalade, add some Jelly of Pippins, and allow Sugar for it.

White Marmalade.

PARE and core the Quinces as fast as you can, and take to a Pound of Quinces (being cut in Pieces less then half Quarters) three quarters of a Pound of double refin'd Sugar beat small, throw half the Sugar on the raw Quinces, set it on a very slow Fire, till the Sugar is melted, and the Quinces tender, then put in the rest of the Sugar, and boil it up as fast as you can, and when it is almost enough, put in some Jelly and boil it apace, then put it up, when it is quite cold cover it with white Paper.

To preserve Oranges whole.

TAKE the best *Bermudas* or *Seville* Oranges you can get, and pare them with a Penknife very thin, and lay your Oranges in Water three or four Days, shifting them every Day; then put them in a Kettle with fair Water, and put a Board on them to keep them down in the Water, and have a Skillet on the Fire with Water, that may be ready to supply the Kettle with boiling Water; as it wastes it must be filled up three or four Times, while the Oranges are doing; for they will take up seven or eight Hours boiling; they must be boiled till a Wheat-straw will run through them, then take them out, and scoop the Seeds out of them very carefully, by making a little Hole in the Top, and weigh them, to every Pound of Oranges put a Pound and three quarters of double refined Sugar, beat well and sifted thro' a clean lawn Sieve, fill your Oranges with Sugar, and strow some on them, let them lie a little while, and make your Jelly thus.

Take two Dozen of Pippins or John Apples, and slice them into Water, and when they are boiled tender, strain the Liquor from the Pulp, and to every Pound of Orange you must have a Pint and half of this Liquor, and put to it three quarters of the Sugar you left in filling the Orange, set it on the Fire and let it boil, and skim it well, and put it in a clean Earthern Pan till it is cold, then put it in your Skillet, put in your Oranges, and with a small Bodkin job your Oranges as they are a boiling to let the Syrup into them, strew on the rest of your Sugar whilst they are a boiling, and

when

when they look clear take them up, and put them in your Glasses, but one in a Glass just fit for them, and boil the Syrup till it is almost a Jelly, then fill up your Glasses; when they are cold, paper them up, and keep them in a dry Place.

To make red Marmalade.

SCALD the Quinces tender in Water, then cut them in quarters and core and pare the Pieces; to four Pounds of Quince put three Pounds of Sugar, and four Pints of Water; boil the Sugar and Water to a Syrrup, then put in the Quinces and cover it, let it stand all Night over a very little Fire, but not to boil; when they are red enough, put in a Porringer full of Jelly or more, and boil them up as fast as you can, when it is enough put it up, but do not break the Quince too much.

Red Quinces whole.

TAKE six of the finest Quinces, core and scald them tender, drain them from the Water, and when they are cold pare them; then take their Weight in good Sugar, and a Pint of Water to every Pound of Sugar, boil it to a Syrup, and skim it well; then put in the Quinces, and let them stand all Night; when they are red enough, boil them as the Marmalade, with two Porringers full of Jelly. When they are as soft as you can run a Straw thro' them, put them into Glasses, let the Liquor boil till it is a Jelly, and then pour it over the Quinces.

Jelly for the Quinces.

TAKE some of the lesser Quinces and wipe them with a clean coarse Cloth; cut them in Quarters, and put as much Water as will cover them, let them boil apace, till it is strong of the Quinces, then strain it thro' a Jelly-bag; if it be for white Quince pick out the Seeds, but none of the Cores nor Quinces pared.

To make Conserve of Red Roses, or any other Flowers.

TAKE Rose-Buds, or any other Flowers, and pick them, and cut off the white Part from the red, and put the red Flowers and sift them through a Sieve to take out the Seeds; then weigh them, and to every Pound of Flowers, take two Pounds and half of Loaf-sugar; beat the Flowers pretty fine in a Stone mortar, then by degrees put the Sugar to them, and beat it very well, till it is well incorporated together; then put it into Gallipots, and tye it over with Paper, and over that a Leather, and it will keep seven Years.

To make Conserve of Hips.

GATHER Hips before they grow soft, cut off the Heads and Stalks, slit them in Halves, and take out all the Seeds and White that is in them very clean, then put them into an earthen Pan, and stir them every Day, or they will grow mouldy. Let them stand till they are soft enough, to rub them through a coarse Hair-sieve, as the Pulp comes take it off the Sieve, they are a dry Berry, and will require Pains to rub them through; then add its Weight in Sugar, mix them well together without boiling; keep it in deep Gallypots for Use.

To make Syrup of Roses.

INFUSE three Pounds of Damask-Rose-leaves in a Gallon of warm Water, in a well glazed earthen Pot, with a narrow Mouth, for eight Hours, which stop so close, that none of the Virtue may exhale. When they have infused so long, heat the Water again, squeeze them out, and put in three Pounds more of Rose-leaves, to infuse for eight Hours more, then press them out very hard; then to every Quart of this Infusion, add four Pounds of fine Sugar, and boil it to a Syrup.

To make Syrup of Cittron.

PARE and slice your Citrons thin, lay them in a Bason, with Layers of fine Sugar. The next Day pour off the Liquor into a Glass, skim it, and clarify it over a gentle Fire.

To make Syrup of Clove Gilliflewers.

CLIP your Gilliflowers, and sprinkle them with fair Water, put them into an earthen Pot, stop it up very close, and set it in a Kettle of Water, and let it boil for two Hours; then strain out the Juice, put a Pound and half of Sugar to a Pint of juice, put it into a Skillet, set it on the Fire, keeping it stirring till the Sugar is all melted; but let it not boil, then set it by to cool, and put it into Bottles.

To make Syrup of Peach Blossoms.

INFUSE Peach Blossoms in hot Water, as much as will handsomely cover them. Let them stand in Balneo, or in Sand, for twenty-four Hours covered close; then strain out the Flowers from the

Liquor,

Liquor, and put in fresh Flowers. Let them stand to infuse as before, then strain them out, and to the Liquor put fresh Peach-Blossoms the third time, and if you please, a fourth time. Then to every Pound of your Infusion, add two Pounds of double-refined Sugar; and setting it in Sand or Balneo, make a Syrup, which keep for Use.

To make Syrup of Quinces.

GRATE Quinces, pass their Pulp through a Cloth to extract their Juice, set their Juice in the Sun to settle, or before the Fire, and by that means clarify it: For every four Ounces of this Juice, take a Pound of Sugar, boiled to a blown Degree. If the putting in the Juices of the Quinces should check the boiling of the Sugar too much, give the Syrup some boiling, till it becomes pearled; then take it off the Fire, and when it is cold, put it into the Bottles.

To preserve Apricots.

TAKE your Apricots, stone and pare them thin, and take their Weight in double-refined Sugar beaten and sifted, and put your Apricots in a Silver Cup or Tankard, and cover them over with Sugar, and let them stand so all Night. The next Day put them in a Preserving-pan, and set them on a gentle Fire, and let them simmer a little while, then let them boil till tender and clear, taking them off sometimes to turn and skim. Keep them under the Liquor as they are doing, and with a small clean Bodkin or great Needle, jobb them sometimes, that the Syrup may penetrate into them. When they are enough, take them up, and put them in Glasses. Boil and skim your Syrup; and when it is cold, put it on your Apricots.

To preserve Damsons Whole.

TAKE some Damsons and cut them in Pieces, and put them in a Skillet over the Fire, with as much Water as will cover them. When they are boiled, and the Liquor pretty strong, strain it out: Add for every Pound of your whole Damsons wiped clean, a Pound of single refined Sugar, put the third Part of your Sugar into the Liquor, and set it over the Fire, and when it simmers, put in your Damsons. Let them have one good boil, and take them off for half an Hour, covered up close; then set them on again, and let them simmer over the Fire, after turning them, then take them out and put them in a Bason, and strew all the Sugar that was left on them, and pour the hot Liquor over them, and cover them up, and let them stand till next Day; then boil them up again till they are enough. Take them up, and put them in Pots; boil the Liquor till it jellies, and pour it on them when it is almost cold, so paper them up.

To candy any Sort of Flowers.

TAKE the best treble-refined Sugar, break it into Lumps, and dip it, Piece by Piece, in Water, put them into a Vessel of Silver, and melt them over the Fire. When it just boils, strain it, and set it on the Fire again, and let it boil, till it draws in Hairs, which you may perceive by holding up your Spoon; then put in your Flowers, and set them in Cups or Glasses; and when it is of a hard Candy, break it in Lumps, and lay it as high as you please. Dry it in a Stow, or in the Sun, and it will look like Sugar-Candy.

To preserve Gooseberries whole without stoning.

TAKE the largest preserving Gooseberries, and pick off the black Eye, but not the Stalk, then set them over the Fire in a Pot of Water to scald, cover them very close to scald, but not boil or break; and when they are tender take them up into cold Water, then take a Pound and half of double refin'd Sugar to a Pound of Gooseberries, clarify the Sugar with Water; a Pint to a Pound of Sugar, and when your Syrup is cold, put your Gooseberries single in your Preserving-pan, and put the Syrup to them, and set them on a gentle Fire, and let them boil, but not too fast, lest they break, and when they have boiled, and you perceive the Sugar has enter'd them, take them off, cover them with white Paper, and set them by till the next Day. Then take them out of the Syrup, and boil the Syrup till it begins to be ropy, skim it, and put it to them again, and set them on a gentle Fire, and let them preserve gently, till you perceive the Syrup will rope; then take them off, set them by till they are cold, cover them with Paper, then boil some Gooseberries in fair Water, and when the Liquor is strong enough strain it out, let it stand to settle, and to every Pint take a Pound of double-refin'd Sugar, and make a Jelly of it, and put the Gooseberries in Glasses, and when they are cold, cover them with the Jelly, the next Day paper them wet, and then half dry the Paper that goes in the inside, it closes down better, and then white Paper over the Glass; set it in your Stove or a dry Place.

To preserve white Walnuts.

FIRST pare your Walnuts till the White appears and nothing else, you must be very careful in the doing them that they don't turn black, and as fast as you do them, throw them into Salt and Water, and let them lye till your Sugar is ready. Take three Pounds of good Loaf Sugar, put it into your Preserving-pan, set it over a Charcoal Fire, and put as much Water as will just wet the Sugar,

let

let it boil, then have ready ten or a dozen Whites of Eggs strain'd and beat up to a Froth, cover your Sugar with the Froth as it boils, then skim it, and boil it, and skim it, till it is as clear as Chrystal, then throw in your Walnuts, and just give them a Boil till they are tender, then take them out, and lay them in a Dish to cool, when cool put them into your Preserving-Pan, and when the Sugar is as warm as Milk pour it over them; when quite cold paper them down.

Thus clear your Sugar for all Preserves, Apricots, Peaches, Gooseberries, Currants, &c.

To preserve Walnuts green.

WIPE them very clean, and lay them in strong Salt and Water twenty-four Hours, then take them out and wipe them very clean, have ready a Skillet of Water boiling, throw them in, and let them boil a Minute, and take them out, lay them on a coarse Cloth, and boil your Sugar as above; then just give your Walnuts a scald in the Sugar, take them up and lay them to cool, put them in your Preserving-pot, and pour on your Syrrup as above.

A nice Way to preserve Peaches.

PUT your Peaches in boiling Water, and just give them a Scald, but don't let them boil, take them out and put them in cold Water, then dry them in a Sieve, and put them in long wide mouth Bottles; to half a Dozen Peaches take a quarter of a Pound of Sugar, clarify it, pour it over your Peaches, and fill the Bottles with Brandy, stop them close, and keep them in a close Place.

To make Quince Cakes.

YOU must let a Pint of the Syrrup of Quinces, with a quart or two of Rasberries, be boiled and clarified over a clear gentle Fire, taking Care that it be well skimm'd from time to time; then add a Pound and half of Sugar, cause as much more to be brought to a Candy-height, and pour'd in hot; let the whole be continually stirred about till it is almost cold, then spread it on Plates, and cut it out to Cakes.

CHAP. XIX.

To Make Anchovies, Vermicella, Ketchup, Vinegar, and to keep Artichokes, French Beans, &c.

To make Anchovies.

TO a Peck of Sprats, two Pounds of common Salt, a quarter of a Pound of Bay-salt, four Pounds of Salt-petre, two Ounces of Salprunella, twopenny-worth of Cochineal, pound all in a Mortar, put them in a Stone-pot, a Row of Sprats, and a Layer of your Compound, and so on to the Top alternately. Press them hard down, and cover them close, and let them stand six Months, and they will be fit for Use. Observe that your Sprats be very fresh, and don't wash nor wipe them, but just take them as they come out of the Water.

To pickle Smelts, where you have Plenty.

TAKE a quarter of a Peck of Smelts, half an Ounce of Pepper, half an Ounce of Nutmeg, a quarter of an Ounce of Mace, half an Ounce of Petre-salt, a quarter of a Pound of common Salt, beat all very fine, wash and clean the Smelts, gut them, and lay them in Rows in a Jar, and between every Layer of Smelts, strew the Seasoning with four or five Bay-leaves, boil Red Wine, and pour over them enough to cover them. Cover them with a Plate, and when cold, tye them down close, they exceed Anchovies.

To make Vermicella.

MIX Yolks of Eggs and Flower together into a pretty stiff Paste, so as you can work it up cleverly, then roll it as thin as it is possible to roll the Paste. Let it dry in the Sun; and when it is quite dry, with a very sharp Knife cut it as thin as possible, and keep it in a dry Place, it will run up like little Worms, as Vermicella does; though the best way is to run it through a coarse Sieve, whilst the Paste is soft. If you want some to be made in haste, dry it by the Fire, and cut it small. It will dry by the Fire in a quarter of an Hour. This far exceeds what comes from abroad being fresher.

To make Ketchup.

TAKE the large Flaps of Mushrooms, pick nothing but the Straws and Dirt from it, then lay them in a broad earthern Pan, strow a good deal of Salt over them, let them lie till next Morning; then with your Hand brake them, put them into a Stew-pan, and let them boil a Minute or two, then strain them thro' a coarse Cloth, and wring it hard. To take out all the Juice, let it stand to settle, then pour it off clear, and run it thro' a thick Flannel Bag, (some filter it thro' brown Paper, but that is a very tedious Way) then boil it, to a Quart of the Liquor put a quarter of an Ounce of whole Ginger, and half a quarter of an Ounce of whole Pepper, boil it briskly a quarter of an Hour, then strain it, and when it is cold, put it into Pint Bottles; in each Bottle put four or five Blades of Mace, and six Cloves, cork it tight, and it will keep two Years. This gives the best Flavour of the Musherooms to any Sauce, if you put to a Pint of this Ketchup a Pint of Mum, it will taste like foreign Ketchup.

Another Way to make Ketchup.

TAKE the large Flaps and salt them as above, boil the Liquor, strain it through a thick Flannel-Bag; to a Quart of that Liquor put a Quart of Stale Beer, a large Stick of Horse-redish cut in little Slips, five or six Bay-leaves, an Onion stuck with twenty or thirty Cloves, a quarter of an Ounce of Mace, a quarter of an Ounce of Nutmegs beat, a quarter of an Ounce of black and white Pepper, and a quarter of an Ounce of All-Spice, four or five Rases of Ginger, cover it close, and let it simmer very softly, till about one third is wasted, then strain it thro' a Flannel-Bag, and when it is cold bottle it in Pint Bottles, and cork it close, it will keep a great while. You may put Red Wine in the Room of Beer; some put in a Head of Garlick; but I think that spoils it. The other Receipt you have in the Chapter for the Sea.

Articoakes to keep all the Year.

BOIL as many Artichoaks as you intend to keep, boil them so as just the Leaves will come out, then pull of all the Leaves and Choak; cut them from the Strings, lay them on a Tin Plate, and put them in an Oven where Tarts are drawn, and let them stand till the Oven is heated again, take them out before the Wood is put in, and set them in again after the Tarts are drawn; so do till they are as dry as a Board, then put them in a Paper-Bag, and hang them in a dry Place; when you use them lay them in warm Water, three or four Hours before you use them, shifting the Water often. Let the last Water be boiling hot, they will be very tender, and eat as fine as fresh ones; you need not dry all your Bottoms at once as the Leaves are good to eat, so boil a Dozen at a time, and save the Bottoms for this Use.

To keep French Beans all the Year.

TAKE fine young Beans, gather them of a very fine Day, have a large Stone-jarr ready clean and dry, lay a Layer of Salt at the Bottom, and then a Layer of Beans, then Salt, and then Beans, and so on till the Jarr is full, cover them with Salt, tye a coarse Cloth over them, and a Board on that, and then a Weight to keep it close from all Air; set them in dry Cellar, and when you use them take some out and cover them close again, wash them you took out very clean, and let them lie in soft Water twenty-four Hours, shifting the Water often, when you boil them don't put any Salt in the Water. The best Way of dressing them is, boil them with just the white Heart of a small Cabbage, then drain them, chop the Cabbage, and put both into a Sauce-pan, with a Piece of Butter as big as an Egg roll'd in Flour, shake a little Pepper, put in a quarter of a Pint of good Gravy, let them stew ten Minutes, then dish them up for a Side Dish. A Pint of Beans to the Cabbage, you may do more or less just as you please.

To keep Green Peas till Christmas.

TAKE fine young Peas shell them, throw them into boiling Water with some Salt in, let them boil five or six Minutes, throw them into a Cullender to drain, then lay a Cloth four or five times double on a Table and spread them on, dry them very well, and have your Bottles ready, fill them and cover them with Mutton Fat try'd, and when it is a little cool fill the Necks almost to the Top, and cork them, tie a Bladder and a Lath over, and set them in a cool dry Place. When you use them boil your Water, put in a little Salt, some Sugar, and a Piece of Butter; when they are boiled enough, throw them into a Sieve to drain, then put them into a Sauce-pan with a good Piece of Butter, keep shaking it round all the time till the Butter is melted, then turn them into a Dish, and send them to Table.

To keep Green Gooseberries till Christmas.

PICK your large green Gooseberries on a dry Day, have ready your Bottles clean and dry, fill the Bottles and cork them, set them in a Kettle of Water up to their Neck, let the Water boil very softly till you find the Gooseberries are coddled, take them out, and put in the rest of the Bottles till all is done; then have ready some Rosin melted in a Pipkin, dip the Necks of the Bottles in, and that will keep all Air from coming in at the Cork, keep them in a cool dry Place, where no Damp is, and they will bake as red as a Cherry. You may keep them without scalding, but then the Skins will not be so tender, nor bake so fine.

To keep Red Gooseberries.

PICK them when full ripe, to each Quart of Gooseberries put a quarter of a Pound of *Lisbon* Sugar, and to each quarter of a Pound of Sugar put a quarter of a Pint of Water, let it boil, then put in your Gooseberries and let them boil softly two or three Minutes, then pour them into little Stone Jarrs, when cold cover them up, and keep them for Use; they make fine Pyes with little Trouble. You may press them through a Cullender, and to a Quart of Pulp put half a Pound of fine *Lisbon* Sugar, keep stirring over the Fire till both be well mix'd and boil'd, then pour it into a Stone Jarr, when cold cover it with white Paper, and it makes very pretty Tarts or Puffs.

To keep Wallnuts all the Year.

TAKE a large Jar, a Layer of Sea-sand at the Bottom, then a Layer of Wallnuts, then Sand, then the Nuts, and so on till the Jar is full; and be sure they don't touch each other in any of the Layers. When you would use them, lay them in warm Water for an Hour, shifting the Water as it cools; then rub them dry, and they will peel well, and eat sweet. Lemon will keep thus covered better than any other way.

Another Way to keep Lemons.

TAKE the fine large Fruit that are quite sound and good, and take a fine Pack-thread about a quarter of a Yard long, run it through the hard Nib at the End of the Lemon, then tye the String together, and hang it on a little Hook, in a dry airy Place; so do as many as you please; but be sure they don't touch one another, nor any thing else, but hang as high as you can. Thus you may keep Pears, &c. only tying the String to the Stalk.

To keep White Bullice, or Pear-Plumbs, or Damascens, &c. for Tarts, or Pies.

GATHER them when full grown, and just as they begin to turn. Pick all the largest out, save about two thirds of the Fruit; the other third put as much Water as you think will cover the rest. Let them boil, and skim them; when the Fruit is boiled very soft, then strain it through a coarse Hair-sieve; and to every Quart of this Liquor, put a Pound and half of Sugar, boil it, and skim it very well; then throw in your Fruit, just give them a Scald, take them off the Fire, and when cold, put them into Bottles with wide Mouths, pour your Syrrup over them, lay a Piece of white Paper over them, and cover them with Oil. Be sure to take the Oil well off when you use them, and don't put them in larger Bottles than you think you shall make use of at a time, because all these Sorts of Fruits spoil with the Air.

To make Vinegar.

TO every Gallon of Water, put a Pound of coarse *Lisbon*-sugar, let it boil, and keep skimming of it, as long as the Scuim rises; then pour it into Tubs, and when it is as cold as Beer to work, toast a good Toast, and rub it over with Yeast. Let it work twenty-four Hours; then have ready a Vessel Iron-hooped, and well painted, fixed in a Place where the Sun has full power, and fix it so as not to have any Occasion to move it. When you draw it off, then fill your Vessel, lay a Tile on the Bung to keep the Dust out. Make it in *March*, and it will be fit to use in *June* or *July*. Draw it off into little Stone-Bottles the latter End of *June* or Beginning of *July*, and let it stand till you want to use, and it will never foul any more. But when you go to draw it off, and you find it is not four enough, let it stand a Month longer before you draw it off. For Pickles to go abroad, use this Vinegar alone; but in *England*, you will be obliged, when you pickle, to put one half cold Spring-water to it, and then it will be full four with this Vinegar. You need not boil, unless you please, for almost any Sort of Pickles, it will keep them quite good. It will keep Wallnuts very fine without boiling, even to go to the *Indies*; but then don't put Water to it. For green Pickles, you may pour it scalding hot on two or three times. All other Sorts of Pickles you need not boil it. Mushrooms only wash them clean, dry them, and put them into little Bottles, with a Nutmeg just scalded in Vinegar, and sliced (whilst it is hot) very thin, and a few Blades of Mace; then fill up the Bottle with the cold Vinegar and Spring-water, pour Mutton-Fat try'd over it, and tye a Bladder and Leather over the Top. These Mushrooms won't be so white, but as finely tasted, as if they were just gathered; and a Spoonful of this Pickle will give Sauce a very fine Flavour.

White

White Wallnuts, Suckers and Onions, and all white Pickles do in the same manner, after they are ready for the Pickle.

To fry Smelts.

LAY your Smelts in a Marinade of Vinegar, Salt, Pepper and Bay-leaves, and Clives for a few Hours; then dry them in a Napkin, drudge them well with Flour, and have ready some Butter hot in a Stew-pan. Fry them quick, lay them into your Dish, and garnish with fry'd Parsley.

To roast a Pound of Butter.

LAY it in Salt and Water two or three Hours, then spit it, and rub it all over with Crumbs of Bread, with a little grated Nutmeg, lay it to the Fire, and as it roasts, baste it with the Yolks of two Eggs, and then with Crumbs of Bread all the Time it is a roasting; but have ready a Pint of Oysters stewed in their own Liquor, and lay in the Dish under the Butter, when the Bread has sock'd up all the Butter brown the Outside, and lay it on your Oysters; your Fire must be very slow.

To raise a Sallat in two Hours at the Fire.

TAKE fresh Horse-Dung hot, and lay it in a Tub near the Fire, then sprinkle some Mustard-seeds thick on it, and lay a thin Lay of Horse-Dung over it, cover it close and keep it by the Fire, and it will rise high enough to cut in two Hours.

CHAP. XX.

DISTILLING.

To distill Walnut-water.

TAKE a Peck of fine green Walnuts, bruise them well in a large Mortar, put them in a Pan, with a Handful of Balm bruised, and put two Quarts of good French Brandy to them, cover them close, and let them lye three Days; the next Day distill them in a cold Still, from this Quantity draw three Quarts, which you may do in a Day.

How to use this ordinary Still.

YOU must lay Wood Ashes thick at the Bottom, on that the Plate, then the Iron-pan, which you are to fill with your Walnuts and Liquor, then put on the Head of the Still, make a pretty brisk Fire till the Still begins to drop, then slacken it so as just to have enough to keep the Still at Work, and mind all the Time to keep a wet Cloth all over the Head of the Still all the Time it is at Work, and always observe, not to let the Still work longer than the Liquor is good, and take great Care you don't burn the Still; and thus you may distill what you please. If you draw the Still too far it will burn, and give your Liquor a bad Taste.

To make Treacle-Water.

TAKE the Juice of green Walnuts four Pound, and of Rue, Carduce, Marygold and Balm, of each three Pound, Roots of Butter-bur half a Pound, Roots of Burdock one Pound, Angelica and Masterwort, of each half a Pound, Leaves of Scordium six handfuls, Venice Treacle and Mithridate of each half a Pound, old Canary Wine two Pounds, White-wine Vinegar six Pounds, Juice of Lemons six Pounds, distill this in a Lembick.

To make Black Cherry-Water.

TAKE six Pounds of black Cherries, and bruise them small, then put to them the Tops of Rosemary, sweet Marjorum, Spear-mint, Angelica, Balm, Marygold Flowers, of each a handful, dry'd Violets one Ounce, Anniseeds and sweet Fennel Seeds, of each half an Ounce bruised, cut the Herbs small and mix altogether, and distill them off in a cold Still.

To make Hysterical Water.

TAKE Redony, Roots of Sovage, Seeds of wild Parsnips, of each two Ounces, Roots of single Piony four Ounces, of Mysletoe of the Oak three Ounces, Myrrh a quarter of an Ounce, Castor

The Art of Cookery, made Plain and Easy.   159

stor half an Ounce, beat all these together, and add to them a quarter of a Pound of dried Mellipedes, pour on these three Quarts of Mugwort-water, and two Quarts of Brandy, let them stand in a close Vessel eight Days, then distil it in a cold Still posted up. You may draw off nine Pints of Water, and sweeten it to your Taste. Mix all together, and bottle it up.

To distil red Rose-Buds.

WET your Roses in fair Water; four Gallons of Roses will take near two Gallons of Water, then still them in a cold Still, and taken the same stilled Water, and put it into as many fresh Roses as it will wet, then still them again.

Mint, Balm, Parsley, and Pennyroyal Water distil the same Way.

To make Plague-Water.

Roots.	Flowers.	Seeds.
Angelico,	Wormwood,	Hart's Tongue,
Dragon,	Suckery,	Whorehound,
Maywort,	Hysop,	Fennel,
Mint,	Agrimony,	Melolett,
Rue,	Fennel,	St. John Wort,
Carduus,	Cowslips,	Cumfery,
Origany,	Poppy,	Featherfew,
Winter Savory,	Planting,	Red Rose-leaves,
Broad Thyme,	Setfoyl,	Wood-sorrell,
Rose-mary,	Buglofs,	Pilotory of the Wall
Pimpernell,	Vocvain,	Harts-ease,
Sage,	Maidenhair,	Sentory,
Fumetory,	Motherwort,	Seadrink, a good Handful of each of
Coltsfoot,	Cowage,	the above-mentioned Things.
Scabeous,	Golden-rod,	Gention-root,
Burridge,	Gromwell,	Dock-root,
Saxafreg,	Dill.	Butter-bur-root,
Bittony,		Piony-root,
Liverworth,		Bay-berries,
Jarmander.		Juniper-berries, of each of these a Pound.

One Ounce of Nutmegs, one Ounce of Cloves, half an Ounce of Mace, pick the Herbs and Flowers, and shread them a little. Cut the Roots, bruise the Berries, pound the Spices fine, take a Peck of green Walnuts, chop them small; then mix all these together, and lay them to steep in Sack-Lees, or any White Wine-Lees, if not in good Spirits; but Wine-Lees are best. Let them lye a Week or better; be sure to stir them once a Day with a Stick, and keep them close covered; then still them in a Lembick with a slow Fire, take care your Still does not burn. The first, second, and third Running, is good, and some of the fourth; let them stand till cold, then put them together.

To make Surfeit Water.

TAKE Scurvy-grass, Brook-lime, Watercresses, Roman Wormwood, Rue, Mint, Balm, Sage, Clivers, of each one Handful; green Merery, two Handfuls; Poppies, if fresh, half a Peck, if dry, a quarter of a Peck; Scuchenel, Six Penny-worth; Saffron, Six Penny-worth; Anaseeds, Carraway-seeds, Coriander-seeds, Cardamon-seeds, of each an Ounce; Liquorish, two Ounces scraped; Figg split, a Pound; Raisins of the Sun stoned, a Pound; Juniper-berries, an Ounce bruised; Nutmeg, an Ounce beat; Mace, an Ounce bruised; Sweet Fennel-seeds, an Ounce bruised; a few Flowers of Rosemary, Marigolds, and Sage-flowers. Put all these into a large Stone-jar, and put to them three Gallons of French Brandy, cover it close, and let it stand near the Fire for three Weeks. Stir it three times a Week, and be sure to keep it close stopped; then strain it off; bottle your Liquor, and pour on the Ingredients a Gallon more French Brandy. Let it stand a Week, stirring it once a Day; then distill it in a cold Still, and this will make fine white Surfeit-water.

You may make this Water at any time of the Year, if you live at *London*, because the Ingredients are always to be had, either green or dry; but it is best made in Summer.

To make Milk Water.

TAKE two good Handfuls of Wormwood, as much Cardus, as much Rue, four Handfuls of Mint, as much Balm, half as much Angelica, cut these a little, put them into a cold Still, and put to them three Quarts of Milk. Let your Fire be quick, till your Still drops; then slacking your Fire, you may draw off two Quarts. The first Quart will keep all the Year. This is good in Fevers sweetned with Sugar, or Syrup of Cloves.

How to distil Vinegar, you have in the Chapter of Pickles.

R r   CHAP.

CHAP. XXI.

How to market, and the Seasons of the Year for Butcher's Meat, Poultry, Fish, Herbs, Roots, &c. and Fruit.

A Bullock.

THE Head, Tongue, Palate, the Entrails are the Sweet-Breads, Kidneys, Skirts, and Tripe; there is the Double, the Role, and the Reed-Tripe.

The Fore Quarter.

First is the Haunch, which includes the Clod, Marrow, Bone, and Shin, and the Sticking-piece, that is the Neck-end. The next is the Leg of Mutton-piece, which has Part of the Blade-bone; then the Chuck-piece, the Brisket, the four Ribs and Middle Rib, which is called the Chuck-rib.

The Hind Quarter.

First Surloin and Rump, the Thin and Thick-flank, and Veiny-piece, then the Chuck-bone, Buttock and Leg.

A Sheep.

THE Head and Pluck, which includes the Liver, Lights, Heart, Sweet-breads, and Melt.

The Fore Quarter.

The Neck, Breast, and Shoulder.

The Hind Quarter.

The Leg and Loin; the two Loins together is called a Saddle of Mutton, which is a fine Joint when it is the little fat Mutton.

A Calf.

THE Head and Inwards are the Pluck, which contains the Heart, Liver, Lights, Nut and Melt, and what they call the Skirts, which eats finely broiled, the Throat Sweet-bread, and the Windpipe Sweet-bread, which is the finest.

The Fore Quarter is the Shoulder, Neck, and Breast.

The Hind Quarter is the Leg, which contains the Nuckle and Fillet, then the Loin.

House Lamb.

THE Head and Pluck, that is the Liver, Lights, Heart, Nut and Melt. Then there is the Fry, which is the Sweet-breads Lamb-stones, and Skirts, with some of the Liver.

The Fore Quarter is the Shoulder, Neck and Breast together.

The Hind Quarter the Leg and Loin. This is in high Season at *Christmas*, but lasts all the Year. Grass Lamb comes in, in *April* or *May*, according to the Season of the Year, and holds good till the Middle of *August*.

A Hog.

THE Head and Inwards, and that is the Haslet, which is Liver and Crow, Kidney and Skirts. It is mixed with a great deal of Sage and Sweet Herbs, Pepper, Salt, and Spice, so rolled in the Caul and roasted; then there are the Chitterlans, and the Guts, which are cleaned for Saufages.

The Fore Quarter is the Fore Loin and Spring; if a large Hog, you may cut a Sparib off.

The Hind Quarter, only Leg and Loin.

A Bacon Hog.

THIS is cut different, because of making Ham, Bacon, and pickled Pork. Here you have fine Sparribs, Chines, and Griskins, and Fat for Hog's-lard. The Liver and Crow is much admired fry'd with Bacon; the Feet and Ears of both are equally good soused.

Pork comes in Season at *Bartholomew*-Tide, and holds good till *Lady-Day*.

How to chuse Butcher's-Meat.

To chuse Lamb.

IN a Fore Quarter of Lamb, mind the Neck Vein; if it be an azure Blue it is new and good, but if greenish or yellowish, it is near tainting, if not tainted already. In the Hinder Quarter, smell under the Kidney, and try the Knuckle; if you meet with a faint Scent, and the Knuckle be limber, it is stale killed. For a Lamb's Head, mind the Eyes if they be sunk or wrinkled; it is stale; if plump and lively, it is new and sweet.

Veal.

If the bloody Vein in the Shoulder looks blue, or a bright red, it is new killed; but if blackish, greenish, or yellowish, it is flabby and stale; if wrapped in wet Cloaths, smell whether it be musty or not. The Loin first taints under the Kidney, and the Flesh, if stale killed, will be soft and slimy.

The

The Art of Cookery, made Plain and Easy.

The Breast and Neck taints first at the upper End, and you will perceive some dusky, yellowish, or greenish Appearance; the Sweet-bread on the Breast will be clammy; otherwise it is fresh and good. The Leg is known to be new by the Stiffness of the Joint; if limber, and the Flesh seems clammy, and has green or yellow Specks, 'tis stale. The Head is known as the Lamb's. The Flesh of a Bull-Calf is more red and firm than that of a Cow Calf, and the Fat more hard and curdled.

Mutton.

If Mutton be young, the Flesh will pinch tender; if old, it will wrinkle and remain so; if young, the Fat will easily part from the Lean; if old, it will stick by Strings and Skins; If Ram-mutton, the Fat feels spungy, the Flesh close grained and tough, not rising again, when dented by your Finger; if Ewe-mutton, the Flesh is paler than Weather-mutton, a closer Grain, and easily parting. If there be a Rot, the Flesh will be palish, and the Fat a faint whitish, inclining to yellow, and the Flesh be loose at the Bone; if you squeeze it hard, some Drops of Water will stand up like Sweat; as to Newness and Staleness, the same is to be observed as by Lamb.

Beef.

If it be right Ox-beef, it will have an open Grain, if young, a tender and oily Smoothness; If rough, and spungy, it is old, or inclining to be so, except Neck, Briscuit, and such Parts as are very fibrous, which in young Meat will be more tough than in other Parts. A Carnation pleasant Colour betokens good spending Meat, the Suet a curious white, yellowish is not so good.

Cow-beef is less bound and closer grained than the Ox, the Fat whiter, but the Lean somewhat paler, if young, the Dent you make with your Finger will rise again in a little Time.

Bull-beef is of a closer Grain, a deep dusky red, tough in pinching, the Fat skinny, hard, and has a rammish rank Smell, and for Newness or Staleness, this Flesh bought fresh, has but few Signs, the most material is its Clamminess, the rest your Smell will inform you. If it be bruised, these Places will look more dusky or blackish than the rest.

Pork.

If it be young, the Lean will break in pinching between your Fingers, and if you nip the Skin with your Nails, it will make a Dent; also if the Fat be soft and pulpy, in a manner like Lard, and if the Lean be tough, and the Fat flabby and spungy, feeling rough, it is old, especially if the Rind be stubborn, and you cannot nip it with your Nails.

If of a Boar, though young, or of a Hog, gelded at full Growth, the Flesh will be hard, tough, reddish, and rammish of Smell; the Fat skinny and hard, the Skin very thick and tough, and pinched up it will immediately fall again.

As for old or new killed, try the Legs, Hands, and Springs, by putting your Fingers under the Bone that comes out; for if it be tainted, you will there find it by smelling your Finger; besides, the Skin will be sweaty and clammy when stale, but cool and smooth when new.

If you find little Kernels in the Fat of Pork, like Hail-shot; if many, 'tis measly, and dangerous to be eaten.

How to choose Brawn, Venison, Westphalia Hams, &c.

BRAWN is known to be old or young by the extraordinary or moderate Thickness of the Rind; the thick is old, the moderate is young; if the Rind and Fat be very tender, it is not Boar Bacon, but Barrow or Sow.

Venison.

Try the Haunches or Shoulders under the Bones, that come out, with your Finger or Knife, and as the Scent is sweet or rank, it is new or stale; and the like of the Sides in the most fleshy Parts. If tainted, they will look greenish in some Places, or more than ordinary black. Look on the Hoofs, and if the Clifts are very wide and tough, it is old; if close and smooth it is young.

Westphalia Hams and English Bacon.

Put a Knife under the Bone that sticks out of the Ham, and if it comes out in a manner clean, and has a curious Flavour, it is sweet and good; if much smeered and dulled, it is tainted or rusty.

English Gammons are tried the same way; and for other Parts try the Fat, if it be white, oily in feeling, and does not break or crumble, and the Flesh sticks well to the Bone, and bears a good Colour, it is good; but if the contrary, and the Lean has some little Streaks of yellow, it is rusty, or will soon be so.

Butter, Cheese, and Eggs.

When you buy Butter, trust not to that which will be given you to taste, but try it in the Middle, and if your Smell and Taste be good, you cannot be deceived.

Cheese is to be chosen by its moist and smooth Coat; if old Cheese be rough coated, rugged, or dry at Top, beware of little Worms or Mites: If it be over full of Holes, moist or spungy, it is subject to Maggots. If any soft or perished Place appear on the Outside, try how deep it goes, for the greater Part may be hid within.

Eggs hold the great End to your Tongue, if it feels warm, be sure it's new; if cold, it is bad; and so in Proportion to the heat and cold, so is the Goodness of the Egg. This way you never can be deceived. And as to the keeping of them, pitch them all with the small End downwards in fine Wood-Ashes, and they will keep some Months.

Poultry.

Poultry.

January.—Hen Turkeys, Capons, Pullets with Eggs, Fowls, Chickens, Hares, all Sorts of Wild Fowl, Tame Rabbits, and Tame Pigeons.

February.—Turkeys and Pullets with Eggs, Capons, Fowls, Small Chickens, Hares, all Sorts of Wild Fowl (which in this Month begin to decline) Tame and Wild Pigeons, Tame Rabbits, Green Geese, Young Ducklings, and Turkey-Pouts.

March.—This Month the same as the preceding Month; and in this Month Wild Fowl goes quite out.

April.—Pullets, Spring Fowls, Chickens, Pigeons, young Wild Rabbits, Leverets, Young Geese, Ducklings, and Turkey-Pouts.

May.—The same.

June.—The same.

July.—The same, with young Partridges, Pheasants, and Wild Ducks, called Flappers or Moulters.

August.—The same.

September, *October*, *November*, and *December*.—In these Months all Sorts of Fowls, both Wild and Tame, are in Season; and in the three last, is the full Season for all manner of Wild Fowl.

How to choose Poultry.

To know whether a Capon is a true one, young or old, new or stale.

IF he be young his Spurs are short, and his Legs smooth; if a true Capon a fat Vein on the Side of his Breast, and the Comb pale, and a thick Belly and Rump; if new he will have a close hard Vent, if stale, a loose open Vent.

A Cock or Hen-Turkey, Turkey-Poults.

If the Cock be young, his Legs will be black and smooth, and his Spurs short; if stale, his Eyes will be sunk in his Head, and the Feet dry; if new, the Eyes lively and Feet limber. Observe the like by the Hen, and moreover if she be with Egg, she will have a soft open Vent, if not, a hard close Vent. Turkey-Poults are known the same way, their Age cannot deceive you.

A Cock, Hen, &c.

If young, his Spurs are short and dubbed, but take particular Notice, they are not pared or scraped; if old, he will have an open Vent, but if new a close hard Vent; and so of a Hen for Newness or Staleness; if old, her Legs and Comb are rough; if young, smooth.

A Tame Goose, Wild Goose, Bran Goose.

If the Bill be yellowish, and she has but few Hairs, she is young; but if full of Hairs, and the Bill and Foot red, she is old; if new, limber footed; if stale, dry footed; and so of a Wild Goose and Bran Goose.

Wild and Tame Ducks.

The Duck, when fat, is hard and thick on the Belly, but if not, thin and lean; if new, limber footed; if stale, dry footed. A true Wild Duck has a reddish Foot, smaller than the Tame one.

Goodwits, Marle, Knots, Ruffs, Gull, Dotterels, and Wheat Ears.

If these be old, their Legs will be rough; if young, smooth; if fat, a fat Rump; if new, limber footed; if stale, dry footed.

Pheasant, Cock and Hen.

The Cock, when young, has dubbed Spurs; when old, sharp small Spurs; if new, a fast Vent, if stale, an open flabby one. The Hen if young, has smooth Legs, and her Flesh of a curious Grain; if with Egg, she will have a soft open Vent, if not, a close one. For Newness or Staleness as the Cock.

Heath and Pheasant Pouts.

If new, they will be stiff and white in the Vent, and the Feet limber; if fat, they will have a hard Vent; if stale, dry footed and limber, and if touched they will peel.

Heath-Cock and Hen.

If young, they have smooth Legs and Bills; if old, rough; for the rest they are known as the foregoing.

Partridge, Cock or Hen.

The Bill white and the Legs bluish, shew Age; for if young, the Bill is black and Legs yellowish; if new, a fast Vent; if stale, a green and open one. If their Crops be full, and they have fed on green Wheat, they may taint there; and for this smell in their Mouth.

Woodcock and Snipe.

The Woodcock, if fat, is thick and hard; if new, limber footed; when stale, dry footed; or if their Noses are snotty, and their Throats muddy and moorish, they are nought. A Snipe, if fat, has a fat Vein in the Side under the Wing, and in the Vent feels thick; for the rest like the Woodcock.

Doves and Pigeons.

To know the Turtle-Dove, look for a bluish Ring round his Neck, and the rest mostly white; the Stack-Dove is bigger, and the Ring-Dove is less than the Stock-Dove. The Dove-house Pigeons, when old are red legged; if new and fat, they will feel full and fat in the Vent, and are limber footed; but if stale, a flabby and green Vent.

And thus of green or grey Plover, Felfare, Blackbird, Thrush, Larks, &c.

Of

The Art of Cookery, made Plain and Easy.

Of Hare, Leveret, and Rabbit.

Hare will be whitish and stiff, if new and clean killed; if stale, the Flesh blackish in most Parts, and the Body limber; if the Cleft in her Lips spread very much, and her Claws wide and ragged, she is old, and the contrary young. To know a true Leveret, feel on the fore Leg near the Foot, and if there be a small Bone or Knob it is right, if not, it is a Hare; for the rest observe as in the Hare. A Rabbit if stale, will be limber and flimy; if new, white and stiff; if old, her Claws are very long and rough, the Wool mottled with grey Hairs; if young the Claws and Wool smooth.

Candlemas Quarter.

FISH in Season.

LOBSTERS, Crabs, Crawfish, River Crawfish, Guardfish, Mackerel, Breams, Barbel, Roch, Shad or Alloc, Lamprey or Lamper-Eels, Dace, Bleek, Prawnes, and Horse-Mackerel.

The Eels that are taken in Running Water, are better than Pond Eels; of those the Silver ones are most esteemed.

Midsummer Quarter.

TURBUTS and Trouts, Soals, Grigs, Shaflins and Glout, Tones, Salmon, Dolphin, Flying-Fish, Sheep-Head, Tollis both Land and Sea, Sturgeon, Seale, Chubb, Lobsters and Crabs.

Sturgeon is a Fish commonly found in the Northern Seas; but now and then we find them in our great Rivers, the *Thames*, the *Severn*, and the *Tyne*. This Fish is of a very large Size, and will sometimes measure eighteen Feet in length. They are much esteemed when fresh, cut in Pieces and roasted or baked, or pickled for cold Treats. The Cavier is esteem'd a Dainty, which is the Spawn of this Fish. The latter End of this Quarter comes Smelts.

Michaelmas Quarter.

COD and Haddock, Coalfish, White and Pouting Hake, Lyng, Tuske and Mullet, Red and Grey, Weaver, Gurnet, Rocket, Herrings, Sprats, Soales and Flounders, Plaise, Dabs and Smeare Dabs, Eels, Chare, Scate, Thornback, and Homlyn, Kinson, Oysters and Scollops, Salmon, Sea Pearch and Carp, Carp, Pike, Tench, and Sea Tench.

Scate Maides are black, and Thornback Maides white. Gray Bass comes with the Mullet. In this Quarter are fine Smelts, and holds till after *Christmas*.

There are two Sorts of Mullets, the Sea Mullet and River Mullet, both equally good.

Christmas Quarter.

DOREY, Brile, Gudgeons, Gollin, Smelts, Crouch, Perch, Anchovy, and Loach, Scollop and Wilks, Periwinkles, Cockles, Muscles, Geare, Bearbet and Hollebet.

How to choose Fish.

To choose *Salmon, Pike, Trout, Carp, Tench, Grailing, Barbel, Chub, Ruff, Eel, Whiting, Smelt, Shad, &c.*

ALL these are known to be new or stale by the Colour of the Gills, their Easiness or Hardness to open, the hanging or keeping up their Fins, the standing out or sinking of their Eyes, &c. and by smelling their Gills.

Turbut.

He is chosen by his Thickness and Plumpness, and if his Belly be of a Cream Colour, he must spend well; but if thin, and his Belly of a bluish White, he will eat very loose.

Cod and Codling.

Choose him by his Thickness towards his Head, and the Whiteness of his Flesh when it is cut. And so of a Codling.

Ling.

For Dried Ling, choose that which is thickest in the Pull, and the Flesh of the brightest Yellow.

Scate and Thornback.

These are chosen by their Thickness, and the She-Scate is the sweetest, especially if large.

Soals.

These are chosen by their Thickness and Stiffness, when their Bellies are of a Cream Colour they spend the firmer.

Sturgeon.

If it cuts without crumbling, and the Veins and Gristle gives a true Blue where they appear, and the Flesh a perfect White, then conclude it to be good.

Fresh Herrings and Mackerel.

If their Gills are of a lively shining Redness, and their Eyes stand full, and the Fish is stiff, then they are new; but if dusky and faded, or sinking and wrinkled, and Tails limber, they are stale.

Lobsters.

Choose them by their Weight, the heaviest are best, if no Water be in them: If new, the Tail will full smart, like a Spring; if full, the Middle of the Tail will be full of hard, reddish, skinned Meat.

S f   Cock

Cock Lobster is known by the narrow back Part of the Tail, and the two uppermost Fins within his Tail are stiff and hard; but the Hen is soft, and the back of her Tail broader.

Prawns, Shrimps, and Crabfish.

The two first, if stale, will be limber, and cast a Kind of slimy Smell, their Colour fading, and they slimy: The two latter will be limber in their Claws and Joints, their red Colour turn blackish and dusky, and will have an ill Smell under their Throats: Otherwise all of them are good.

Plaise and Flounders.

If they are stiff, and their Eyes be not suck, or look dull, they are new, the contrary when stale: The best Sort of Plaise look bluish on the Belly.

Pickled Salmon.

If the Flesh feels oily, and the Scales are stiff, and shining, and it comes in Fleaks, and parts without crumbling, then it is new and good, and not otherwise.

Pickled and Red Herrings.

For the first, open the Back to the Bone, and if the Flesh be white, fleaky, and oily, and the Bone white, or a bright Red, they are good. If Red Herrings carry a good Gloss, part well from the Bone, and smell well, then conclude them to be good.

January *Fruits which are yet lasting, are*

SOME Grapes, the Kentish, Russet, Golden, French, Kirton and Dutch Pippins. John Apples, Winter Queenings, the Marygold and Harvey Apples, Pom-water, Golden-dorset, Renneting, Love's Pearmain, and the Winter Pearmain. Winter Purgomat, Winter Boucretien, Winter Mask, Winter Norwich, and Great Surrin Pears. All Garden Things much the same as in *December*.

February *Fruits which are yet lasting.*

THE same as in *January*, except the Golden Pippin, and Pom-water; also the Pomery, and the Winter Pepperning, and Dagobent Pear.

March *Fruits which are yet lasting.*

THE Golden Ducket Dauset, Pippins, Rennetings, Love's Pearmain, and John Apples. The latter Bon Chretien, and Double Blossom Pear.

April *Fruits which are yet lasting.*

YOU have now the Kitchen Garden and Orchard, Autumn Carrots, Winter Spinage, Sprouts of Cabbage and Colliflowers, Turnip Tops, Asparagus, young Reddishes, Dutch Brown Lettice and Cresses, Burnet, young Onions, Scullions, Leeks, and early Kidney-Beans. On hot Beds, Purslane, Cucumbers, and Mushrooms. Some Cherries, Green Apricots, and Gooseberries for Tarts.
Pippins, Deuxons, Westbury Apple, Russeting, Gilliflower, the latter Bon Chretien, Oak Pear, &c.

May, *the Product of the Kitchen, and Fruit Garden this Month.*

ASparagus, Colliflowers, Imperial Silesia, Royal and Cabbage Lettice, Burnet, Purslain, Cucumbers, Nasturtiam Flowers, Pease and Beans, sown in *October*, Artichokes, Scarlet Strawberries, and Kidney-Beans. Upon the hot Beds, May Cherries, May Dukes. On Walls, Green Apricots, and Gooseberries.
Pippins, Deuxans or John Apple, Westbury Apples, Russetting, Gilliflower Apples, the Codling, &c.
The Great Kairvile, Winter Bon Chretien, Black Worcester Pear, Surrein, and Double Blossom Pear. Now the proper time to distil Herbs, which are in their greatest Perfection.

June, *the Product of the Kitchen, and Fruit Garden this Month.*

ASparagus, Garden Beans and Pease, Kidney Beans, and Colliflowers, Artichokes, Battersea and Dutch Cabbage, Melons on the first Ridges, young Onions, Carrots and Parsnips sown in *February*, Purslain, Burrage, Burnet, the Flowers of Nasturtian, the Dutch Brown, the Imperial, the Royal, the Silesia and Coss Lettices, some Blanched Endive and Cucumbers; and all Sorts of Pot-herbs.
Green Gooseberries, Strawberries, some Rasberries, and Currans white and black, Duke Cherries, Red Hearts, the Flemish and Carnation Cherries, Codlings, Jennatings, and the Masculine Apricot. And in the forcing Frames all the forward Kind of Grapes.

July, the Product of the Kitchen and Fruit Garden.

RONcival and Winged Peafe, Garden and Kidney-Beans, Colliflowers, Cabbages, Artichokes, and their fmall Suckers, all Sorts of Kitchen and Aromatick Herbs. Sallads, as Cabbage Lettice, Purflane, Burnet, young Onions, Cucumbers, Blanched Endive, Carrots, Turnips, Beets, Nafturtian Flowers. Musk Melons, and Wood Strawberries, Currans, Goofeberries, Rasberries, Red and White Jennatings, the Margaret Apple, the Primat Ruffet, Summer Green Chiffel and Pearl Pears, the Carnation Morella, Great Bearer, Morocco, Erigat and Begarreaux Cherries. The Nutmeg, Ifabella, Perfian, Newington, Violet, Mufcal and Rambouillet Peaches. Nectarines the Primodial, Myrobalan, Red, Blue, Amber, Damask Pear, Apricot, and Cinnamon Plumbs; alfo the King's and Lady Elizabeth's Plumbs, &c. Some Figs and Grapes. Walnuts in high Seafon to pickle; and Rock Sampier.———The Fruit yet laft of the laft Year are, the Deuxans and the Winter Ruffeting.

August, the Product of the Kitchen and Fruit Garden.

CAbbages, and their Sprouts, Colliflowers, Artichokes, Cabbage Lettice, Beets, Carrots, Potatoes, Turnips, fome Beans, Peafe, and Kidney-Beans, all Sorts of Kitchen Herbs, Reddifhes, Horfereddifh, Cucumbers, Creffes, fome Taragon, Onions, Garlick, Rocumboles, Melons, and Cucumbers for pickling.
Goofeberries, Rasberries, Currans, Grapes, Figs, Mulberries and Filberts, Apples, the Windfor Sovereign, Orange Bergamot Sliper, Red Catherine, King Catherine, Penny Prufian, Summer Poppening, Sugar and Louding Pears. Crown Bourdeaux, Lavur, Difput, Savoy and Walacotta Peaches, The Muroy, Tawny, Red Roman, little Green Clufter and Yellow Nectarines.
Imperial Blue, Dates, Yellow late Pear, Black Pear, White Nutmeg late Pear, Great Anthony or Turkey and Jane Plumbs.
Clufter Grapes, Mufcadine and Cornelian Grapes.

September, the Product of the Kitchen and Fruit Garden.

GArden and fome Kidney-Beans, Roncival Peafe, Artichokes, Radifhes, Colliflowers, Cabbage Lettice, Creffes, Chervile, Onions, Tarragon, Burnet, Salary, Endive, Mufhrooms, Carrots, Turnips, Skirrets, Beats, Scorzonera, Horfe-reddifh, Garlick, Shalotts, Rocombole, Cabbage and their Sprouts, with Savoys, which are better, when more fweetened with the Froft.
Peaches, Grapes, Figs, Pears, Plumbs, Walnuts, Filberts, Almonds, Quinces, Mellons and Cucumbers.

October, the Product of the Kitchen and Fruit Garden.

SOME Colliflowers, Artichokes, Peafe, Beans, Cucumbers, and Melons; alfo *July* fown Kidney-Beans, Turnips, Carrots, Parfnips, Potatoes, Skirrets, Scorzonera, Beets, Onions, Garlick, Shallots, Rocombole, Churdones, Creffes, Chervile, Muftard, Reddifh, Rape, Spinage, Lettice fmall and cabbaged, Burnet, Tarragon, Blanched Salary and Endive. Late Peaches and Plumbs, Grapes and Figgs. Mulberries, Filberts and Walnuts. The Bullace, Pines and Arbuters ; and great Variety of Apples and Pears.

November, the Product of the Kitchen and Fruit Garden.

COlliflowers in the Green-houfe, and fome Artichokes, Carrots, Parfnips, Turnips, Beets, Skirrets, Scorzonera, Horfe-reddifh, Potatoes, Onions, Garlick, Shallots, Rocombole, Salary, Parfley, Sorrel, Thyme, Savory, Sweet Marjoram dry and Clary. Cabbages and their Sprouts, Savoy Cabbage, Spinage, late Cucumbers. Hot Herbs on the Hot Bed. Burnet, Cabbage Lettice, Endive blanched ; feveral Sorts of Apples and Pears.
Some Bullaces, Medlars, Arbutas, Walnuts, Hazel Nuts, and Chefnuts.

December, the Product of the Kitchen and Fruit Garden.

MANY Sorts of Cabbages and Savoys, Spinage, and fome Colliflowers in the Confervatory, and Artichokes in Sand. Roots we have as in the laft Month. Small Herbs on the Hot Beds for Sallads, alfo Mint, Tarragon, and Cabbage Lettice preferved under Glaffes ; Chervile, Salary, and Endive blanched. Sage, Thyme, Savory, Beet-leaves, Tops of young Beets, Parfley, Sorrel, Spinage, Leeks and Sweet Marjoram, Marigold Flowers, and Mint dried. Afparagus on the Hot Bed, and Cucumbers on the Plants fown in *July* and *Auguft*, and Plenty of Pears and Apples.

CHAP.

CHAP. XXII.

A certain Cure for the Bite of a Mad Dog.

LET the Patient be blooded at the Arm nine or ten Ounces. Take of the Herb, called in *Latin*, *Licken Cinereus Terrestris*, in *English*, Ash-coloured Ground Liverwort; cleaned, dried, and powdered, half an Ounce. Of black Pepper powdered, two Drachms. Mix these well together, and divide the Powder into four Doses; one of which must be taken every Morning fasting, for four Mornings successively, in half a Pint of Cow's Milk warm. After these four Doses are taken, the Patient must go into the cold Bath, or a cold Spring, or River, every Morning fasting for a Month: He must be dipt all over, but not stay in (with his Head above Water) longer than half a Minute, if the Water be very cold. After this he must go in three times a Week for a Fortnight longer.

N. B. The Licken is a very common Herb, and grows generally in sandy and barren Soils all over *England*; The right time to gather it, is in the Months of *October* and *November*.   *D. Mead*.

Another for the Bite of a Mad Dog.

FOR the Bite of a Mad Dog for either Man or Beast; Take six Ounces of Rue, clean picked and bruised; four Ounces of Garlick, peeled and bruised; four Ounces of *Venice* Treacle, and four Ounces of filed Pewter, or scraped Tin, Boil these in two Quarts of the best Ale, in a Pan covered close over a gentle Fire, for the Space of an Hour, then strain the Ingredients from the Liquor. Give, eight or nine Spoonfuls of it warm to a Man, or a Woman, three Mornings fasting; eight or nine Spoonfuls is sufficient for the strongest; a lesser Quantity to those younger, or of a weaker Constitution, as you may judge of their Strength. Ten or twelve Spoonfuls for a Horse, or a Bullock; three, four, or five to a Sheep, Hog, or Dog. This must be given within nine Days after the Bite; it seldom fails in Man or Beast.—— If you can conveniently bind some of the Ingredients on the Wound, it will be so much the better.

A Receipt *against the* Plague.

TAKE of Rue, Sage, Mint, Rosemary, Wormwood and Lavender, a Handful of each, infuse them together in a Gallon of White Wine-Vinegar, put the whole into a Stone-pot closely covered up, upon warm Wood Ashes for four Days: After which draw off (or strain through fine Flannel) the Liquid, and put it into Bottles well corked; and into every Quart Bottle, put a Quarter of an Ounce of Camphire. With this Preparation, wash your Mouth, and rub your Loins and your Temples every Day; snuff a little up your Nostrils when you go into the Air, and carry about you a Bit of Spunge dipped in the same, in order to smell to upon all Occasions, especially when you are near any Place or Person that is infected. They write, that four Malefactors (who had robbed the infested Houses, and murdered the People during the Course of the Plague) owned, when they came to the Gallows, that they had preserved themselves from the Contagion, by using the above Medicine only; and that they went the whole time from House to House, without any fear of the Distemper.

How to keep clear from Buggs.

FIRST take out of your Room all Silver and Gold Lace, then set the Chairs about the Room, shut up your Windows and Doors, tack a Blanket over each Window, and before the Chimney, and over the Doors of the Room; set open all Closets and Cupboard-doors, all your Drawers and Boxes, hang the rest of your Bedding on the Chair-backs, lay the Feather-bed on a Table, then set a large broad Earthen-pan in the Middle of the Room, and in that set a Chaffindish, that stands on Feet, full of Charcoal well lighted. If your Room is very bad, a Pound of rolled Brimstone; if only a few, half a Pound: Lay it on the Charcoal, and get out of the Room as quick as possibly you can, or it will take away your Breath. Shut your Door close, with the Blanket over it, and be sure to set it so as nothing can catch Fire. If you have any *India* Pepper, throw in with the Brimstone. You must take care to have the Door open whilst you lay in the Brimstone, that you may get out as soon as possible. Don't open the Door under six Hours, and then you must be very careful how you go in to open the Windows; therefore let the Doors stand open an Hour before you open the Windows. Then brush and sweep your Room very clean, and wash it well with boiling Lee, or boiling Water, with a little unslacked Lime in it, and get a Pint of Spirits of Wine, a Pint of Spirit of Turpentine, and an Ounce of Camphire; shake all well together, and with a Bunch of Feathers wash your Bedstead very well, and sprinkle the rest over the Featherbed; and about the Wainscot and Room.

If you find great Swarms about the Room, and some not dead, do this over again, and you will be quite clear. Every Spring and Fall, wash your Bedstead with half a Pint, and you will never have a Bugg; but if you find any come in with new Goods, or Box, *&c.* only wash your Bedstead, and sprinkle all over your Bedding and Bed, and you will be clear; but be sure to do it as soon as you find one.—If your Room is very bad, it will be well to paint the Room after the Brimstone is burnt in it. This never fails if rightly done.

F I N I S.

CPSIA information can be obtained
at www.ICGtesting.com
Printed in the USA
BVHW020535211222
654406BV00041B/199